Voices from S-21

A

Philip E. Lilienthal (signature)

B O O K

The Philip E. Lilienthal imprint
honors special books
in commemoration of a man whose work
at the University of California Press from 1954 to 1979
was marked by dedication to young authors
and to high standards in the field of Asian Studies.
Friends, family, authors, and foundations have together
endowed the Lilienthal Fund, which enables the Press
to publish under this imprint selected books
in a way that reflects the taste and judgment
of a great and beloved author.

David Chandler

Voices from S-21

Terror and History in Pol Pot's Secret Prison

University of California Press

Berkeley

Los Angeles

London

University of California Press
Berkeley and Los Angeles, California

University of California Press, Ltd.
London, England

© 1999 by the Regents of the University of California

Library of Congress Cataloging-in-Publication Data

Chandler, David P.–.

Voices from S-21 : terror and history in Pol Pot's
    secret prison / David Chandler.
        p.   cm.
    Includes bibliographical references (p.   )
    and index.
    ISBN 0-520-22005-6 (alk. paper).
    1. Torture—Cambodia.   2. Political prisoners—
Cambodia.   3. Political persecution—
Cambodia.   4. Genocide—Cambodia.
5. Cambodia—Politics and
government—1975–79.   I. Title.
II. Title: Voices from S-Twenty-one.
HV8599.C16C48   1999
303.6'09596—dc21   99-13924
                                                        CIP

Manufactured in the United States of America

08   07   06   05   04   03   02   01   00   99
10   9   8   7   6   5   4   3   2   1

The paper used in this publication meets the
minimum requirements of ANSI/NISO Z39.48-1992
(R 1997) *(Permanence of Paper).* ∞

Contents

Photographs follow page 76

Preface

In April 1975 armed Cambodian radicals, known to the outside world as the Khmer Rouge, were victorious in a five-year-long civil war. Almost at once, and without explaining their rationale, the Khmer Rouge forcibly emptied Cambodia's towns and cities, abolished money, schools, private property, law courts, and markets, forbade religious practices, and set almost everybody to work in the countryside growing food. We now know that these decisions were made by the hidden, all-powerful Communist Party of Kampuchea (CPK) as part of its plan to preside over a radical Marxist-Leninist revolution. The Khmer Rouge regime of Democratic Kampuchea (DK), led by a former schoolteacher using the pseudonym Pol Pot, was swept from power by a Vietnamese invasion in January 1979. By then, perhaps as many as 1.5 million Cambodians were dead from malnutrition, overwork, and misdiagnosed and mistreated diseases. At least another 200,000 people, and probably thousands more, had been executed without trial as "class enemies." Overall, roughly one in five Cambodians died as a result of the regime. Because so many of the victims were ethnic Cambodians, or Khmer, the French author Jean Lacouture coined the term *auto-genocide* to describe the process.

In August 1981, two years after the collapse of the Pol Pot regime, I traveled to Phnom Penh with four academic colleagues. It was the first time in ten years I had been in the city. During our three-day sojourn we were struck by the way that the city and its people seemed to be recovering from their catastrophic experiences in the 1970s, when foreign invasions, a ruinous civil war, and the Khmer Rouge regime had successively swept through Cambodia with typhoon force. The people's courage and resilience in 1981, however, could not diminish the horrors of the Khmer Rouge era.

On our second day in Phnom Penh, we were taken to see the Tuol Sleng Museum of Genocidal Crimes, located in a southern section of the city. The museum had been set up by the pro-Vietnamese regime that had replaced the Khmer Rouge. It had been open to the public for about a year and was a prominent feature of government-organized tours for foreign visitors. In prerevolutionary times, we learned, a high school had occupied the site. Under the Khmer Rouge the abandoned school became the headquarters of the regime's internal security police or *santebal*. This secret facility, known as S-21, was an interrogation center where over fourteen thousand "enemies" were questioned, tortured, and made to confess to counterrevolutionary crimes. All but a handful were put to death. The existence of S-21 was known in the DK era only to the people inside it and to the country's leaders, who were themselves concealed from view.

Two Vietnamese photographers had stumbled across the compound in January 1979, in the aftermath of the invasion. They discovered the bodies of "about fifty" recently murdered prisoners, instruments used for torture, and a huge, hastily abandoned archive. It was clear to them that under the Khmer Rouge S-21 had been an important and horrific institution. Within days the site was cleaned up and shown to sympathetic foreign visitors. Over the next few months, under Vietnamese guidance, it was transformed into a museum.

On our guided tour we were first taken to small classrooms on the ground floor. We saw metal beds, fetters, and photographs of murdered prisoners taken by the Vietnamese when they had entered the compound in 1979. In other ground floor rooms instruments of torture were displayed, alongside paintings by a survivor that depicted prisoners being interrogated, tortured, and killed. Hundreds of enlarged mug shots of prisoners were also posted on the walls.

On the second floor we saw the tiny cells assigned to prisoners being questioned and larger rooms where groups of less important captives were held. In a suite of smaller rooms we were shown what remained of S-21's archive. Stacks of documents, some of them several feet high, were piled into glass-fronted cabinets, on tables, and against the walls. The vast majority, it seemed, consisted of typed or handwritten confessions. There were over four thousand. Some covered only a page or two. A few, drawn from high-ranking prisoners, were several hundred pages long. Other documents in the archive included entry and execution records, interrogators' notes, copies of speeches by DK officials, Khmer Rouge periodicals, cadre study notebooks, and biographical data about workers at the prison. We spent a few minutes riffling through the papers, taking desultory notes on the prisoners' "treasonous activities" before emerging, numbed, into the darkening afternoon.

Over the next few years, the visit lingered in my mind as other writers, including Elizabeth Becker, Ben Kiernan, and Steve Heder, drew on materials from the archive for their research. In the early 1980s, the human rights activist David Hawk assembled hundreds of documents from S-21 to use as evidence for an unsuccessful campaign to bring the leaders of DK to justice. Throughout the decade, copies of confessions circulated among scholars and journalists interested in the Khmer Rouge. Thanks to the generosity of these people and the cooperation of the museum staff, I used many of these documents for my own research before returning to Cambodia in 1990, when I spent several hours working in the archive, assembling material to be copied.

In 1992 and 1993 the S-21 archive was microfilmed under the auspices of Cornell University and the Cambodian Ministry of Culture, which had jurisdiction over the museum. Judy Ledgerwood, John Marston, and Lya Badgley supervised the microfilming at different times. During this period I visited Cambodia four times and kept track of the microfilming project. When the microfilming was complete, the prospect of examining the S-21 archive in depth and at leisure struck me as tempting, and I began to map out an agenda.

I hoped initially to use the archive as the basis for a narrative history of opposition to DK. I soon discovered, however, that the truth or falsity of the confessions, along with the innocence or guilt of the people who produced them, could rarely be corroborated. For a narrative history of DK, I realized, I would have to cast a wider net, with no assurance that corroborating documentation for the confessions would ever come to light. On the other hand, the challenge of studying S-21 and its archive on their own terms remained attractive, particularly as a means of entering the collective mentality of the Khmer Rouge and also as a way of coming to grips with a frightening, heavily documented institution. Changing direction in this way soon led me to concentrate on those texts that would help me answer such questions as: How did the prison work? Who were the "enemies" being held? How were interrogations structured? When was torture applied? Was S-21 primarily a "Communist" facility or a "Cambodian" one? Were there foreign models for it? And so on. Between 1993 and 1998 I examined over a thousand confession texts, scanned hundreds more, and read all the administrative materials from the prison that had come to light. These included hundreds of documents that were discovered in 1996 and 1997, after the Cornell project was complete. Over the years I supplemented my readings in the archive with research in secondary literature, looking for comparative insights.

This book is the result. Over the years that it took me to write it, I received generous financial support for my research and incurred a multitude of intellectual debts that I am happy to acknowledge.

The greatest of these debts, extending over the past thirty-two years, is to my wife, Susan. During our sojourns in Melbourne, Paris, Washington, D.C., and elsewhere, she has shared the ups and downs of my teaching career and the joys and glooms of my research. She has read successive drafts of everything I've written. Her comments have improved everything she has read. She has accomplished all this with baffling good humor in the midst of her own busy professional life, in the course of raising our three children, and on top of many other interests. This book, like my earlier ones, would never have taken shape without her close reading, her support, and her astute suggestions.

Work on the book was formally set in motion when the vice chancellor of Monash University, Professor Mal Logan, underwrote the purchase of a set of S-21 microfilms for me to work with. John Badgley, the curator of the Southeast Asia collection at Cornell University, saw to it that all 210 reels were waiting for me in 1994 when I took up a fellowship at the Woodrow Wilson Center in Washington, D.C. Over the next eight months I familiarized myself with the archive, copied hundreds of confessions, and gave several seminars that helped me to refine my research focus and my conclusions. Back in Australia, the Australian Research Council provided me with a generous grant that defrayed the cost of research assistance and allowed me to copy hundreds of confessions onto paper. In 1995 a fellowship from the Harry Frank Guggenheim Foundation paid for further research assistance and a trip to Cambodia. The fellowship also allowed me to reduce my Monash teaching load for a semester. In March 1996, when I was ready to start writing, a resident fellowship at the Rockefeller Foundation's study center at

Bellagio gave Susan and me an unimpeded month to consider how my research might be turned into a book.

At every stage of my work I have been favored with excellent libraries, assiduous administrative support, and superb research assistance. Library staff at Monash University and the University of Wisconsin were helpful in tracking down secondary materials. I am particularly grateful for the administrative support provided as the book was being written, first at Monash by Val Campbell and Wendy Perkins, and later at the University of Wisconsin by Danny Streubing and at the University of Oregon by Martina Armstrong.

My talented research assistants at the Wilson Center, Thong-Chi Ton Nu and Tim O'Connell, refined the computerized index to the archive and hunted down invaluable secondary materials. For the next three years my research assistant in Australia was Sok Pirun, a survivor of the DK era who had been trained as a historian in Phnom Penh in the 1960s. Pirun gave unstintingly of his time, arranged some fascinating interviews for me, and translated dozens of key documents from the archive. As we worked together, he provided a running commentary on the project and thereby gave me an invaluable entrée into the murky thought-world of the Khmer Rouge. Another survivor of the DK regime, Mouth Sophea, took an interest in my work when I was teaching in Madison and helped me over several hurdles of interpretation.

Over the years I have been buoyed up by friends and colleagues who have read all or part of the manuscript. These include Sara Colm, May Ebihara, Craig Etcheson, Kate Frieson, Alexander Hinton, Charles F. Keyes, Judy Ledgerwood, Alfred W. McCoy, and Keith W. Taylor. Steve Heder in particular has been unstinting in his help, sending me hundreds of pages of unpublished translations, several unpublished essays, numerous interview transcripts, and invaluable comments on the full text and on specific points. Several of Richard Arant's graceful translations from the S-21 archive have found their way into the book, and I am grateful for his interest in the project. Henri Locard shared his findings about "the Khmer Rouge gulag" with me in 1995–1997, and my more recent discussions with Alexander Hinton about the collective psychology of the Khmer Rouge have helped me to reformulate some of my ideas.

In 1994 I came to know Douglas Niven and Chris Riley, two intrepid photojournalists who formed the Photo Archive Group in Phnom Penh to clean, index, and reprint over six thousand photographs—the vast majority of them mug shots—from negatives that they discovered in woeful condition at S-21. Along with their friend Peter Maguire, Doug and Chris provided me with transcripts of interviews they conducted in 1995 and 1996, and Doug arranged several interviews with former workers at S-21 that we conducted together in 1997 and 1998. Additional interview transcripts were kindly provided at various times by Richard Arant, David Ashley, Chhang Youk, Sara Colm, David Hawk, Steve Heder, Alexander Hinton, Ben Kiernan, Nate Thayer, and Lionel Vairon.

Soon after I began writing, I learned that the Cambodia Genocide project administered by Yale University had gained access to a range of new materials dating from the Lon Nol period (1970–1975) and the DK era. Thanks to Dr. Timothy Castle in the Office of the DPMO-MIA in the U.S. Department of Defense, I was given a contract to examine these materials to see whether they contained information useful to the MIA program. In 1997 I visited Cambodia three times to review the materials, now housed in the Documentation Center–Cambodia (DC–Cam) under the able supervision of Chhang Youk, whose enthusiastic help in 1997 and 1998 was crucial to DPMO-MIA and to my S-21 project. During these visits, Lach Vorleak Kaliyan, the archivist at the Tuol Sleng Museum, located and copied several hundred pages of materials that had been found at S-21 after the Cornell University microfilming project had been completed.

Many other people have been helpful to me along the way, clearing up specific points, making comparative suggestions, and sharing their ideas about the Khmer Rouge.

In addition to those named already, and at the risk of offending anyone I might forget to single out, I am happy to acknowledge the help of Norman Aiblett, Susan Aitken, Lya Badgley, Elizabeth Becker, Andy Brouwer, Frederick Brown, Mary Brown Bullock, Timothy Carney, Susan Cook, Robert Cribb, Thomas Cushman, Stephen Dunn, Penny Edwards, Craig Etcheson, Joseph Fraley, Lindsay French, Edward Friedman, Jörg Friedrich, David Garrioch, Christopher Goscha, Bailey Gunther, Eleanor Hancock, Anne Hansen, Iem Sokhim, Helen Jarvis, David Jenkins, William Joseph, Ben Kiernan, J. D. Legge, Suzanna Lessard, John Marston, Robin McDowell, Kevin McIntyre, Paul McNellis, Robert Moeller, Rudolf Mrazek, Seth Mydans, Irina Paperno, Kong Peng, Christophe Peschoux, Craig Reynolds, John Rickard, Michael Schoenhals, Daniel Schwartz, Bruce Sharp, Sok Sin, Larry Stross, Nate Thayer, Serge Thion, Ton-that Quynh-Du, William Turley, Khatarya Um, Lionel Vairon, Walter Viet, Eric Weitz, Thongchai Winachikul, and Yang Lian.

My editors, Patrick Gallagher of Allen and Unwin and Reed Malcolm and Cindy Fulton of the University of California Press, have been supportive and enthusiastic. I am also grateful for the comments prepared by anonymous readers for the Press and for the inspired and assiduous copyediting of Erika Büky. All but two of the photographs, those by Kelvin Rowley and Carol Mortland, were generously provided by the Photo Archive Group. Gary Swinton, of the Monash Geography Department, prepared the diagram of S-21.

Putting the book together, in spite of its horrific subject matter, has been a pleasurable, cooperative effort. Without the copious help I have mentioned it could never have been written.

CHAPTER ONE

Discovering S-21

On 7 January 1979, a bright, breezy day in Cambodia's cool season, heavily armed Vietnamese forces, accompanied by lightly armed Cambodian allies, reached the outskirts of Phnom Penh after a blitzkrieg campaign that had begun on Christmas Day. For over a year, Vietnam had been at war with the Maoist-inspired regime of Democratic Kampuchea (DK), known in the West as the Khmer Rouge. Their invading force of over one hundred thousand troops, including armored units, was reinforced by a sustained aerial bombardment.[1]

The rapidity of the Vietnamese success took their commanders by surprise. After barely two weeks of fighting, Cambodia cracked open like an egg. The leaders of DK, most of their army, and tens of thousands of their followers fled or were herded out of the city. The invaders were welcomed by nearly everyone who stayed behind. These were people terrorized and exhausted by nearly four years of undernourishment, back-breaking labor, and widespread executions. A similar welcome, tragically misplaced, had greeted the Khmer Rouge themselves when they had occupied Phnom Penh in April 1975 and ordered its population into the countryside to become agricultural workers. In both cases, people were longing desperately for peace.[2]

By late afternoon the Vietnamese forces had occupied the city. Aside from a few hundred prisoners of war and other people—including some of the workers at S-21—who were in hiding, waiting to escape, Phnom Penh was empty.[3]

After the Khmer Rouge had emptied the city in 1975, Phnom Penh had remained the country's capital, but it never regained its status as an urban center. The bureaucrats, soldiers, and factory workers quartered there probably never numbered more than fifty thousand. During the DK era, the country had no stores, markets, schools, temples, or public facilities, except for a warehouse in the capital serving the diplomatic community. In Phnom Penh, barbed-wire fences enclosed factories, workshops, barracks, and government offices. Street signs were painted over, and barbed-wire entanglements blocked many streets to traffic. Banana trees were planted in vacant lots. Automobiles abandoned in 1975 were rusted in piles along with refrigerators, washing machines, television sets, and typewriters. Scraps of paper in the gutters included prerevolutionary currency, worthless under the Khmer Rouge. On 7 January 1979, no people or animals could be seen. As in 1975, the central government, such as it was, had disappeared. Once again, Cambodians were being made to start at zero.[4]

The effect of the desolation on the newcomers was phantasmagoric. Chey Saphon, for example, was a forty-seven-year-old Cambodian Communist who had fought against the French in the 1950s. He had lived in Vietnam since 1955 and had been trained as a journalist. On 7 January he was thrilled to be returning home with the Vietnamese troops. He was so unnerved by what he saw, however, that years later he recalled that he "spent the whole afternoon in tears."[5]

Over the next few days Vietnamese troops fanned out across Phnom Penh. On 8 January, in the southern sector of Tuol Svay Prey, two Vietnamese photojournalists who had accompanied the invasion were drawn toward a particular compound by the smell of decomposing bodies.[6] The silent, malodorous site was surrounded by a corrugated tin fence topped with coils of barbed wire. Over the gate was a red placard inscribed in yellow with a Khmer slogan: "Fortify the spirit of the revolution! Be on your guard against the strategy and tactics of the enemy so as to defend the country, the people and the Party." The place carried no other identification.[7]

Pushing inside, the two photographers found themselves on the grounds of what appeared once to have been a high school. The spacious, dilapidated compound measured roughly four hundred meters from east to west and six hundred meters from north to south (see illustrations). It consisted of four whitewashed concrete buildings, each three stories high, with balcony corridors running along each upper story. A fifth, single-story wooden building, facing west, split the compound into two identical grassy spaces. To the rear of each of these, one of the taller buildings faced east, toward the entrance. Similar buildings marked off the northern and southern boundaries of the compound.[8] The purpose of the compound was unclear to the two men, although the single-story building, littered with papers and office equipment, had obviously been used for some sort of administration.

In rooms on the ground floor of the southernmost building, the two Vietnamese came across the corpses of several recently murdered men. Some of the bodies were chained to iron beds. The prisoners' throats had been cut. The blood on the floors was still wet. Altogether the bodies of fourteen people were discovered in the compound, apparently killed only a couple of days before.[9]

In large classrooms on the upper floors of the western buildings, the patrol found heaps of shackles, handcuffs, whips, and lengths of chain. Other rooms on the upper floors had been divided by clumsily bricked partitions into small cells where each prisoner's foot had been manacled, as William Shawcross later wrote, "to a shackle large enough to take a ship's anchor." Ammunition boxes in some of the cells contained human feces.[10] On the third floor were slightly larger, more elaborately constructed cells with wooden walls and doors.

The two intruders took photographs of all the rooms in the facility, adding photos of the corpses. They then "informed the Vietnamese authorities" of what they had found. That evening the corpses were burnt "as a sanitary measure." Some of the photographs taken at that time now hang in the rooms where the bodies were found.

Over the next few days the Vietnamese and their Cambodian assistants discovered in nearby houses thousands of documents in Khmer, thousands of mug-shot photographs and undeveloped negatives, hundreds of cadre notebooks, and stacks of DK publications. In a workshop near the front gate they found several recently completed, oversized concrete busts of the DK prime minister, Pol Pot, a concrete mold for the statues, and some portraits of him, apparently painted from photographs.

The Vietnamese had stumbled into a vicious and important Khmer Rouge facility. Documents found at the site soon revealed that it had been designated in the DK era by the code name S-21. The "S," it seemed, stood for *sala,* or "hall," while "21" was the code number assigned to *santebal,* a Khmer compound term that combined the words *santisuk* (security) and *nokorbal* (police). "S-21," and *santebal,* were names for DK's security police, or special branch.[11]

Over the next few weeks the history of the site was pieced together. In the early 1960s, when Cambodia had been ruled by Prince Norodom Sihanouk, it had been a high school. It was named after Ponhea Yat, a semilegendary Cambodian king associated with the foundation of Phnom Penh.[12] After Sihanouk was overthrown in 1970—the event that sparked Cambodia's civil war—the school had taken the name of the surrounding district, Tuol Svay Prey (hillock of the wild mango). An adjoining primary school was called Tuol Sleng (hillock of the sleng tree). This name was used to designate the entire compound after it became the Museum of Genocidal Crimes in 1980, perhaps because the sleng tree bears poisonous fruit.[13]

The code name S-21 began to appear on Khmer Rouge documents in September 1975. For the next nine months, until the facility came into operation in May or June 1976, the security service's work was spread among several units in Phnom Penh, the southern suburb of Ta Khmau, and in Sector 25, north of the capital.[14] By the end of 1975, according to a former guard, Kok Sros, interviewed in 1997, *santebal* coalesced under the command of Kang Keck Ieu (alias Duch), a former schoolteacher who had been in charge of security in the so-called special zone north of the capital during the civil war. Duch became the director of the Tuol Sleng facility in June 1976. He remained in command until the day the Vietnamese arrived.[15]

Sensing the historical importance and the propaganda value of their discovery, the Vietnamese closed off the site, cleaned it up, and began, with Cambodian help, to examine its voluminous archive. On 25 January 1979, a group of journalists from socialist countries was invited to Cambodia by the Vietnamese to report on and celebrate the installation of the new Cambodian government, known as the People's Republic of Kampuchea (PRK). The journalists were the first official visitors to see Tuol Sleng. Chey Saphon accompanied them to the site. One of the journalists, the Cuban Miguel Rivero, wrote later that "there were still traces of blood on the floor. The smell was even more penetrating. There were thousands of green flies circling the room." Rivero added that he saw documents "written in Sanskrit" and "several" copies of Mao Zedong's *Little Red Book* at the "Dantesque" site.[16]

Soon afterwards, in February or March 1979 (his own memory is uncertain), Mai Lam, a Vietnamese colonel who was fluent in Khmer and had extensive experience in legal studies and museology, arrived in Phnom Penh. He was given the task of organizing the documents found at S-21 into an archive and transforming the facility into what David

Hawk has called "a museum of the Cambodian nightmare."[17] The first aspect of Mai Lam's work was more urgent than the second. It was hoped that documents found at the prison could be introduced as evidence in the trials of Pol Pot and Ieng Sary, DK's minister of foreign affairs, on charges of genocide. These took place in Phnom Penh in August 1979. Although valuable information about S-21 was produced at the trials, none of the documents in the archive provided the smoking gun that the Vietnamese and PRK officials probably hoped to find. No document linking either Pol Pot or Ieng Sary directly with orders to eliminate people at S-21 has ever been discovered, although the lines of authority linking S-21 with the Party Center *(mochhim pak)* have been established beyond doubt.

Because of his penchant for history, his experience with museums (he had organized the Museum of American War Crimes in Ho Chi Minh City), and the criminality of what had happened at S-21, Mai Lam approached his work with enthusiasm and pride. His genuine, somewhat patronizing fondness for Cambodia and its people, based on his experiences in Cambodia in the first Indochina war, also inspired him. "In order to understand the crimes of Pol Pot–Ieng Sary," he told interviewers in 1994, "first you should understand Cambodians, both the people and the country."[18]

In turning S-21 into a museum of genocide, Mai Lam wanted to arrange Cambodia's recent past to fit the requirements of the PRK and its Vietnamese mentors as well as the long-term needs, as he saw them, of the Cambodian people. Because numbers of the "Pol Pot–Ieng Sary genocidal clique," as the Vietnamese labeled them, had been Cambodians themselves, the message that Mai Lam was trying to deliver was different from the one that he had hoped to convey in the Museum of American War Crimes, but it was just as harsh. The history that he constructed in the exhibits at S-21 denied the leaders of the CPK any socialist credentials and encouraged viewers to make connections between the DK regime and Tuol Sleng on the one hand, and Nazi Germany and what Serge Thion has called the "sinister charisma" of Auschwitz on the other. The comparisons were fitting insofar as S-21, like the Nazi death camps, was a secret facility where all the inmates were condemned to death, but any more explicit links between Nazism and DK, although seductive, were inexact.[19]

A Cambodian survivor of S-21, Ung Pech, became the director of the museum when it opened in 1980. He held the position for several years and traveled with Mai Lam to France, the USSR, and Eastern Europe in the early 1980s to visit museums and exhibits memorializing the Holocaust. Although Mai Lam remained in Cambodia until 1988, working at Tuol Sleng much of the time, he concealed his "specialist-consultant" role from outsiders, creating the impression that the initiatives for the museum and its design had come from the Cambodian victims rather than from the Vietnamese—an impression that he was eager to correct in his interviews in the 1990s.[20]

Over the next few months, people working at the prison constructed a rough history of the facility, drawing on entry and execution records, memoranda by prison officials, and the memories of survivors. Between April 1975 and the first week of 1979, they discovered, at least fourteen thousand men, women, and children had been held by S-21. Because the entry records for several months of 1978 were incomplete, the true number of prisoners was undoubtedly higher. Of the documented prisoners, all but a dozen specially exempted ones, including Ung Pech, had been put to death. Since 1979, seven of these survivors have come forward. Their memories, corroborated by those of former workers at the prison, have been invaluable for this study.[21]

The records from S-21 also showed that most of the lower-ranking prisoners had been held for a few days or weeks, whereas more important ones, and lesser figures suspected of grave offenses, had been incarcerated for several months. Thousands of the prisoners, regardless of their importance, had undergone interrogation, prepared "answers" (*chomlaoy*) or confessions admitting counterrevolutionary crimes, and submitted lists of their associates, titled "strings" or "networks of traitors" (*khsae kbot*), that sometimes ran to several hundred names. The texts range from a single page to several hundred pages. Roughly 4,300 of them have so far come to light, including those of nearly all the important DK figures known to have been purged.[22]

Confession texts, survivors' memories, and the grisly instruments discovered at the site made it clear that torture was widely inflicted at S-21. Tortured or threatened with torture, few prisoners maintained their innocence for long. Considered guilty from the moment they arrived—the traditional Cambodian phrase for prisoner, *neak thos*, translates literally as "guilty person"—thousands of these men and women were expected to confess their guilt in writing before they were taken off to be killed. This bizarre procedure drew some of its inspiration from the notion of revolutionary justice enshrined in the Reign of Terror in eighteenth-century France and enacted in the Moscow show trials in the 1930s and also from the land reform and "reeducation" campaigns in China in the 1940s and in Vietnam a decade later. In spite or perhaps because of these manifold influences, no precise or overriding foreign model for S-21 can be identified. Moreover, the severity of practices at S-21 and the literalness with which interrogators went about their business also reflected prerevolutionary Cambodian punitive traditions, by which prisoners were never considered innocent and crimes of lèse-majesté were mercilessly punished.

Although DK's economic and social policies do not fit into a fascist framework, the resemblances between S-21 and Nazi death camps are striking. Works discussing the Holocaust provide insights into the psychology of torturers, administrators, and victims at the prison, as do more recent works that deal with torturers in the "dirty war" in Argentina in the 1970s and early 1980s. The list of materials that I have found useful for comparative purposes could easily be extended.[23]

The most striking difference between the German and Cambodian cases lies in the extent of the documentation produced at S-21. Prisoners both under the Nazis and in DK were removed from any semblance of legal protection; but whereas those in the Nazi death camps were simply exploited for physical labor while awaiting execution, those in S-21 were treated almost as if they were subject to a judicial system and their confessions were to provide evidence for a court of law. In this respect they resemble the alleged counterrevolutionaries who went on "trial" in the Soviet Union in large numbers in the 1930s. In Nazi Germany, political prisoners were kept in separate camps from those targeted for execution and were somewhat better treated. At S-21, all were charged with political offenses, and all were to be killed.

Like the Nazi extermination camps and the Argentine torture facilities, S-21 was a secret facility, and the need for secrecy influenced much of what happened inside its walls. The prison's existence was known only to those who worked or were imprisoned there and to a handful of high-ranking cadres, known as the Party Center, who reviewed the documents emerging from S-21 and selected the individuals and the military and other units to be purged. Interrogators, clerks, photographers, guards, and cooks at the prison were forbidden to mingle with workers elsewhere, and the compound soon earned an eerie reputation. A factory worker in a nearby compound, interviewed in 1989, referred to S-21 as "the place where people went in but never came out."[24] The factory workers were uncertain about what went on inside its walls but were ready to think the worst. Party leaders never referred to S-21 by name. In 1997, when questioned by the journalist Nate Thayer, Pol Pot denied any knowledge of "Tuol Sleng," hinting that the museum and its archive were Vietnamese concoctions. "I was at the top," he said:

> I made only big decisions on big issues. I want to tell you—Tuol Sleng was a Vietnamese exhibition. A journalist wrote that. People talk about Tuol Sleng, Tuol Sleng, Tuol Sleng. . . . When I first heard about Tuol Sleng it was on the Voice of America. I listened twice.[25]

Guided tours of S-21 were first organized in March 1979, but for over a year, as the museum took shape, only foreigners were admitted because, as a PRK Ministry of Culture, Information, and Propaganda document from 1980 asserted, the site was intended primarily "to show . . . international guests the cruel torture committed by the traitors to the Khmer people." In the meantime, Mai Lam and his associates were slowly transforming the site into a museum. In July 1980 the ban on Cambodian visitors was lifted, and tens of thousands visited S-21, many of them seeking information about relatives who had disappeared. They consulted hundreds of enlarged mug shots of prisoners on view on the ground floor of the prison, which formed a major component of the museum display. As Judy Ledgerwood has written, many of the visitors were also "searching for meaning, for some explanation of what had happened. A visit would not have been an easy task; people who went through the museum in the first year said that the stench of the place was overwhelming."[26] Some thirty-two thousand people visited the museum in the first week it was open to the public. By October 1980, over three hundred thousand Cambodians and eleven thousand foreigners had passed through the facility.[27]

Mai Lam always had high ambitions for S-21. He wanted to establish a museum and organize an archive that would be useful to the Cambodian people and would prevent them from forgetting what had happened under "the contemptible Pot" *(a-Pot)*. One of his more melodramatic exhibits was a large map of Cambodia, composed of skulls with the rivers shown in blood red. In the early 1980s, after S-21's killing field at Choeung Ek, west of the capital, had been excavated under his direction, he supervised the exhumation of thousands of bodies and ordered the construction of memorial stupa at the site, fronted with glass and filled with skulls. Talking to Sara Colm in 1995, Mai Lam said:

> For seven years I studied . . . to build up the Museum . . . for the Cambodian people to help them study the war and the many aspects of war crimes. . . . For the regular people who cannot understand, the museum can help them.

> Even though they suffered from the regime, as a researcher I want them to go [to the museum]. Even though it makes them cry. . . . The Cambodian people who suffered the war could not understand the war—and the new generation also cannot understand.[28]

For many Cambodians, as Ledgerwood points out, there are problems of "authenticity" in a museum established by foreigners to press home fortuitous parallels between the "genocidal regime" of DK and Hitler's Germany. At the same time, for the survivors the vast and seemingly random cruelties of the DK regime easily became encapsulated in the museum's displays. Nazism seemed as good a label as any other for the horrors that the survivors of the regime had undergone. The indifference of DK officials to their victims, exhibited in room after room, recurs in the memories of many survivors. Cambodians' interpretations of the Pol Pot era slip easily into Manichean frameworks that make poor history but are emotionally satisfying and consistent with much of what they remember. This point has been driven home by the French psychiatrists Jean-Pierre Hiegel and Colette Landrac, who worked in Khmer Rouge refugee camps in Thailand in the 1980s:

> It is always more comfortable to have a Manichean vision of the world, for that allows us not to ask too many questions or at least to have the answer readily at hand. In this fashion, representing the Khmer Rouge as an homogenous group of indoctrinated fanatics, the incarnation of absolute evil, responsible for all the unhappiness of the Khmer people, is a reductive vision of a complex phenomenon but one which a good many people find satisfying.[29]

Within just such a Manichean framework, the PRK regime worked hard to focus people's anger onto the "genocidal clique" that had governed Cambodia between April 1975 and January 1979. While the new government based its legitimacy on the fact that it had come to power by toppling the Khmer Rouge, it was in no position to condemn the entire movement, since so many prominent PRK figures had been Khmer Rouge themselves until they defected to Vietnam in 1977 and 1978. The continuing existence of DK's leaders and their armed followers on the Thai-Cambodian border, however, gave the Vietnamese a rationale for keeping their troops in the country and allowed the PRK to label its political opponents as Khmer Rouge.

Like their predecessors in other Cambodian regimes, PRK spokesmen arranged history to suit their day-to-day requirements. In their formulations, the Cambodian Communist movement had been an authentic revolutionary one, up to and including the liberation of Phnom Penh in 1975, when the movement had suddenly and inexplicably spun out of control. This contorted narrative enabled the PRK to celebrate the socialist "triumph" of 17 April 1975 while condemning the people who brought it about. PRK historiography also stressed a long-standing official friendship between Khmer and Vietnamese movements and regimes that was hard to locate in the historical record.[30]

These tangled readings of the past made sense to Party faithful. After all, only an authentic revolutionary movement could have defeated the United States; and, once the wheel of history had turned, no such movement could have been so cruel to ordinary people or could have opposed the genuinely revolutionary Vietnamese. These ex post facto explanations, however, were of little interest to most nonrevolutionary Khmer. They found it easier to focus their memories on "the contemptible Pot," whose bizarre, unpardonable crime was not that he had been a Communist (or a "fascist") but that he had presided over the deaths of so many of his own people. If the Vietnamese wanted to call Pol Pot a fascist, people would go along with it, without knowing much about the subject. Thus, talking with Lionel Vairon in 1995, the S-21 survivor Pha Thachan, by then a general in the Cambodian army, stated:

> Yes, what happened under Pol Pot was "Communism," but it was of a "fascist" kind, and it surpassed fascism. In fascism the Germans never killed their own people, they only killed foreigners. They killed French and Poles and so on. Pol Pot on the other hand killed his own people, three million of them. The fascists never did this.[31]

In annual "days of hate," the government mobilized public opinion and refreshed people's memories of the DK period. On these occasions, anti–Pol Pot demonstrations were organized for school children, PRK officials made speeches condemning the DK, and Vann Nath and other survivors of S-21 were called on to recite their experiences at the prison.[32]

By the mid-1980s visitors to the archive, relocated to the second floor of one of the western buildings at Tuol Sleng, were impressed by the mass of documentation collected there. Many of the dossiers were over a foot thick. Hundreds were typed and duplicated. Glass-fronted cabinets in the archive were stuffed with cadre notebooks recording political meetings, military seminars, and sessions of paramedical training. Stapled "summaries" of confessions, stacked in piles, sometimes ran to hundreds of pages. Journalists and scholars were encouraged to photocopy confession texts and other materials. In the 1980s, the human rights activist David Hawk assembled a daunting collection of materials from Tuol Sleng that provided ample evidence of the extrajudicial crimes of the DK regime.[33] His efforts and those of others to bring DK's leaders to justice then and later were stymied by Thai intransigence and political considerations. Thoughts about bringing the Khmer Rouge leaders to trial gathered steam again in the 1990s as the Khmer Rouge movement lost momentum.[34]

After 1989, when the Vietnamese withdrew their troops from Cambodia, the fate of the archive, and even of the museum, looked uncertain. In 1991 Cornell University, noted for the richness of its Southeast Asian library holdings, proposed to catalogue and microfilm the S-21 archive, which came under the Ministry of Culture's jurisdiction. The work was completed in two years. A full set of the microfilms was deposited in the Cornell University library; another set was retained by the museum.

The microfilmed materials cover 210 reels of film, including eleven reels of retakes. The reels contain all the confession texts discovered at the site, including those by foreign prisoners (filmed on separate reels). Foreigners' confessions were primarily those of Vietnamese prisoners of war but also included statements from Thai and Vietnamese fishermen, some Vietnamese civilians, and a handful of American, British, and Australian sailors who were arrested when their boats strayed too near the Cambodian coast.[35]

Among the most revealing confessions in the archive are those of seventy-nine former workers at the prison. Twenty-four of these prisoners had been interrogators, and twelve had been document workers. Most of the others had been guards. These texts provide valuable biographical data about the young men working at the prison. They are also helpful in documenting work patterns at S-21, the style of interrogations, and the practice of torture *(tearunikam)* there.

The microfilmed reels also reproduce a range of nonconfessional materials that were discovered at the prison. These include entry and execution records, typed summaries of confessions broken down by region, and military unit and government office and study notebooks that cover such diverse subjects as politics, aircraft identification, mathematics, medicine, artillery, and small arms. The nonconfessional materials also include copies of the CPK's statutes, speeches, and directives from the Party Center and copies of DK's theoretical journals, *Revolutionary Flags (Tung Padevat)* and *Revolutionary Youth,* distributed to

Party members. Materials stemming from the prison itself include a report for the first three months of 1977, written notes from interrogators reporting the torture of prisoners, rules for guards, and notes by Duch, the prison director, on a range of issues, including his analysis of the confession texts in a handwritten document probably written in early 1978, titled "The Last Plan." Probably the most revealing nonconfessional text microfilmed by Cornell is a fifty-five-page study notebook compiled by an interrogator, prepared in 1976. This text is discussed in detail in chapter 5.[36]

When the microfilming at S-21 was completed in 1993, it was thought that the reels included all the significant surviving material from the prison. In 1995, however, another S-21 archive, held in the Cambodian Ministry of the Interior, was presented to the Documentation Center–Cambodia (DC–Cam), an affiliate of the Cambodia Genocide Program established by Yale University, with a grant from the U.S. Department of State, with a view to gathering documentation of the DK regime. The new material, held by DC–Cam in Phnom Penh, seems to be have been drawn from the archives of the DK minister of defense and national security, Son Sen, who also oversaw the operations of the prison. Over fifty confession texts in this collection contain annotations in Son Sen's writing. Many of the confession cover sheets also bear handwritten annotations in Vietnamese, suggesting that they had been reviewed under the Vietnamese protectorate of Cambodia in the 1980s.

The newly discovered materials included dozens of confessions that had not survived in the S-21 archive, as well as valuable administrative materials, such as notes from self-critical study sessions held for cadres at the prison and notebooks compiled by senior interrogators. DK materials unrelated to S-21 are also housed in DC–Cam and will undoubtedly be of interest to scholars of the regime.

Several hundred documents from S-21 itself that were not microfilmed have also found their way into the DC–Cam collections since 1996. These include miscellaneous, fragmentary interrogation schedules, lists of prisoners who were ill, documents transmitted with prisoners to S-21, and over two hundred additional study notebooks. Two that are of special interest were prepared in 1977 and 1978 by the chief interrogator, Mam Nay (alias Chan) and, in a shared notebook, by two senior interrogators known by their pseudonyms Tuy and Pon (henceforth the Tuy-Pon notebook).

Discovering S-21, in other words, is a process that began in January 1979 and is still under way. The mass of material now available seems sufficient to support a detailed study of the prison. The Yugoslav writer Milovan Djilas has observed that "the way prisons are run and their inmates are treated gives a faithful picture of society, especially of the ideas and methods of those who dominate the society"—a remark that seems particularly appropriate to S-21 and Democratic Kampuchea.[37] As we pore through the materials and listen to the voices of so many people living under extreme conditions, we may also learn something about ourselves.

I first visited Tuol Sleng for less than an hour in August 1981. Since 1990, I have returned to the museum many times. In spite or perhaps because of the courtesy and friendliness of the staff, I am always disoriented by the place. On every visit, I've been struck by the contrast between the peaceful, sun-soaked compound and the horrific exhibits on display, between the whitewashed classrooms with their yellow and white tile floors and the instruments of torture they contain, between the children at play outside the buildings and the mug shots of other children en route to being killed.

In the museum, the eyes of the mounted mug shots, and especially those of the women and children, seem to follow me. Knowing as we do, and as they did not, that every one of them was facing death when the photographs were taken gives the photos an unnerving quality that is more affecting, for me at least, than the photographs of dead prisoners or the grisly portrayals of torture painted after 1979 by the S-21 survivor, Vann Nath, that are also included in the display.[38]

On most of my visits mynah birds have hopped along the overgrown paths. Roosters have crowed around the neighborhood, the sound competing with the hum of traffic on Monivong Boulevard to the east or, in the dry season, with music broadcast over loudspeakers from Buddhist wedding celebrations nearby. The noises in the 1970s were different. Almost every night in the pitch-dark, silent city, workers at the prison who were quartered on the boulevard heard the screams of people being tortured. Indeed, all the survivors and people who worked at the prison share the memory of hearing people crying out in pain at night.

Moving through the museum, absorbing its archive and listening to survivors and to people who worked at the prison, we can still hear many of these ghostly voices. They control the narrative that follows.

CHAPTER TWO

S-21: A Total Institution

The sociologist Erving Goffman, in his illuminating book *Asylums,* defines a total institution as "a place of residence and work where a large number of like-situated individuals, cut off from the wider society for an appreciable period of time, together lead an enclosed, formally administered round of life."[1] Goffman goes on to call such institutions—which can include schools, monasteries, prisons, hospitals, military units and so on—"forcing houses for changing persons; each is a natural experiment on what can be done to the self."[2]

Under the Communist Party of Kampuchea (CPK), which was itself a total institution par excellence, all of Cambodia soon became what Irving Louis Horowitz has called a "sealed environment," cut off from the outside world. The country was administered by a handful of politically obsessive men and women, many of them former schoolteachers, who saw it as their long-term duty to oversee, punish, and transform the people under their control. The cadres in charge of S-21, in turn, were under the surveillance of the Party Center *(mochhim pak),* similarly concealed from view, and, as members of an independent regiment, they worked under military discipline. S-21, the Party Center, the CPK, and the state of Democratic Kampuchea (DK), in other words, can be seen as successively more inclusive "forcing houses for changing persons."

By Goffman's definition S-21 was an extreme example of a total institution. Its mission was to protect the Party Center. It accomplished this task in part by killing all the prisoners and in part by altering their autobiographies to align them with the requirements and suspicions of the Party. Control over biographies, inmates, and the personnel working at S-21 was absolute and followed a complex "discipline" *(viney)* that enabled the keepers to dominate the kept and to preside over their refashioning.[3]

S-21 combined incarceration, investigative, judicial, and counterespionage functions. Some documents refer to it as a "ministry" *(kro-suong)*, others as an "office" *(munthi)*. Counterparts of *santebal* in other Communist countries would be the Soviet NKVD, the East German Stasi, and the Central Case Examination Group in China. Parallels also exist between S-21 and such bodies as the American FBI and the British MI5. In fact, most twentieth-century nations have a national security apparatus. Unlike many of its counterparts, however, S-21 deployed no agents in the countryside or overseas and had no central policymaking office. After mid-1976, its functions were carried out almost entirely at Tuol Sleng. For these reasons I use the names "S-21," *santebal*, and Tuol Sleng interchangeably.

Although S-21's mission and the duties of people working there were not spelled out in law, for DK had no legal code and no judicial system, they resembled those of the Soviet secret police, empowered by the Soviet law of February 1936 "to uncover and combat all tendencies and developments inimical to the state and to take for this end all measures deemed necessary and expedient."[4]

Strictly speaking, S-21 was an interrogation and torture facility rather than a prison. Although people were confined and punished there, no one was ever released. The facility served primarily as an anteroom to death.

The two men who ran *santebal* reported directly to the collective leadership of DK, known as the Upper Organization *(angkar loeu)*, the Organization *(angkar)*, or the "upper brothers"*(bong khang loeu)* to outsiders and as the Party Center *(mochhim pak)* or leading apparatus *(kbal masin)* to members of the CPK. The Party Center was the nerve center of the country. Its membership altered over time, but its highest-ranking members, who were also those most directly concerned with the operations of S-21—Pol Pot, Nuon Chea, Ta Mok, Son Sen, and Khieu Samphan— remained members throughout the regime and, indeed, into the 1990s.[5]

Secrecy at S-21

S-21's task of defending the Party Center was given the highest priority by DK's leaders. Speaking to sympathetic Danish visitors in July 1978, the Deputy Secretary of the CPK, Nuon Chea ("Brother Number Two"), explained: "The leadership apparatus must be defended at any price. If we lose members but retain the leadership, we can continue to win victories. . . . There can be no comparison between losing two or three leading cadres and 200–300 members. Rather the latter than the former. Otherwise the Party has no head and cannot lead the struggle."[6] The Party's theoretical journal, *Tung Padevat* (Revolutionary Flags) had taken a similar position earlier in the year when an editorial had asserted, "If there is damage to the Center, the damage is big. . . . The leading *apparati (kbal masin)* must be defended absolutely. If we can defend them, we can defend everything else."[7]

The existence of S-21, the location of the Party Center, and the identity of those inside it were closely guarded secrets. Talking to the Danes, Nuon Chea insisted that "it is secret work that is fundamental. We no longer use the terms 'legal' and 'illegal'; we use the terms 'secret' and 'open.' Secret work is fundamental to all we do. . . . Only through secrecy can we be masters of the situation and win victory over the enemy who cannot find out who is who."[8] Secrecy was always fundamental at S-21. In mid-1976, when a prisoner managed to escape from S-21, a study document prepared at the prison viewed the incident with alarm:

> Secrecy was broken. The secrecy we had maintained for the last 3–4 months has been pierced. When there's no secrecy, there can be no *santebal*, the term has lost its meaning. . . . If they were to escape they would talk about their confessions. The secrecy of *santebal* would be broken at exactly the point where it must not be broken.[9]

Secrecy was maintained at S-21 by keeping outsiders away from the compound, clearing the neighborhood, limiting the distribution of the documents produced, burning papers instead of throwing them away, blindfolding prisoners when they were moved from place to place, and forbidding contact between the interrogation and document groups in the prison on the one hand and less privileged employees on the other. Guards were forbidden to talk to prisoners, and prisoners were forbidden to talk to one another. High-ranking prisoners were held and interrogated in buildings separate from the main complex. Finally, nearly all interrogations took place in buildings to the east of the compound, supposedly out of earshot of prisoners and personnel. An S-21 document from September 1976, setting up day and night guard rosters, noted that guards were not allowed to follow interrogators into interrogation rooms or to "open windows to look at enemies" being questioned.

Most brutally, secrecy about S-21 was maintained by killing nearly all the prisoners.[10]

S-21's existence was known only to those who worked or were confined there, to a handful of high-ranking Party figures, and to cadres charged with *santebal* duties in the zones and sectors. When briefing their subordinates, Pol Pot, Nuon Chea, Son Sen, and Ta Mok—by 1978, Brothers One through Four—occasionally named important "enemies" who we know had already been interrogated at S-21 and had confessed to counterrevolutionary crimes. None of these statements, however, ever referred to S-21 or *santebal* by name.

No documentary evidence survives to tell us when, why, by whom, and under what guidelines *santebal* was formally established. Predecessor units existed in the Khmer Rouge army during the Cambodian civil war (1970–1975); S-21's immediate forebear, it seems, had operated in Sector 25 north of the capital from 1973 to 1975. The two men most intimately concerned with such operations at that time were Son Sen (1930–1997, alias Brother 89 and Khieu), a ranking military commander, and his subordinate, a former schoolteacher named Kang Keck Ieu (c.1942–, alias Duch), charged with security matters. Under DK, Son Sen was the deputy prime minister, responsible for defense and national security. *Santebal* was one of his responsibilities. Duch, who reported to him, was the commandant of S-21 itself.

Workers at S-21

S-21 had three main units: interrogation, documentation, and defense. A photography subunit operated within the documentation unit. Subunits operating within the defense unit, the largest at S-21, included one that guarded the prisoners, another that brought prisoners in and took them to be executed, a third that provided rudimentary medical services, and a fourth that was responsible for economic support.

A helpful guide to the higher-ranking personnel at S-21 is an internal telephone directory containing forty-six names. It must have been prepared before November 1978, when one of the interrogators listed in it, Chea Mai, was arrested.[11] The directory lists twenty-four names in a "hot" *(kdau)* section of the interrogation unit, fourteen in "documents," five in a "separate" (administrative) category, and six others, probably also interrogators, in an unlabeled group.

The titles that preceded names in the telephone directory paralleled the three-tiered ranking system that operated within the CPK, whereby Party members progressed from belonging to the Communist Youth League *(yuv'kok)* through candidate membership *(triem)* to "full-rights" membership *(penh set)*. The names in the directory proceed in seniority from eight people listed by their full names, with no ranking prefix, through ten whose revolutionary pseudonyms are prefixed with the word *mit* (friend or comrade), to nine whose pseudonyms appear with the prefix *bong* (older brother). The last category was reserved for people with the greatest authority. An even more respectful classification, *ta* (grandfather), was used for Duch in a few documents, even though he was only in his thirties.

Freed from the "exploiting classes" of the past, CPK members and workers at the prison followed deferential rules that were as complex, hierarchical, and baffling as those they might have encountered on their first day of school or as Buddhist novice monks. The analogies are appropriate because Duch and his colleagues in the interrogation unit had been schoolteachers for many years, and nearly all the workers at the prison were males in their late teens and early twenties, just the age when many of them, in prerevolutionary times, would have spent some time as monks. Moreover, those in charge of the prison, like Buddhist monks, were accustomed as teachers to unquestioning respect. The discipline of S-21 was based on the memorization of rules; it induced reverence for authority and unquestioning obedience.

The hierarchy of the names in the telephone directory suggests that Duch and his close associates were unwilling or unable to forsake the rankings and the deference that had marked prerevolutionary Khmer society and that the revolution had promised to overturn. Those beneath them might also have been reluctant to see the ranks abolished. The former guard Kok Sros, for example, recalled that on one occasion, "Duch told me I had done a good job, and I felt that he liked me. I was pretty sure from then on that I was going to survive, because I had been admired from above."[12]

With the constraints of hierarchy in mind, we can examine the lives and characters of Son Sen and Duch before turning to the people in charge of the various units at the prison.

Son Sen

In 1975 Son Sen was a slender, bespectacled man in his mid-forties. Like DK's foreign minister, Ieng Sary, he had been born into the Cambodian community in southern Vietnam, where his parents were prosperous landowners. After moving to Phnom Penh as a boy, Son Sen

soon attracted attention for his academic talent. He received a scholarship for study in France in 1950, shortly after Saloth Sar (later known
as Pol Pot) had been awarded one. As a student of philosophy and history in Paris, Son Sen joined the French Communist Party alongside
Saloth Sar, Ieng Sary, and several other Khmer. Returning home in
1956, he embarked on a teaching career and became part of the clandestine Cambodian Communist movement. In the early 1960s he was
the director of studies of the Pedagogical Institute attached to the University of Phnom Penh. He was dismissed from his post in 1962 for his
anti-Sihanouk views but was allowed to continue teaching.

In 1963, after Saloth Sar had been named secretary of a reconsti-
tuted Communist Party, Son Sen joined him on the newly formed, concealed central committee. In 1964 he was spirited out of the capital in
the trunk of a Chinese diplomatic vehicle and joined Saloth Sar and a
handful of others in a Vietnamese Communist military base known as
"Office 100," which moved back and forth across the Cambodian-
Vietnamese border in response to battle conditions in Vietnam.[13]

Son Sen did not return to Phnom Penh until April 1975. During his
twelve years in the maquis he bonded with the men and women who
would later make up the Party Center, several of whom he had known
in France. When armed struggle against Sihanouk broke out in 1968,
Son Sen became a field commander. He soon revealed a talent for
battlefield operations. By early 1972, he was chief of the general staff.
His colleagues in the Party sometimes found him peremptory and his
point of view "bourgeois,"[14] but by August 1975 he was given responsibility for Cambodia's security and defense.

His new responsibilities included *santebal*. Son Sen monitored its
operations closely. He read and annotated many confessions from the
prison and ran study sessions for S-21 cadres in which he discussed its
goals, the interrogations, and the use of torture. Three sets of notes by
S-21 officials from these sessions have survived. They suggest that Son
Sen's interest in history, cultivated in France, persisted into the DK era.
Like many Cambodians born in Vietnam, Son Sen also seemed to find it
easy (or prudent) to be stridently anti-Vietnamese.[15]

Many documents routed from S-21 to the Party Center passed
through Son Sen's hands, and dozens of memoranda addressed to him
by Duch have survived. So have many of his replies. These display a
schoolmasterish attention to detail and unflinching revolutionary zeal.
Son Sen's wife, Yun Yat (alias At), also a former teacher, worked closely
with him and had access to some of the confessions.

In 1975 and 1976, Son Sen worked hard to mold the regionally based units that had won the civil war into a national army. In 1977 and 1978, he took charge of the fighting with Vietnam and supervised the purges of "disloyal" cadres in the Eastern Zone. In the closing months of the regime, when the war went badly, he came under suspicion himself. Had the Vietnamese invasion been delayed, he might have been cut down by the "upper brothers" and by his own remorseless institution.[16] However, Son Sen retained his balance and in 1979 resumed command of the Khmer Rouge military forces after their defeat. In the aftermath of the Paris Peace Accords in 1991 he emerged as the "public face" of the Khmer Rouge, but he faded from view when his superiors decided to stonewall the United Nations–sponsored national elections. He never regained his former status. In a brutal case of poetic justice Son Sen, his wife, Yun Yat, and a dozen of their dependents were murdered on Pol Pot's orders in northern Cambodia in June 1997, accused of being "spies" for the Phnom Penh regime.[17]

Duch

Kang Keck Ieu (alias Duch), the commandant of S-21 throughout its operation, was born around 1942 into a poor Sino-Cambodian family in Kompong Chen (Kompong Thom). Like Son Sen, he attracted attention as a boy for his intellectual abilities. His mother, interviewed in 1980, said that her son's head was "always in a book." Aided by a local entrepreneur he earned a scholarship to the Lycée Sisowath. Specializing in mathematics, he ranked second in the national *baccalauréat* examinations in 1959. In those days, a classmate has recalled, he was a studious young man with no hobbies or political interests.[18]

For the next few years, he taught mathematics at the *lycée* in Kompong Thom. One of his former students later recalled that "he was known for the precision of his lectures as if he were copying texts from his mind onto the board." One of his colleagues at the school, who taught biology, was an exceptionally tall, almost albino Cambodian named Mam Nay (alias Chan). Years later, when both men were members of the CPK, Duch invited him to head the interrogation unit at the prison. Duch and Chan emerge from the record as strict, fastidious, totally dedicated teachers—characteristics that they carried with them, to altered purposes, when they worked together at the prison.[19]

In 1964, Duch was rewarded with a posting to the Pedagogical Institute. Son Sen had already left. According to Duch's Lycée Sisowath classmate, Nek Bun An, the young mathematician was drawn toward Communism by a group of Chinese exchange students enrolled to study Khmer at the University of Phnom Penh. Duch was inspired and politicized by these sharply focused, idealistic young men and women, all of whom were to play important roles in Sino-Cambodian relations during the DK era and beyond.[20]

After leaving the Institute, he taught briefly at Chhoeung Prey *lycée* in Kompong Cham, where he enrolled at least one of his students, Ky Suk Hy, into the revolutionary movement and was soon arrested as a "Communist" by Sihanouk's police. He was held without trial for several months—a normal procedure for political prisoners at the time— but he managed to obtain his release through the intervention of his childhood patron. Soon after Sihanouk was overthrown, Kang Keck Ieu had gone into the maquis.

In the early 1970s, known as Duch, he was in charge of security in Sector 33, north of Phnom Penh. A French ethnographer, François Bizot, was arrested by Communist guerrillas there in 1970. Duch interrogated Bizot repeatedly for two months, accusing him of being a CIA agent and making him write several detailed autobiographies before allowing him to go free. Bizot came away chastened by Duch's fanaticism. In his view, "Duch believed Cambodians of differing viewpoints to be traitors and liars. He personally beat prisoners who would not tell the 'truth.'"[21]

In 1973 Duch moved to Sector 25, north of Phnom Penh. His superior there was Sok Thuok (alias Von Vet), a Communist militant since the 1950s who was executed at S-21 in 1978. Sok Thuok's deputy in 1973, charged with military affairs, was Son Sen, whose favorable attention Duch probably attracted at this time.

Duch picked up his expertise in security matters as he went along; there is no evidence that he ever traveled abroad or received any training from foreign experts. He may well have developed his elaborate notions of treachery involving "strings of traitors" between 1972 and 1973, when a secret operation was set up by the Khmer Rouge to purge the so-called Hanoi Khmers—Cambodians who had come south in 1970 after years of self-imposed exile in North Vietnam, ostensibly to help the revolution. Hundreds of them were secretly arrested and put to death in 1973, after the Vietnamese had withdrawn the bulk of their troops from Cambodia. A few managed to escape to Vietnam after detention; and others were arrested after April 1975. Many were arrested in the Special Zone. The stealth and mercilessness of the campaign may have owed something to Duch's emerging administrative style. The campaign, indeed, foreshadowed the modus operandi of S-21.[22]

Santebal operations were transferred to the capital soon after the Khmer Rouge victory in April 1975, but for several months the entity went under the name of Office 15; annotations by Duch appear on documents emanating from this office.[23] The earliest documents connecting Duch with S-21 date from October 1975. For the next six months or so, Duch divided his time between a *santebal* prison at Ta Khmau, south of the capital, and interrogation centers scattered throughout Phnom Penh. The Ta Khmau facility, code-named S-21 Kh, was located on the grounds of what had been Cambodia's only psychiatric hospital.[24]

As the man in charge of S-21, Duch worked hard to control every aspect of its operations. His experiences and instincts from teaching were helpful. He was used to keeping records, ferreting out answers to problems, earning respect, and disciplining groups of people. He drove himself and his subordinates very hard. "He was strong. He was clear. He would do what he said," the former guard Him Huy has recalled. Duch often frightened workers at the prison. When asked what kind of a man Duch was, another guard replied, "Ha! What kind of man? He was beyond reason [*huos haet*]." In this man's view, Duch's worst crime was not to have presided over the deaths of fourteen thousand prisoners, but to have allowed two of his own brothers-in-law to be brought to S-21 and put to death. "Duch never killed anyone himself," the former guard recalled, but he occasionally drove out to the killing field at Choeung Ek to observe the executions.[25]

Duch's neatly written queries and annotations, often in red ink, appear on hundreds of confessions. They frequently correct and denigrate what prisoners confessed, suggest beatings and torture, and urge interrogators to unearth the buried "truth" that the prisoners are hiding. Duch also summarized dozens of confessions, pointing out the links he perceived with earlier ones and suggesting fresh lines of inquiry. The most elaborate of his memoranda, written in 1978, was titled "The Last Plan"; it attempted to weave two years' worth of confessions into a comprehensive, diachronic conspiracy that implicated the United States, the USSR, Taiwan, and Vietnam. Like the late James Jesus Angleton of the CIA, Duch was mesmerized by the idea of moles infiltrating his organization. As a mathematician, he enjoyed rationally pleasing models. "The Last Plan" was his chef d'oeuvre.[26]

Duch lived close to S-21 with his wife and their two young children, and he remained at the prison until the evening of 7 January 1979, when he walked out of Phnom Penh and soon disappeared from sight. In 1996, no longer affiliated with the Khmer Rouge, Duch met some American evangelical missionaries in northwestern Cambodia and converted to Christianity. He was working as a medical orderly in April 1999 when a journalist discovered his past identity. Duch was later interviewed by Nate Thayer and spoke freely about his past before he was arrested by Cambodian police and imprisoned in Phnom Penh.[27]

Duch's Assistants

Duch's deputy *(anuprotean)* at S-21 was Khim Vat (alias Ho), a soldier in his mid-twenties who served concurrently as the head of the prison's defense unit. Ho had been born and raised in Prek Touch, south of the capital, and had joined the revolutionary ranks as a teenager in 1966. Serving in the 11th (later the 703d) Division, he lost an eye in combat. His signature appears on many entry and execution lists. In 1978, he often joined forces with Chan to interrogate Vietnamese prisoners of war. Ho was a fierce disciplinarian feared by his subordinates. Kok Sros recalled:

> I was scared of him. If I looked him in the face he looked mean, and if he gave us instructions and we made a mistake he would beat us. If we said something wrong, he beat us. We had to be careful when we spoke; whatever we said had to be to the point. I knew he was strict, so I was always careful.[28]

Nothing is known of Ho's career after 1979. His deputy, Peng, hailed from the same district as Ho and had served with him in Division 703. Peng, a Sino-Khmer, had been born in 1950. At S-21 he commanded the guards. He also kept track of arriving prisoners and assigned them to rooms and cells. According to Khieu Lohr, a former guard, Peng had "keys to all the cells." He reported to Duch, who decided whether prisoners were to be interrogated, ignored, or taken off to be killed. Peng accompanied Duch on his tours of the prison and acted as his bodyguard. Vann Nath was so frightened of Peng, whom he called a "brutal young butcher," that he "never dared to look him in the eye." Ung Pech, in his testimony at the trial of Pol Pot and Ieng Sary in 1979, called Peng "savage and cruel," adjectives not applied to any other S-21 employee at the trial. Peng seems to have been demoted in 1978, when his duties were taken over by Him Huy, but, according to Kok Sros, Peng survived the Vietnamese invasion and died in southwestern Cambodia in the 1980s.[29]

After Duch, Ho, and Peng, the most important person at S-21 was probably Chan, who headed the interrogation unit. Aside from his stint of teaching in the 1950s, we know nothing about his early life, although his fluency in Vietnamese, rare among Cambodians, suggests that he was born and raised in Vietnam. He arrived at S-21 with Duch in 1975 and remained there until the Vietnamese invasion. In 1990, he was still working with the Khmer Rouge as an interrogator. Nate Thayer, who saw him questioning prisoners at that time, recalled that Chan "was the most frightening-looking character" he had ever seen. When sighted again by an United Nations official in 1996, Chan was semi-retired and engaged in market gardening.[30]

Chan's deputy was another former mathematics teacher, Tang Sin Hean (alias Pon), a Sino-Khmer from Sector 25 who had served under Duch during the civil war. He was already working for *santebal* by July 1975. In a self-criticism session at the prison in December 1976, he deplored his "middle bourgeois" class background, confessed that he was often "individualistic" in his thinking, and admitted that because he worked so hard on *santebal* matters he had failed to "build himself" or learn as much as he should have done from the "masses." The document closed with warm testimonials about his performance at S-21 from Chan and Duch.[31]

Pon interrogated many prominent prisoners, including Keo Meas, Ney Saran, Hu Nim, Tiv Ol, and Phouk Chhay. Several documents signed by Pon and attached to these interrogations propose extensive torture. At a biweekly self-criticism meeting held at the prison in 1978, staff claimed to be "frightened" of Pon, who criticized himself for not "following the masses," probably a euphemism for his top-down, authoritarian style.[32]

The documents unit *(krom akkesa),* closely linked to the interrogations unit, was headed in 1977 and 1978 by Suos Thi, a former soldier in his mid-twenties who came from the same district as Ho and Peng. Suos Thi had "joined the revolution" *(choul padevat)* in August 1971. He had served with Ho in Division 703 before coming to S-21 in November 1975. In his self-critical autobiography Suos Thi claimed that he had become a revolutionary because he was "angry about imperialism, privilege, and capitalism that exploited poor people." Among his "shortcomings," he admitted that he "enjoyed going to movies," "liked to laugh," "quarreled with his siblings," and "got angry quickly." Among his virtues, he said, was a "willingness to perform any tasks for the Party." He survived into the 1990s, when he was twice interviewed by journalists. Asked if he "regretted" working at S-21, he said that he was "very sorry for the killings, for the children and women. In fact, some of the people weren't guilty at all." At another point in the interview, he was more laconic. "When they gave you a job," he said, "you had to do it."[33]

In the "separate" category in the telephone directory, listed with Duch, Pon, and Chan, appears the name of "Brother Huy." Two men with this name were working at S-21 in 1978. The one named in the directory was probably Him Huy, a self-described "lower-middle" peasant from Sector 25 who became a Khmer Rouge soldier in 1972 because, he wrote in his self-critical autobiography, he was "sick of capitalism and privilege." Serving under Ho, he had been wounded in the final assault on Phnom Penh. He came to S-21 in early 1977 as a guard, and in 1978 he took charge of documenting prisoners entering the facility and those executed at Choeung Ek, duties previously carried out by Peng. In late 1978 Huy was put in charge of security matters at the prison, placing him fifth or sixth in the chain of command. "After they killed all the [other] bosses," he told Peter Maguire, "they promoted me."[34]

In many interviews with journalists and scholars since 1985, Him Huy has admitted that he drove truckloads of prisoners to Choeung Ek and also killed "several" prisoners there. He claims that he was imprisoned after 1979 for "a year" for these offenses. Vann Nath, however, remembers Huy as a "very cruel" member of the assassination squad that accompanied prisoners to Choeung Ek. Another survivor said that Huy had been responsible for "hundreds" of deaths. These grim views were echoed by Nhem En and others interviewed by a British journalist in Phnom Penh in 1997. In interviews Huy has often stressed his repentance, remarking at one point, "I don't feel that [working at S-21] is what my parents intended me to do."[35]

The second Huy at S-21, Nun Huy, was nicknamed "Tall Huy" (Huy k'puh) or "Rice field Huy" (Huy srae). He ran Office 24, the prison farm at Prey So affiliated with S-21. In the hierarchy of the prison, he was an important figure. In 1976, for example, he supervised some study sessions for Communist Youth Group members working at the prison. His wife, Prak Khoeun, a "full-rights" member of the CPK, worked as a part-time interrogator at S-21. The two were arrested in November 1978. Nhem En claimed that Huy was arrested for sexual offenses, but his confession does not mention these.[36]

The Interrogators

In November 1976, the interrogation division consisted of at least eleven six-man interrogation groups. These evolved into ten six-person units by mid-1977, which were further divided into three-man teams, led by a unit supervisor. Each team included a chief, an annotator-deputy, and a third member, in the manner of Communist Party cells and other triadic organizations throughout DK. The third member, sometimes referred to as a guard, may have been the person assigned to inflict torture. By 1978, most interrogators worked in a "hot" *(kdau)* contingent. This was directed by a senior interrogator, Pu, about whom no biographical data have come to light. In 1976 and 1977 there had also been a "gentle" *(slout)* subunit, whose members were apparently prohibited from using torture. The "hot" subunit was referred to in one confession as the "cruel" *(kach)* contingent. Its members were allowed to torture prisoners. In 1978, the "gentle" group was no longer mentioned in confessions, although it may have been replaced by a "cool" *(trocheak)* unit. An eight-person "chewing" *(angkiem)* unit under Prak Nan, an experienced interrogator, dealt with tough, important cases.[37]

In 1977 and 1978, it seems that at least one interrogator, Prak Khoeun, the wife of "Rice-field" Huy, was a woman. Prak Khoeun came from Sector 25 and classified herself as a "lower-middle peasant." She had joined the revolution in 1972, she wrote, because she was angered by the "way the power-holding classes exploited and looked down on poor peasants." Having transferred to S-21 in 1977 after marrying "Rice-field" Huy, she admitted torturing "several" prisoners "until they couldn't function." There may have been other female interrogators at the prison. Ung Pech remembered one whom he nicknamed "the Monster" *(a-yeak)*, and the archive reveals that Kun, who was the wife of a senior Khmer Rouge cadre and arrested with him at the end of 1978, was interrogated by two women, Li and Kon. On the other hand, Kok Sros, interviewed in 1997, could recall no women regularly employed to question prisoners.[38]

Most of the interrogators and document workers had fought in the 1970–1975 war, often serving as messengers *(nir'sa)*—a perilous, respected job. In most cases, their education had been limited to a few years in rural primary schools or sojourns in Buddhist *wat*s, where a premium was placed on memorization, obedience, and neat calligraphy, all virtues in demand at S-21. However, the transitions from schooling to warfare to S-21, where political acuity was also prized, were often difficult for these young men, as the ex-interrogator Ma Meng Kheang confessed:

> It's difficult to think so much. You get so tired [at S-21] and you get headaches, and besides, it's a political place, it's not easy to work there, it's different from rice or vegetable farming or working in a factory. You never know when the day is finished. You never know if you are "correct." With farming, on the other hand, you either have a crop or you don't, in a factory a machine starts up or it doesn't.[39]

The hours for interrogators were long, and the work was exhausting. Questioning often extended far into the night. Interrogators resented the conditions under which they were forced to work and sometimes compared them unfavorably to the relative freedom they had enjoyed as soldiers in the civil war.[40]

The Documentation Workers

The telephone directory lists fourteen men in the documentation unit, but it was undoubtedly larger than that, and those listed were probably in charge of three-man teams. The unit was responsible for transcribing tape-recorded confessions, typing handwritten ones, preparing summaries of confessions, and maintaining the prison's voluminous files. Unsurprisingly, given what we know of the consequences for "sabotage" in DK, typographical errors are almost nonexistent. Even so, between 1976 and 1978 at least ten documents unit staff were arrested, interrogated, and put to death. They confessed to being "lazy," preparing "confused" documents, "ruining" machines, and beating prisoners to death when they assisted with interrogations.[41]

The photography subunit at S-21 operated under the supervision of Suos Thi. People in this group took mug shots of prisoners when they arrived, pictures of prisoners who died in captivity, and pictures of important prisoners after they were killed. According to Nhem En, who worked in the subunit, photographs in this final category were taken by specially selected cadres (the prisoners' throats had been cut) and forwarded in single copies to the "upper brothers." The unit also produced identification photographs of the staff. Over six thousand photographs taken by the unit have survived. Hundreds of the mug shots, selected and enlarged by East German photographers in 1981, have been posted on the walls of the Tuol Sleng Museum since 1980.[42]

The photography subunit used cameras, film, paper, and developing chemicals that they discovered at various locations in the capital. Nhem En, who defected from the Khmer Rouge in 1996, was interviewed several times. En was a peasant boy from Kompong Cham who joined the

Khmer Rouge forces in 1970, when he was ten years old. He was selected
to study photography in China in 1975 and 1976 and then came to work
at S-21. Five Khmer worked with him in the photography unit, and one
of them was purged. En himself came under suspicion in a December
1977 study session for "playing the radio" and "taking bad photographs"—offenses he recalled spontaneously twenty years later. One of
his photographs, developed from a negative processed during Pol Pot's
visit to China in October 1977, appeared to show "Brother Number
One" with an unseemly blotch above one eye. Chan accused Em of doctoring the photo to insult Pol Pot, and Em was packed off to the "reeducation office" *(munthi kay pray)* at Prey So. In early 1978 he was released,
he says, after Chan had found the flaw in the original, Chinese negative.[43]

The Guards

The defense unit, not included in the telephone directory, was the largest
at the prison. In 1978 it had 169 members: 127 assigned to the main
facility and the rest attached to the "special prison" to the south reserved
for high-ranking cadres. In 1976 and 1977 guards were organized into
six four-hour shifts a day, but in 1978 guards worked in ten-man units
for eight-hour shifts. They were expected to follow a set of thirty rules
designed to keep them alert and to prevent them from fraternizing with
prisoners. The rules enjoined them to keep prisoners from escaping,
obtaining weapons, attempting suicide, or talking to each other.[44]

Guards were not allowed to talk to prisoners, to learn their names,
or to beat them, but as a former guard admitted in his confession, "If
you're on guard at night, you can beat the prisoners without anyone
noticing it." Kok Sros has recalled that while guards were forbidden to
beat prisoners, only those who beat them "severely" were punished.
Moreover, "If a prisoner didn't obey our orders, we had authority to
beat them." As for casual chatting, which inevitably took place, Kok
Sros went on to say that

> we could talk to them, but we weren't allowed to pity them. . . . Some of
> them asked us to release them, but if we did that we would take their place.
> Some of the prisoners said, "I didn't do anything wrong, why did the Orga-
> nization bring me here?" I didn't know what to do. . . . I told them I was
> afraid to help them.[45]

Guards were also forbidden to observe or eavesdrop on interrogations,
and they were expected to be constantly alert: "While on duty," an S-21

regulation reads, "[guards] must not sneak naps or sit down or lean against the wall. They should [always] be walking, guarding, examining things carefully." Guards seldom had enough sleep. In their self-critical autobiographies, they overwhelmingly list "drowsiness" *(ngok nguy)* as the greatest flaw affecting their work. Elaborate routines governed the disposal of weapons and ammunition and the disposition of prisoners' chains, shackles, and locks. There were also complex procedures for transferring prisoners from their cells to interrogation sessions and between cells and the trucks that took them to Choeung Ek.[46]

Rules for guards prohibited humane behavior. High spirits and levity in the contingent also worried those in charge. A self-criticism document prepared at the prison in 1977 accused some guards of "laughing together in their free time" and "lacking a firm revolutionary stance." The same "offenses" crop up in the self-critical autobiographies that the guards prepared from time to time and also in guards' confessions.[47] Nhem En has recalled friendly rough-housing with his colleagues in the photography group, and Kok Sros has referred warmly to the friendships he developed in his three years of working at the prison. None of this is surprising, when we recall that many of the workers were rural teenagers unaccustomed to any kind of institution, much less one where laughter was viewed as a "shortcoming."

An Evening at S-21

In the early days of the prison the rules for guards were apparently more relaxed. A night-watch report from October 1976, which suggests as much, is the only surviving document recording conversations between guards and prisoners. This report provides a rare glimpse of prisoners and guards in relatively humane interaction and also records some examples of prisoners' courage and resistance, sadly lacking from most of their torture-induced confessions.[48]

SUMMARY SENT TO THE OLDER BROTHER
IN CHARGE OF THE GUARD GROUP

I. Interior Guards

a. *Activities of Enemies*

—Building K, Room 5, cell 5, the prisoner Pun Suphoal told the guard that mosquitoes were biting excessively.

—Room 4, cell 3, the prisoner Ngai Yet said that he couldn't sleep, between sunset and 2 A.M.

—In the room under the stair, to the west, a sleepless prisoner stole frequent looks at the guard and at the electric wiring.

—Room 5, cell 4, the prisoner Suk Hoeun, alias Hom, managed to shift a table, noisily, without informing a guard.

—Room 3, cell 4, the prisoner Yim Phoeung, at the time when our comrade was distributing rice gruel, said maliciously that he'd not yet eaten and had just come in from work but [in fact] he wasn't [ever] working, he's wearing shackles.

—In the cookhouse, Room 6, cell 3, the four prisoners Mau Hung, Yu Nan, Pun Leang, and Di Somat intend to break their locks and escape. . . . One of them said: "This is not the Organization's place, it's a place for individuals." Mau Hung said, "This is the place where the Organization caught me, it's a place where I won't survive, because the Organization consists of outlaws" [*chao prey*, literally "wild robbers"]. That's what Mau Hung said to one of our fellow guards.

—Building Kh, room 5, cell 10, when the guard asked the prisoner Som Saravuth to stretch, the prisoner claimed to be unable to rise, but when the guard left his room he stood up.

Subunits at the Prison

Three subunits and the prison farm at Prey So operated under the aegis of the defense unit. One of the subunits included eight "capturers" (sometimes called "messengers," or *nir'sa*) and ten in a "motorized section." According to Nhem En, the "capturers" accompanied prisoners to S-21 from the countryside and executed them all, including important cadres, who were killed and buried near the prison. Nhem En's memory is corroborated by Kok Sros. In 1977, Him Huy worked in this unit and earned a fearsome reputation among other members of the staff. A "motorized section" drove batches of prisoners into S-21 and conveyed others to the execution grounds at Choeung Ek.

A twenty-six person "economic support" subunit, affiliated with the defense unit, provided food and custodial services for guards, interrogators, and prisoners. Two of its members were barbers, and five others were responsible for raising chickens, rabbits, pigs, ducks, and vegetables within the compound. Four "excrement bearers" in the unit provided a plumbing and sewage system of sorts. The duty was given to guards as a punishment for minor infractions.[49] Excrement was removed in buckets from the prison and used for fertilizer.

Seven employees in the economic support unit prepared and delivered food for a prison population that averaged a thousand or more for most of 1977 and 1978. Six others performed the same task for less than a hundred interrogators and document workers, and thirteen more took care of perhaps two hundred guards. In Duch's report on the prison in the first three months of 1977, he takes seven lines to deplore the deaths of ducks and chickens at the prison and only two lines to report fourteen prisoners' deaths from torture. In the looking-glass world of S-21, ducks were mourned more than people.[50]

Rice for S-21 and probably for other units in the capital was grown at Prey So. In the DK era, men and women were sent there from units, factories, and work sites in Phnom Penh for minor offenses or pending transfer to Tuol Sleng. In the first ten months of 1977, according to a document prepared by "Rice-field" Huy, over two thousand prisoners passed through Prey So. One hundred ninety-two of them, "mostly under twenty years of age," a report from the facility asserted, had died of "illness." Eighty had managed to escape. All but twenty-seven of these were recaptured and sent on to S-21. Some of the remaining prisoners listed in the document were probably also sent along to S-21, whereas others—Nhem En and Him Huy among them—returned to duty at S-21 after serving short sentences at Prey So.[51]

Ho's defense unit also supervised the work of fifteen paramedical personnel who treated sick prisoners undergoing interrogation, patched up those who had been severely beaten, and certified deaths. One of the paramedics, Phoung Damrei (alias Phoeun), complained in his confession that there were only three trained medical personnel at S-21 to deal with thousands of prisoners. It was "impossible" to treat them, he said, and large numbers of them died. The man in charge of the detachment, Pheng Tri, was later arrested himself and made a similar admission at a study session in 1977, whereupon he was reproved by Chan for "not believing in revolutionary medicine." Prison records list prisoners as succumbing to malaria, diarrhea, "emaciation," "tiredness," and mistreatment. In a document listing twenty-one deaths in a short period, five are attributed to "wounds" and one to "torture, suffocated inside a plastic bag." Fifty-two prisoners are said to have died of "illness" between April and September 1976, a period when the prison housed less than 300 people at any one time, and a cadre notebook from 1977 recorded that 30 deaths had occurred at the prison in July, 88 in September, 49 in October, and 67 in November, making a total of 234 deaths over four months. Many those who died had already been worn down by wounds, malnutrition, and torture; several photographs of corpses in the archive show that they were all severely undernourished.[52]

Several medical study notebooks were recovered at S-21, but the teachers, students, and locations of the medical lessons are unknown. A pocket-sized notebook discovered near the prison suggests that bizarre experiments were sometimes carried out by prison personnel. These included bleeding prisoners to death and seeing how long dead bodies took to rise to the surface of a tank of water. Elsewhere in the country, fatal surgery was sometimes carried out on anaesthetized prisoners to teach anatomy to medical cadres. It is possible that experiments of this kind were also conducted on prisoners at S-21 and hardly surprising if the records have not survived.[53]

Profile of Prison Personnel

What kinds of people worked in the units at the prison? Duch, Chan, and Pon were Sino-Cambodians in their thirties who had worked as schoolteachers; the senior interrogators Pu and Tuy probably came from similar backgrounds. Most of their subordinates at S-21 were young ethnic Khmer from rural areas. Before joining the revolution in the civil war they had been students in primary school, apprentice monks, or helpers on their parents' farms. Hardly any had lived in cities or worked for pay.

Of some 166 S-21 employees who completed biographical statements in 1976 when they came to work at the prison, 44 classified themselves as "poor peasants," 99 as "lower middle peasants," 16 as "middle peasants," 1 as a "worker," and 6 as "petty bourgeois." Five of the latter had been students when they joined the revolutionary ranks; the sixth had been a teacher. Allowing for a male gender bias in the sample, the profile of workers at S-21 replicated the class structure of prerevolutionary rural Khmer society, in which the vast majority of rural families owned land, and would have been categorized as "middle" peasants.[54]

The Khmer Rouge, like its counterpart in Mao's China, made virtues of inexperience and ignorance, preferring young people who were, in Mao's phrase, "poor and blank" to those corrupted by capitalism or extensive schooling. In praising the "poor and blank" Mao asserted that "a sheet of blank paper carries no burden, and the most beautiful characters can be written on it, the most beautiful pictures painted." In Cambodia, the "upper brothers" were in charge of such inscriptions, and the "brothers" who ran the prison, accustomed to commanding respect—a respect derived in several cases from their own extensive schooling—enjoyed inscribing their ideas on others. They chose their subordinates from the least-trained members of society and demanded their respect.[55]

Duch, Chan, Ho, and Pon were indeed "older brothers" to most of their subordinates. Only twenty-five of those completing the S-21 personnel forms in 1976 were over twenty-five years old; twenty were under eighteen. One hundred eight were between the ages of eighteen and twenty-two. Kok Sros, who was twenty-five when he came to S-21, has said that guards recruited after mid-1977 were markedly younger than those assigned to the prison earlier.

Nearly all of the lower-ranking workers at the prison were young, unmarried men. Throughout world history, young men have been easily uprooted or have uprooted themselves to pursue new lives among others of their own age. Stints of travel, military service, religious life, banditry, pilgrimage, wage labor, and university study have often served to mark the transition between childhood and maturity. In the Cambodian revolution thousands of young women were also "liberated" to take up duties as soldiers, cadres, and district leaders—positions unthinkable for Khmer women in prerevolutionary times. Many young Cambodians fighting on both sides had found the war exciting, and while several soldiers confined to S-21 had deserted the ranks because they "missed their mothers and fathers," one prisoner in his confession claimed to have joined the revolution because he was angry with his parents. Many survivors of the DK era, now in their mid-thirties, enjoyed the freedom of moving around the country as teenagers, much as the young Red Guards in Maoist China had done.[56]

Many of the S-21 workers had "joined the revolution" *(choul padevat)* when they were very young. Nhem En was only ten. Six years later, when he came to S-21, others his age were working there. Photographs of these self-satisfied, smiling teenagers, many wearing oversized Mao-style caps, adorn the walls of the Museum of Genocidal Crimes. For many of them, the "Organization" had replaced their mothers and fathers. Responding to its desires, filtered through the commands of their "older brothers," they were often capable of extreme cruelty.[57]

Adolescents have earned a reputation in many countries for their malleability, idealism, their hunger for approval, and their aptitude for violence. Talking to Philip Gourevitch in 1996, the psychiatrist Richard Mollica discussed the Hutu warriors in Rwanda, whose age and background resembled those of the workforce at S-21. "In my opinion," he said, "the psychology of young people is not that complicated, and most of the people who commit most of the atrocities in these situations are young males. Young males are really the most dangerous people on the planet, because they easily respond to authority and they want approval. They are given the rewards for getting into the hierarchical system, and they're given to believe they're building heaven on earth. . . . Young people are very idealistic and the powers prey on them."[58]

Problems arose at the prison with young people precisely because they were "poor and blank." Their exposure to revolutionary discipline, to say nothing of Marxist-Leninist ideas, had been hortatory, brief, and haphazard. What they had learned in study sessions was no guarantee of good work habits. Their raw energy, so attractive in its revolutionary potential, was difficult for older people to harness. In the short time they were at DK's disposal, many of these boys and girls were impossible to educate. As a Party spokesman noted ruefully at a cabinet meeting in May 1975:

> Speaking of young, untrained people, they are honest, dedicated, and vigorous. These are their strong points. As for shortcomings, our young brothers and sisters play around too much; their culture is weak and they are illiterate and innumerate to the extent that the places where they work encounter difficulties.[59]

After the regime collapsed, Ieng Sary explained the disastrous history of DK to the American journalist Henry Kamm. "We did not choose our public servants well," he said disingenuously. "We lost some control." He neglected to say that DK "chose" its "public servants" from among the least qualified people in the country after all the incumbents had been dismissed and thousands of them had been summarily put to death.[60]

Very few of the workers at S-21 had been "revolutionaries" for long. Only twenty-nine of those completing personnel forms in 1976 had "entered the revolution" before 1973, when Vietnamese forces withdrew from Cambodia and a massive U.S. bombing campaign forestalled Khmer Rouge attacks on Phnom Penh. Fifty-eight of the workers joined in that year, forty-three in 1974, and forty-two in the first few months of 1975. The remaining five had "joined the revolution" after the capture of Phnom Penh. The only training that any of them received for working at S-21 was a two-week session of studying "politics" *(nay-obay)* at a "technical school" run at Ta Khmau in Sector 25 by "Brother [Kim] Tuy," who later became an interrogator and administrator at S-21.

For many, the school may have been their first encounter with a total institution. If study sessions from the DK era serve as any guide, those that Kim Tuy conducted would have involved listening to hortatory lectures, memorizing slogans, and preparing brief, self-critical autobiographies. Students would have marched from place to place singing revolutionary songs. They would have been allowed very little sleep. Like newly enrolled members of a religious movement, they were expected to emerge from the school with an intensified focus and a shared sense of exaltation.[61]

The cohort of workers at the prison appears geographically cohesive. Of those who completed biographical statements, one hundred one of the men and thirty-two of the women had been born and raised in the region designated as Sector 25, north of Phnom Penh, while twenty-nine came from Sector 31, three from Sector 32, thirteen from Sector 33—all northwest of the capital—and one from Sector 41, to the north. They were drawn from military units that were relocated to the capital in 1975.

Sector 25 was a thickly settled, relatively prosperous area housing thousands of Chinese and Sino-Khmer market gardeners and town dwellers as well as a majority of ethnic Khmer rice farmers. In the 1960s the region had been represented in the National Assembly by Khieu Samphan, who was popular in the electorate and encouraged followers to join the clandestine Communist Party. "Everyone in the region loved Khieu Samphan," Him Huy has recalled. Four years after his flight to the maquis in 1967, when many had thought him dead, Samphan became a key member of the Party Center. Until his defection to the Phnom Penh government in 1998, he was a formidable, malevolent survivor.[62]

In summary, making an exception for the "older brothers," most of whom sprang from Cambodia's minuscule intelligentsia, S-21 workers were of similar age, class, experience, and geographic origins. They also resembled the majority of the people incarcerated in the prison.

Prisoners at S-21

The number of prisoners at S-21 varied, reflecting the waxing and waning of the purges that swept through DK from mid-1976 onward. These are discussed in detail in chapter 3. The prison's maximum capacity, reached in 1977, was around 1,500 prisoners. On 20 April of that year, the prison held 1,242 prisoners, of whom 105 were female. It was probably in this period that Nhem En saw truckloads of prisoners arrive at S-21 and be taken off almost immediately to be killed, without being photographed or interrogated, presumably because they were considered unimportant and there was no space in the prison.[63]

At other times, S-21 held only a few hundred people. In 1975, fewer than 200 people were held by *santebal*. The number rose to 1,622 in 1976, with more than three-quarters of these arrested between May, when serious purges began and the Tuol Sleng facility was brought into operation, and the end of the year. In 1977, when many DK government offices and all geographic zones were purged, at least 6,300 people entered the prison. On some days, more than 300 prisoners were brought to the prison; on others, none came in.[64] From mid-February to mid-April 1977 alone, 1,249 men and women were brought in during purges of the Northern and Northwestern Zones.

In 1978 prisoners' photographs included placards giving their names and numbers in a monthly admission sequence. Entry records, although incomplete, suggest that at least 4,352 prisoners came to S-21 in 1978. Only 59 prisoners are listed in the scattered records for May, although the mug shot numbers for that month go up to 791. Although there are many lacunae in the photo archive for 1978, the highest number for all the months except May and August (for which no photographs survive) corresponds roughly with the entry records. I have added 732 to the recorded May entries, to arrive at a total estimate of 5,084 prisoners in 1978.

The high intake from April through June reflected the purges in the eastern part of Cambodia. By the end of the year, the prison population had dropped dramatically. In December 1978, as a note from Huy to Duch suggests, there were 279 prisoners in the "big prison" (presumably the main, western buildings), as well as 45 "Vietnamese," undoubtedly prisoners of war, and 33 other prisoners in the "special prison." There were also 14 prisoners "working" at that time. These would have included the 7 men known to have survived incarceration at S-21. Although the totals listed here come to only 13,206, given the lacunae in the data it seems prudent to estimate the prison population between 1975 and 1979 as approximately 14,000.[65]

The vast majority of prisoners at S-21 were young, ethnic Khmer males from rural backgrounds. They were socially and ethnically indistinguishable from the people who held them captive. With some exceptions, people labeled "class enemies" or "new people" and those suspected of minor crimes were generally held in provincial prisons.[66] Only

238 of the prisoners whose confessions survive, or 6.4 percent, were women. This disparity can be explained by the fact that far fewer women than men served in the military units so heavily targeted by *santebal,* and very few held positions of responsibility in DK and so could be accused of serious counterrevolutionary crimes. The number of women in the prison population, however, was undoubtedly higher than the number of women's confessions would suggest. We know that dozens of higher-ranking prisoners' wives and even some of their mothers were incarcerated at S-21 and put to death, often without undergoing interrogation. Those female prisoners who wrote confessions, on the other hand, included several holding high rank, such as district chiefs, factory and hospital administrators, and military cadres, as well as representatives of more traditional female callings such as nurses and cooks.[67]

Roughly 500 of the prisoners whose confessions have survived, or slightly more than 10 percent of the total, had held positions of responsibility in DK. In this category I include the political secretaries of military units and government offices, the secretaries of individual sectors and their assistants, regimental and divisional military commanders, cadres running industrial enterprises such as factories and railways, and those working in such government ministries as foreign affairs, information, industry and trade. Thirty of those purged had at one time been members of the Party's Central Committee.[68]

Although their fates were the same, higher-ranking prisoners at S-21 often received special treatment. Kok Sros has recalled that the cadres quartered in the so-called "special prison" slept on beds and received the same rations as the staff. After they had been interrogated and tortured, he said, they were bathed and patched up by S-21 paramedical personnel and given time to compose more "accurate" confessions. Hoping to postpone or lessen torture, and perhaps in some cases hoping to be released, many senior cadres decided to cooperate and wrote confessions of several hundred pages. The guards assigned to them, Kok Sros recalled, were chosen from the best in the contingent. The special treatment that the cadres received can be explained in part by lingering feelings of respect for high-ranking figures, but it is more likely to have been connected with the Party Center's requirement that they be kept healthy and comfortable enough to compose plausible confessions.[69]

None of the confessions provide descriptions of day-to-day life at the prison or any details about prisoners' relations with each other. In this respect the sources from S-21 are much sparser from those we can consult in studying the Holocaust, or the Argentine "dirty war," or the Chinese and Soviet prison camps, not only because survivors of these facilities are far more numerous but also because the secrecy and the "discipline" of S-21 shut off the prisoners from each other and shut us off from nearly everything that was produced at the facility except confessions, memoranda, and self-critical autobiographies. In addition, unlike the Nazi camps, S-21 had very few "trusties." The better treatment accorded some high-ranking prisoners did not include permission to fraternize with the staff. Instead, to use Wolfgang Sofsky's phrase, the prisoners "existed in a tertiary social region, a world of misery and namelessness."[70]

After mid-1976, when Tuol Sleng expanded, prisoners deemed to require extensive interrogation, but not senior enough to be confined in the "special prison," were kept in cinder-block cubicles measuring two meters by eighty centimeters, where they were shackled by one ankle to the floor. Less important prisoners, like Vann Nath, were confined in large classrooms on the second floor of the complex, "lined up in rows and shackled to the floor with ankle irons. . . . A long pole was inserted into the sprockets of each ankle iron and secured at the end of the room."[71]

Male and female prisoners were segregated, and women with small children stayed with them while their husbands underwent interrogation and before all the family members were taken off to be killed. Scattered entry records reveal that wives and children were often kept at S-21 for very short periods—sometimes as little as two days—before their executions, and one document suggests that in early July 1977 seventy-five prisoners, identified only as sons or daughters of those previously executed, were "smashed" *(komtec)* at Prey So. Confessions of prison personnel suggest that female prisoners were frequently harassed and occasionally assaulted. Vietnamese female prisoners were especially vulnerable to attack.[72]

Isolation, poor food, and silence were crucial to breaking the prisoners down in preparation for their interrogations, for as Foucault has suggested, "solitude is the primary condition of total submission."[73] The prisoners' day began at 5:00 A.M., when they were awakened and strip-searched. They were then encouraged to engage briefly in awkward calisthenics, without being unshackled from the floor. Nearly twenty years later, Vann Nath recalled the "gymnastics" vividly:

> Then we heard a voice order, "All of you get up." When I sat up I saw a small boy, about thirteen years old, standing with a rod made of twisted electric wire, maybe a meter long.

"Why are you sleeping? It's nearly dawn," the boy said. "Don't be lazy. Do some exercises."

"How can I exercise, brother?" a prisoner asked.

"How stupid you are, you old coot," the boy said. "Get the shit buckets, put them under the bars, and jump together."

All the prisoners followed his instructions. The noise of the shackles and buckets clanged throughout the room. I tried to jump a few times with the others. How could we do that, with one ankle fastened to the shackles and the other foot jumping?[74]

Those scheduled for interrogation could be taken off to as many as three sessions a day, scheduled from 7:00 A.M. to noon, from 1:00 P.M. to 6:00 P.M., and from 8:00 P.M. to midnight. Those who stayed behind were forbidden to communicate with each other; they were allowed to address guards only when they needed to relieve themselves.[75]

Prisoners in the large classrooms were "washed" every three or four days by being hosed down en masse through open windows. Food consisted of a few spoons of watery rice gruel, garnished with bits of water convolvulus *(trokuon)* or banana leaves, served up at eight in the morning and eight at night. Prisoners soon lost weight and suffered from diarrhea, "numbness" *(spuk)*, swollen limbs, and a range of skin diseases. As their resistance weakened, they were infected by other prisoners. Many of them died before they could be questioned, and others died after questioning but before they could be taken off to be killed. If they died at night, their bodies were not removed until the next morning. The contradiction between treating prisoners like animals and expecting them to provide detailed, supposedly rational confessions was central to the culture at S-21, and it was never resolved. Would more humane treatment have led to "truer" confessions? There is no way of knowing, but humane treatment of prisoners was almost always out of the question. There was no need, from the administrators' point of view, even to keep the prisoners healthy.

After a month of confinement Vann Nath recalled:

After they starved us for so long and we were unable to walk, unable even to sit up, we had no resistance, we had no strength in our hearts for resistance. It was all gone. We just lay there waiting for the day that we would die.[76]

Over the lifetime of the prison, conditions for prisoners varied in response to the number being held and the intensity of the Party Center's fears. In 1975, before *santebal* moved to Tuol Sleng and its operations became secret, several inmates were released and either sent to the prison's agricultural facility at Prey So or returned to their former units.[77] Later on a handful of prisoners, like Ung Pech and Ruy Nikon, were unshackled and allowed to perform manual work on the outskirts of the prison. In early 1978, a dozen other men—including Vann Nath and three other known survivors—were detailed by Duch to paint and sculpt images of Pol Pot. In the closing months of DK, as conditions worsened in the fighting with Vietnam, Pol Pot seems to have toyed with the idea of establishing a cult of personality similar to those that surrounded his mentors Mao Zedong and Kim Il Sung. The "trusties" at S-21 were recruited to provide a fitting monument. Talking to David Ashley in 1995, Vann Nath recalled:

> Near the end we had to design a revolutionary monument. The design was first taken to Nuon Chea who approved it and was then supposed to be taken to Pol Pot for his approval. The monument was like those in China and Korea and featured Pol Pot at the front of a line of people with his right hand stretched skywards and his left arm grasping a copy of the revolutionary works, the red book. Pol Pot was the only figure depicted as a particular individual and behind him were a number of people indicating the progress of the revolutionary struggle, beginning with axes and knives and ending with abundance, with guns and B-40s. Duch said that the plan was to destroy the temple at Wat Phnom and replace it with this monument. If the Vietnamese hadn't invaded, I think that's what would have happened.[78]

For over fourteen thousand men, women, and children confined in S-21, there was no revolutionary struggle "beginning with axes and knives and ending with abundance." For days or months on end they inhabited an anteroom to death. Their struggle ended not with abundance but when their skulls were smashed with ox-cart axles at the killing field of Choeung Ek.

CHAPTER THREE

Choosing the Enemies

S-21 was a total institution whose mission was to locate, question, and destroy the enemies of the Party Center. Given its prisoner intake and the number of inmates who were executed by the facility, S-21 was probably the most efficient institution in the country. Considering the emphasis the Party Center placed on protecting itself from "enemies," it was also one of the most important.

The theory of the regime posited the existence of enemies, and the search for them was a crucial ingredient of its practice. Because Cambodia's leaders subscribed to the Maoist doctrine of permanent revolution, counterrevolutionary "enemies" were continuously created, and purges (the Cambodian compound verb, *boh somat,* translates as "sweep and clean") were continuously needed to assure the safety of the Party Center and to maintain the revolution's purity and momentum.[1] Enemies were thought to be everywhere. "Sweeping and cleaning" them could never stop. Building and defending the country went hand in hand. As a CPK motto put it, "One hand is for production, the other for beating the enemy."[2]

To Pol Pot and his associates, friends and enemies posed a "life-and-death contradiction" *(tumnoas slap ruos).* In making this distinction, Pol Pot drew on Mao Zedong's 1957 speech "On the Correct Handling of Contradictions among the People," in which Mao had classified "the problem of eliminating counterrevolutionaries" as an example of "the first type of contradiction" (i.e., between the enemy and ourselves).[3]

Twenty years later, in a five-hour speech announcing the existence of the Communist Party of Kampuchea (CPK), Pol Pot said:

> Within the new Kampuchean society there exist such life-and-death contradictions as enemies who belong to various spy networks working for the imperialists, and international reactionaries are still planted among us to carry out subversive activities against our revolution. . . . These elements are small in number, only 1 or 2 percent of the population.

From Pol Pot's perspective, in other words, 140,000 Cambodians at most (2 percent of an estimated seven million people) were real or potential enemies of the regime. "Contradictions with these elements," he continued, "must be dealt with the same way we deal with any enemy." These measures included "winning over" and "educating" some of the enemies and "neutralizing" others. Finally, Pol Pot proposed to "isolate and eradicate only the smallest number of elements, those who determinedly oppose the revolution and the people and collaborate with foreign enemies to oppose their own nation, people, and revolution."[4] As he spoke, several thousand people had already been questioned, tortured, and put to death at S-21.

DK divided its enemies, as Stalin and Mao had done, into those outside and those within the country.[5] External enemies included powers opposed to socialism, led by the United States, and "revisionists" or "hegemonists" like the Soviet Union, Vietnam, and their allies. Pol Pot and his colleagues frequently suggested that the destruction of Cambodia was so important to these enemies that they had set aside their antagonisms to achieve it. In the same vein, a document prepared at S-21 in March 1976 fantasized that recently deposed South Vietnamese and Communist Vietnamese forces were happily cooperating with each other in Vietnam with a view to overthrowing DK, coordinating their efforts with those of Thailand and the U.S. Seventh Fleet.[6] Six months later another S-21 document, drawing on information from former Lon Nol soldiers who had undergone training in the United States, described SEATO (the South East Asia Treaty Organization)—whose principal policy objective was to destroy DK—as having Taiwan, South Korea, Indonesia, and "the Viet Cong" as its members.[7] In 1978 Nuon Chea, the second-ranking official in the Party Center, told sympathetic Danish visitors that

> It is . . . widely known that the USA planned to seize power from us six months after liberation. The plan involved joint action on the part of the USA, the KGB and Vietnam. There was to be a combined struggle from inside and outside. But we smashed the plan.[8]

External enemies were relatively easy to identify. They could be held in check by vigilant defense and by Cambodia's powerful friends. "China can help us scare our enemies," Pol Pot told CPK cadres in 1977. "Having friends like the Chinese is a good thing."[9]

Internal opponents of the regime, on the other hand, were hard to locate and considered more dangerous. Those operating in the open posed no special problems. They included the "new" or "April 17" people evacuated from the towns in 1975 and men and women from the "old society" whose class origins or biographies were inimical to the revolution. After April 1975, tens of thousands of these people were kept under informal surveillance in the countryside or were held in "education halls" *(sala oprum),* indistinguishable from prisons, where conditions were harsh and thousands died.[10]

Internal Enemies

What concerned the Party Center more than these remnants of the past were those designated as "hidden enemies burrowing from within" *(khmang bonkop si rong phtai knong).* Although these men and women had joined the revolution, they were now working to betray it. In May 1975 Nuon Chea attacked such enemies at length when he spoke to Party cadres.[11] A few months later, an editorial in *Tung Padevat* claimed that internal enemies had "tried to make the revolution change its colors."[12] In 1978, an editorial in the journal railed against people who

> were able to carry the signboard *(plaque)* "Revolution" temporarily, masquerade as revolutionaries, burrow away, build up their treasonous forces inside our revolutionary ranks and damage our revolution at a time when our revolution wasn't strong, hot or battlehardened, when it still took the form of a secret network or when it was cut off from the masses. But at the moment when the revolutionary mass movement sprang out seethingly, resplendent with power, when the secret networks awoke, at that point the buried enemies boring from within no longer had a place to hide, no matter how important they were. Every single one of their silent, shielded, masked activities aimed at destroying the revolution could be seen clearly by the revolutionary masses and could be smashed at once.[13]

Toward the end of the regime, talking to the Danes, Nuon Chea remarked in passing that "we are not worried about . . . external, military aggression. We worry most of all about the enemy inside."[14]

The hunt for internal enemies was deeper, more complex, and more relentless than merely finding and "smashing" treacherous individuals.

Insidious "bourgeois" ideas, preferences, and attitudes were thought to be buried in everybody's consciousness—an idea that Pol Pot inherited from Stalin and Mao. In 1977 Pol Pot declared, "We all carry vestiges of our old class character, deep-rooted for generations." These had to be destroyed before socialism could be achieved. A year earlier, a writer in *Tung Padevat* had said:

> We must rid each Party member, each cadre of everything that is of the oppressor class, of private property, stance, view, sentiment, custom, culture which exists in ourselves, no matter how much or how little.[15]

In "sweeping clean" Cambodia of its traitors and all citizens of their potentially "bourgeois" thinking, *santebal*'s work had to be wide-ranging, open-ended, and merciless. As a DK adage put it, "It is better to arrest ten people by mistake than to let one guilty person go free."[16]

Once they were identified, arrested, and brought to S-21, suspects of the Party Center became "guilty people"—guilty because they had been arrested rather than arrested because they were guilty. Dehumanization of the prisoners was immediate and total. Just as Lon Nol had seen his opponents as nonbelievers or *thmil* (i.e., "Tamils"), and just as the U.S. Congress until recently regarded indigenous Communists as "un-American," Pol Pot and his colleagues thought of Cambodia's internal enemies as intrinsically foreign and impure. Internal enemies could wreak enormous damage. In his "Last Plan," Duch compared their strategy to "the way that weevils bore into wood" or "the way oil permeates" and likened them to "worms" *(dongkeau)* or "germs" *(merok)* that had come from the CIA, Vietnam, and so on to attack healthy, revolutionary people.[17]

Once infected, anyone could infect others. Counterrevolution, unless it was nipped in the bud, could become an epidemic. In December 1976 Pol Pot drew on this quasi-medical imagery in a passionate address to CPK cadres. "There is a sickness in the Party," he said:

> We cannot locate it precisely. The sickness must emerge to be examined. Because the heat of the people's revolution and the democratic revolution were insufficient at the level of people's struggle and class struggle . . . we search for germs within the Party without success. In the Party, the army, and among the people we can locate the ugly germs. They will be pushed out by the true nature of the socialist revolution.[18]

Like many of Pol Pot's statements, this one was a volatile mixture of hubris, paranoia, and wishful thinking. It failed to define the "true nature" of the revolution, explain how the sickness might "emerge," or, most important, demonstrate any proof that the Party had "treacherous, secret elements" buried inside it. Instead, the speech referred vaguely to "observations over the last ten years."

The 1975 Purges

The purges conducted by the Party Center and enacted at S-21 can be broken into two broad phases. The first lasted from September 1975 until September 1976. The second extended until the collapse of DK. Most of those targeted in the first wave of purges were civilian and military officials affiliated with the defunct Lon Nol regime. In the backwash of victory, thousands of these people were rounded up and killed. In Vietnam, by contrast, such people were normally sent off to "reeducation" camps; many died, but tens of thousands eventually emerged. The 1975 killings in DK, like reeducation in Vietnam, were ordered from the top. According to Cho Chhan's 1977 confession, after the "liberation of the entire country,"

> the Organization put forth a policy of successively exterminating officers, starting from the generals and working down through to the lieutenants, as well as government security agents, policemen, military police personnel and reactionary civil servants.[19]

These killings extended the civil war and reflected its brutality. Historical precedents can be found in the Soviet Union after 1917, in China in 1949–1950, and in Vietnam after 1954. Another parallel, pointed out in 1979 by Noam Chomsky and Edward Hermann, might be the "purification" (épuration) of suspected collaborators and "enemy agents" that followed the Allied victory in France in 1944–1945. In both France and Cambodia, popular anger, the sudden empowerment of former victims, and the absence of judicial safeguards combined to encourage a range of extrajudicial behavior that included widespread killings.[20]

In Cambodia, the killing campaign was curtailed in June 1975 by the Party Center. Soon afterward more formal and more extensively documented procedures for dealing with "enemies," centered on santebal, came into effect. From October 1975 onward, instead of being summarily put to death, people suspected of working against the revolution were interrogated and required to prepare confessions. Prisoners included officials of the defunct regime, Cambodians who had studied abroad, deserters, malingerers, Khmers with links to the deposed Thieu regime in Saigon, and the so-called Hanoi Khmer, who were viewed by the Party Center with particular suspicion and had been subjected to CPK purges since 1972.[21]

In 1976, as the purges gathered momentum, the Khmer Rouge worked hard to consolidate their control over the country and to burnish their reputation overseas. In January, Democratic Kampuchea's constitution was promulgated. In April national elections were held, a central government was formed, and steps were taken to set up a national army. Phnom Penh Radio announced that a "rubber plantation worker" named Pol Pot, unknown by that name to anyone outside the Party, was the country's new prime minister. In May, *santebal* shifted most of its operations to Tuol Sleng. Soon afterward, the second wave of purges began.

Because Tuol Sleng functioned as the capital's main political prison, the sorts of victims targeted earlier continued to be brought in, questioned, and killed, but as Elizabeth Becker has phrased it, "The Party leaders [now] shifted their attention from eliminating or transforming the bourgeoisie to eliminating the bourgeois tendencies in the Party." The alteration ushered in a full-scale reign of terror that continued until the collapse of DK. As Hannah Arendt has suggested, "Only after the extermination of real enemies has been completed and the hunt for 'objective' enemies begins does terror become the actual content of totalitarian regimes."[22]

The Second Wave of Purges

The new search for enemies was accelerated by two unnerving, inexplicable events. On 25 February 1976, an explosion occurred in the city of Siem Reap, accompanied by sightings of foreign aircraft. In early April a series of what were probably random explosions in Phnom Penh seemed to Pol Pot and his colleagues to foreshadow a full-blown coup d'état. Exactly what happened on these two occasions is still unclear. Publicly the regime blamed the Siem Reap explosion on "CIA agents"— a charge sustained as late as 1978—and the incident in the capital on DK troops manipulated by Vietnam. In private, the Party's leaders suspected the secretary of the Northern Zone, Koy Thuon (alias Khuon), of involvement in the Siem Reap explosion. They also came to suspect the secretary of the Eastern Zone, the veteran revolutionary Sao Phim (alias Sovanna) of masterminding the incident in the capital. Both men, remained at large, although soon after the explosion Koy Thuon was summoned to Phnom Penh, ostensibly to take charge of the nation's foreign trade but also to be questioned about alleged sexual misconduct. On 8 April 1976, less than a week after the explosions in Phnom Penh, Koy Thuon was placed in protective custody in a "special building" *(sala pises)* near the Royal Palace, not far from the heavily guarded buildings occupied by the "upper brothers." In May and June, the second wave of purges began in earnest.[23]

In presenting the sequence of these purges, using data drawn to a large extent from successive confessions, I have taken no position on the truth of the texts or on the prisoners' innocence or guilt. Because these decisions may disappoint readers looking for a reliable history of opposition to DK, my rationale needs to be spelled out.[24]

First, without corroboration from other sources, very few of the "facts" contained in the confessions, aside from strictly autobiographical ones, can be taken at face value. Whether prisoners told the truth under torture, said what they were told to say, said what they thought their interrogators wanted to hear, or produced a mélange of truth, half-truth, and fantasy is impossible to determine. It is safe to assume, however, not only that in their broad outlines most confessions were fabricated to suit what S-21 officials assumed to be the wishes of the Party Center but also that strands of genuine conspiratorial narrative, and actual angry conversations are sometimes woven into the confessions.[25]

Second, very few documents have survived about the decisions made by the Party Center regarding "enemies." We can seldom determine why prisoners were arrested, aside from tracing their associations with others already arrested or with units that had performed badly and had come under suspicion. For low-ranking prisoners, the essence of their "crimes" was often the company they kept. Higher-ranking prisoners, on the other hand, were made to confess to planning to overthrow or sabotage the revolution by forming rival parties, plotting to assassinate the Party's leaders, or openly criticizing the Party Center's policies. Whether these conspiracies were genuine, or the conspirators accurately named, is impossible to determine.

Although there were no courts or judges in Democratic Kampuchea, the confessions resemble briefs for the prosecution, or more precisely the kinds of evidence assembled for an examining magistrate under the French system of justice practiced in prerevolutionary Cambodia. The confessions were prepared at S-21 for the invisible "judges" in the Party Center. Because of the infallibility asserted by the Party Center and the secrecy surrounding S-21, the possibilities of error, innocence, and release were all foreclosed.

Moreover, using the words "guilty" or "innocent" to describe the prisoners at S-21 is misleading. Using these words lends judicial legitimacy to a macabre project whereby all the prisoners, regardless of their actions and before they started talking, were condemned to death. Procedures followed at S-21 indeed sometimes seem to have been inspired by the Red Queen in *Alice in Wonderland* or by Kafka's *The Trial*. At another level, those prisoners genuinely "guilty" of opposing DK might well deserve to be seen—in hindsight, to be sure—as heroes, while those victims who were "innocent" of opposition and thus complicit in the regime's guiding ideas and practices should not necessarily be honored as law-abiding citizens of a humane regime, swept up in error by a responsive judicial system. In the topsy-turvy world of DK, as in the French Revolution and in occupied Europe in World War II, guilt and innocence were always affected by the ebb and flow of power at the top.

The diverse responses of French citizens to the German occupation in World War II provide a useful parallel to what happened in Cambodia, with diverse meanings opening up for "selfishness," "nationalism," and "betrayal" depending on who was involved in politics as well as where, when, and to what extent. To extend the comparison, it certainly occurred to a number of CPK cadres after 1977, or even earlier, that some form of foreign, (Vietnamese) patronage or even a more "Vietnamese" style of revolution would be preferable to the ongoing depredations, endemic poverty, and apparently random, open-ended violence of DK. By 1978 thousands of Cambodians were cutting their losses, drawn to the greater power of the Vietnamese and the possibility of new patrons. None of them, it seems, had judged DK as evil from the start. Similarly, very few French citizens had opposed Pétain in 1940, whereas many had come to do so by 1943. In DK in 1977 and 1978, however, the defectors from DK, like latter-day Gaullistes, became guilty, from the government's perspective, of choosing what turned out to be the winning side. The purges of the Eastern Zone in Cambodia in 1978, which aimed to stamp out resistance and prevent more people from fleeing to Vietnam, had the unintended effect of generating opposition among survivors. Those who escaped these purges, including such post-1979 Cambodian luminaries as Heng Samrin, Chea Sim, and Sar Kheng, joined surviving "Hanoi Khmers" and some earlier defectors to form the regime that took office after the Vietnamese invasion.

Finally, the awesome cruelty of the DK regime toward its citizens, so vividly documented in the archive of S-21, does not foreclose the possibility that Pol Pot and his associates in some cases (but which ones?) had evidence about real conspiracies to overthrow them. As Steve Heder has suggested, many of the confessions ring true, even without corroboration, and it would be wrong to label all the prisoners at S-21 "innocent" of involvement in conspiracy because their confessions contain absurdities, because the regime was evil, or because they were all so cruelly treated.

Rationale for the Archive

Putting questions of justice, truth, innocence, and guilt aside, we still need to ask why the S-21 archive was so voluminous and why it was maintained at all when its contents were kept secret, so much of the material was untrue, and all the prisoners were killed.

We now know that DK was far more heavily documented than observers had thought likely in the 1980s, when hardly any DK documents except those from Tuol Sleng were accessible to outsiders. Impressed at the time by the sheer bulk of the S-21 archive and the supposedly primitive character of the regime, many of us believed that other documentation from DK, if it existed, would not alter the general picture that was emerging from survivors' descriptions.[26] Since 1994, however, hundreds of thousands of pages of DK materials, including thousands more dealing with S-21, have come to light. Most of these were released by the Cambodian government to the Cambodia Genocide Program managed by Yale University. Others were discovered at S-21 itself after the microfilming of the archive was completed in 1993.[27]

Many of these recently discovered documents are typed; some survive in several carbon copies. The clatter of typewriters in derelict buildings, indeed, was probably one of the few sounds of human activity in Phnom Penh. Moreover, we know that the mountain of DK material now accessible to scholars represents only a fraction of what was produced. Sizable collections of DK documents still closed to outsiders are known to exist in Cambodia and Vietnam.[28]

The S-21 archive, therefore, is not unusual in its volume or its technical sophistication, but why it was maintained? Why were such lengthy and detailed confessions extracted from people already condemned to death and kept on file after the prisoners had been killed? An obvious, perhaps overriding answer is that workers at S-21 wanted at all costs to avoid the wrath of their superiors. Playing it safe, they processed the regime's "enemies" as thoroughly as they could and maintained the voluminous files as proof of their hard work. Another likelihood is that the administrators of the prison, every one a true believer, were genuinely curious about betrayals of their "beloved Party" and hoped, by documenting what the prisoners confessed, to plumb the depths of counterrevolutionary schemes. A third possibility is that prisoners hoped by spinning out their confessions to avoid or postpone torture and execution. Finally, its seems clear that Son Sen and the other former schoolteachers running the prison wanted to administer a modern, meticulously documented security operation, worthy of an internationally recognized Communist regime and pleasing to themselves.

These explanations are helpful, but a more fruitful one was suggested to me some time ago by Steve Heder, who argued that the archive was assembled to provide the Party Center with raw material for a massive, unwritten history of the Party.[29] Detailed accounts of so many conspiracies would have assuaged the curiosity of Pol Pot and his colleagues—lifelong conspirators themselves—about what was going on behind their backs while they were underground in the 1950s, in hiding in the 1960s, and on the move during the civil war. Moreover, because everyone held at S-21 was eventually "smashed," their confessions would testify not only to their crimes but also to the Party's power and omniscience. As induced historical texts, they provided the Party's leaders with intriguingly dark areas that threw the triumphal history of the Party into sharp relief. The model that Pol Pot and his colleagues were following, it seems, was the *History of the Communist Party of the Soviet Union,* as published in 1939—a document with which several of them had probably become familiar during their time in France. This document tells the story of Stalin's triumph over the Party's internal enemies.[30]

At a psychological level, reading confessions and execution reports and looking at photographs of their executed enemies must have made the "upper brothers" feel temporarily secure. Like many authoritarian leaders, Pol Pot and his colleagues believed that they were surrounded by enemies conspiring to overthrow them. The prisoners at S-21 objectified these fantasies and brought their dreams to life just long enough for the dreamers to know that their enemies were being subdued. Ruling the country by terror, the DK leaders seem to have been terrified themselves, echoing what Engels had observed to Marx in September 1870, during the siege of Paris: "We take the reign of Terror to mean the rule of people who inspire terror. On the contrary, it is the rule of people who are themselves terror-stricken. *La Terreur* implies mostly needless cruelties perpetuated by terrified men."[31]

The interrogators at S-21 also acted like poorly trained therapists excavating the buried "memories" of their prisoners just as therapists examine the manias of their patients. The patients in question were not the prisoners, as one might expect, although the interrogations included elements of Chinese-style thought reform. Instead, the patients, or at least the beneficiaries of the therapy, were those in the Party Center whose anxieties and resentments were embodied by the prisoners and in the crimes that the prisoners were encouraged to "remember" and confess. As ring after ring of enemies was smashed at S-21, the leaders of DK may have felt vindicated and reassured. In the meantime, however, another ring of enemies had sprung to life.

The interrogation procedures followed at S-21 bear some rudimentary and fortuitous resemblances to psychoanalytic practices. As sources for an unwritten Party history and as tools of therapy beneficial to the Party Center, the interrogations and the confessions provided the Party Center with what the psychiatrist Donald Spence has called the "narrative truth" that they needed to function as political leaders and perhaps as human beings.[32] The relation of the confessions to Spence's contrasting notion of "historical truth," however, cannot be clarified until more DK archival materials come to light or more former party members speak their minds. In the meantime, reading the confessions takes us inside the thought processes of a schizophrenic regime that was at once terrified and terrifying, clairvoyant and delusional, omnipotent and perpetually under threat. The confessions provide a narrative of the Party Center's evolving fears and obsessions as these beleaguered, vindictive, visionary men and women struggled to maintain the nation on a war footing, impose collectivization, achieve economic independence, stifle dissent, and centralize their control.

The Events of April 1976

On 30 March 1976, at a meeting convened by the Party Center, procedures were established "to smash [people] inside and outside the ranks." These delegated control over "smashing" enemies to appropriate bodies so as "to strengthen our state power"; the bodies in question were to be accountable to the Party Center. The gnomic reference is as close as researchers have yet come to a smoking gun that implicates the leaders of DK in the mass killings perpetrated under their regime. The meeting also dealt with such questions as pushing Sihanouk aside as chief of state, tearing down the Catholic cathedral in Phnom Penh, Party history, economic planning, official holidays, and government organization. Reading it today, one senses the helter-skelter enthusiasm of the newly empowered regime, whose leaders were looking forward to extending their victory of April 1975 "over the United States" to Cambodian society as a whole.[33]

Three days later, shortly before dawn, grenades exploded near the Royal Palace, and shots were fired at the National Museum in Phnom Penh. The palace and the museum were not far from the heavily guarded compound occupied secretly by the "upper brothers." There is no evidence, however, of casualties, material damage, or further conspiratorial activity. The motives behind the explosions are unclear, but the "upper brothers" took them, and their timing, very seriously indeed. Prince Sihanouk was scheduled to resign as head of state later in the day, and, while the hapless soldiers who threw the grenades were probably unaware of the coincidence, the country's jittery leaders saw the incident as foreshadowing a coup d'état. The grenade-throwers were arrested within a week, and tape recordings of their confessions, with a covering note by Duch, were rushed to the Party Center.[34]

The culprits belonged to Division 170, a unit formed after April 1975 out of Division 1, which had been recruited in the Eastern Zone during the civil war. At the time of the explosions, elements of the division were stationed on the outskirts of Phnom Penh, where its soldiers were assigned to growing rice—a task many of them found demeaning. In keeping with S-21 practice, which it shared with police operations everywhere, the culprits were pressed to implicate their superiors. Suspicions soon coalesced around Chan Chakrei, a flamboyant Eastern Zone military figure and former Buddhist monk who was acting as Division 170's political commissar. Chakrei, thirty-three years old, was also deputy secretary of the newly formed national army's general staff, working under Son Sen.[35]

Chan Chakrei had switched sides at least once before; he had come under CPK scrutiny in 1975. Arrested on 19 May, he was designated in S-21 documents by the Roman numeral I, at the head of a "string" of alleged conspirators that ran to twenty by the end of the year. In the course of a four–month interrogation he confessed to links with the Lon Nol regime and to membership in the Khmer Serei, a quasi-military, anti-Sihanouk movement based until 1975 in South Vietnam.

He also claimed to have planned to assassinate Sihanouk and to poison the "upper brothers." In the wake of Chakrei's arrest, Ly Vay, the deputy secretary of Division 170 (Number II), was hauled in. In his confession, Ly Vay spoke vaguely of "wanting to disrupt security in Phnom Penh." Chakrei, for his part, implicated Ly Phen (Number IV), the political commissar of the Eastern Zone armed forces, Ros Phuong of Division 170 (Number VII), and Suas Neou (alias Chhouk, Number VIII), the secretary of Sector 24 in the Eastern Zone. Ly Phen was arrested in June 1976, Ros Phuong in July, and Chhouk in August.

Chhouk was a long-time protégé of the Zone secretary, Sao Phim, a senior revolutionary who was close to the Party Center but already suspected of disloyalty because of his friendly relations, dating back to the 1950s, with Vietnamese Communist cadres. Sao Phim at this time belonged to the so-called Central Military Commission *(kanak kammatikar santesuk-yothea)*, which allegedly set policies for purges in DK.[36]

Chhouk's confession was of special interest to the Party Center because of his connections with Sao Phim. A passage dated 28 September 1976—which may of course be fictional, like so much of the archive—suggests that Sao Phim had prepared him for the possibility of interrogation. We know from Phuong's 1978 confession that Chhouk's arrest in 1976 had been delayed until Sao Phim returned from a mission to China, so such a briefing may well have taken place. The passage reads:

> During the second stage when the Party interrogated me using torture [Chhouk wrote] I stuck to Brother [Sao] Phim's instructions by agreeing to implicate Keo Meas. [The Organization] still did not believe me, since I could not provide exact answers about treasonous activities, I did not know where any Party Center standing committee traitors were. I did not know how many there were ... or how they acted. I implicated Keo Meas but I didn't know where he was. I implicated Vietnam, but incorrectly in the details. Then my situation gradually deteriorated as the Organization asked to uncover the apparatus leaders. I tried to evaluate and balance between two things: Who was stronger, my group or the Party? ... I stuck to the hope that no matter how the security people educated and questioned me I could protect the treasonous elements [of Sao Phim], evade up and down to implicate the Hanoi group, the old resistance group and miscellaneous small elements. But because of the Party's inspired judgment, the Party refused to accept my reports, saying they were unclear and asking me to do them again. This was the final word of the Party, asking me to reconsider. Then ... even if I was to lose my life, I was determined to answer the Party truthfully about [Sao Phim's] treason. ... I pledge absolutely to follow the Party's road.[37]

Purging Senior Cadres, 1976

Those besides Sao Phim implicated in Chhouk's confession included three senior Party figures: Ney Saran (alias Ya, Number IX), the secretary of the Northeastern Zone; Keo Meas (Number X), a veteran revolutionary then under house arrest; and Non Suon (alias Chey, Number XII), who was serving in effect as DK's secretary of agriculture. They were not informed of the Party's suspicions, of course, and for the time being they remained at large. In July and August the CPK convened meetings to acclimatize Party members to its Utopian Four-Year Plan, scheduled for promulgation in September. In that month, Ney Saran and Keo Meas were brought into S-21. Non Suon was arrested at the beginning of November.[38]

These three men had much in common with each other. Aside from their age, they had almost nothing in common with Pol Pot. They had joined the anti-French resistance in 1945 and 1946. They had learned about Marxism-Leninism from Vietnamese Communist cadres or from Cambodians trained in Vietnam. None of them had studied in France. Unlike Brothers Number One and Two, Non Suon and Keo Meas had operated in the open in the 1950s; Ney Saran had taught at the same school as Saloth Sar. Keo Meas had twice run as a radical candidate for the National Assembly, and Non Suon had been imprisoned by Sihanouk in 1962. Both men had joined the Party's Central Committee in September 1960, alongside Saloth Sar, whom they knew well. In 1963, Ney Saran and Keo Meas had joined Pol Pot and a handful of others in Office 100, the Vietnamese base on the Cambodian-Vietnamese border, where they remained until 1965. From then on, their paths diverged. Non Suon, released from prison in 1970, joined the maquis near Phnom Penh, Ney Saran became a military leader in the northeast, and Keo Meas worked in Beijing and Hanoi on behalf of the United Front government in exile. When he returned to Cambodia in 1975, Keo Meas, probably suspected of being pro-Vietnamese, was placed under house arrest.

At S-21, the three were accused of having formed the Workers' Party of Kampuchea (WPK) to oppose the CPK from within. Belonging to WPK, it seems, was shorthand for treason committed by CPK members after Pol Pot had been brought into the Party Center in 1960. In 1977 and 1978, the dissident "party" became the focus for accusations leveled at many prisoners at S-21. The party was a moving target, and WPK had the same portmanteau usefulness as "CIA" or "KGB."

Because WPK was seen as a permanent source of enemies, its leaders were always said to be at large. In July 1978, for example—almost two years after Keo Meas had been arrested and put to death and a month after Sao Phim had killed himself—Pon wrote in his notebook: "Find the leaders of the WPK. This is crucial."

Ironically, as many high-ranking prisoners knew perfectly well, Pol Pot's own party had chosen the Workers' Party of Kampuchea as its name in 1960. Although the name change had probably been approved, if not imposed, by the Vietnamese, there is no evidence that a rival Party using this name was ever established. Instead, the Party was known as the WPK until mid-1966, when Pol Pot, again in secret, renamed it the CPK.[39]

Despite these contradictions, the idea that Keo Meas had founded a concealed party called the WPK was still current in 1978, when Von Vet, the deputy prime minister, was arrested and wrote in his confession that the subversive party

> was put together with the help of the Vietnamese, who had Keo Meas create it so that the Vietnamese could build up their forces in Kampuchea. The important CIA people joined this party. In form it belonged to the Vietnamese, but [in] reality . . . it belonged to the CIA. It took the form of the Communist Party in order to proceed with its work.[40]

Keo Meas and Ney Saran were arrested in a bewildering sequence of events that began in August 1976, when the CPK's Four-Year Plan was discussed at a cadre meeting, and closed in October with a controversy over the founding date of the CPK, manipulated by the Party Center, that was resolved in Pol Pot's favor. Taken together, the events and arrests marked a turning point in the histories of DK and S-21. By the end of the year, perhaps as a result, the Party Center's pronouncements had become pessimistic and bellicose. By the beginning of 1977, purges reached the central nervous system of the CPK. For these reasons, the sequence of events that occurred from August to October 1976 must be set out in detail.

On 21–23 August, CPK cadres assembled in Phnom Penh to be briefed by Pol Pot on the Party's "Four-Year Plan to Build Socialism in All Fields," a 110-page document compiled earlier in the month. The plan proposed to expand Cambodia's agricultural production so dramatically that exports, especially rice, could earn enough foreign currency to pay for imported agricultural machinery and later, when agricultural outputs increased, to finance industry. To overcome the obstacles in its path, the Party Center counted on the revolutionary fervor supposedly generated by the leveling of Cambodian society, the collectivization of the means of production, and the collective empowerment deriving from the Khmer Rouge's victory in April 1975. These dogmatic assumptions were untested. The plan made no allowances for variations in world markets, paid little heed to the types of soil or the availability of water within Cambodia, and overlooked crippling shortages of workers, tools, and livestock. Most importantly, the plan failed to acknowledge that most Cambodians were prostrate after five years of war and that hardly any of them had enough to eat. Instead, the Party Center assumed that nearly everyone in the country was ready, able, and willing to grow enormous quantities of rice.[41]

In political terms, the plan offered Pol Pot and his colleagues an opportunity to grasp the wheel of history *(kong pravatt'sas)* and thereby to display the purity and strength of Cambodia's revolution to allies and enemies overseas. Study notebooks prepared by S-21 cadres suggest that the Party Center seriously believed the Cambodian revolution was the most successful in world history. The Four-Year Plan, in turn, was the CPK's most detailed policy document. The Party's leaders probably hoped to unveil it at anniversary celebrations scheduled for 30 September, when it seems likely that they also hoped to proclaim the CPK's existence.

In Pol Pot's address to the August gathering dealing with the plan, the language of his "preliminary explanation" echoed the breezy self-assurance of the plan itself. In passing, he singled out the "contemptible people to the east and to the west" (Vietnam and Thailand) as causes for vigilance and alarm. He said nothing about internal enemies.

Mao Zedong's unexpected death on 8 September triggered some uncertainty in the Party Center. A former DK cadre told Steve Heder in 1980 that "after Mao's death there was apprehension in Kampuchea. . . . People were afraid that chaos and confusion in China might affect our solidarity with China."[42] On 18 September, at a memorial service for Mao in Phnom Penh, Pol Pot admitted publicly for the first time that Cambodia was being governed by a Marxist-Leninist Party. He praised Mao's writings, including "On the Correct Handling of Contradictions among the People." On the same occasion, the Chinese ambassador, Sun Hao, noted that Mao had reached "the scientific conclusion that there are bourgeois elements even inside the Communist party"—a key tenet of Chinese radicalism that was used to justify the continuing purges there.[43]

Pol Pot's "Resignation"

On September 20, Pol Pot "resigned" as prime minister on grounds of ill-health. The announcement of the resignation was made by Phnom Penh Radio a week after it had supposedly occurred. Pol Pot's place was taken, the announcement said, by Nuon Chea, "Brother Number Two," who had occupied the position since 1963 and was to do so until Pol Pot's eclipse in 1997. Pol Pot's "resignation," if it ever occurred, may have been caused by genuine illness—he suffered from recurrent bouts of malaria and dysentery—or because he feared assassination and wanted to go into hiding. It is more likely, however, that Pol Pot never resigned and that the announcement was intended to throw some of his internal enemies off balance and to draw others into the open. This explanation seems plausible given that neither Nuon Chea nor Ta Mok, interviewed by Nate Thayer in 1997, had any recollection of the event.[44]

Ney Saran was arrested on the same day that Pol Pot resigned. Keo Meas was apprehended five days later. From a study session convened at about this time, perhaps to coincide with the anniversary of the Party's foundation, a brief, anxiously worded document emerged, titled "Summary of the Results of the 1976 Study Session." The text, which consists of notes taken from a speech by a Party spokesman, is much darker in tone than Pol Pot's August speech describing the Four-Year Plan. It is tempting to associate its pessimism with suspicions or information emerging from the two arrests.[45]

Whereas the August speech had mentioned foreign enemies, the September "Summary" referred more ominously to "instruments and agents" of foreign powers who "furtively steal their way into and hide themselves in our revolutionary ranks." The speech foreshadowed the one delivered in December that deplored "a sickness in the Party." It also inaugurated a new phase of class conflict in DK, which, the speaker said, would be "sharp . . . uncompromising, bitter, thorough, and life and death . . . long into the future."[46]

Ney Saran: "The Contemptible Ya"

The full-blown reign of terror that ensued from September onward was probably linked in some way to what Keo Meas, Ney Saran, and other prisoners were being forced to "confess" at S-21. It is impossible to determine whether these prisoners had been involved in genuine plots, although documents that survive from S-21 about them are suspiciously skimpy and may have been culled after 1979 to conceal evidence of connivance with the Vietnamese. As they stand, the documents do little to explain the paranoia that seems to have gripped the Party's leaders from then on.

Ney Saran's confession covers only thirty-one pages, drawn from seven interrogation sessions. Several viciously worded memoranda from Pon to Duch and from Duch to Ney Saran supplement the slim dossier.[47] On 23 September, for example, Pon reported to Duch that he had beaten Ney Saran with rattan whips and electric wires. In a four-page memorandum written to the prisoner on the following day, Duch addressed Saran disingenuously as "Older Brother, in Anticipation," and noted that

> you are a person in whom the Organization has placed the greatest confidence, because you have been closer to the Organization and closer to our revolutionary movement of Kampuchea when compared with other people whom the Organization has recently arrested. The Organization has made it clear to us that you cannot hide anything that has happened in the past. The Organization knows what is good and what is evil. You can't lie or blame other people as you have done. . . . The Organization . . . has clear views about stubborn people.

Two days later, Duch wrote to Pon that "if [Ney Saran] continues to hide his treacherous linkages . . . he should be executed and not allowed to play games with the Party any more." Torture was stepped up, and Pon wrote to Duch:

> In the afternoon I asked Brother Duch to give permission to use both hot and cool techniques; having received permission toward the early evening I went in to threaten him, telling him to prepare himself at 8 or 9 P.M. for the torture to be continued. At about 10 P.M. I went in to get ready to carry out torture with [my] bare hands. IX [Ney Saran] started to confess by asking us to summarize what he was to report. We clarified this as follows: "Please write a systematic account of your treasonous activities from beginning to end."

Keo Meas

The confrontation between Pon and Ney Saran is easy to imagine, but a "systematic account" of his activities, if it was ever written, has not survived. Similarly, no full confession by Keo Meas has come to light. The ninety-six pages in his handwriting in the S-21 archive consist of letters that he addressed to Pol Pot over a relatively brief period.[48] Several of them carry Duch's notation "Don't summarize," which suggests that they never left the prison. Keo Meas's dossier also contains questions posed by Pon and Duch, directives to Keo Meas in Pon's handwriting signed "*santebal*," and cruel annotations by Duch demanding information, revisions, and retractions.[49] Even under intense pressure, Keo Meas continued to protest his innocence. He had almost thirty years' experience in the cut and thrust of Communist debate, and in his letters to Pol Pot he was fighting for his life. "These accusations are absurd," he wrote. "They are totally incomprehensible to me. I knew and did nothing of the sort."

As far as the Party's anniversary was concerned, he wrote on 29 September, the day before it was to be celebrated, that

> my view is in favor of maintaining 1951, and if anyone wants to go down a different path from this, I'm not willing to go along. I will . . . oppose it by maintaining that the Pracheachon Group and the Pracheachon newspaper were legal organs of a Marxist-Leninist Party, which was founded in 1951.

When Was the Birthday of the Party?

Keo Meas's stance on the anniversary issue exposed a major contradiction in the CPK's perceptions of its history, one that had been papered over for many years and was to be resolved in Pol Pot's favor. The contradiction had been noted in passing in the 30 March meeting of the Party Center: "Set the birth of the Party at 1960; do not use 1951 . . . make a clean break."[50]

At stake in what seems like a semantic argument were the large questions of the Party's leadership and Cambodia's relations with Vietnam. From 1960 to 1975, the anniversary of the CPK had been celebrated on 30 September 1951, a date that blended 30 September 1960, when a Party meeting in Phnom Penh had constituted the Workers' Party of Kampuchea (WPK), with the year 1951, when its predecessor party, the Khmer People's Revolutionary Party (KPRP), had been founded at the instigation of Vietnam.[51]

A CPK cadre who defected to Vietnam from the Eastern Zone in 1978 reported that preparations were being made in mid-September 1976 to celebrate the Party's twenty-fifth anniversary. As these were underway, however,

> we received an urgent message from higher authorities ordering us to suspend the preparations. Later on a circular from the central office informed us that the Party had been founded on 30 September 1960. Anyone who had

joined the Party prior to that date should consider himself not a Party member, and his years with the Party before 30 September 1960 were invalid. If he agreed, he would be redeemed by the Central Committee. Otherwise, he would be sent to a re-education camp.[52]

The September issue of the CPK's journal, *Revolutionary Youth,* carried an article anticipating the twenty-fifth anniversary, while an article in the September–October special issue of *Tung Padevat* declared that the CPK had been founded in 1960, because "we have made a new numeration." The rationale for the change, the author said, was that

> the Revolutionary Organization has decided that from now on we must arrange the history of the Party into something clean and perfect, in line with our policies of independence and self-mastery.[53]

This passage marked another stage in the ascendancy of Pol Pot and his colleagues. Since articles in both journals were always vetted and largely written by Pol Pot and Nuon Chea, the possibility of an uncoordinated disagreement between them is remote. It seems more likely that the *Revolutionary Youth* article was published to draw the "1951" faction into the open, where they could be "smashed," whereas the article in *Tung Padevat* represented the considered thinking of the Party Center.

In early November, Non Suon, a longtime associate of both men, was arrested as he disembarked from an airplane bringing him home from an official mission to China. At S-21 he protested his innocence at first, but after three weeks of interrogation he succumbed and wrote:

> I am a termite boring from within . . . and wrecking the Party in every way I can. No matter how the Party has educated and nurtured me, I have not abandoned my dark and dirty intentions. . . . I would like to present myself to the Party Organization for punishment for the serious crimes I have committed in willingly betraying the Party so that the Party can strengthen and expand [its] ranks . . . and advance toward the construction of a Communist society.[54]

Purging Diplomats and Intellectuals

By December 1976, when Pol Pot delivered his "sickness in the Party" speech, the Party Center had decided to keep the CPK's existence secret from outsiders and to shelve the Four-Year Plan. The rationale for these decisions, given at the December meeting, was that unspecified "documents have revealed that enemies have tried to defeat us using every possible method"—probably a reference to the confessions that had recently been extracted at S-21. At about the same time, although the documents are lacking and the reasons for the timing unclear, the Party Center probably decided to inaugurate sustained hostilities against Vietnam. In early 1977 DK launched a series of vicious cross-border raids from the Eastern and Southwestern Zones. Hundreds of civilians were massacred in these incursions, which were not publicized in either country.[55]

As DK prepared itself for war, the CPK also purged people in the diplomatic service and the ministry of foreign affairs suspected of being "pro-Soviet" or "pro-Vietnamese." Prominent victims included the DK ambassador to Vietnam, Sean An, and Hak Seang Lay Ni, a foreign ministry official accused of founding yet another rival Communist party, with Soviet encouragement, in the 1960s. Several other diplomats were also rounded up. These punitive measures also reflected the distrust felt within the Party Center for anyone except themselves who had had professional training, extensive residence overseas, or contacts with non-Khmer.[56]

The purges also foreshadowed the campaign against intellectuals (neak cheh dung) inside the Party that gathered steam in the first half of 1977. In February, two prominent Party intellectuals, Koy Thuon and Touch Phoeun, were brought into S-21. Both members of the CPK's Central committee, they were the first cadres at this level to be purged. Santebal's targets soon included military and civil cadres in the Northern Zone, where Koy Thuon had served as secretary until early 1976, and other intellectuals in the CPK who were associated with both prisoners. In the words of the "Last Plan," these were people "who pretended to be progressive and infiltrated the revolution to gain information."[57]

Koy Thuon was born in 1933 and entered the Lycée Sisowath in 1949. After graduation he embarked on a teaching career. In 1959 or 1960, inspired by Tiv Ol, a fellow teacher who was "like a brother" to him, Koy Thuon was drawn toward revolutionary ideas. Sponsored by another teacher, Son Sen, he joined the CPK. In 1960 he worked with Khieu Samphan on Samphan's short-lived weekly, L'Observateur. After a stint of teaching in Kompong Cham, where he recruited Sua Va Si (alias Doeun) and others into the Party, Koy Thuon fled to the maquis. During the civil war, he was active in the Northern Zone, where he earned a reputation as a womanizer and bon vivant. In the words of the "Last Plan," "the group [around] Koy Thuon . . . created an atmosphere of pacifism, luxury and excitement entertained by arts, girls, receptions and festivities . . . stimulated prestige, ranks and relations with the enemy."[58]

Koy Thuon's copious, neatly written confession implicated over a hundred people. These included senior Party figures, civil and military cadres who had worked with him in the North, and his subordinates in the commerce committee. His confession also implicated a cohort of former schoolteachers, including the minister of information, Hu Nim; the director of Office 870, Suas Va Si; his assistant, Phok Chhay; the ex-minister of the interior, Hou Youn (purged in 1975); and Koy Thuon's former mentor, Tiv Ol, who was working in 1977 with Hu Nim. Koy Thuon also implicated Tiv Ol's wife, Leng Sim Hak, but she was not arrested for another six months. In closing, his confession listed "networks of traitors" in the northeast, the northwest, the port of Kompong Som, and Phnom Penh.[59]

In his confession Koy Thuon was forced to devalue his career and to blacken the reputations of everyone he had worked with except those in the Party Center. His numerous intellectual acquaintances constituted a new category of targets. The purge against them began soon after his arrest. Following Laura Summers's suggestion, Steve Heder has referred to these men and women as "democracy activists" and has characterized them as "ex-petit bourgeois associated with Son Sen either directly or via Koy Thuon." Heder locates the most sustained, coherent opposition to Pol Pot's policies in the DK era, within this group.[60]

Koy Thuon's confinement coincided with a serious uprising against the regime that had broken out in Chikreng, near Siem Reap, in March. Refugees escaping to Thailand later reported widespread unrest in the Northern Zone and the replacement of local cadres there by cadres from the Southwest. Suspects from the Northern Zone and the military forces associated with it—Divisions 310 and 450—were heavily purged. The S-21 archive contains over three hundred confessions from people associated with these units, and an 1178-page dossier amalgamates references to soldiers in Division 310 mentioned in all the confessions. In March 1977 alone, some 1,059 people arrived at S-21, straining its capacity. An overwhelming number of them had Northern Zone connections.[61]

In questioning Koy Thuon, interrogators sought out or created multiple connections with people already purged. The prisoner also confessed to meetings with two American CIA agents whom he identified as "Furkley" and "Cerutti," with Vietnamese "agents," and with non-Communist Cambodian colleagues from the 1960s during the civil war.[62]

Koy Thuon brought out the worst in his interrogators. On 2 March Duch wrote him an ominously deferential letter which closed by asking

why your faith was so strong, given that the CIA, Vietnam and the Khmer
Serei all have stinking reputations and given that their concrete forces have
disintegrated under attack to an extent you had not imagined? On this question you have not yet reported correctly. This is the question you are avoiding.

Two days later, Koy Thuon wrote an abject response to these demands.
For another month, before he was killed, he doled out hundreds of
names and detailed narratives of his own and other people's treasonous
behavior.

His confession was a mirror image of the Party's triumphal narrative. At every turn, his feckless "plans" to assassinate Pol Pot, to
"gather forces," to form rival parties, to assemble Thai, American, and
Vietnamese patronage and support, to demoralize his own troops, and
to "produce confusion" by reinstituting private property came to nothing. His "treasonous activities," which should have been sufficient to
unnerve or smash any incumbent regime, had no effect on DK. Instead,
his powerlessness and his abject confession provided further evidence
of the Party's clairvoyance.

Echoing the passage in the *Tung Padevat* article, study sessions at
S-21 at this time concluded that Koy Thuon's arrest and the data in his
confession had dramatically reduced tensions in the country. The senior
interrogator Tuy wrote in his study notebook:

> In the old Northern Zone before the problem of Khuon's "strings" or "net-
> works" was solved there were problems of defense and construction and
> problems affecting people's livelihood. After the contemptible Khuon's
> "strings" were clear, the movement was able to leap along in every aspect.[63]

Two weeks after Koy Thuon's arrest, Doeun was brought into S-21.
Doeun had worked closely with Thuon in the civil war and had
replaced him briefly as commerce secretary. In 1975 he became the
administrative officer of Office 870, the CPK's Central Committee. He
visited Koy Thuon often in 1976 and 1977 to discuss commerce ministry affairs. The visits had certainly been approved by higher-ups
beforehand, but by the time of Doeun's arrest, they had become occasions for conspiratorial talk. While the "offenses" of both men may
have been woven together from the suspicions of the Party Center, the
possibility of a genuine conspiracy between these two old friends, one
close to the Party Center and the other maintaining extensive "strings"
of loyal people in the countryside, cannot be discounted.[64]

Rummaging in his memory for offenses, Doeun claimed that he had
shirked combat in the civil war, encouraged subordinates to "lose faith

in the revolution," and planted fruit trees without permission. He also confessed to extensive dealings with Vietnamese cadres (normal practice at that stage of the civil war) and to plotting outright against DK.

Of the prisoners arrested so far, with the possible exception of Ney Saran, Doeun was the closest to the Party Center, and the importance of his position in Office 870 is confirmed by the fact that he was replaced by Khieu Samphan, DK's ostensible chief of state. It is possible, as Heder has argued, that Khieu Samphan played a key role in Doeun's downfall. He was certainly the major beneficiary.[65]

Koy Thuon's confession also implicated Hu Nim (alias Phoas), DK's minister of information and propaganda and a longtime associate of Khieu Samphan, who was arrested in April 1977.[66] Born into a poor peasant family in Kompong Cham in 1930, Hu Nim had overlapped with Khieu Samphan (and missed overlapping with Saloth Sar) at school in Kompong Cham. He studied in France from 1955 to 1957, while Khieu Samphan was there, before taking up a government position in Phnom Penh. Along with Samphan and Hou Youn, Hu Nim had served in Sihanouk's National Assembly until he had attracted the prince's wrath for his outspoken pro-Chinese views. Threatened with arrest in 1967, Hu Nim fled the capital. Hou Youn and Khieu Samphan had preceded him. For several years, nothing was heard of the three men. Their supporters assumed that they were dead, and they came to be known as the "three ghosts."

Soon after the March 1970 coup d'état, the ghosts reappeared via a radio broadcast recruiting people into the resistance. During the civil war, they occupied "cabinet" positions in the United Front government, forming a façade that concealed those who held genuine power in the Party Center.

Hu Nim was a dedicated revolutionary. Even at S-21, it seems, he was still prepared to accept the rulings of the Party. In his own handwriting he spelled out a lifetime of counterrevolutionary activity, but because his revolutionary career was so well known, much of the treason that he was made to adduce had to be subjective and related to unspoken "bourgeois" attitudes.

As the Dutch scholar R. A. Burgler has suggested, there are hints in Hu Nim's confession that he had some genuine objections to CPK policy and had heard objections from others. According to Kiernan, Hu Nim had suggested reintroducing money into DK.[67] In his confession, Hu Nim said that Nhem Ros, the secretary of the Northwestern Zone, had criticized the Party Center's policy of "self reliance, using the labor force as the basis and using very little machinery." Hu Nim stated that

Sao Phim shared similarly subversive views. Nhem Ros had also complained, accurately enough, that armed struggle in the northwest in the 1960s, beginning with the quasi-spontaneous Samlaut uprising of 1967, which had been savagely repressed, had been ignored in the Party history. Hu Nim promised to produce sympathetic propaganda materials about the northwest that would defy the Party Center's reading of history.[68]

Hu Nim's confession foreshadowed the arrests that soon swept through the Northwestern Zone. The purges in fact responded to the food crisis affecting the zone, where thousands of "new people" evacuated from the cities had already died of malnutrition and overwork and where unrealistic grain quotas set by the Party and enshrined in the Four-Year Plan had not been met, resulting in famine. The purges constituted a classic case of scapegoating by the Party Center, whose programs could fail only if they had been betrayed. As Nhem Ros put it, quoted in Hu Nim's confession:

> "Now for the year 1976, the Party has assigned us the task of achieving three tons [of paddy] per hectare. As for the northwest . . . the Party has assigned us four tons per hectare. . . . How can we [fulfill the Plan] if there is no solution to the problem of machinery? We cannot. This is not my fault, it's the fault of the Standing Committee."[69]

For Hu Nim to write the last sentence in this passage, even placing it in the mouth of someone else, took extraordinary courage. On 28 May 1977, he wrote in his last confession that

> over the twenty–five years that have passed [1952–1977] I gave myself over very cheaply into the service of the enemy's activities. Strong private property habits, imposed on me by the feudal and capitalist classes and the imperialists, suppressed me and made me become an enemy agent. I served the . . . CIA and the American imperialists who have now been shamefully defeated, and I have received my present fate. Over the past month and a half I have received a lot of education from the Party. I have nothing to depend on, only the Communist Party of Kampuchea. Would the Party please show clemency toward me. My life is completely dependent on the Party.

In late April 1977, Hu Nim was followed into S-21 by Siet Chhe (alias Tum), who had replaced Chan Chakrei on the military general staff in 1976 after serving as secretary of Sector 22 in the Eastern Zone. There, as a known protégé of Pol Pot, he may have been expected to keep tabs on Sao Phim and other cadres. Siet Chhe had studied under Saloth Sar at the Chamraon Vichea middle school in the 1950s. He had been brought into the Communist movement by Saloth Sar and his wife, Khieu Ponnary. He had accompanied Sar to Office 100 in 1963 and had nursed him through bouts of malaria and other ailments. By 1977, however, probably because of his association with the Eastern Zone and with intellectuals of his generation in the Party then being purged, Siet Chhe's credit had run out. Perhaps, as he suggested in his confession, other Party members were jealous of his high status. His arrest was a clear indication that loyalty in the CPK was never a two-way street. Indeed, because Siet Chhe was thought to have betrayed his trust—or perhaps, as he claimed, because he was innocent and still hoped for intercession from Pol Pot—his interrogations were particularly severe. Moreover, just before his arrest he had been working closely with Son Sen. His former mentor, to avoid being implicated himself, was probably zealous in pushing for a confession.

Like Keo Meas, Siet Chhe tried to send private memoranda to the "upper brothers" from S-21. The fact that these documents survive in the archive suggests that they never left the prison. Siet Chhe's high status, however, probably kept Duch and his colleagues from destroying them. They are worth quoting in detail.[70]

In the first of them, written a week after his arrest, Siet Chhe denied the charges leveled against him. Three days later, he wrote to "Brother 89," Son Sen:

> I am suffering horribly, brother! Never in my life have I run into anything like this! When my daughter was in the enemies' [Lon Nol's] prison, I thought it was a normal thing—a struggle between the enemy and us! Now that I'm confined in the revolution's prison *(kuk padevat)* on the other hand, I can't understand it, it's enormously confusing, but in the end I can see clearly that it was the CIA group, the Vietnamese consumers of territory, and people working for the KGB who have dropped me into the revolution's prison.

Siet Chhe told Son Sen that "three traitors" had slandered him. He claimed to have reported everything about the issue "to the Organization in detail through S-21." By communicating directly with the "upper brothers" he hoped to negotiate his fate. Later in the memorandum, however, he noted that "I have always understood without any firsthand knowledge [of the place] that once entering S-21, very few leave; that is, there's only entering; leaving never happens. Brother, if this is the case, I have no way out."

His appeal for mercy is rendered more poignant by what seems to be its transparent honesty, its breathlessness, and, as we shall see, by the brutality of Duch's response. Siet Chhe was terrified. He knew that he was about to be tortured. He wrote:

> At S-21 for a week now, the staff have not used any methods at all against my body. I have only been shackled. The staff have taken good care of me. According to the people responsible for me, after five to seven days I would enter stage 2, that is, the stage of being tortured.
>
> Beloved brother! I know I am finished! No matter how the comrades take me and beat me, break my bones to bits, there will be nothing new to report. It is certain that there will be only the flow of blood and feces, or death.
>
> Please rescue me in time, brother. No matter how I die, I will be loyal to the Party to the end.
>
> If you don't rescue your younger brother, he will certainly die! And I will agree to die by my own hand, not allowing the Party Security (santesuk pak) to smash me [and thus] saving the honor of Party Security for smashing of [genuine] enemies . . .
>
> This is the final time. . . . Brother, please rescue your younger brother in time. I would be happy to grow rice with my wife and children on a collective farm. I don't need to have any official position. You need not think of that. . . . Please save me, just let me live.

Duch's reply, written after Chhe had been tortured, took issue with the prisoner's contention that he had been framed by treacherous associates. "Painting people black" was an enemy trick, Duch wrote, but the CPK was "so far advanced" that it was always able to detect and overcome such trickery. He went on to say that

> in my historical observations, I have never seen a single cadre victimized by trickery aimed to paint him black. The Party doesn't pretend to be worried by this issue. Speaking to be easily understood, [let me say that] there has never been a single cadre who has come into santebal because of trickery to paint him black. . . . What's your understanding of the problem, brother?
>
> Looking at the problem: does it arise because the CPK has been deceived by the enemy into painting you black, or because you haven't been straightforward with the CPK? It's my understanding that you haven't been straightforward with the CPK. What's your understanding? I ask you to consider this problem and resolve it. When we agree, we can work together.

Siet Chhe was hard to crack. In June Duch altered his approach. In what may be the cruelest document in the S-21 archive, the interrogator Tuy wrote to Siet Chhe:

> Write out the story of [your] sexual activities with your own child in detail because from the standpoint of the masses, this [offense] has been clearly observed. You don't need to deny this. Don't let your body suffer more pain because of these petty matters.

The person involved was Siet Chhe's only daughter, a young woman of twenty who was already a dedicated revolutionary. Siet Chhe denied the charges and insisted that his favorite child was still a virgin. His eloquent denial appears in an appendix to this book. Something seems to have snapped inside him after he was psychologically invaded in this manner. For the remainder of the year, until he was killed, he wrote no more memoranda. Instead, his confessions implicated dozens of former colleagues.

Purging the Northwest

At some point in 1977, probably when confronted with the mixed results of the agricultural expansion envisaged by the Four-Year Plan, and probably using information that was reaching him from confessions extracted at S-21, Pol Pot decided to place more emphasis on ferreting out enemies of the state than on economic development. The Four-Year Plan itself seems to have been quietly abandoned.[71]

In April and May 1977, *santebal*'s attention shifted to the Northwestern Zone, where civil and military cadres were accused of sabotaging the economic aspects of the revolution by imposing harsh conditions on the populace so as to lower everyone's morale and to undermine their confidence in the revolution. In 1977, because of a poor harvest and a poorly equipped and ill-fed labor force, the expected deliveries of rice from the northwest had not arrived in Phnom Penh. Cadres in the zone were accused of hoarding or destroying the harvest, deliberately starving the people under their jurisdiction, allowing others to flee the country, offering Cambodian territory to the Thais, plotting with Cambodian exiles, and trading rice to Thailand.[72]

In prerevolutionary times, the northwest had been Cambodia's rice bowl, producing the bulk of the country's rice exports. Much of the region had been under Thai control in World War II, and with Thai encouragement it had become a breeding ground for the anti-French Khmer Issarak in the late 1940s. In 1967, a rebellion against Sihanouk's army had broken out in a former Issarak stronghold in Samlaut. The uprising led to severe repression and thousands of deaths. Armed struggle against Sihanouk was inaugurated in the zone in February 1968. During the civil war, however, much of the region had remained in the hands of the Phnom Penh regime.[73]

After 1975, its population included hundreds of thousands of "new people" evacuated to the countryside from Phnom Penh, Battambang,

and other towns. CPK cadres in the northwest tended to be inexperienced at administration, and many of them lacked local ties. Their
counterparts in zones bordering Vietnam, in contrast, had enjoyed years
of revolutionary training and, after 1970, uninterrupted periods of
political control. Many of the cadres put in charge of the Northwest
Zone in 1975 and 1976 were either former schoolteachers like Khek
Pen (alias Sou), the popular secretary of Sector 4 who was purged in
1977, or former combatants from other zones without much education.
In some cases, "new people" were given responsibilities, but these
people were regarded as potential saboteurs because of their class origins and previous activities. "Cooperatives administered by bad class
elements," *Tung Padevat* declared in October 1977, "are without rice
to eat." The article suggested that the "bad class elements" were to
blame.[74] On the other hand, the secretary of the zone, Muol Sambath
(alias Nhem Ros), was a veteran revolutionary who hailed from the
northwest and had built up a following there.[75] Like Sao Phim in the
east, he had remained in the region during the civil war. What Pol Pot
and his colleagues disliked about the northwest, aside from its proximity to Thailand, was that its leader was quasi-independent and linked
by marriage to Sao Phim. Because he was so popular, the Party Center
held off arresting him for several months.

Within the zone itself, conditions varied from sector to sector. In the
main rice-growing area, located primarily in Sector 3, there was usually
enough to eat, and relatively few executions took place. In the more
sparsely populated sectors 1, 4, 5, and 6, "new people" were assigned
to clearing often malarial forest, conditions were much worse, and
death tolls from disease and malnutrition were among the highest in
DK.[76] In formulating the Four-Year Plan, Pol Pot and his associates had
high hopes for the northwest, which was expected to produce 30 percent of the nation's annual yield for every year of the plan. The Party
Center expected the zone's "new people," most of whom had no experience in farming, to fulfill the regime's unrealistic hopes to harvest three
tons of rice per hectare.[77]

In mid-1976 Khieu Thirith, who was Ieng Sary's wife and Pol Pot's
sister-in-law, visited the northwest and was distressed by what she saw.
"Conditions were very queer," she told Elizabeth Becker in 1980. "The
people had no homes and they were all very ill." Instead of blaming
these conditions on commands emanating from the Party Center, she
told Becker, as she had probably told Pol Pot, that "agents had got into
our ranks."[78]

One of these "agents," presumably, was Phok Sary, a sector official who was arrested in 1978 and was made to shoulder the blame for some of the problems in the zone:

> I gave instructions to wreck the paddy harvest by harvesting it unripe. There was also to be wrecking when it was threshed. I designated Chaet to burn paddy . . . and a lot of already harvested paddy was burnt. I told forces in the districts that robbers and new people were burning the paddy. My goal was to create turmoil among the people, between the base people and the new people. This stymied the Party's [Four-Year] Plan. . . . When the paddy was being farmed, the only action was to wreck it along with the equipment used for planting and harvesting. In addition, the forces attached to the district secretary were instructed to starve the people of rice, to make them eat gruel, so as to get them to make demands on the Organization.[79]

In April and May 1977, cadres from the northwest began to be brought into S-21. Some had "intellectual" connections; others were purged for sabotaging the Four-Year Plan.[80] By the end of the year the secretaries and their assistants of all seven sectors in the Northwest Zone had been purged, and tens of thousands of citizens had been killed. Before the year was out several thousand "base people" (those who had not lived under Lon Nol during the civil war) had been brought into the Northwest Zone by train from the southwest. Cadres from the west and southwest followed, and in several northwestern districts they purged and replaced "disloyal" officials. In some districts they instituted communal eating, and they set often impossibly high standards for rural work. The purges and the harsh policies of the new arrivals generated hundreds of refugees, who spoke to journalists and diplomats in Thailand.[81]

Throughout 1977 relations between DK and Vietnam had deteriorated as Vietnam refused to negotiate border issues on DK's terms and DK increased its pressure through anti-Vietnamese propaganda broadcasts and cross-border raids. In September 1977 the Vietnamese ambassador to Cambodia, Phan Van Ba, speaking with Pol Pot, took issue with DK claims that the regime wished to "retake" areas of southern Vietnam known to the Khmers as Kampuchea Krom, or "lower Cambodia." Pol Pot replied: "That would not be in our real interests. The problem is that we have enemies in our ranks." His response defies analysis: were the "enemies in our ranks" people who wanted to attack Vietnam, or those who counseled him against it? And how was the ambassador to discern Cambodia's "real interests"?[82]

War with Vietnam

On 27 September 1977, in a five-hour speech broadcast on DK's national radio, Pol Pot announced and celebrated the role of the CPK in Cambodian history. His decision to bring the CPK into the open had probably been forced on him by China, which he was about to visit. The speech was broadcast on 30 September to coincide with the Party's "seventeenth" anniversary. By then Pol Pot was already in Beijing. In the speech, he referred to an "infamous handful of reactionary elements" working to undermine DK, but he named no names and struck an optimistic note appropriate to the occasion. In the meantime, Eastern Zone forces had inaugurated a series of unpublicized attacks on Vietnam.[83]

In late October, soon after Pol Pot returned from China, Vietnamese forces mounted a serious offensive against Cambodia. They remained on Cambodian soil, in the vicinity of Svay Rieng, until the end of the year, and they herded several hundred prisoners (many of whom would probably have fled Cambodia in any case) into Vietnam when their campaign was over. Neither country publicized the conflict, but shortly before the Vietnamese forces withdrew in early January 1978, DK broke off diplomatic relations with Hanoi. Soon afterward the Party Center formally declared victory. Pol Pot visited Sao Phim's headquarters at Suong to celebrate the event. He called on his listeners to engage in all-out warfare against Vietnam, echoing an inflammatory document titled "Guidance from 870" issued earlier in the month that compared Vietnamese troops to "monkeys shrieking in the forest" and noted that the war could be won easily if every Khmer combatant killed thirty Vietnamese.[84] Later in the month Pol Pot cited "flaming national hatred and class hatred" as weapons in the struggle. According to the Tuy-Pon notebook, he told supporters on 17 January: "When you fight the Vietnamese, if you attack his legs, he can't crawl; if you attack his arms, he can still walk."[85] Where the "legs" and "arms" were located was left for his listeners to decide.

Racially based nationalism had emerged as the basis of DK propaganda, and the "enemies" brought into S-21 in 1978 were overwhelmingly accused of collusion with Vietnam. Son Sen and the secretary of the newly named Central (formerly Northern) Zone, Ke Pauk, who had been sent to the Eastern Zone in November 1977 to supervise the fighting, were asked to remain there to reorganize its military forces and to purge anyone who was thought to have "aided" the Vietnamese. By mid-February, the Vietnamese had formulated secret plans to overthrow DK either internally or by force. There is no evidence that the Party Center was aware of this decision, but their worst nightmare—that Vietnam would "swallow" Cambodia—was coming true.[86]

For the first half of 1978, the "enemies" targeted by the Party Center were often said to have "Cambodian bodies and Vietnamese heads," and at S-21 particularly stubborn prisoners were made to pay homage to a drawing of a dog whose head was Ho Chi Minh's.[87] Most of the "traitors" were thought to be in the Eastern Zone, where the Vietnamese incursion had been most successful and where veteran cadres, from Sao Phim down, had a history of associations with the Vietnamese dating from the early 1950s.[88]

Sao Phim was a popular figure in the zone. He had been a Communist since the 1950s. Although comfortable with Marxism-Leninism as he understood it, Sao Phim had been slow to introduce the more radical aspects of CPK policy, such as communal eating, into the zone. In some areas he allowed people to wear their own clothes instead of peasant costumes. In December 1978, several months after Sao Phim's suicide, the deputy prime minister, Sok Thuok (alias Von Vet), confessed to a conversation he claimed to have had with Sao Phim in 1977, when both of them had allegedly been members of the subversive WPK:

> He informed me of the good situation in the East Zone. [The WPK] had been able to build itself up in the ranks of the military and among the people. Cooperatives had already been established, but the harvest was distributed and there was a private standard of living in accordance with the demands of the people [who] did not want to eat in common because they perceived that this meant shortages of everything. If they . . . lived privately, eating in families as in China, the people would be very happy.[89]

Von Vet went on to say that the notion of following Chinese models of socialism had "been disseminated among the people . . . especially in the East, the Northwest and the Northeast, starting from the end of 1977"—that is, when the survival of the Cambodian "race" (puch) began to take priority over the development of socialism.

Between March and May 1978, while scattered fighting against Vietnam persisted, the Party Center continued its purge of the Eastern Zone. Sao Phim seemed to know what was happening but was unable to raise the energy or gather the forces to resist.[90] In March, he was suffering from intestinal troubles and a skin disease. Half-suspecting that he was a target of the Party Center, he spent some time recuperating in the 17 April Hospital in Phnom Penh before traveling by train to the northwest with the zone secretary, Nhem Ros.

On 25 March, while Sao Phim was hospitalized or possibly visiting the northwest, the secretary of the Western Zone, Chou Chet (alias Si) was arrested and brought to S-21. Along with Nhem Ros and Sao Phim, Chou Chet was a holdover from the pre–Pol Pot period of Cambodian radicalism. Several of his CPK colleagues from that period, as we have seen, had been purged in 1976. Chou Chet seems to have been a loyal revolutionary unwilling to adopt the strident rhetoric of the regime and concerned about people's welfare. His wife, Im Nan, held the prestigious post of party secretary in Sector 32 in the Northern Zone. She was arrested with him. In her confession, she claimed to have cooked for Pol Pot in Office 100 in the 1960s and to have repeatedly tried, without success, to poison him.[91]

The Party Center then embarked on a wholesale purge of cadres in the Eastern Zone. In April 1978, so many were brought into S-21 that some of the trucks bearing prisoners had to be turned away. The prisoners were presumably taken off to be killed without any interrogation.[92] The purges were conducted by senior members of the CPK, led by Son Sen and supported by loyal troops dispatched from the Southwest and the Central Zones under Ke Pauk.

In mid-May 1978, Ke Pauk invited senior Eastern Zone cadres, from Sao Phim down to officials at the battalion level, to a meeting at Sao Phim's headquarters at Suong, which been occupied by Ke Pauk and reinforced with tanks and infantry from other zones. Sao Phim, sensing a trap, refused to go. Those who went were arrested, and some were executed on the spot. Several divisional commanders and the secretaries of Sectors 20, 21, and 22 were bundled off to S-21. Over the following days, Pauk sent messages summoning Phim to meetings. The subordinates whom Phim sent to ascertain Pauk's intentions were arrested one by one. Their failure to return provoked Sao Phim's suspicions. Unable or unwilling to believe that Pol Pot was behind the attacks—he preferred to consider Son Sen and Pauk as traitors—Sao Phim prevaricated.

On 25 May Pauk launched an attack from Suong against recalcitrant Eastern Zone units. He ran into spirited resistance, later characterized by some participants as a rebellion against DK control. On 31 May, Sao Phim decided to go to Phnom Penh to plead his cause with Pol Pot. When he reached Chrui Changvar opposite the city and sent a messenger to announce his arrival, forces were sent from Phnom Penh by boat to capture him. He fled by Jeep and sought refuge in a *wat*. In the meantime, helicopters dispatched from Phnom Penh dropped leaflets throughout the zone naming him as a traitor and asking combatants to lay down their arms. Three days later, when a 300-man force recruited locally was on its way to arrest him, Sao Phim shot and killed himself.[93]

Fighting between government forces and Eastern Zone units continued for several weeks, during which several Eastern Zone cadres, including the divisional commander Heng Samrin (later Cambodia's president), sought refuge in Vietnam, where they were enrolled in a force being assembled to invade Cambodia. In June and July, in what Heder has called "massive, indiscriminate purges of Party, army and people alike," pro-government forces massacred thousands of people in the east. In the most extended and systematic outburst of state-sponsored violence in the DK era, they killed off entire villages suspected of harboring "traitors." Tens of thousands of other civilians were evacuated from the zone and told that they would be resettled. Many of these were massacred either en route or when they arrived in the southwest, the zone from which the cadres who had purged the east had predominantly come. Some were in fact resettled in the northwest. By September 1978 the Eastern Zone had been "swept clean."[94]

The Final Purges

The closing months of DK were marked by the regime's desperate attempts to seek military support from China and political backing from non-Communist countries while playing down some of the harsher aspects of DK rule. The purges continued, but at a slower pace. In the process, previously immune entities were targeted. Prisoners were brought into S-21 from the railroads, the factories, and even from the supposedly loyal southwest, where a tightly focused, xenophobic anti-intellectual, Ta Mok, had been in command for many years. Toward the end of 1978, the factory workers were joined in S-21 by nearly a hundred Vietnamese prisoners of war. Von Vet, a deputy prime minister, and his long-time associate, Cheng An, the deputy minister for industry, were also purged in November, charged respectively with plotting a coup and with mobilizing factory workers, many of whom were former soldiers. Any organized group of young men was now potentially a nest of traitors.

In December suspicions fell on Son Sen, who had been made secretary of the Eastern Zone in addition to his other duties, following Sao

Phim's suicide. Because of these new responsibilities and the burden of the fighting with Vietnam, Son Sen may have been exercising less control than usual over the operations of S-21. He had been closely associated with Von Vet since the civil war, and scattered evidence suggests that the two men might have been considering a self-defensive coup d'état against the Party Center. The Vietnamese invasion and the collapse of DK probably saved Son Sen's life.[95]

Without such extraordinary interventions, no mechanisms at S-21 or in the Party Center could stop or decelerate the process of "sweeping clean." Any command to do so would have had to emanate from the "upper brothers," and until the last few months of 1978 it never came. At that time, while fewer and fewer prisoners were being targeted, those who were tended to be high-ranking cadres. As conditions throughout the country worsened, suspicions deepened in the upper ranks of the Party, and as fighting with Vietnam went badly, scapegoats were needed. Inevitably, as the lower ranks of the CPK were eliminated, suspicions fell on increasingly senior figures. Even Ta Mok and the Southwestern Zone cadres whom he commanded came under scrutiny in the regime's closing weeks. Who might have come next? Where could the persecutions end? The all-consuming purges made macabre sense: how could anyone ever be sure that the last concealed enemy had been found?

A larger, more experienced, and more self-confident Communist Party might have been able to restrain the purges when they got out of hand. Belated efforts along these lines were made in the closing months of 1978, when the prisoner intake at S-21 dropped off sharply. However, the Party Center still felt itself surrounded by enemies. There was ample evidence from S-21 to prove it: *santebal*'s mission had always been to validate the Party Center's worst suspicions. After the Vietnamese invasion of 1977–1978 and the purges in the Eastern Zone, the Party Center was beset by fears and racing against time.

Reigns of terror and continuous revolutions (in DK, the two phenomena overlapped) require a continuous supply of enemies. When these enemies are embedded in a small, inexperienced political party, ethnically indistinguishable from the majority of the population, attempting to purge *all* its enemies can have disastrous effects. As Duch and his colleagues did what they were told, they undermined Cambodia's military effectiveness, dismantled the administrative structure of the country, and destroyed the Party. The killing machine at S-21 had no brakes because the paranoia of the Party Center had no limits. The

half-hearted reforms instituted in 1978—the amnesty proclaimed by
Pol Pot and the reduction of torture at S-21—[96] were counterbalanced
by the fact that several of the revolution's highest-ranking figures were
arrested at that time, just when the Party needed experienced cadres to
present a united front in the conflict with Vietnam. By the end of the
year, the Party's administration of the geographic zones had largely broken down; Ta Mok had assumed command of several zones at once.

When the Vietnamese launched their invasion in late December
1978, the CPK's Central Committee had been decimated. Except for Ta
Mok, all the original zone secretaries and most of their replacements
had been purged, as had the administrators of nearly all the nation's
factories and hospitals and hundreds of military cadres. By the end of
1978, there were not enough experienced people to run the country or
enough military leaders to organize a coherent defense. As the one-time
Communist Mey Mann told Steve Heder in 1997, recalling this period,
"Everybody was accusing everybody else of treason, and nobody knew
what was really happening."[97]

In July 1997, when Pol Pot was placed on trial at the Khmer Rouge
base at Anlong Veng—ironically, his crime was ordering the murder of
Son Sen—one of his accusers blamed him for encouraging a generalized
paranoia among his followers. Although the accusation focused on the
1990s, its vivid wording suggests, in hindsight, some of the destructive
energies unleashed at S-21:

> [Pol Pot] saw enemies as rotten flesh, as swollen flesh. Enemies surrounding.
> Enemies in front, enemies behind, enemies to the north, enemies to the south,
> enemies to the west, enemies to the east, enemies in all eight directions, ene-
> mies coming from all nine directions, closing in, leaving no space for breath.
> And he continually had us fortify our spirit, fortify our stance, fortify over
> and over, including measures to kill our own ranks . . . even strugglers of the
> same rank in the movement.[98]

Between 1975 and the collapse of the regime, tens of thousands of its
"enemies" were arrested and killed throughout the country. At least
fourteen thousand had been held, questioned, tortured, and put to
death by *santebal*. Had the Vietnamese invasion been delayed, the end
of the spiraling, destructive process at S-21 is impossible to envision.
The "wheel of history" had developed an inexorable momentum,
crushing everyone in its path. Indeed, as an interrogator from the prison
arrested at this time asked plaintively in his confession: "If *angkar*
arrests everybody, who will be left to make a revolution?"[99]

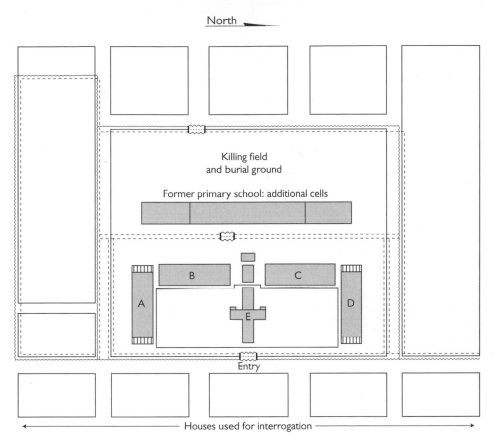

North

Killing field
and burial ground

Former primary school: additional cells

A   B   C   D

E

Entry

← Houses used for interrogation →

A–D: Cells for mass-detention   E: Administration and archive

Tuol Sleng Prison (S-21).

The Tuol Sleng Museum of
Genocidal Crimes. Photo by
Carol Mortland.

Kang Keck Ieu (alias Duch),
the director of S-21. Photo
Archive Group.

Staff photograph from S-21 (1976). Mam Nay (Chan) is in back row, at left; Duch is in back row, third from left. Women and children are unidentified. Photo Archive Group.

Group of guards at S-21
(1977). Him Huy is fourth
from right. Photo Archive
Group.

Him Huy in 1995. Photo by
Chris Riley, Photo Archive
Group.

Koy Thuon (alias Khuon),
high-ranking DK cadre
imprisoned in 1977. Photo
Archive Group.

Bedroom on ground floor of
S-21, reserved for important
prisoners. Photo Archive
Group.

Unidentified prisoner in front
of wooden cell, S-21. Photo
Archive Group.

Mug shot and postmortem
photographs of Voeuk Peach.
Photo Archive Group.

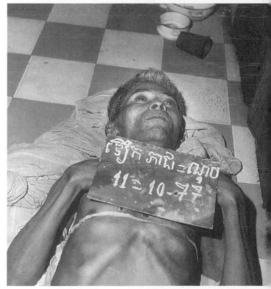

Prisoner 259 (1977?) showing
the room where unimportant
captives were held en masse.
Photo Archive Group.

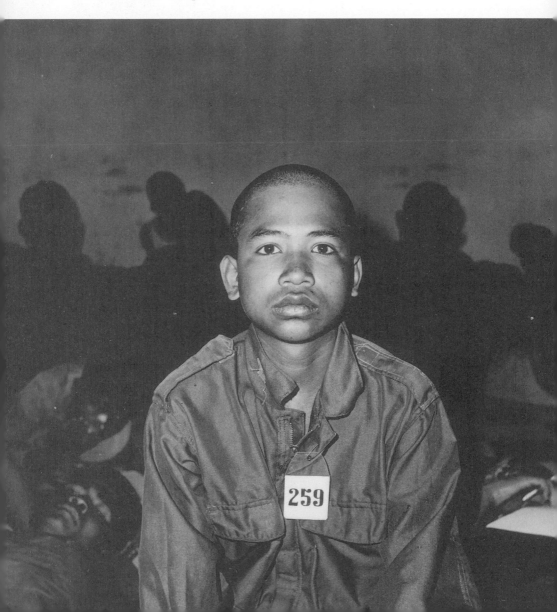

Chan Kim Srun (alias
Saang), the wife of DK
foreign ministry official,
and her baby. Photo
Archive Group.

Overleaf: Skulls of S-21
prisoners, Choeung Ek.
Photograph by Kelvin
Rowley.

Nhem En at the Tuol Sleng
Genocide Museum, 1997.
En was the first Khmer
Rouge photographer to
take mug shots of S-21
prisoners. Photograph by
Douglas Niven.

Framing the Questions

In January 1978, Vann Nath, a commercial painter in Battambang, was arrested there and interrogated for several days before being shackled and driven in a truck to S-21. In 1978, he had no idea why he was arrested. He still doesn't. Talking with Sara Colm in 1995, he recalled his first interrogation:

> "What was the problem that caused them to arrest you?" the interrogator asked.
> I said I didn't know.
> "The Organization isn't stupid," he said. "It never catches people who aren't guilty. Now think again—what did you do wrong?"
> "I don't know," I said again.[1]

Many other prisoners at S-21 were asked to explain why they had been arrested and therefore why they were guilty. Like Joseph K in Kafka's novel *The Trial*, they had not been accused because they were guilty; they were guilty because they had been accused. The questions were intended to throw the prisoners off balance, but the interrogators themselves were often genuinely curious and sincere. They believed that the prisoners were guilty, but they had no idea what offenses they were supposed to uncover. The first encounter, which was bewildering on both sides, resembled interrogation techniques used by police officials everywhere, and also drew on the practices of other Communist regimes.[2] As in the USSR and Maoist China, many of the prisoners' hidden "crimes" had taken place only in the minds of their accusers. The interrogators' duty was to validate the Party's verdict by extracting full confessions. These documents, once recorded, became induced historical texts that supposedly demonstrated a given prisoner's "objective" connection to serious offenses, the assiduousness of the staff at S-21, and the clairvoyance of the Party.

In addition to Communist models, there are also striking parallels between the techniques used at S-21 and those employed in the Spanish Inquisition, seventeenth-century witch trials, the French Reign of Terror in the 1790s, and, more benignly, in the early, "archaeological" phases of Freudian psychoanalysis. Freud noticed one of these parallels himself. Writing to his friend Wilhelm Fleiss in January 1897, he asked, "Why are [the witches'] confessions under torture so like the communications made by my patients in psychic treatment?"

One answer to Freud's question might lie in the confident, lopsided relationship imposed by many judges, interrogators, and analysts onto their prisoners and patients. Moreover, analysts and interrogators frequently claim to know what they are looking for, while patients and prisoners often have no idea what is supposed to be "hidden." One of Freud's own youthful heroes was the archaeologist Heinrich Schliemann, who "knew" where the ancient city of Troy was located and was proved right when he began to dig.[3]

When combined with other kinds of pressure, including torture, a skillful interrogator at S-21 could often induce memories that had little or no relation to "historical truth." In some cases, the prisoner concocted them to please the interrogator and to validate the latter's insistence that they were true. The vexed issues of "recovered" memories and transference then come into play.[4]

At S-21, some prisoners came to believe that they were genuinely guilty of counterrevolutionary crimes. This is hardly surprising, for under extreme conditions, as Richard Ofshe and Ethan Watters have written in another context, "We desire to create a comprehensive cause and effect story out of our lives and . . . when we are unable to do this we are most vulnerable to the . . . suggestions offered by others." At the same time, echoing a prevailing belief in the USSR in the 1930s, counterrevolution in DK was not an activity but a "state of mind from the point of view of the state."[5] Whatever the prisoners had actually *done,* in other words, they were forced to agree with the Party's assumption that they were guilty because they had been caught. Thus, Suy Chheng Huot, a former electrical worker, stated frankly at the end of his confession:

I am not a member of the CIA. I confessed to being CIA when confronted with my guilt. I beg the Organization to [kill] me because I have not followed the revolution. . . . I deserve to die because the Organization had [once] trusted me. I no longer wish to live, make no protests to the Organization, by way of seeking justice. But I must declare that in my heart I have not betrayed the Organization at all. I declare my guilt . . . because I am dying. Long live the glorious revolution! Long live the Revolutionary Organization![6]

The Party's efforts to obtain admissions of guilt were not always so successful. Sbauv Hin (alias Euan), the secretary of Division 310, was arrested in May 1977. After admitting that he harbored unrevolutionary concerns about his family and was partial to his military unit at the expense of national priorities, he veered off in a dangerously triumphant fashion:

I am supposed to report my plans for a coup d'état against the Party. In my nineteen years of revolutionary life I have fulfilled assignments as a Communist in which I was ready to sacrifice . . . my life for the cause of the liberation of my class and my nation. Under the Party's leadership I have repeatedly refashioned [kay pray] myself. . . . I have nothing to hide from the Party. I have therefore had no thoughts of carrying out a coup d'état against the Party. I find this question preposterous because the thought has never occurred to me. . . . I regret very much that I had no advance knowledge that I was going to be arrested, in which case I could have proven my loyalty to the Party. However, it's too late now. I'm shackled in S-21.[7]

Sbauv Hin was also shackled by his knowledge that there was no resisting the authority of the Party, even (or especially) when it was being nourished with so much false, but pleasing, information. When Sbauv Hin closed this section of his confession with the sentence, "Only the Party knows my biography," he was simultaneously pleading innocent and acknowledging the Party's right to declare him guilty.[8]

For days or months, interrogators at S-21 invaded the prisoners' bodies, minds, and histories, teasing out, inducing, and inventing memories to coincide with prepackaged accusations and adjusted to the format of confessions. Prisoners and interrogators were engaged in shadow-boxing, with the interrogator trying to get at the "truth" (without revealing what it was) and the prisoner trying to please or in some cases—but which ones?— to obfuscate the interrogator by concealing, spinning out, or doctoring his or her story.

The interrogators were expected to coax and terrify the prisoners until they produced a document that coincided with the Party's "knowledge" of their "crimes" and the Party's readings of its oscillating history. In Milan Kundera's Kafkaesque formulation, it was always a case of the "punishment seeking the crime."[9] The prisoners, in turn, had to blend, amplify, or suppress what they actually remembered in order to construct the admissions demanded of them. For interrogators and prisoners alike, as Alexander Solzhenitsyn has written, the process resembled "a grandiose game of solitaire whose rules are . . . incomprehensible to its players." The Party Center, to extend the metaphor, kept the rules concealed, and interrogators were encouraged to frame their questions in such a way that "the enemies can't grasp our intentions." The ensuing dialogue, unsurprisingly, came to resemble a game of blind man's buff.[10]

Many prisoners, it seems, were arrested primarily to force them to betray their superiors. Thus, several cadres arrested in 1976 were questioned to build a case against the Eastern Zone secretary, Sao Phim, and in 1978, Kheang Sum Han (alias But), was pressed by his interrogators to implicate Son Sen.[11]

All the prisoners in S-21, with a handful of exceptions, were killed not only because of their alleged guilt but also because the existence of the prison, its location, and its purposes needed to be kept secret. The exigencies of secrecy overrode the advantages, never taken seriously, of letting innocent prisoners out.[12]

Prisoners were brought to S-21 for many reasons: because they had been named in other confessions, because their unit commanders were suspected of being "enemies," or because they had come under the suspicion of security services in the zones. Hu Nim's confession suggests that "enemies" were sometimes exposed at regular self-criticism meetings for cadres. The "enemies" were sent off to S-21 after they had been pushed into admitting treasonous behavior.[13]

By and large, however, the ways in which prisoners were chosen, summoned, collected, and delivered to the facility are unclear, and so are the administrative relationships between S-21 and "education halls" (the word "prison" was not used elsewhere in the country, but we know that every zone in DK had its own *santebal* office, organized along lines similar to those of S-21). These bureaus apparently reported to the zone secretaries rather than to S-21 or the Party Center in Phnom Penh. Aside from the confessions themselves, we know little about what written evidence was used as the basis for arresting people or was made available to interrogators at the prison. The narrow range of questions to which most of the prisoners responded suggests that little documentation had accompanied them to S-21.[14]

Lower-ranking figures were usually inculpated by their membership in military or production units that had performed badly or by the arrest of their superiors, but the prisoners who were interrogated at length had to confess to treasonous crimes of their own as well as to crimes of association. Many of these individual crimes are completely implausible.

In their confessions, prisoners were always asked to implicate their associates. The "strings of traitors" *(khsae kbot)* appended to nearly all of the confessions occasionally run to several hundred names, creating the impression of a vast, nationwide conspiracy. This is exactly what Duch and his superiors had in mind. "The world view of the [S-21] confession," as Steve Heder has noted, "includes the individual who is confessing, the people above him who persuaded him to betray the revolution and the people below him whom he persuaded to betray it. Everything is seen in terms of networks and forces."[15] Very few prisoners admitted to making decisions on their own. Instead, they usually confessed to being enticed to join or to betray the revolution by the rhetoric and friendly manner of higher-ranking people. Em Choeurn, for example, heard someone talk about the failure of the revolution to deliver material prosperity. "I heard such a clear explanation," he confessed a year later, "I became angry at the Party and began to take action to destroy it."[16] Hak Kim Chheang, beaten by his teacher as a boy, claimed that he had been recruited that very afternoon by a "Chinese spy" who saw him weeping, while Khim Phuong, a teenage girl, was attracted to treasonous conduct by descriptions of the plentiful possessions that might come from espousing "freedom."[17]

Often, the sponsors who brought people into the revolution later were accused of encouraging them to betray it. Many prisoners, probably because they were frightened and in pain, betrayed the people who had brought them into the Party, supposing that this information was what the interrogators wanted most. The regime's naïveté in filling the CPK's ranks with so many "enemies" is never mentioned. Instead, the sequences of betrayal in the confessions were intended to emphasize the conspiratorial character of society outside the Party and to cut short and discredit any genuine revolutionary activity by prisoners or their erstwhile patrons.

In this fashion, many men and women who had devoted their lives to the revolutionary cause, including several who had been closely associated with Pol Pot, were made to confess longstanding "CIA" affiliations. The prisoner Re Bo at least knew what was expected of him and confessed: "I was a traitor from the day I entered the revolution until the day I was arrested." How could it be otherwise? In the eyes of the Party Center, someone who had truly joined the revolution could never conceivably have betrayed it. Someone who betrayed the revolution, conversely, could never have been loyal.[18]

The "weak points" in confessions at S-21 were seen by Duch and his colleagues not as proof that prisoners had nothing to remember but as occasions when they were most strenuously attempting to conceal something. A prisoner's moments of indecision or vagueness struck interrogators as deliberately "complicated" *(smok smanh)* and thus as further evidence of the prisoner's guilt. In many cases, of course, isolation, sleeplessness, torture, and fear had already made the prisoners incoherent, suggestible, or both.[19]

The two methods consistently used by interrogators at S-21 to obtain results were called "doing politics" *(tvoeu nayobay)* and "imposing torture" *(dak tearunikam),* which is discussed in chapter 5. "Doing politics" involved insulting the prisoners, asking them questions, and persuading them that the Party knew their crimes already. The 1976 study notebook set out a seven-point procedure for interrogations:

1. First, extract information from them.
2. Next, assemble as many points as possible to pin them down with and to prevent their getting away.
3. Pressure them with political propaganda.
4. Press on with questions and insults.
5. Torture.
6. Review and analyze the answers so as to ask additional questions.
7. Review and analyze the answers so as to prepare documentation.[20]

The opening and closing pairs of suggestions recall police procedures anywhere, but problems arise with suggestions 2 through 5. The difference between "political propaganda" and "insults" and the borderline between "pressure" and "torture" are not defined. The dehumanization of the prisoners, the lopsided power relations at S-21, the permissiveness of its culture, and the urgency with which the interrogations were carried out encouraged widespread violence. Long before torture was applied, interrogations were routinely accompanied by kicks and punches. The former guard Kok Sros has recalled that prisoners were often "covered with blood" when they were taken back to their cells, an observation corroborated by the S-21 survivor Pha Thachan, and mug shots of many prisoners show signs of recent beatings.[21]

As far as "doing politics" is concerned, a parallel from Vietnam in the 1950s is instructive. In the land-reform campaign launched by the newly installed Communist government, what were called *truy buc* methods were used to extract confessions from alleged "landlords" in the countryside. *Truy buc*, which has been translated as "the constant repetition of demands and questions over a long period," aptly describes the procedures used in "doing politics" at S-21 and in other interrogation facilities.[22]

The forms of verbal pressures used are difficult to recapture. In nearly all the confessions the interrogator's questions have been removed. The kind of interrogation dialogue so vividly depicted by Artur London, Solzhenitsyn, Jacobo Timerman, and others is missing. Moreover, no interrogators have been interviewed so far, and none of the survivors of S-21 was interrogated for very long, whereas we know that some senior figures were questioned at S-21 on dozens of occasions over several months. Over this length of time, relationships between interrogators and prisoners and patterns of questioning were bound to develop, as a few key confessions, like Ney Saran's, make clear, but these relationships are missing from the archive. An exception proving the rule is the confession of Thong Vann, a Party member arrested in September 1977. Describing his interrogation, Thong wrote:

When I first arrived [at S-21] a representative of the security office came and questioned me. He accused me of being CIA on the basis of the accusations of others who had said that I was CIA. At that point I lost mastery completely and said, "Negative." He said, "If [you say] 'negative' [there would be] a beating [that] would lead to our getting clear information."

To start off with, I wrote a detailed summary of my revolutionary activities to date. When I had written it, the representative of the security office said, "How come I don't see any treacherous story [here]?"

"Because I've done no treacherous activities," I replied.

And the representative said, "If your answer is negative, you will be beaten." I asked if I could write the truth.

"If you write about treacherous activities, that would be good."

I knew that I could not withstand torture, so I decided to write a made-up story about my treasonous activities. I wrote that I had been a traitor since 1970 and about my connections with Non Suon when we were together in . . . Oural.

I listed all the comrades who had carried out revolutionary activities with me in 1976. After I did this the security representative asked me to clarify my story: "What about treasonous activities when you were in the city?" he said.

I answered, "[There were] none."

The security representative said, "If you say 'none' you get beaten with an electric cord."

When I heard about torture, my body began to shake. I began to write a made-up story.[23]

Several months earlier, Siet Chhe (alias Tum) wrote a memorandum to *santebal* that offers another glimpse of a prisoner's psychology in the early stages of interrogation and torture (see chapter 3). Siet Chhe believed that he had been falsely accused and that Duch should allow him to communicate directly with the "upper brothers"—a proposal that Duch repeatedly brushed aside. His memorandum of 8 May revealed his oscillating, unsteady state of mind.[24]

On the evening of 7–8 May 1977 [i.e., tonight] my state of mind has been unstable in a way I cannot describe. I can't see any road to the future. I beg the Party to show pity on its child at this time.

[These are] developments in my state of mind: Stage 1. The period after the Organization first arrested me until 4 May 77 was one of report writing on every point that the Organization wanted explained. Using those reports, I hoped that the Organization would inquire and investigate at the bases where I had been involved and would [thereby] verify my statements. I had hoped that the *santebal* ministry, as the responsible ministry, would follow up and validate these documents and submit summaries of them to the Organization. Make a foundation for any of my large and small mistakes and care for me.

Stage 2. From the evening of 4 May until [today] I underwent all kinds of torture according to *santebal*'s procedures. *Santebal*'s perception [so far] has been that I am a 100 percent traitor and that there is no way at all that I am not a traitor.

So, given their stance, the level of torture has gradually been increased so that as I face this situation my feelings fluctuate wildly. I do not see any way to get out. [Tonight] my feelings are as follows:

1. If I admitted to being a traitor when I was not, I would not know how to report any [genuine] activities with collaborators in a reasonable, continuous way. This is one thing. Moreover if I did that, considering my stance toward the Party since 26 May 59 and toward Brother Number 1 [Pol Pot], who brought me up all along, and wrote according to torture, well, I could not do that!

2. Weighing this back and forth, I see the best way out as death . . . sudden death to escape the pain . . . and be with the Party until the end. But there is no possibility of sudden death. Again, no way out . . . I fear torture and death. If I was connected with any traitors, I would immediately tell the Organization and I would be free from this torture immediately.

3. After considering this back and forth, and finding no way out, this morning I struggle to write to let the Organization know about the development of my feelings and pity me. This last request is to ask the Organization to kindly delay my torture and to reconsider the three traitors' testimony

that accused me. These enemies made this up. I know there must be contradictions in some important points.

Prisoners were encouraged to corroborate previous confessions and to incriminate people who had already been arrested and killed, and it is possible that higher-ranking prisoners were given other confessions to read. In other words, if prisoner A confessed to taking part in a conspiracy, his confession seemed to ring truer if he admitted conspiring in the past with C, P, and G, who had been arrested and executed months before. Thus Baen Chhae, interrogated in the Eastern Zone in June 1977 before being brought to S-21, was encouraged to name "anyone the Organization has [already] arrested." The interrogators, he continued, "further said that anyone I could think of who had been arrested in any sector or zone I should say that they were all my connections."[25]

"Doing politics" was always more difficult for workers at S-21 than beating up the prisoners. For one thing, the "upper brothers" to whom the confessions were routed were impossible to consult. Moreover, the interrogators were poorly trained and poorly informed. The prisoners were always frightened but seldom helpful. Indeed, an entry in Tuy and Pon's notebook suggests that the relations between prisoners and interrogators often came to an ominous, unpromising halt when violence was called for. "In the matter of questioning enemies their strong point is that we don't know their story, so they can say anything they want," the entry read, adding: "Their weak point is that they are in our hands."[26]

Everyone at the prison was also handicapped by the volatility of the Party's stance toward "enemies." As the 1976 study notebook declared:

> The Party changes frequently. The Party changes the prisoners to be interrogated in no fixed pattern. The Party goes from one group to another and sometimes changes our duties. The Party also changes its methods for making documents, for interrogation, for doing politics, for propaganda, for torture. We must adjust ourselves to the situation, leaping along with the movement of three tonnes [of rice] per hectare [a slogan from DK's Utopian Four-Year Plan].[27]

Interrogators at S-21 were often whipsawed by instructions of this kind. How could any of them feel safe or competent when they were told to "[leap] along with the movement of three tonnes per hectare"? Sau Kang, the former secretary of Sector 37 in the Western Zone, put the point succinctly in his confession when he complained that "if the higher-ups keep modifying things back and forth suddenly like this, those lower down will be unable to keep up."[28]

The Party's insistence that practice overshadowed theory had the effect of ignoring inconvenient precedents and legitimizing anything that the Party Center did or had in mind. Only the leaders were free from blame and free to change direction. A Khmer Rouge cadre, interviewed on the Thai border in 1980, told Steve Heder:

> [The cadres] blame everything on others. They say everything depends on the concrete situation, but they're the ones who conclude what the concrete situation is and even sometimes create the concrete situation.[29]

In a similar fashion, the 1976 study notebook told interrogators to "root out the stance" of believing or disbelieving what enemies confessed, but to continue "believing completely in the Party as far as enemies . . . are concerned"—an impossible proposition, when the Party Center's position "as far as enemies are concerned" was normally concealed. Interrogators were also told to approach what the prisoners said "from a progressive standpoint and from a nonprogressive one, from a revolutionary standpoint and from one that is not revolutionary at all"—a rat's nest of positions that left the interrogators' superiors free to maneuver and the interrogators open to rebuke. They were urged to use torture and propaganda in "proper" proportions that were not made clear.

On some occasions even Son Sen and Duch were uncertain how to proceed. Writing to Duch in October 1977, for example, Son Sen suggested that prisoners left to their own devices might "implicate all kinds of people." He added:

> In any case, each and every response must be carefully reviewed, because some [of the prisoners] attack us (i.e., high-ranking functionaries). Some of them attack consciously. Some are frightened and merely talk.[30]

To make things worse for the interrogators, a study notebook from S-21 compiled in 1978 suggested that a large number of enemies were embedded inside the facility itself:

> The task of searching out and purging (somrit somrang) enemies inside Office S-21 has not been resolved among either combatants or cadres. Our soldiers study the teachings of the Party, but when they emerge from studies, nothing has changed in their outlooks. They are still subservient to their elders (bong). When they are frightened they stop being relaxed and they stop smiling. Although there are enemies all around them they do nothing to seek them out.[31]

The menacing contradictions in this passage must have unsettled anyone who read or overheard it. How could the workers at S-21 be inde-

pendent, insubordinate, or suspicious, after all, while cleaving unques-
tioningly to their superiors' commands? What would happen to them if
they "relaxed" or "smiled"? Were attacks on Duch, Pon, and Chan
really to be the order of the day? Where precisely were the ubiquitous
enemies to be found?

Workers at S-21 were thrown off balance by documents like this and
by the uncertainty of daily life, encapsulated by the disappearance, from
time to time, of friends, relatives, and coworkers. As Kok Sros told
Douglas Niven:

> I was losing some of the people who were working with me. One day we
> were working together and then they were taken away. And they were killed.
> I felt anxious. I thought: "Today it's their turn. I don't know what will hap-
> pen tomorrow."[32]

Everyone at S-21 was encouraged to be suspicious; as Him Huy told
Peter Maguire, "We were all spying on each other." Everyone was looking over everyone else's shoulder and also looking in all directions. Family members were far away. Friendships provided little or no security,
and patronage could be withdrawn at any moment. Every act could be
construed as political. The nation was at war with its external enemies,
society was at war with itself, the Party was at war with "hidden enemies," and people were at war with their shortcomings. The Organization's authority and legitimacy were unquestioned, but its principal
message was that there were people concealed inside the Organization
seeking to destroy it. By definition, these "enemies" were simultaneously known and unknown, visible and unseen, outside and inside
S-21. To cap things off, everyone might well be lying. A former DK
cadre told Steve Heder in 1980, putting the situation rather mildly:
"People were insecure psychologically [in the DK period]. People feared
being wrong unconsciously or being fingered, [we] just kept smiling but
[we] were tense inside."[33]

The confessions that survive from S-21 vary in length, completeness,
and interest. Roughly 4 percent of the microfilmed ones and an even
smaller percentage of those in the DC–Cam archive are less than three
pages long. Most of these were composed soon after the prisoners'
arrival, before any interrogation had taken place. They usually contain
skeletal biographical data and mention no offenses. In several cases, the
data sheets are annotated: "Of no interest. Discard"*(boh chaul)*. Since
the documents have survived, the "discard" orders may have referred

to the prisoners themselves; "discard" was one of the euphemisms used at S-21 for "kill."[34]

While 2,013 of the microfilmed confessions, or roughly half the total of those in the microfilmed archive, were obtained after a single interrogation session, the remainder were composed in successive versions, those of cadres sometimes stretching over weeks or months. Most of the confessions in the microfilmed archive and at DC–Cam run between ten and forty pages. The prisoners I categorize as "cadres"— those who were over thirty years old and had revolutionary pseudonyms—often wrote confessions of several hundred pages.[35]

Over time, the format and style of the confession documents changed. Some of them were written by the prisoners themselves, and a few early ones were composed by prisoners and interrogators on alternating pages, but most of the handwritten confessions appear to have been transcribed by interrogators or document workers from tape recordings or notes. None of the tapes, which probably included questions as well as answers, has survived. Some confessions are obviously first drafts, with excisions and corrections by the prisoners, document workers, or senior cadres. In a few cases the drafts have survived alongside subsequent, typed versions, while other confessions, annotated "Don't use" or "Don't summarize," exist in draft form and presumably never left the prison. Several confession texts from 1976 include questions written in an interrogator's hand—even, on two occasions, Duch's[36]—followed by answers written by the prisoner. In nearly all cases, however, the questions and suggestions have disappeared.

By 1978 most confessions were typed. A number were prepared in multiple copies and stapled into booklets. We know from the Tuy-Pon notebook that by 1978 six copies of important confessions were normally prepared. Two of these were sent to "the Organization," and the remaining copies were sent to the prisoner's former work unit, the security office in the prisoner's sector, and its counterpart in the relevant zone. The sixth copy was retained for the S-21 archive.[37]

Many of the early confessions at S-21 resemble prerevolutionary Cambodian police reports. Drawing on the French police tradition of the *procès verbale,* they recorded a prisoner's initial, often self-incriminating declaration. Many of them include such colonial-era idiosyncrasies as spelling out dates, calling the prisoner "the named," and so on. Most confessions at S-21 were authenticated by being signed or thumbprinted and dated by the prisoner on each page, another carryover from prerevolutionary police practice. When an interrogator wrote out the confession, it was usually authenticated by the prisoner and countersigned by a document worker present at the interrogation. The elaborate format of the confessions and the files of which they formed a part suggest that Duch and his colleagues were proud of their thoroughness, modernity, and sophistication. They wanted S-21 to be considered a model interrogation center and saw themselves as professional security experts.[38]

We know very little about the way prisoners were processed for interrogation when they arrived or how interrogators were briefed from one day to the next, but forms relating to nineteen prisoners under interrogation in August, September, and December 1976, the only ones of their kind to come to light, provide a glimpse of these procedures.[39] The headings on the forms asked for the prisoner's name, pseudonym, work unit, and "strings" *(khsae),* the word used for patronage networks. Handwritten comments then set out the questions that had been asked on that day and suggested a line of questions for the next interrogation session. For several prisoners, forms survive from as many as six successive interrogation sessions. Interrogators recorded the prisoners' health (five were listed as "weak" and three as "normal"), indicated whether torture had been used (in these cases it had not), and noted the condition of each prisoner's shackles and the key needed to open them. In one case, the interrogator observed that the prisoner had written ten pages of his confession the preceding day.[40]

By the end of 1976, most confession texts at S-21 were in a four-part format that endured with few alterations until the collapse of the regime. In the first part, prisoners provided their "life stories," named their relatives and associates, and listed their work units. These curricula vitae were normally followed by a section titled "history of [my] treasonous activities" or "my political biography," with data arranged in chronological order. A third section, called "plans," described what the prisoners would have done had they not been arrested. Most confessions closed with lists of a prisoner's associates, or "strings of traitors," with indications of their whereabouts. In some cases, the "strings" included everyone, even dead people, who had been named in the confession.

The autobiographies were inspired by a peculiarly Communist genre of writing, the self-critical life story or *pravatt'rup*.[41] Before 1975, autobiographical narratives had been rare in Cambodia, and the biographical genre itself enjoyed no particular status. In DK, on the other hand, as in other Communist countries, self-critical autobiographical narratives of Party members were repeatedly solicited, compared, and kept on file. The practice of writing autobiographies and their occasional use as heuristic texts seems to have been more important in the Chinese and Vietnamese Communist parties than elsewhere. The practice was widely used by the Chinese in the 1940s. David Apter and Tony Saich, writing about the phenomenon at that time, suggest that its goal was "exigetical bonding."[42]

In Cambodia, self-critical autobiographies were featured in the regular "livelihood" meetings. Many non-Communists encountered the genre for the first time when they were evacuated from the towns and cities in April 1975 and asked at roadblocks to compose them. When the procedure became a national routine in 1976, people were periodically asked to name their family members and associates, to describe their class origins, to list their political activities, and to set out their strengths and weaknesses. Finally, participants were made to suggest ways in which they might improve their own and others' attitudes and behavior.[43]

The process of self-exposure, attested in many secret societies, was intended to purify the participants, reinforce the solidarity of the group, and display the Organization's empathy and vigilance. For Party members, of course, the Party replaced the Organization. As Apter and Saich describe the experience of self-criticism in Maoist China, "One begins with sin and blemish, the purging removal of which is essential for enlightenment, not only for the self but for the collectivity, lest others become contaminated and polluted. Indeed, the notions of pollution and purification are endemic in rectification."[44] The biographies thus induced could also be used as incriminating evidence or to justify promotion. Everyone in DK was constantly on trial. A person's trustworthiness could evaporate if information in a *pravatt'rup* was found to be incomplete, misleading, "complicated" *(smok smanh),* or incorrect. Conversely, a "good" biography that included a "good" class background and praiseworthy activities could lead to Party membership, better work assignments, and enhanced personal security. Kok Sros has said that he owed his own rise within the Party (he became a "full-rights" member in 1978) to his hard work and his "good biography." Nhem En, the S-21 photographer, has made a similar assertion.[45]

The autobiographies were measured against the Party's requirements of the moment, which is to say against the Party's history up to the time when they were written and against the ever-altering tactical requirements of the revolution. Study sessions in DK repeatedly stressed the importance of preparing "clean" biographical statements, and in early 1976 readers of *Tung Padevat* were warned against people with "systematically complicated biographies." On the occasion later in the same year when he described the Party's internal enemies as "germs," Pol Pot told his subordinates that "life stories must be good and must conform to our requirements."[46]

Senior cadres solicited biographies from their subordinates. In his confession, Non Suon dutifully regretted his incompetence in this respect:

> My shortcomings included the fact that I did not follow up the biographical records of Party and core members in detail and then take measures to purge the Party. All I could see was the appearance of their actions. I was unable to grasp each of their essential origins, I failed to delve deeply into family roots. This provided the enemy with easy opportunities to penetrate and undermine the Party from within.[47]

By 1977, hundreds of thousands of ordinary Cambodians as well as Party members had written *pravatt'rup*. Thousands had written more than one. Over two hundred autobiographies prepared by S-21 personnel, for example, have survived in a booklet form that was apparently used throughout the country. These autobiographical booklets consist of questionnaires whose format so closely resembles that of the biographical sections of the confessions as to suggest that the questions in the booklets formed the basis of many interrogations.

The questionnaires open by asking about the subject's name, revolutionary pseudonym if any, date and place of birth, sex, nationality or ethnic group, and marital status. The next item, "means of livelihood before entering the revolution," was used to determine a person's class status *(vannakpheap)*. Most urban inhabitants of prerevolutionary Cambodia, known as "new people" after 1975, were lumped together as "royalists," "capitalists," or "petit bourgeois." The class categories for rural inhabitants, on the other hand, took account of their material wealth, which was calculated on the basis of the dimensions of the land they owned, the materials of which the family house was constructed, the number of people in the family, and the quantity of livestock, ox carts, and farm equipment the family possessed. Suos Thi, the head of the documentation unit at S-21, for example, called himself a "middle-level middle peasant," and Him Huy defined himself as a "lower-middle peasant."[48] In the confessions, references to a prisoner's class origins are almost always missing, presumably because a "good" class background had been blacked out or a "bad" one confirmed by the prisoner's treacherous actions.[49]

Before 1975, few if any Cambodians outside the clandestine Communist movement had engaged in class analysis. Instead, most of them distinguished broadly among the "haves" *(neak mean),* those with "enough" *(neak kuosom),* and the "poor" *(neak kroo),* groups roughly consonant with people who commanded *(neak prao),* "free people" *(neak chea),* and those who received commands *(neak bomrao).*[50]

The revolutionary potential and intrinsic worth of Cambodians after 1975, it was thought, reflected their class origins. Those with the fewest resources had the best "life stories" and supposedly the highest status. Conversely, those with too many relationships or possessions had "complicated" biographies and constituted potential enemies. The class origins of the "upper brothers" were prudently concealed. Most of them—Ta Mok being the most important exception—sprang from Cambodia's minute bourgeoisie. They had prepared self-critical biographies about themselves, but by leading the country to victory in 1975, they had clearly already overcome the stigma of their past. In their lifelong search for enlightenment, as it were, they had reached the outskirts of nirvana, the highest level of Buddhist consciousness (a connection they would have scoffed at). Like those embodiments of the Buddha known as *bodhisattva,* they were uniquely equipped to assist others toward enlightenment. In this context, it is of interest that Ho Chi Minh chose his pseudonym ("Ho the enlightened one") in 1943 before taking command of the "liberation" of Vietnam.

The next question asked respondents to list membership in "nonrevolutionary political organizations." S-21 personnel whose questionnaires I have examined wrote "none." Prisoners, on the other hand, were often nudged at this point to admit connections with the Lon Nol regime, with fictional or defunct political parties, and with foreign intelligence agencies.

The questionnaire then asked when the respondent had "entered the revolution" *(choul padevat).* This event had presumably consisted of swearing allegiance to the Organization and expressing a willingness to bear arms. In most of the questionnaires and the majority of confessions, joining the revolution coincided with joining the Khmer Rouge army between 1970 and 1975. After listing the date, S-21 workers and many low-ranking prisoners named the people who had vouched for them. The sponsors were usually village officials or military cadres.

The next questions provided space for "reasons for entering the revolution." In the confessions this often revealing item was almost always missing. Instead, immediately or shortly after they "entered the revolution," most prisoners admitted to having entered the service of the CIA or another foreign power. Ironically, the austere ceremonies that some of the prisoners connect with joining the CIA resemble those set out in Party statutes for joining the CPK. Prisoners remember swearing allegiance and facing a flag in the presence of their sponsors. Forced to admit joining something that most of them had never heard of, they resurrected the only political step that any of them (or their interrogators) had ever taken.[51]

Some older prisoners, to be sure, identified the CIA specifically with the United States. They claimed to have been recruited by American agents and confessed to being paid enormous salaries in dollars. Other claims were equally fantastic. Phe Di, arrested in the Northern Zone in June 1976, for example, sketched an identity card he claimed he had been given in the Lon Nol era, signed by "the Chief of the CIA" in Phnom Penh, John B. Devine (?).[52] Another prisoner said he had been recruited by an American named "Kennedy" in the 1960s and confessed that one of his high school teachers, Khieu Thirith (who had been Ieng Sary's wife since 1952), had been a CIA agent. This bizarre accusation led Duch, when he read it, to scribble nervously in the margin: "Whose wife is she? What evidence do you have?"[53]

Another prisoner, knowing only that the "CIA" was in some sense the opposite of DK, asserted that the acronym meant "having enough to eat"; others claim to have been told by their recruiters that "with CIA there will be women and liquor and theaters and markets, stone houses and automobiles to ride" or that after joining the CIA they would be "be free to move around [because] there aren't any rules (viney)." A more acceptable definition to the CPK came from Penh Sopheap, the daughter of Sok Thuok (alias Von Vet), a high-ranking CPK cadre. She was arrested with her father in 1978. She recalled her mother telling her that "CIA is a person who burrows inside the Party."[54]

Steve Heder has suggested that in S-21 confessions, "words like CIA and KGB . . . became generic descriptions of enemies. If you said somebody was CIA, you didn't mean that he was organizationally a member of the CIA, you just meant that he was an enemy." Similarly, in the Cultural Revolution in China, it was not important what an enemy was called, so long as he or she was dramatically read out of society and effectively condemned. "To discredit a person," a document at the time asserted, "the following can be used: rightist, ultra-leftist, counter-revolutionary, bad element, agent of the USSR, USA, KMT, etc."[55] In a similar vein, Lynn White has argued that "measures for labeling people" constituted an aspect of Chinese policy in the Cultural Revolution that was conducive to widespread violence. His insight can be applied to DK, where anyone labeled repeatedly as an "enemy," regardless of corroboration, was brought to S-21 or executed on the spot.[56]

In affiliating offenders with foreign intelligence agencies, the interrogators at S-21 were following precedents from the Soviet Union in the 1930s, where prisoners were accused of working for foreign intelligence agencies trying to overthrow Stalin's regime. Since no loyal Soviet citizen could conceivably oppose the regime, people who did so were by definition "non-Soviet."[57] In Cambodia, people accused of betraying the revolution were similarly thought to be non-Khmer. A speech by Pol Pot in December 1977 noted that

> we have [expelled] the international spy networks. The three big ones are the American CIA, the Soviet KGB, and the network belonging to the Vietnamese consumers of territory. These espionage networks have been buried inside our party, inside our army, and inside our people for more than twenty years.[58]

In 1997, Pol Pot told Nate Thayer that "Vietnamese agents" had been responsible for most of the deaths that occurred under DK. How could it be otherwise, given the purity of the Party's intentions, the intrinsic innocence of ethnic Khmer, and the scientific basis of the Party's vision?[59]

The next sections in the autobiographical questionnaires asked for lists of "strong points" and "shortcomings." In the confessions, a person's "strong points" disappeared, and "shortcomings" were absorbed into the "history of [my] treasonous activities."[60] The "histories of treasonous activities," in turn, not only listed actions by the prisoners but often also reported conversations in which acquaintances complained about life in DK. Many of these complaints foreshadow the criticisms of DK by people who escaped or survived the regime. They depict a nation whose people were plagued by poor, inadequate food, who wore ragged clothing and worked too hard, who were subjected to constant surveillance and bullying, and who suffered from endemic distrust, excessive puritanism, and restrictions on freedom of movement.

What the prisoners missed most, it seems, was *happiness,* an elusive but almost palpable condition that they connected with family life, abundant food, and the freedom to go where they pleased. This nostalgia also affected prison workers. When the prisoner Yos Thoeurn complained that in DK "we live like animals in a cage" and Huy Savorn compared the revolution to "being in jail," the workers recording the accusations must have silently concurred. Similar statements surfaced later in some of their own confessions.[61]

Most of the prisoners were young combatants with a limited knowledge of the world. None of the confessions that I have seen, for example, took issue with such DK policies as the closing of schools and newspapers, the disempowerment of the rich and educated, the abolition of law courts and elections, or the forced evacuation of the towns. Three that I have located complained about the suppression of religion, but they lamented the loss of festivals rather than of Buddhist teaching or monasticism. Those that mourned the loss of ranks *(sakdi),* prestige *(muk mo't),* and honors *(ket'yuos)* did not regret the disappearance or humiliation of high-ranking people or the destruction of Cambodia's bourgeoisie. Instead, the prisoners who regretted the loss of privilege confessed that they wanted it for themselves.[62]

Prisoners also complained frequently about the harsh discipline imposed by revolutionary life. Under DK, they said, they were unable to "go where they wanted" *(teu tam chet),* to "stroll" *(dao lenh),* or simply to "play" *(lenh)* with their families and friends. Under DK, they were always working and always pushed around. Nop Nuon, a former interrogator, complained that "the Organization orders us around like cows or buffaloes," and Kim Chhoeung noted sourly that "we live under the leadership of others. You need permission to do this, you need permission to do that . . . In the [1970–1975] war we soldiers had difficulties, too. We never thought of them in the life-and-death battlefields, though, because what we wanted [in the end] was to be free or happy, but when the war stopped, suddenly everything was just as difficult [as ever]."[63]

Many prisoners missed having the freedom to decide what they might do next. While they were willing to condemn "freedomism" *(sereipheap)* in political meetings and obediently connected this form of evil with the United States, many of them fondly remembered the personal freedoms they had enjoyed before the civil war. Prum Yon described his "counterrevolutionary" stance as follows: "If I want to eat something, I eat it; if I want to do something, I do it; if I want to go somewhere, I go." Another prisoner recalled that "in the old society, there were no secrets, and if you had some money you could be happy"; a third confessed to the "crime" of "encouraging people to love the happiness that they had enjoyed in the past."[64]

Prisoners also missed the pleasures of living among relatives and friends. Some of them expressed nostalgia for gambling, dancing, theaters, movies, alcohol, and extramarital sex—"sinful" pleasures that were frowned on and curtailed in DK. These regrets crop up so often in the confessions of young prisoners as to suggest that they were saying what they imagined their interrogators wanted to hear. While it is unlikely that many of the young prisoners had ever had the time, money, or leisure to become gamblers, alcoholics, or libertines, "crimes" of this kind were perhaps the only ones they could readily imagine.[65] Asked to write about "counterrevolutionary" actions, prisoners dredged up or invented sexual encounters, playful conversations, card games, or drinking bouts. Several female prisoners were coaxed into confessing serial liaisons; males owned up to a series of one-night stands.

Many prisoners expressed a generalized nostalgia for prerevolutionary life. Complaints of this kind often recur word for word in documents written several months apart. It seems likely that copy deemed suitable for confessions was spooned into the texts by the interrogators or document workers regardless of what a given prisoner had done or said. It is also possible that the confessions of many low-ranking prisoners were cobbled together by document workers without much interrogation, once the general outline of appropriate "crimes" and what constituted acceptable complaints was clear. Indeed, the former interrogator Chhim Chhun admitted in his confession that he "only wrote the [prisoners'] stories that were easy to write. If a story had too many relationships [in it] and was hard to write I threw it out."[66]

Even with these constraints, the confessions that describe the shortcomings of the revolution are often extraordinarily frank. For example, in July 1977, Chhin Cheap, formerly a soldier in Division 310, recalled a conversation with one of his friends.

> Chhun of Division 310 made me see that the revolution was pitch dark *(ngongut)*. He said, "Doing a revolution these days is difficult and confusing, from the standpoint of clothing and nourishment; there's never enough of either." He said, "When the war was on, that was difficult enough, but when it stopped things became even more difficult. There was no time to rest. To make a comparison, it's like they order us around like cattle but

don't even let us eat grass. What's more you can't live where you like, there's no freedom, you can't even walk a short distance without permission. The way we live now is unhappy. There's no fun. . . . If we look at the old society, on the other hand, sure, our parents used to work, but not too hard, and they never lacked food, they were happy, they were independent, easy. If we wanted to do something we could do it, provided we had money."[67]

A month earlier, Dith Kung, also a soldier, had remembered:

In February 1976, Sung told me, "If you do a socialist revolution, food isn't tasty, and you work without stopping to the point where young people collapse at their work places. You work all day and all night, there's no time to rest, you have no freedom at all. Doing a revolution means eating rice gruel morning and afternoon, and there's not even enough of that. To go some place or come from some place you need a letter. There's a rule for going out and a rule for coming in. When you do a socialist revolution there are no wages, either, no ranks, no women, no alcohol, no gambling, no cars to travel in. You just walk everywhere."[68]

Several confessions compared the fate of Cambodian soldiers after their victory in April 1975 with that of Vietnamese soldiers soon afterward. In Vietnam, former combatants were allowed to rest and visit their families. In Cambodia, on the other hand, they were immediately forced to go to work growing rice. As Vann Khoeurn put it, "In other countries they fight the enemy for a month and then they rest. We fight the enemy without stopping."[69] "When the war was won," Prum Phorn observed, "the Vietnamese army had clothes to wear and food to eat." This idea was echoed by Norn Nal, who wrote, "Neighbors [i.e., in Vietnam] fought imperialism too, but they have enough to eat." The comparisons with DK, although not spelled out, are obvious.[70]

Chou Ny of Regiment 411 used information gleaned from CPK study sessions to paint the Cambodian revolution in a unfavorable light. In his confession he assigned these subversive views to a senior cadre, whom he quoted:

"Soldiers in Vietnam don't grow rice like we do. Their soldiers are happy, and move about freely, as they wish. They have enough to eat, and, unlike us, they lack nothing. To be sure, they're engaged in a revolution, but it's only the outer husk. Inside, they're not happy with socialist ways, because [socialism] is no way for people to live. They're aroused and they struggle ceaselessly against socialist ways, because they're confused, they can't keep going. And that's not all. In the Soviet country, which has had a socialist revolution for a long time now, they haven't begun to do what we do, they never started out as we did. They are reexamining things today, because they can't keep up the hot class struggle that a revolution involves. Waging a revolution is really hard. . . . When we waged a national democratic revolution, they said it was difficult, against the enemy. When the war ended, we went on into a socialist revolution, and they said we would be happy. In fact it was still difficult, from the point of view of food, clothing, freedom to move around. None of this was like other countries."[71]

Victory had brought Cambodian soldiers very few rewards. In many cases victory had actually lowered the victors' painfully earned new status. Young men and women had run away from their parents' farms to "liberate" Cambodia as well as themselves, and they were unwilling to revert to growing rice once victory had been achieved. The regime's pro-peasant rhetoric was lost on young people who felt that as revolutionary combatants they were entitled to leave to others the mud, backaches, and low status of growing rice. To compound the irony, those meting out the punishments had seldom grown any rice themselves.

Kae San (alias Sok), a high-ranking Party member, was displeased by these developments and made a play on words to underscore his point:

[In May 1975] the one named Chhas said: "Friend, do you see, we'd been liberated a month without any rest (somrak). All we did were storming attacks (vay samruk). We grew rice all day and all night, you can imagine the problems and the confusion."[72]

A few months later, Khloeung Run, also a soldier, reported a friend's distress when confronted by the ragged appearance of so many people:

Som said, "Doing a revolution is difficult and complicated (smok smanh). . . . There are difficulties in living and in clothing. Let's look at clothing for a moment. We've never had new clothes at all. Cadres and ordinary soldiers were the same. You go to the battlefield, all you saw was rags and tatters, nothing clean, and that wasn't all. Whatever day month or year it was you saw people sleeping on the ground, their bodies never touched water, they were spattered with mud for a month at a time."[73]

Older combatants complained that they were separated from their wives and children. The breaking up of their families made no sense. As Keng Bak put the problem, using someone else's voice:

Han said that he missed his wife, and I replied, "Friend, if you examine the revolutionaries, and especially your own friends, you'll soon see that when the Organization says 'We have been liberated into freedom,' freedom is nowhere to be seen. If there were any freedom you'd be allowed to see your wife; what reason can there be for not seeing her?" Han answered, "That's up to the Organization. If the Organization doesn't take care [of us] one day we'll desert the ranks, just wait, one of these days I'll look for a new place myself."[74]

Although these complaints about DK are succinct, eloquent, and powerful, there are few examples in the archive of what James Scott has
called the "hidden transcripts" of resistance to oppression. Examples of
confrontation, outrage, and ironic backchat between oppressors and
oppressed, so frequent in memoirs of the Holocaust or the Russian and
Chinese gulags, for example, are rare.[75]

Because they are so rare in the archive, the occasions when prisoners
attacked the revolution head-on are courageous and moving. Prak
Chhean, a low-ranking soldier from Division 310 said frankly: "The
Organization is shit";[76] Ho Tong Ho, a former teacher who had visited
the United States in the 1950s, used his confession to deliver a wither-
ing attack on the ideology and practice of the CPK, remarking that "I
can't see how Communism can succeed in the future if technical workers are dismissed, industrial production stops, and factories close their
doors."[77] Neak Ang Kear, a radio operator, confessed that his work had
suffered because of his "hot anger at the revolution,"[78] and Tan Douern
noted crisply that as far as he was concerned, "Communism means
eating one can of rice a day and following the ideas of uncivilized
people."[79]

Many "hidden transcripts" would have been delivered orally and so
would not have found their way into the documentary archive. Nhem
En, who lived with his colleagues in a house several hundred yards from
the prison, has recalled hearing a prisoner shout out at night, when the
city was completely quiet: "If you want to kill me, go ahead: *you* are
the real traitor!"[80]

Very few of the prisoners questioned DK's top-down style of rule or
its violence, characteristics that DK shared with prerevolutionary Cambodian regimes. Insulting senior figures by name was taboo. The closest
anyone came in the confessions I have examined was In Van, who
worked for an elite battalion "guarding the Organization" until he was
arrested in March 1977. In his confession he berated Khieu Samphan,
probably Brother Number Six or Seven:

> Khieu Samphan is conducting an oppressive socialist revolution, attacking
> the free spirit of the people and pitilessly exploiting them. For these reasons,
> we must fight to liberate our brothers and sisters among the people from the
> exploitation of this group, whose revolution is impure.[81]

More calmly, Phuong, a senior cadre from the Eastern Zone who had
been targeted at *santebal* since 1976 but was not arrested until 1978,
attacked the regime head-on:

The people are losing all popular democratic rights and freedoms, all the cadres and the entire state power are under the control of the CPK at all times. . . . Day by day the people and cadres are being imprisoned and chained, massacred by the hundreds, and there's not the slightest bit of organization or law to guarantee the people's rights. The people are silent as if they were in so much pain that they don't dare utter a thing.[82]

The secretary of the Western Zone, Chou Chet, arrested in March 1978, confronted his captors directly at several points, delivering a stinging attack on the CPK and its policies without mentioning anyone in the Party Center by name:

[I said that] the current regime was a highly dictatorial one, too rigid and severe, one that overshot the comprehension and consciousness of the people. Therefore a lot of people were muttering . . . that they were doing a lot of work and getting little back for it, how they couldn't get together with their families, couldn't rest, never had any fun, and so on.[83]

We know from Vann Nath's account that prisoners whispered to each other and from former workers at the prison that they sometimes talked to prisoners, even though doing so was against the rules. Pha Thachan remembers tapping on the brick walls of his cell to draw the attention of prisoners on either side. He never saw them and had no idea who they were. What was said or tapped out on these occasions— a "hidden transcript" if there ever was one—remains a mystery. Similarly, records of conversations among the interrogators about their work or about the prisoners are very rare and otherwise impossible to reconstruct. Most of the victims and all the perpetrators can be over-heard only through the papers that survive.[84]

The "treacherous activities" of prisoners, as opposed to their complaints about the regime, are impossible to corroborate, but in many cases they call to mind the genuine problems that hard-pressed cadres were encountering in the countryside as they struggled to impose the policies of the Party Center. A November 1976 memorandum to Son Sen from Roeun, the political secretary of Division 801, stationed outside the capital, described the "activities of those who serve the enemy" in military units:

1. They agitate among cadres and other ranks not to believe in our revolution, raising the issue of insufficient food.
2. They stir up combatants to desert military ranks, or to desert the cooperatives, saying that cooperatives are difficult.

3. At worksites, they encourage people to steal whatever they can; what they can't eat they throw away.

4. They stir people up people to be "free": wandering around, speaking their minds, mentioning freedom in Vietnam and Laos.

5. They agitate people with tales of rank, privilege, and wages in Vietnam and Laos, where [people] are happy with wages, whereas the Kampuchean revolution isn't happy and will be unhappy for a long time.

6. They stir up people to be lazy at their work, saying, "If you can't eat your fill, you have no strength to work."[85]

These "activities of those who serve the enemy" resembled those to which Party cadres and ordinary soldiers repeatedly confessed. The words the prisoners used to describe their "treacherous activities" were often Leninist ones they had absorbed from CPK study sessions. For example, prisoners claimed to have "educated" *(op rum)* and "organized" *(chat tang)* their treacherous followers: these are both key Marxist-Leninist terms, crucial to CPK thinking. Other examples of Party-inspired language include the prisoners' claims that they had "nourished secret work" *(cenhchom ka somngat)*, "built forces" *(kosang komlang)*, "expanded forces" *(bongrik komlang)*, conducted "storming attacks" *(vay samruk)*, and engaged in "propaganda" *(khosna)*.

The prisoners often confessed to imitating the subversive tactics that the CPK had used en route to gaining power. Unsurprisingly, most of the so-called subversive "parties" *(pak)* that the prisoners founded or joined were organized exactly like the CPK. Indeed, some of the "enemies" admitted that they had been "buried inside" the CPK for many years, when the CPK itself was "buried inside" Cambodian society. Unlike the CPK, however, the treacherous parties had identifiable leaders—usually important cadres who had already been arrested or were dead—to whom members had directed their "feudal" loyalties and onto whom the Party Center could pour its disdain.

In response to questions asking what they were hiding from the interrogator, many prisoners came up with improbable stories of hidden weapons, bullets, medicines, packets of poison, and in more than twenty cases, Vietnamese. Pok Pha confessed to "gathering forces," otherwise unidentified, whom he had "concealed in deep holes." Sixty-one confessions involving hidden objects or persons were accompanied by neatly drawn maps, prepared by S-21 personnel, locating the hiding places precisely, down to bureau drawers. The confessions that mention concealed Vietnamese were all written in 1978, after hostilities with

Vietnam had broken out. They are suggestive of the mass hysteria that swept through the Party Center at this time. Invisible Vietnamese were thought to be everywhere, "burrowing from within," waiting to pounce, while in the countryside Vietnamese forces confronted the DK army in the open. Concealed enemies were always the most dangerous. In July 1978, after a study session titled "On the Problem of Hidden Vietnamese," the senior interrogator Pon wrote:

> There are surely Vietnamese hidden in Phnom Penh because Phnom Penh is not yet cleared of traitors. Documents at *santebal* reveal that traitors have hidden Vietnamese in Phnom Penh, in the Northwest and in other zones.[86]

According to some confessions, the Vietnamese were hidden in houses or concealed in vacant lots within sight of important ministries in Phnom Penh. None of these confessions was rejected by Duch and his associates as fanciful, and yet none of the Vietnamese prisoners of war and "spies" questioned at the prison ever stated that they had been hidden by Khmer. These cases are perhaps the clearest examples in the archive of objectified fantasies known by prisoners, interrogators, and the Party Center to have had no basis in fact. At the same time, betraying the regime was tantamount to concealing Vietnamese within oneself, in the same way that treason necessarily implied "bourgeois" tendencies.[87]

Just as the maps showing the hiding places of weapons, medicine, poison, and Vietnamese confirmed the narrative truth of the confessions, most of the confessions were up-to-date in the sense that prisoners were encouraged to admit working for the sorts of enemies who were then being targeted by the Party Center. No one "hid Vietnamese" in 1976, in other words, and in 1978 no one confessed to working for Lon Nol. Naturally enough, prisoners' "crimes" were also related to their work. Thus, prisoners who had been engaged in agriculture confessed to wrecking farm machinery, flooding, burning, stealing and uprooting crops, maiming, killing and losing track of livestock, and arbitrarily cutting down fruit trees. Factory workers confessed to wrecking machinery, stealing materials, making faulty goods, and plotting with coworkers to sabotage production. Cooks confessed to repeatedly attempting to poison high-ranking figures, smashing crockery, serving Chinese experts food on dirty plates so as "to destroy relations with China," or putting pebbles or feces in vats of soup. A woman who prepared food for Chinese "guests" attached to the ministry of foreign relations claimed to have "sought to destroy the policy of the guests" by serving them overcooked soup and providing them with broken spoons.[88] Those employed by the capital's electrical works confessed to short-circuiting the system, while people employed in the ministry of foreign affairs confessed to contact with foreign diplomats in Phnom Penh or with "enemy agents" while on duty overseas. Workers in DK hospitals confessed to injecting patients with poison, stealing or misusing medicine, and having sexual relations with patients and with each other. Former patients, in turn, confessed to malingering and to seducing nurses. Drivers confessed to "intentional" accidents, dock workers to breakage and pilferage, and railway workers to damaging rolling stock. Soldiers confessed to desertion, hiding weapons and ammunition, and to having conversations wth their colleagues that belittled the regime, while those working at S-21 confessed to working slowly, preparing "confusing" documents, encouraging prisoners to escape, forbidding them to defecate, and beating them to death. People who had lived abroad said that they had fallen under malign foreign influences, such as "freedomism"; diplomats confessed to conversations with officials in foreign countries.

Once the "guilty people" had been brought to S-21, none of their previous actions, real or concocted, significant or not, was considered accidental. How could they be, if the Party's leaders were following the laws of history? The prisoners' counterrevolutionary frame of mind, evidenced by their arrest, had from the interrogators' standpoint influenced everything they did, including what might appear to others as loyal service to the Party. "Offenses" that were hardly punishable under a code of law were ratcheted up to the level of "treason" by adducing treasonous motives to everything the prisoners had done.

Terrified into creativity but constrained by their unpracticed imaginations, prisoners struggled to "remember" the kinds of crimes that the relentless and similarly terrified interrogators wanted them to confess. Some of the prisoners came up with revelations so bizarre as to cast doubt on the whole archiving exercise at S-21. Noeun Moeun, a soldier in Regiment 171, for example, confessed:

> In 1.1977 I shot three bullets at the Vietnamese Embassy. After I had done so I reported to [my patron] Sovanna.
>
> In 2.77 Sovanna ordered me to shoot at the Chinese Embassy. I fired three bullets at the Chinese Embassy and then I fired two more bullets at the hostel for Chinese workers so as to disable the policies of Cambodia and China. Afterwards I reported to Sovanna about the problems I had in gathering forces. . . . After I had informed Sovanna in 3.1977, Chut and I went to fire

three bullets at the Albanian Embassy, three bullets at the Korean Embassy, and one bullet to the west of the Independence Monument. When that was done I went to inform Sovanna about the difficulty I was having in firing these shots. When I told him, Sovanna said, "Comrade, you should take on some secret characteristics. You mustn't let them know that you are involved in the shootings. We should plan some strong activities in the future and use the forces that you have gathered. We need to shoot at embassies, at the Organization's place, at factories and at various ministries in Phnom Penh." After receiving this guidance I returned home, and on 27.3.77 I was arrested.[89]

None of the macabre "offenses" described in this and many other confessions would have been punishable by death in prerevolutionary times. Some would not have even have attracted the attention of the offender's family or neighbors. Yet it was crucial for the staff of S-21 to extract confessions that admitted *something*. Oeur Iep, for example, confessed to having a "narrow attitude," forgetting to water plants, and failing to respect communal living. Mol Moeun confessed to the offense of "eating too much, like cadres," and Peou Chhim admitted that he was "lazy and incorrect and talked about women."[90]

Most post-1976 confessions include a section labeled "plans" *(phaenka)*, which enumerated counterrevolutionary activities that the prisoners had hoped to carry out but that had been foiled by their incarceration. For many prisoners, "plans" proved impossible to remember or imagine. As a result, interrogators frequently complained in their notes to confessions that the prisoners' "plans" were "confused," "lacking," or "unclear." Some of them were "revealed" only after extensive torture. The exigencies of the interrogation format were such, however, that no prisoner interrogated at length could be documented without a "plan." It was important for the Party's history and for the well-being of those in the Party center that the "plans" be simultaneously numerous and ineffective.

Many of the "plans," as recounted in the confessions, are absurd, and in many cases they probably reflect what the interrogators believed would fit the bill. Thus, soldiers from the countryside confessed to plotting to assassinate "the Organization" or "Brother Number One," whom they had never seen, or sought to "overthrow the revolution" with a handful of unarmed associates. A former guard at S-21, Tum Thun, claimed to have plotted with some associates to loosen prisoners' shackles and handcuffs, to leave prison doors open, to fall asleep at the gate of the prison so that prisoners could escape—and also to beat prisoners to death.[91] Interestingly, he did not confess to *committing* any of these offenses, which constitute a kind of wish list. Another S-21 guard, An Hot, confessed that he "planned to fall asleep on duty." A film projectionist, Khim Yu, planned to "cause contradictions among foreign guests" by bungling film presentations. Chuon of Division 450 confessed that he planned to "alter the consciousness" of thirty colleagues, without specifying how this would be accomplished, and another prisoner planned to urge his friends to flee to Thailand or Vietnam. By and large, the "plans" sections of the confessions seem in many cases to have been slapped together by workers at S-21. They are the least revealing and probably the most consistently concocted portions in the texts.[92]

The autobiographical pamphlets close with the names and addresses of family members who might be called on to vouch for the person writing the life story. In the confessions, these names are usually replaced at the end of the text by "strings of traitors" and "secret networks" (khsae somngat). The lists seem to have been relatively easy for the interrogators to obtain, and the data they contained were also usually easy to confirm from other sources. In many cases, prisoners provided the names of people already captured or purged by the Organization, and these names were then annotated with the word "caught" (chap), while others were marked with an X, perhaps to indicate that they had been put to death. Names listed in the "strings" were used as the bases for additional arrests. They were also consolidated into typewritten summaries, bringing together the names of people affiliated with certain military units, sectors, offices, factories, or work sites.[93]

Why go to such trouble to compile and concoct these mountains of material? One plausible rationale, as I suggest in chapter 3, was that the Party's leaders wanted the confessions on file as raw material for an ongoing, triumphant history of the Party. Another is that the confessions and mug shots objectified the leaders' paranoid fantasies and were used to convince them that their innumerable enemies were being found, questioned, and put to death. However, other possible explanations have their roots in Cambodia's historiography and traditions.

In prerevolutionary Cambodia, centralized power and control over historical documents were intimately linked. Historical chronicles were prepared at court to celebrate and legitimize the genealogy of a ruler and his accession to power.[94] Held in the palace, these heroic documents became parts of a dynasty's regalia. Throughout Cambodian history writing itself was highly valued, in part because literacy was a skill closely guarded by priests and their students and in part because so many written texts had intrinsic (and therefore secret) religious content or power. In a broader Buddhist context, history was perceived as proceeding in an inexorable decline over the five thousand years following the Buddha's death and enlightenment in 543 B.C. Inside this *longue durée,* history was dynastic, anecdotal, and cyclical, focusing on the actions of those in power and incorporating anecdotes (often imported, with the proper names altered, from other chronicles) that gave pleasing accounts of battles, ceremonies, and intrigues.

Under Pol Pot, historical texts were also composed, controlled, and held by the "ruling apparatus" *(kbal masin),* and historical narratives still described the defeat of enemies. At the same time, the writing of history began to be conceived in a different way. While both genres related events that reflected favorably on a given ruler, Marxist-Leninist history was teleological, dialectical, and collective, a modern genre that supposedly followed scientific laws. By mastering these laws, it was thought, a Marxist-Leninist party like the CPK could seize power and maintain itself thereafter. Thus when a Party spokesman declared in 1976 that "two thousand years of history" had ended, he probably meant not only that past practices were dead but also that progressively oriented, Party-centered history could now replace the chronicles and everything they stood for. Cambodia's history-writing, as well as its social relations, had been overturned.

In an undated document titled "Characteristics of the CPK," a Party spokesman made these points after outlining the Party's history:

> The exploiting group wrote history so as to exploit the people even more. When we write the history of our country we write about the struggle of our Party and our people for independence and not to be the slaves of others any more. For example, when we write the history of Angkor we write that the people made it, and that is the truth: the people made it, not the kings.[95]

Several Party histories from the 1970s reflect this altered focus and new approach.[96] With what Timothy Carney has called its "unexpected victory" in April 1975, the CPK achieved the closure that had been lacking in these earlier texts and grasped the "wheel of history" *(kong pravatt'sas).* With victory, Cambodia's "two-thousand-year" history became coterminous with the Party's rise to power. Put another way, the Communists' victory in 1975 illuminated the Party's past. Alternative readings of the past, along with the Party's flesh-and-blood opponents, were unthinkable and had to be "swept clean."

The involvement of S-21 in the historiography of the Party became important after April 1976, when, as we have seen, a military disturbance in Phnom Penh was interpreted by the CPK's leaders as a revolt that threatened the hegemony of the Party and undermined its hitherto triumphal history. Thanks to the voluminous "evidence" about the conspiracy reaching the Party Center from S-21, the Party's history from then on was conceived largely in terms of an open-ended struggle against internal enemies. S-21 became the regime's cutting edge.

As I suggested earlier, the confessions extracted at S-21 also served a psychological purpose by objectifying the paranoid fantasies of the Party's leaders. In this regard, the resemblances between the interrogators' methods and objectives and Freud's notions of therapeutic "archaeology," while fortuitous, are striking.[97] Interrogators at S-21, like psychoanalysts, excavated the memories of each "guilty person" who was assumed to be hiding a history (which is to say, a memory) of counterrevolutionary activities, plans, and associates. Like many psychoanalysts, the interrogators pretended to know what they were looking for and had some idea of the "memories" that they wanted the prisoners to "recover." They also knew the format that a completed confession had to take, whereas the prisoners, like many psychiatric patients, did not.

In several other respects, of course, comparisons between what happened at S-21 and what sometimes takes place in psychoanalysis are invalid. Analysts, to begin with, seldom resort to violence, whereas S-21 was steeped in it. Analysis patients are usually free to get up and leave, thereby abandoning the procedure or seeking a more sympathetic interlocutor; all the prisoners at S-21 were killed, and their confessions were in effect their wills, last letters from the death house. Another aspect of the interrogations at S-21 that sets them apart from their psychoanalytic counterparts is that the fantasies being excavated, objectified, and spoken about in Pol Pot's secret prison were not those of the prisoners but those projected onto them by the interrogators on behalf of their patrons (and, in a sense, their patients) in the Party Center. Perhaps the major difference between analysis and interrogation, of course, is that analysis is aimed, in theory, at the betterment of the patient, whereas interrogations aim to extract evidence from a prisoner for use in a legal proceeding. Insofar as interrogations at S-21 had a heuristic purpose, in line with the Maoist theory of reeducation, the two forms of questioning tended to overlap.

With these reservations, however, there are still uncanny resemblances between the two kinds of conversation and between the lopsided power relationships that they display. In a disturbing passage, Freud himself once suggested:

> We must not believe what they say, we must always assume, and tell them,
> too, that they have kept something back. . . . We must insist on this, we must
> repeat the pressure and represent ourselves as infallible, until at last we are
> really told something.[98]

The S-21 interrogator's manual, even more chillingly than Freud, when
we recall the prisoners' fates, makes a similar point:

> They must write confessions in their own voice, clearly, using their own sen-
> tences, their own ideas. We should avoid telling them what to write. When
> they have finished telling their story or writing it down, only then can we
> raise their weak points, press them to explain why they did things, why they
> are lying, concealing, abbreviating things.[99]

A third reason why the S-21 archives were maintained has been suggested, in another context, by Peter Holquist, writing about the amass-
ing of "all encompassing information" about "political moods" in the
USSR and the relationship between information-gathering and surveillance by police services on the one hand and what Holquist calls the
Bolshevik notion of "sculpting" twentieth-century society on the other.
Seen in this way, the information collected at S-21 could be used by the
Party Center to gauge the "political moods" of the people, so as to forestall opposition and reconstruct those who were not yet imprisoned
along proper revolutionary lines. Collecting everyone's biography, so as
to "know" everyone in the country, fits into such a scheme. Indeed, DK
seems to have been seduced by the notion that gathering masses of
information per se increased its capacity to influence events. Unfortunately for the regime but fortunately for many survivors, information at
the regime's disposal was often incomplete or falsified, and hundreds of
thousands of "enemies" were never found.[100]

If for argument's sake we assume the S-21 confessions to be "true,"
an ungenerous reading is that the Party's leaders, in the dark for so long
about so many conspiracies and betrayals, displayed colossal naïveté,
misplaced trust, and a consistent misreading of people's priorities and
motives. Indeed, this is the line that Pol Pot took, somewhat plaintively,
after 1979 in talking about his time in power. What went wrong, Pol
Pot told some followers in 1981, was that he had "trusted people too
much." In 1995, he said that the deaths that occurred under DK could
be traced to the fact that "we were like babies, learning to walk." Pol
Pot's evasion of responsibility is easy to understand, and so is his self-
pity, but the comparison between DK and a gigantic baby stumbling

across the Cambodian landscape, inflicting colossal damage, defies analysis.[101]

When they were extracted, of course, the confessions were not intended as demonstrations of the Party Center's naïveté but as evidence of the CPK's knowledge of everything that went on, however tardily obtained, and its leaders' consummate ability to grasp the wheel of history and thereby create and control the Party's triumphant narrative. Just as multiple "national" and personal stories flowed together into the governing narrative of the CPK's triumph over what it called "the United States" in April 1975, the records of "treasonous activities," "plans," and the "strings of traitors" being unmasked were also absorbed into that history, and the "enemies" neutralized, before their treasonous acts or any of their "plans" could take effect. Seen in this way, the confessions are mantras protecting the Party Center not only from its enemies but also from any genuine effort to understand what was going on. Duch, Pon, Chan, and their associates were simultaneously priests, therapists, miners, vivisectors, and historians. In concocting history out of their leaders' fantasies, which were probably also their own, they served their masters well.

CHAPTER FIVE

Forcing the Answers

As in the Nazi concentration camps examined by Wolfgang Sofsky, "excessive violence was an everyday phenomenon" at S-21.[1] Some of the documents from the prison, and especially those that deal with torture, exude so much horror and speak so calmly about pain that they are difficult to absorb, even as they draw us toward the victims. For example, in July 1977 an interrogator appended the following unsigned note to the confession of Ke Kim Huot, the former secretary of Sector 7 in the Northwest Zone:

1. In the morning of 18.7.77 I decided to employ torture. I told the prisoner that I was doing this because I had not grasped the weak points of what he had said, and my pressure had not had any results. This was my stance. I watched his morale fall when I administered torture, but he had no reaction. When questioning began, it was still the same. As for his health, he ate some gruel, but he was not able to sleep. The doctor looked after him.

2. On the morning of 20.7.77 I beat him again. This time his reaction was to say that he was not a traitor but that the people who had accused him were the traitors. His health was still weak, but was not a serious problem.

3. In the afternoon and evening of 21.7.77 I pressured him again, using electric cord and shit. On this occasion he insulted the person who was beating him: "You people who are beating me will kill me," he said. He was given 2–3 spoonfuls of shit to eat, and after that he was able to answer questions about the contemptible Hing, Chau, Sac, Va, etc.

4. That night I beat him with electric cord again.

At present he is a little weak. The doctor has seen him. He has asked to rest.[2]

Another interrogator's comment vividly illustrates the lopsided relationship between torturers and their victims, which Michel Foucault has somewhat luxuriantly compared both to a "duel" and to a game of chess.[3]

> I first asked the enemy about his life and associations. When I had done this, I spoke about the discipline of the office [S-21], and I told him that his body, tied up with fetters and handcuffs, was worth less than garbage.
>
> I had him pay respect to me. I told him that if I asked him to say a single word to me, he had to say it. I made him pay homage to the image of a dog [a common torture, involving an image of a dog with the head of Ho Chi Minh]. I beat him and interrogated him until he said that he had once been CIA. After I beat him some more, he admitted that he had joined the CIA in 1969.
>
> Once he had confessed I didn't have to beat him to obtain the rest of his story, but when he hesitated or came to weak points in his story I beat him, and I also beat him to clarify the points in his story where the information about important matters was confused.[4]

Coming face to face with documents like these, or with the harrowing photographs from S-21, we are at a loss for words. Indeed, Jean Améry, E. Valentine Daniel, and Elaine Scarry have eloquently demonstrated that the *experience* of torture is impossible to put into words; Scarry even suggests that pain destroys language. Perhaps this is one reason why there seems to be no precise legal definition for torture. Why, then, do so many authors persist in trying to write about it ? Why should we? There is something unsettling about "fine writing" about pain. As Améry has remarked, "Torture is the most horrible event a human being can retain within himself." He adds that "the howl of pain defies communication through language." In spite of or perhaps because of such warnings, writers and readers alike are drawn inexorably toward a subject that is ugly, frightening, seductive, and ultimately inexpressible.[5]

We can be emotionally worn down by the idea of torture merely by visiting the site of S-21, looking at the mug shots, or leafing through the archive. It is tempting to take refuge in the received wisdom that the all-pervasive "evil" in the DK period was epitomized by the prison. Looking at every photograph and every confession, we know the prisoner's fate. Repeatedly and with hindsight we confront descriptions of violence and the repetitive fact of death. At the same time, we are insulated from what really happened to the minds and bodies of the victims and to the personalities of the perpetrators later on. What happened is awful, but it happened long ago to other people. "Evil," we like to think, takes place elsewhere.

The Problem of Studying Torture

In studying torture at S-21 we are restricted not only by our distance from what happened but also by the relative silence of available sources on the subject. Since the early 1980s, only three survivors of the prison have talked at length about their experiences. Their testimonies are valuable and heartfelt, but they have limitations that spring from their repeated use as propaganda in the 1980s, from the survivors' interview fatigue, and from the blurring of their memories over time. Moreover, the survivors cannot describe conditions in the prison in 1976, before they were arrested.

Similarly, only six former workers at the prison—Duch, three guards, a photographer, and the man who was in charge of the documentation unit—have been interviewed in depth in recent years. Only one of them, the former guard Him Huy, has admitted killing people. He says that he was not a torturer. No one who has admitted torturing prisoners has come forward, and although some ex-workers at the prison, like Huy, were arrested and "reeducated" in the 1980s for their activities at the prison, none of them has ever spoken at length about their activities, and none has gone on trial.[6]

The scarcity of survivors and the dearth of oral testimony or transcribed memories of prison life contrasts sharply with the voluminous literature and numerous survivors from such comparable institutions as the Soviet and Chinese gulags and the Nazi concentration camps, or with materials dealing with torture and cruelty in other countries. The work of Christopher Browning, Daniel Goldhagen, Raul Hilberg, and Gitta Sereny concerning German perpetrators of the Holocaust, for example, would be impossible to duplicate for S-21. So would the memoirs of Jean Améry, Primo Levi, Alexander Solzhenitsyn, and Jacobo Timerman, or E. Valentine Daniel's haunting study of Sri Lanka, which is based in part on interviews with former torturers and victims. To study torture at S-21, we are thrown back onto documents that were extracted from tortured men and women now dead, or confessions that reflect the boastful, evasive, or exculpatory views of the torturers themselves. Without corroboration from other sources, it is impossible to say whether these documents exaggerate or play down what was happening at the prison. My guess, after years of immersion in the archive, is that innumerable random cruelties and hundreds of instances of torture went unrecorded. What we can read are faint traces of what was going on, and they give only an inkling of the mayhem perpetrated at the prison every day.[7]

In spite of these obstacles, torture and violence are central to S-21 and to our ability to understand prison. We need to establish the dynamics by which the confessions were extracted. We need to penetrate the thinking of the prison administrators and to understand the rationale they used for torture. Most important, as Alexander Hinton has suggested, we need to "rehumanize" the victims by bearing witness to their suffering.[8]

What is striking about the imposition of torture *(tearunikam)* at the prison, however, is not its brutality—although the tortures inflicted were severe—but its use within a graduated, supposedly rational process. The coolness with which torture is chosen, inflicted, and written about is unnerving. We can easily understand outbursts of cruelty in ourselves or others, but we tend to back away from cruelty that is so carefully meted out. One explanation for this coolness, as Darius Rejali observes in his study of torture in Iran, is that torture is not so much a fruitful means of obtaining valid evidence and confessions, nor a form of unchecked sadism, as an instrument that serves to display and rationalize the power of those inflicting it, especially when they are representatives of the state. Other writers on torture have presented similar views.[9]

With Rejali's formulation in mind, we can see that torture at S-21 was not simply a matter of young men and women inflicting their will on defenseless prisoners, although they often did so, nor was it a straightforward extension of prerevolutionary police procedures, although elements of these, such as mug shots, thumbprinting, and the preliminary pummeling known in French argot as a *passage à tabac* were also part of S-21 routine. Instead, most of the tortures at S-21 were purposive and constrained. The beatings and tortures inflicted were merciless, but torture usually required the permission of superiors, which was sometimes withheld. Interrogators who used "excessive" torture (torture that killed prisoners before they completed their confessions) criticized themselves at livelihood meetings and were occasionally punished for the offense. In eight confession texts—all from the closing months of 1978—the interrogator noted that the confession had been extracted without the prisoner in question being beaten or tortured at all.[10] By that time, the prison was operating more smoothly and "rationally" than it had in 1976, when most of the staff were new recruits and when the Party Center had found it necessary to request "less beating" at the prison.[11] In 1977 and 1978 individual interrogators, except when they got out of hand, applied torture selectively at the outset of some interrogations, again when they encountered resistance, and more intensely in "difficult" cases. Torture was a tool, a means to an end, an integral part of what Foucault has called the "authoritarian search for truth." Interrogators who tortured people found it easy to obey the people who ordered them to do it, especially when their own lives were constantly at risk. As far as we can tell, they harbored few regrets.

Limitations on torture at the prison were imposed not out of respect for the victims or because administrators found the practice unpleasant but rather because it was always linked to the other aspect of interrogation, "doing politics" *(tvoeu nayobay),* which meant, ideally, explaining the Party's policies to the prisoners and extracting confessions. A calibrated mixture of torture, inspiration, and propaganda, it was thought, could illustrate the power relations in effect and could also produce the memories, accusations, and documents that the Party needed. Excessive torture would obstruct or delay the production of these necessary texts.

"Imposing Torture" and "Doing Politics"

The tensions that developed between doing torture and doing politics are set out in the interrogator's study notebook prepared at the prison in 1976 and in two notebooks written by senior interrogators in 1977 and 1978. Some of the tensions sprang from the fact that while all the interrogators were encouraged to use violence, very few of them had any training in politics or interrogation. The 1976 notebook stated that torture was "secondary, subsidiary, and supplementary" to politics, but added that "doing politics" alone was insufficient. Violence was always needed. As the notebook puts it: "Take politics as the basis. Keep track of the answers, in a comparative way, and then use torture." Two years later, the chief interrogator's notebook asserted that "insults" were part of doing politics and added that while beating alone was "insufficient," "beating + politics = important."[12]

Prisoners at S-21 were dehumanized from the moment they arrived. Blindfolded and shackled, they were bundled out of trucks, usually at night. They were kicked, shoved, and beaten as they were taken inside to be documented and photographed. They had arrived, as Vann Nath said later, in "a place many times worse than hell."

The distinction between beating *(vay)* and torture *(tearunikam)* lay in the use of weapons, contraptions, or humiliating ceremonies (such as the torture involving obeisance to the image of Ho Chi Minh with the body of a dog, known as *sompeah* or *thvay bongkum rup chkae*), but beatings during interrogation could also be classified as torture, and many documents use the terms *vay* and *tearunikam* interchangeably. Once an interrogation had begun, outside controls were rare, and, as Sofsky points out with regard to German concentration camps, the "transition from torture intended to extract a confession to pure, purposeless torture was fluid." The welfare of the prisoners was never a consideration unless they died before confessing.[13]

Violence and Sadism

Interrogations could be stopped, intensified, or interrupted at the whim of the interrogation team leader. The torturer—usually a different person—could resume using his hands, take up a new weapon, or return the prisoner to his cell. If a confession could be obtained merely by beating or by asking questions, so much the better. If none was forthcoming after extensive torture, so much the worse. Some prisoners were tortured on a daily basis. Ten Chan, a survivor, recalls being beaten and occasionally tortured for twenty-six days in a row.[14]

The victims of torture often died. The prison authorities were unconcerned if death occurred after a confession had been obtained, but if a prisoner died beforehand the interrogator was often suspected of sabotage. Several interrogators imprisoned at S-21 confessed to killing prisoners under interrogation, and so did two of the guards, but in most cases it is unclear whether this crime was the one for which they had been arrested or whether it reflected their own assessment of punishable actions in their recent past. In any case, sadistic emotions occasionally spilled over, as the former guard Son Moeun wrote in his confession:

> After I was assigned to guard this prisoner [in the "special prison" south of Tuol Sleng] I saw the [interrogators] beating him, and when the interrogators were gone I stole inside and beat him too, pushing, kicking, and punching him freely, until the prisoner said, "What are you doing? You'll kill me this way!"

Soon afterwards, the prisoner in question, Bun Than, died from the injuries inflicted by the interrogators and the guard. His confession is incomplete.[15]

In any case, locked inside a total institution that was cross-cut by the competing demands of permissiveness and "discipline," empowerment and mistrust, violence and propaganda, interrogators always walked a fine line between too little and too much. They usually erred in the direction of excess, which was seldom punished, rather than discretion, which was never rewarded.

Like their counterparts in the Nazi death camps, they became callous. Cruelty at the prison, if we can judge from the documents that survive, was often what Randall Collins has called "cruelty without passion," in which "the subject of the violence is simply an instrument or an obstacle, and his suffering is merely an incidental (usually ignored) feature of some other intention."[16] A vivid example of cruelty without passion at S-21 is a note sent by senior interrogator Pon to Duch following a day of vigorous interrogation. The prisoner in question was Keo Meas, a former member of the Party's Central Committee. Pon wrote:

> On the night of 26 September 1976, after threatening [the prisoner] with a few words, I had him remove his shirt and shackled his arms behind him, to be removed only at meals. [I thus] deprived him of sleep and let mosquitoes bite.[17]

Penal and Judicial Torture

The phenomena of torture and violence at S-21 need to be placed in a historical context. Did they have roots in prerevolutionary Cambodian practices, or were they new phenomena traceable to the needs of the Khmer Rouge and less firmly to specific foreign models?

Etymology sheds some light on the issue of torture itself. The Cambodian word for torture, *tearunikam,* shared with Thai, derives from the Sanskrit *daruna,* meaning "fierce" or "savage," and the Pali *kamm,* meaning "action." According to the definitive Khmer dictionary published by the Buddhist Institute in Phnom Penh in the 1960s, its secondary meanings, like those of its Thai counterpart, are "savagery," "cruelty," and "barbarism." The illustrative sentence for *tearunikam* in the Buddhist Institute dictionary reads: "Don't ever torture [i.e., inflict cruelty on] people or animals."[18]

Torture in its Khmer linguistic context, then, implies mere cruelty, carries moral opprobrium, and is not associated with the administration of justice. The phrase *dak tearunikam,* "to impose torture," suggests a cruel ordeal, or what Foucault and Rejali have referred to as *penal* torture, embodying what Foucault has called "the revenge of the sovereign," rather than what Edward Peters has referred to as *judicial* torture, which has been connected throughout history with gathering evidence and obtaining confessions.

Peters's magisterial study traces the practice of judicial torture from Greece in the fifth century B.C., where it was practiced only on slaves, through its development under Roman law and its revival in western Europe in the twelfth and thirteenth centuries A.D. Peters goes on to describe what he calls the "regularizing" of judicial torture that occurred between the thirteenth century and the eighteenth, when the practice came under sustained attack. He closes his book by discussing the revival of judicial torture on a global scale in recent times.

A shortcoming of Peters's absorbing study is its failure to take up Asian examples of judicial torture in any detail. Both judicial and penal torture were widespread in classical China, Japan, and Vietnam, especially in interrogating prisoners of war or when confessions or the names of a prisoner's associates were required. A Chinese term, *kao wen,* breaks down into the characters for "interrogate" and "beat," while the Vietnamese term, *tra tan,* uses the verbs "to examine" and "to question" without implying violence. The notion of blending torture with interrogations to produce confessions—missing from the word *tearunikam*—seems to have been a Sino-Vietnamese concept as well as a European one, but it was not familiar in the Theravada Buddhist parts of Southeast Asia. Evidence for its arrival in Cambodia before DK is lacking.[19]

Even with this neglect of Asia, what Peters writes about judicial torture in Europe prior to 1800 is applicable to S-21. With the rise of Christianity, he tells us, judicial torture became integral to heresy cases. It was justified partly because "heresy was a shared offense [and] besides the salvation of the heretic's soul, inquisitors needed the names of fellow-heretics." Under torture, the suspected heretic produced the names of people who were subsequently tortured and who then produced more names, in widening spirals similar to those constructed centuries later at Tuol Sleng. In a perceptive paper about medieval torture, Talal Asad has suggested that "since the crime of holding heretical views could not be confirmed independently of a confession by the accused, [torture] had to be tried before the existence of the crime could be established. Since the crime itself was deliberately hidden, the hunt for the truth had to employ its own game of deadly secrets."[20] In most of these cases, as at S-21, defendants were assumed from the start to be guilty, were allowed little or no formal defense, and were subject to condemnation on the strength of hearsay.

Torture in Cambodia's Past

In prerevolutionary Cambodia, there is no documentation of torture being used for evidentiary purposes, although suspects were sometimes subjected to painful ordeals to "prove" that they were lying or telling the truth. Instead, scattered evidence suggests that torture took its punitive form, extending or intensifying punishments meted out for crimes of lèse-majesté. Vivid examples of such ordeals can be found in several Angkorean inscriptions and are mentioned as penalties for defiance of oaths sworn by medieval Cambodian officials. Bas-reliefs in the southern gallery of Angkor Wat depict some of the punishments that were thought to await transgressors. In the reliefs Yama, the Hindu deity of the underworld, is shown astride a buffalo dispatching rows of men and women either to an antiseptic heaven or into thirty-two vividly imagined levels of hell, where they are condemned, as in Dante's *Inferno*, to gruesome tortures appropriate to their sins. A guide who pointed out the bas-reliefs to a visitor in 1981 likened Yama to Pol Pot.[21]

In post-Angkorean Cambodia, images of hell, with victims being tortured, were painted as murals in many Buddhist *wat*s. Vann Nath has compared the prison to such a hell *(norok)* and his own experiences to those pictured in Buddhist murals, noting that prisoners were often addressed as *a-pret* ("damned souls") by prison personnel. To complete the circle, Vann Nath's paintings of tortures inflicted at S-21 now adorn the walls of the Tuol Sleng Genocide Museum.

In this context, the prisoners' systematic dehumanization, which Nath has discussed in several interviews, may well have been linked to the fact that they were seen by their captors as irredeemable "unbelievers"—an unconscious carryover, perhaps, from Buddhist thinking, which tends to view nonbelievers (*thmil,* or "Tamils," in Cambodian and Thai) as beyond the pale. Dehumanizing them made things easier for workers at S-21, just as dehumanizing Jews, Gypsies, homosexuals, and other inmates made things easier for workers in the Nazi death camps. Those who were being tortured and killed, like the people in hell in the murals, were *others.* Pol Pot himself, in his marathon speech announcing the existence of the CPK in 1977, made this point succinctly: "These counterrevolutionary elements which betray and try to sabotage the revolution," he said, "are not to be regarded as our people."[22]

Elaborate public executions in precolonial Cambodia, often involving trampling by elephants, demonstrated the power of the king, destroyed the culprits, and awed the onlookers summoned to the scene. It is as if the judgment of their superiors and the fate of the culprits' souls, as depicted at Angkor Wat and in later murals, had to be prefigured by the public destruction of their bodies.[23]

Other physical punishments for crimes in precolonial times were also very severe. Seventeenth-century Cambodian legal codes, for example, list twenty-one time-consuming, extremely painful punishments that were permissible in cases involving people "who seek to become great and seek to betray the king who is the lord of the land."[24] The Khmer narrative poem *Tum Taev,* set in the seventeenth century, first published in the early 1900s, and familiar to generations of Cambodian schoolchildren, closes with the execution of an entire family after one of them is accused of lèse-majesté. Buried up to the neck, the family is decapitated by passing an iron harrow drawn by water buffaloes across their protruding heads.[25]

These precolonial cases and prescriptions resemble the public executions in prerevolutionary France described in detail by Michel Foucault in the opening pages of *Discipline and Punish.* But these cases differ in several ways from what went on in S-21, where tortures were inflicted selectively, in private, and had no connection with executions, which were carried out later, in secret, en masse, and usually at night. By combining elaborate physical torture and total secrecy, heavy documentation and complete surveillance, the practices of S-21 blend what Foucault has argued, in France at least, were separable stages in an evolutionary process, which he calls respectively the "vengeance of the sovereign" and "the defense of society."[26]

In the colonial era in Cambodia (1863–1954), the French set up a career police force that operated under their supervision. By 1900 or so, penal torture had ceased to be practiced by Cambodian officials. Because of French scruples, judicial torture was never openly employed. Instead, the French established procedures, courts, and institutions for the administration of Western-style justice. Within this supposedly rational framework, however, interrogations of prisoners were often very rough. After Cambodia gained its independence, its French-inspired gendarmerie still beat prisoners, and people accused of treason were often tortured before being put to death. In the Lon Nol regime, prisoners of war were routinely tortured to obtain information. There is no evidence, however, that judicial torture was practiced extensively by the police, or used as an instrument of national security, before the Khmer Rouge came to power.

Why was this the case? To begin with, hardly anyone accused of treason under Sihanouk or Lon Nol ever went on trial; thus there was little call under those regimes for the detailed confessions that judicial torture might be expected to produce. Another constraining factor was that until 1975, Western-style police procedures and courts in Cambodia remained in place. Evidence obtained under torture, if its use could be established, might have been challenged in court, and the unwelcome publicity, if it reached foreign observers, might have besmirched Cambodia's reputation. This kind of constraint operated in other countries as well. If judicial torture occurred in postcolonial Cambodia, the absence of documentary corroboration suggests that it was carried out in secret, as has been customary elsewhere in modern times.[27]

Torture in DK

After the Khmer Rouge victory of 17 April 1975, the judicial system in Cambodia disappeared. There were no courts, judges, laws, or trials in DK. The "people's courts" stipulated in Article 9 of the DK Constitution were never established.[28] The absence of laws or safeguards, DK's self-imposed isolation from the world, the importance placed by the Party Center on the confessions of "enemies," and the blend of prestige and secrecy that characterized S-21 encouraged Duch and his associates to use torture and any other means at their disposal to obtain confessions. The staff concealed the practice, however, like everything else they did, from the Cambodian public.

Officials at S-21 believed that when they tortured prisoners they were responding to the country's needs and to the fears of those who led it. The ideology of Democratic Kampuchea, as we have seen, was premised on continuous class warfare and continuous revolution. "Enemies" were everywhere and needed to be destroyed. Some were poised along Cambodia's borders; others were farther off; still others were "buried inside the Party, burrowing from within." Enemies often came disguised as friends. To ferret them out, extreme measures needed to be taken.

Most judicial torture in DK took place inside S-21, perhaps because, ironically, the facility was the only one in the country that had quasi-judicial functions, as reflected by the documentation that the facility produced. S-21 also had authority from the Party Center to deal with crimes of lèse-parti. Thousands of men and women charged with lesser offenses or imprisoned as class enemies succumbed to malnutrition, illness, and savage treatment in provincial prisons, but in general these people were not tortured to produce evidence of their crimes.[29] Prisoners already ticketed for Tuol Sleng, however, were occasionally tortured in a provincial prison beforehand to soften them up and to provide some rudimentary documentation for interrogators in Phnom Penh. Vann Nath, for example, was tortured "for many hours" in Battambang before he came to S-21, and Baen Chhae (alias Chhaom Savath) said in his confession that he was tortured in Kompong Cham before being transported to Phnom Penh.[30]

Judicial torture at S-21, therefore, was linked to crimes which, like heresy in medieval Europe, involved betrayals of the ruling ideology and suspicions of hidden networks of conspirators. As in medieval times, guilt was established primarily by the prisoner's confession, there being no other means of proof. After the Chan Chakrei "uprising" of April 1976, as we have seen, the leaders of DK felt continuously threatened. They needed scapegoats for what the DK Constitution (Article 10) called "hostile and destructive activities which threaten the people's state." The massive failure of their economic master plan soon required more scapegoats. By the middle of 1976, most of the prisoners brought to S-21 had been accused of treason or were connected with others who had been accused. S-21 became crucial to the regime's survival.

The first step in any imprisonment and even more starkly in judicial torture is to dehumanize the prisoner. At S-21 this practice had the double effect of anesthetizing the torturers and cutting the prisoners off from any sense of community or self-respect. Because they were labeled "enemies" (like the *thmil* of prerevolutionary times) the prisoners had lost their right to be treated as Cambodians or as human beings. When they arrived at S-21, they were pitched head-over-heels into hell like the victims in the bas-reliefs of Angkor Wat. Being arrested often involved a sudden change of fortune. With considerable pleasure, Vann Nath recalled being held for a time in the same room as a discredited Khmer Rouge cadre, known for his brutality but now disgraced: "When he was in the cooperative, he acted like a king," Vann Nath recalled. "No one could look at his face. But now he was shackled by the legs, looking like a monkey."[31]

The process of Nath's own dehumanization evokes prisoners' accounts in other countries. In the 1930s Eugenia Ginzburg, a young Russian Communist first imprisoned by Stalin and later sent to

Auschwitz, faced a Soviet judge who told her: "Enemies are not people. We're allowed to do what we like with them. People, indeed!" The judge's words might have served as a motto for S-21.[32]

Elsewhere in DK, most "base people" were given enhanced status. They were placed in the same categories as Communist Party members who had passed the "Communist Youth League" phase either as "candidates" *(triem)* or as having "full rights" *(penh sut)*. In contrast, "new people," as Cambodians with urban or nonrevolutionary backgrounds were called, became known as "depositees" *(pnhao),* a category reflecting their status as people evacuated to the countryside. Prisoners at S-21 had even lower status than "depositees."[33] Before being questioned, they were made to discard their black, revolutionary clothes and wear ill-fitting, ragged clothing tossed at them by the guards. The pronouns that guards used to refer to the prisoners were those normally applied to children and animals. In the autobiographies that opened their confessions, the prisoners no longer noted their class background *(vannakpheap)* as required on other Party documents. Stripped of clothing, humanity, and class, they could be invaded, beaten, and humiliated until their memories coincided with the requirements of the Party, at which point they could be put to death.

The Soviet Show Trials

As we have seen, officials at S-21 worked on the assumptions that prisoners were guilty of something because they had been accused, and subhuman because they had been arrested. Both notions had deep roots in Cambodian culture. At S-21, however, the main inspirations for prolonged interrogation accompanied by judicial torture and leading to copious confessions came from abroad: from the so-called Moscow show trials (sometimes called the Great Terror) of 1936–1938, when hundreds of Soviet Communist Party cadres and military figures had confessed publicly, and often spuriously, to sabotage, espionage, and treason. Thousands more were executed without trial. The elaborate confessions extracted in Moscow were orchestrated to please Stalin. They confirmed his often inchoate fears, preempted "enemy" initiatives, and strengthened his authority. In this respect, the Soviet purges and the confessions stemming from them closely resembled those extracted at S-21. Like Stalin, who spent most of the period of the show trials concealed from public view, Pol Pot made only a few carefully orchestrated appearances throughout the DK era. Moreover, the heavily coached Soviet defendants, like those in Cambodia later on, almost never denied their guilt once they appeared in court, and they seldom offered any defense. The prisoners in both countries were regarded as "less than garbage." After reciting their confessions to the court, most of the Soviet prisoners, like those at Tuol Sleng, were secretly put to death.

In both cases the sentence of death was a foregone conclusion—recalling the Red Queen's "Sentence first, verdict afterwards"—but in Moscow the ordeals were staged openly, in courtrooms, with the trappings of twentieth-century justice, whereas at S-21 everything was kept secret, there were no occasions for dialogue, and neither the prisoners nor the judges were ever on display. One reason for this difference is that Moscow trials were intended, among other things, to demonstrate the Soviet Union's leadership of the world socialist movement, whereas the Khmer Rouge leaders, indifferent to world opinion, believed that secrecy was a key ingredient of their success.

Another difference between the two procedures was that physical torture preceding the Soviet trials seems to have been infrequent and was limited—officially at least—to such practices as sleep deprivation and exposing prisoners to bright lights, prolonged questioning, poor food, and isolation. Solzhenitsyn, referring to his own interrogations in the 1940s, wrote: "My interrogator had used no methods on me other than sleeplessness, lies, and threats—all completely legal." At S-21 these pressures were used along with physical violence. The Soviet methods were enough to break most prisoners; severe physical torture was in any case precluded by the requirement that the prisoners look healthy in court and sound as if they were confessing of their own free will. (However, physical torture was specifically permitted by Stalin in cases involving "known and obstinate enemies of the people," with the justification that it was widely used by "bourgeois intelligence services.") The concealed victims at S-21, on the other hand, could be beaten and tortured as often and as violently as their captors saw fit.[34]

Even when these differences are kept in mind, the resemblances between the Soviet accusations and confessions and their counterparts at S-21 are too numerous to be coincidental. How did the Soviet models reach Cambodia? To begin with, most of the "upper brothers" were familiar with the Moscow trials. Pol Pot, Son Sen, Ieng Sary, and Khieu Samphan would have learned about them in the early 1950s, when they were all students in France and fledgling members of the French Communist Party. They would have read Party documents, journalism, and briefings that justified the purges. They would also have known and approved of the Soviet-orchestrated show trials that were taking place in Czechoslovakia, Hungary, and other Soviet-bloc countries.[35]

Although they never commented publicly on these trials, these young Cambodians must have been struck by the abject self-incrimination of the accused, the comprehensive evidence arrayed against them, and the identification of revolutionary justice with a concealed, all-powerful leader. Their training in the French Communist Party, which was emphatically pro-Stalin, would hardly have led them to sympathize with Stalin's victims or to appreciate the niceties of bourgeois as opposed to revolutionary justice. When the time came, the confessions extracted at S-21 replicated the paranoid ideology, the holistic, accusatory format, and the interrogatory procedures of the Soviet show trials. Since in both cases a Communist Party, obsessed with history, was purging itself to protect its suspicious leaders, the resemblances are not surprising.

Chinese and Vietnamese Models

Another model for S-21's draconian procedures came from Communist Party purges and reeducation campaigns in China, filtered through Vietnam. Cambodian Communists fighting alongside the Vietnamese in the first Indochina war (1946–1954) probably learned about Soviet interrogation techniques, Chinese-style "reeducation," and the proper format for "counterrevolutionary" confessions from their Vietnamese patrons.

Vietnamese training for Khmer cadres in security work, if there was any, would probably have reflected Chinese models. In this early period, these included the rectification *(zhen-fan)* campaigns conducted at Yan'an in 1943 and the land reform campaigns in North China after 1949. Purges swept through China and Vietnam in the mid-1950s. Thousands of people were killed, thousands of careers were ruined, and tens of thousands of people were interrogated and then released. The Chinese and Vietnamese blended Soviet notions of implacable revolutionary justice with ideas of redemptive "thought reform" or "reeducation" that had roots in prerevolutionary China and Vietnam but very little resonance in Cambodian history.[36]

Drawing on this tradition, the Chinese and Vietnamese pursued what Peter Berger and Thomas Luckman have called a "therapy" strategy to deal with deviants, as opposed to that of "nihilation" pursued in the

USSR and later at S-21. In all four countries prisoners were expected to confess fully and openly to accusations, reassessing their past to harmonize with the requirements of the Party. They were also supposed to express profound remorse. Redemption, however, was difficult to obtain and seldom complete. The characters of those accused of counterrevolutionary activities were permanently stained, but after "rectification" far fewer victims were killed in China and Vietnam than in the USSR. Instead, thousands of "enemies" spent long periods in prison.[37]

In the closing months of 1978 Cambodian officials at S-21 toyed with the idea of adapting a similar strategy, perhaps in line with the amnesty offered by Pol Pot to former "enemies" earlier in the year. A document from Office 870, as the Central Committee was called, promised leniency to people who had "joined the CIA, done work for the Vietnamese, or entered the KGB" before 1975; those who had offended later would be judged on a case-by-case basis.[38]

In 1978, perhaps reflecting this change of tactics, S-21 was referred to in some confessions as a "reeducation hall" *(sala kay pray)*, the name used at the time by provincial prisons in DK. According to Pon's notebook, a policy was inaugurated in October 1978 not to beat Cambodian prisoners, instead reserving the fury of *santebal* for "foreigners such as Vietnamese, and CIA agents of imperialist powers." According to Vann Nath, the number of prisoners held at S-21 dropped sharply at about that time, following celebrations honoring the CPK's eighteenth birthday. His memory is corroborated by S-21 entry statistics for October and November. The cells reserved for senior cadres were cleaned and repainted, and rules affecting the prisoners were generally relaxed. Pon claimed in his notebook that confessions could now be extracted without beating from "80 percent" of the prisoners, but added that if political approaches failed interrogators could still "rely on beating." In December he wrote, "Instead of not beating them at all, beat them only a little bit at most." The new policies were not framed in terms of previous errors, and those who had presided over the massive violence of 1977 at S-21 remained in power.

In a case from December 1978, an interrogator referred to the reforms in his notes attached to a confession:

> As for [the prisoner], when I first did politics with him he was willing to talk, but he said he had entered the CIA [only] in 1977. For two days he insisted on this story. After he had spoken and written all this down, right up to 1978, he said he had not betrayed the Party. At this point I took him up [close] to me and pointed out to him the Party's new line about helping

[prisoners], and then I threatened him and said if he didn't speak I would beat him. At that point he agreed to continue telling his story.[39]

No documentation survives to explain the motivation for the reforms, and because the prison closed soon afterward it is impossible to say whether these reforms might have foreshadowed wider ones, conceivably involving the "reeducation" and release of some of the prisoners. For the remainder of the prison's existence, however, death sentences remained in effect, and the prisoners held at S-21 on the eve of the Vietnamese invasion were murdered on the spot. Pon's December 1978 entries, the last in his notebook, close by asking : "If it's necessary to break a particular person, should we use a special torture, special interrogators, or different methods?" Five months earlier, his immediate superior had posed the same question in his notebook, suggesting that interrogators must be "experienced," that beating should coincide with other "work," and that the prisoner's health should be taken into account. Chan closed his notes by asking: "Should an interrogator beat [a prisoner] with his hands?" His answer was, "If it must be done, a little will suffice."[40]

Ironically, although thought reform and other Sino-Vietnamese notions of redemptive justice found few echoes either in prerevolutionary Cambodian culture or in DK, it seems likely that the merciless procedures used at S-21 came to the country through a Chinese official who had observed the Moscow trials in the 1930s, rather than through Vietnam or directly from the USSR.

This official was K'ang Sheng (1898–1975), who had masterminded the Chinese reeducation campaign at Yan'an in 1942 and 1943 and the more sweeping national purges of the 1950s. K'ang Sheng was the head of Mao's secret police. After becoming the head of the Chinese Communist Party's security and spying operations in the Kuomintang-controlled areas in 1931, he had lived for several years in the USSR, where he had studied Soviet security and interrogation procedures and observed the beginning of the purges. Using his Soviet contacts, K'ang himself saw to it that several expatriate members of the CCP were purged. When K'ang Sheng returned home in 1937 his experience proved useful and pleasing to Mao, and he was probably responsible for introducing Soviet purge techniques to China. During World War II K'ang Sheng took charge of the Chinese version of *santebal*; he became known at the time as "Mao's pistol," and the 1942–1943 "rectification" and "rescue" purges he supervised were especially vicious and thorough. When they were over he admitted that fewer than 10 percent of those who had "confessed" were genuine spies or enemies. Emerging from semiretirement in the 1960s, "venerable K'ang" became a senior ideologue of the Cultural Revolution, closely allied with the so-called Gang of Four, and involved in the purges that swept through the Party in 1967 and 1968. When he died in 1975 he received a full state funeral. Five years later, with the downfall of the Gang of Four, he was posthumously expelled from the Communist Party.[41]

A former Chinese official who has been involved in Cambodian affairs since the early 1960s has said that K'ang Sheng befriended Pol Pot when the latter (as Saloth Sar) visited Beijing in 1966. At the time K'ang was in charge of liaison with foreign Communist parties and is known to have favored those that appeared to be sympathetic to Chinese attacks on Soviet "revisionism." During Saloth Sar's visit, K'ang Sheng became a key member of the Case Examination Committee (later renamed the Central Case Examination Group), a secret entity established in May 1966 to "manage the purge of senior counterrevolutionary revisionists." Although there is no way of telling whether Saloth Sar learned about the facility from K'ang Sheng then or later, it may well have provided an institutional model for S-21.

K'ang Sheng and Saloth Sar probably renewed their acquaintance on the Cambodian's subsequent visits to China in 1970 and 1971. When K'ang Sheng died in 1975, the Chinese official said, Pol Pot visited the Chinese Embassy in Phnom Penh to present his condolences in person. If this connection between Pol Pot and K'ang Sheng indeed existed, a plausible line of descent for S-21 can be established from Soviet security procedures and ideology in the 1930s and the Soviet-style Chinese purges later on.[42]

Torture at S-21

Keeping these precedents and continuities in mind, we can return to the practice of torture at S-21 and the rationale given for torture by people working there. No records detailing the frequency of torture at the prison have survived. To study the phenomenon we must rely on the scattered memoranda that passed between interrogators and their superiors, supplemented by interrogators' confessions, marginal notes that appear on some confessions, three study texts written by S-21 officials, and the interrogators' notebook compiled in 1976.

These documents clearly do not reveal the full range of tortures that were inflicted on prisoners at S-21. They also give no clear idea of the frequency with which torture was applied, of any policy developments affecting torture, or of the duration and intensity of the tortures that were imposed. It seems likely that the administration of torture, like everything else at the prison, became routinized as the "system" evolved over time, as interrogators overcame their initial hesitation, and as some methods of torture came to be preferred over others.

By the middle of 1977, as we have seen, S-21 was running relatively smoothly. With a year's experience of trial and error, interrogators had become more adept at both "doing politics" and inflicting torture. They certainly had a clearer idea of what kinds of documentation satisfied their superiors, what tortures "worked," and how prisoners and their confessions could be "processed" expeditiously. As time went on, interrogations became swifter, and confessions became shorter. Increasingly, confessions were tape-recorded and the transcriptions typed. Elaborate summaries were then drawn up to connect confessions, military units, geographical regions, and "strings of traitors." How the wholesale bureaucratization of procedures at the prison affected the frequency or intensity of torture, however, is impossible to say, although we know that torture and beatings continued apace in 1977. The photographer Nhem En remembered "lots of screaming, especially at night, when there was no noise in Phnom Penh. The cries were so loud that we could hear them from half a mile away." In a similar vein, the former guard Khieu Lohr told Alexander Hinton: "I could hear screams, but no words. Sometimes everything went quiet." Kok Sros, interviewed by Douglas Niven, said he heard people screaming under interrogation "every time I went on duty" and also "whenever a prisoner disobeyed a guard."[43]

The cries of people being tortured were treated at the time as an administrative problem that compromised the secrecy of the prison's operations. "Problem of political education," Tuy wrote in his notebook. "Sometimes the sound of prisoners being beaten can be heard outside [the prison]."[44]

Often the interrogators' zeal accomplished nothing. In many cases neither the prisoner nor the interrogators knew what crimes had been committed or what the prisoner's often garbled admissions meant. A key feature of most interrogations was to ask prisoners abruptly why they had been arrested and then to beat the ones who said they didn't know. Lacking information themselves, the interrogators resorted to torture, and, as Aristotle pointed out more than two thousand years ago, confessions that flow from torture often bear little relation to the truth.[45]

Interrogators often lost control. The temptation must have been overwhelming when three young men, armed with heavy sticks, whips, electrical current, and other devices were locked in a room with a helpless, shackled, supposedly treasonous prisoner. "If violence is considered normal in a social collective," Wolfgang Sofsky has pointed out, "it gradually becomes a binding norm."[46] Ma Meang Keng (alias Rin), a former interrogator, confessed that violence was a dead end and its own reward, as he recalled a deceptively relaxed conversation with his colleagues:

> A fortnight later . . . the one named Noeun, the one named Sreng, and I were taking a break on the top floor of the canteen [at S-21]. At that time, Noeun said, "In [interrogation] group 1, all you hear everywhere is the sound of beatings, and [people] asking [prisoners] if they are 'C' [i.e., CIA] or not. . . . With a question like that, what can anyone answer, if some of them don't even know what 'C' stands for? You never hear [people in] Group 1 'doing politics' at all, all they think of is beating, and when all they think of is beating, the enemies answer confusingly, accusing this one, accusing that one. This is the weak point of Group 1." The one named Saeng said that it was the same near where he was: all you ever heard were thuds and crashes and people screaming, "C or not C?" when they don't know "C" chicken from "C" duck.[47]

As this harrowing passage suggests, a balance between torture and politics was often impossible to achieve, especially when the interrogators had so little training in either politics or interrogation, so much administrative leeway, so much testosterone, and so much combat experience. "Doing politics" in DK, reversing Clausewitz, amounted to waging war by other means. Like the Red Guards in Mao's China, the interrogators at S-21 had been taught that the Party's "enemies" were to be "smashed" in "storming attacks." They had also been told that they were the regime's "life-breath" (donghaom). Emerging from bursts of overheated, haphazard training into the secret and supposedly rational world of S-21, they proceeded to "smash enemies" without hesitation, with their bare hands and a variety of weapons.[48]

Prisoners' comments about torture were rare. They were also unwelcome. For example, when Ney Saran wrote in his confession, "The answers I gave on 28.9.76 were given after I had been severely tortured, and I offer them with this in mind," the passage was crossed out by Duch, who sent the document back with the notation: "You have no right to report on such matters to the Organization."[49]

Sun Ty, in his confession, scribbled a private note to the Organization that protested his innocence and said he had been tortured:

> At first I refused to answer, but after I had been beaten with a heavy stick I invented an answer. I beg the Party not to arrest the people I named. Our comrades are good. I am not CIA or Khmer Serei.

The presence of these comments in Sun Ty's file suggests that they never left S-21.[50]

Instances of torture mentioned in the archive and by survivors are given in the following list.

Beating
  by hand
  with a heavy stick
  with branches
  with bunches of electric wire

Cigarette burns

Electric shock

Forced to eat excrement

Forced to drink urine

Forced feeding

Hanging upside down

Holding up arms for an entire day

Being jabbed with a needle

Paying homage to image(s) of dogs (all from 1978)

Paying homage to the wall

Paying homage to the table

Paying homage to the chair

Having fingernails pulled out

Scratching

Shoving

Suffocation with plastic bag

Water tortures
  immersion
  drops of water onto forehead

The list does not include many of the tortures that are depicted in Vann Nath's paintings. Talking to East German filmmakers about S-21 in 1981, Nath recalled:

> This is the room I used to work in. Sometimes I could see through a crack in the window what was happening outside. So I saw them submerging prison-

ers in water. Others were brought to interrogation stark naked. Whatever I observed in secret I tried to record [later] in my pictures.[51]

Of the twenty-one interrogators listed in the 1978 telephone directory for S-21, eighteen were implicated in torture in their own comments to prisoners' confessions, in other interrogators' confessions, or in self-critical study sessions conducted for prison staff. Of the twenty-four interrogators at S-21 who were later arrested, eighteen admitted torturing prisoners. Eleven confessed to beating prisoners to death, as did one of the guards. Some of the confessions implicated others on the staff whose confessions have not survived. The archive suggests that certain interrogators resorted to torture more readily than others. One of them, Buth Heng, who was eventually arrested, confessed to a series of barbaric sexual assaults and to beating several prisoners to death, including one who had already been severely injured after a suicide attempt.[52]

Sexual violations of female prisoners probably occurred frequently, but sexual references seldom surface in the confessions of S-21 personnel. Such offenses were certainly frowned on by the men administering the prison, as an entry in Chan's notebook suggests:

> When questioning females, there must always be two people asking the questions. Don't lie down [with them?], and don't pinch their hair or their cheeks.[53]

All the survivors remember being beaten, and, as the S-21 survivor Ung Pech told David Hawk, "For beating, anything that fell into [the interrogators'] hands was used: different kinds of tree branches, bamboo, whips hurriedly made from electric wire."[54]

Electric shock was administered to prisoners so commonly that a list of instructions drawn up for all prisoners included a request not to scream when electric shocks were applied. The penalty for disobeying an interrogator, said the instructions, could be ten strokes of a whip or "five electric shocks."[55] Vann Nath's memories of electric shock were probably typical:

> [The interrogator] tied an electric wire around my handcuffs and connected the other end to my trousers with a safety pin. Then he sat down again.
> "Now do you remember? Who collaborated with you to betray [the Organization]?" he asked. I couldn't think of anything to say. He connected the wire to the electric power, plugged it in, and shocked me. I passed out. I don't know how many times he shocked me, but when I came to, I could hear a distant voice asking over and over who my connection was. I couldn't get any words out. They shocked me so severely that I collapsed on the floor, my shirt completely drenched with sweat. . . . To this day I don't understand why they arrested me.[56]

Interrogators' notes to some confessions suggest that prisoners often physically collapsed and confessed "fully" when threatened with electric shock. Others succumbed after the shock had been inflicted. One prisoner, the interrogator wrote, "says he can't withstand [any more] electric shock, that his liver and gall bladder have dissolved." Other prisoners were tougher. One of them, an interrogator remarked, "would respond only after strong torture," and another, when "strong torture was applied, refused to talk." Ly Phen, a veteran revolutionary, "refused to say anything about his activities, so I applied torture," his interrogator noted. "When he regained consciousness, all he could do was vomit." Interrogators found one female prisoner "very lascivious" *(khul khoch nah).* "Unable to withstand torture, she removed her sarong and pretended to be sick." Toward anyone offering resistance Duch was merciless, telling an interrogator on one occasion, "Beat [the prisoner] until he tells everything, beat him to get at the deep things."[57]

Another frequently imposed torture at S-21 was that of "paying homage." Vann Nath remembered a drawing of a dog's body with Ho Chi Minh's head tacked to the wall of an interrogation room and recalled interrogators talking about it.[58] *Thvay bongkum,* or "paying homage," as John Marston has argued, is a more "explicit declaration of hierarchy" than the normal Cambodian greeting, with palms together, known as *sompeah.* Both terms were used to describe this particular torture. In prerevolutionary society, the *thvay bongkum* gesture, which involves raising the joined palms above one's head and also occasionally prostrating oneself, was reserved for greeting royalty or Buddhist monks or paying homage to an image of the Buddha.[59] At S-21, the gesture probably involved assuming a painful, groveling posture, perhaps related to the infamous "airplane" that prisoners were made to mimic in the Cultural Revolution in China. One interrogator's note tells of making a prisoner pay homage for half an hour, and another mentions the torture being repeated "five times." "Paying homage" was painful enough in some cases to induce a full confession.[60]

By 1978, an image symbolizing America had been added to that of Ho Chi Minh. The interrogator's notes to Svang Kum's confession identify the second image as one of Lyndon Johnson:

> At first when we came to the interrogation place, after I had asked about her history and asked why the Organization had arrested her, she wept and shouted, saying that her husband was a traitor and that she wasn't a traitor. I applied discipline by making her pay homage to the image of the dogs Ho Chi Minh and Johnson, but she refused to salute [them], so I beat her for

refusing to tell her story and for not respecting the discipline of *santebal*. She gave up hope and began to speak about her secret networks.[61]

Two other passages that discuss "paying homage" to the images occur in notes takes by senior interrogators Chan and Tuy-Pon at a livelihood meeting convened on 28 May 1978. They differ slightly and are worth quoting in full.

TUY-PON TEXT

We test them by getting them to pay homage to two dogs. Dogs have a political meaning. The first dog is America. The second is Vietnam. When they salute them, they acknowledge that they support these two.

From the standpoint of ideology, we cast [the prisoners] aside, and no longer allow them to stay with us.

From the organizational standpoint, we force them to honor *santebal*. We have achieved good results from this already.

The document closes when Tuy-Pon quotes the speaker at the study session as saying: "You should not beat prisoners when they are angry. Beating doesn't hurt them when they are angry." The interrogators also were urged to keep their tempers, for as the interrogators' notebook asserted, "Sometimes we go blind with rage, and this causes us to lose mastery. It causes [the prisoners] to be incomplete, ideologically, spinning around thinking [only] of [their own] life and death." The rights and wrongs of inducing these death-dealing effects are left unmentioned.[62]

CHAN TEXT

We force them to salute the images of two dogs. This is a kind of interrogation. The dogs have political significance.

First dog: American imperialism.

Second dog: Vietnamese consumers of [our] territory.

We have them pay homage so as to hold them firmly, because when they are arrested, 90 percent of them [still] consider themselves revolutionaries. After they have paid homage to the dogs, they will realize that they are traitors.

From an ideological standpoint, we reject their ideology.

From an organizational standpoint: do they respect *santebal,* or not?

Procedures: Say what you can to make them change their minds and obey "older brother." If they argue, don't beat them yet, but wait for a minute before making them say that they served these two dogs: from what year? in what organization? Be careful: they may say that the CIA has no venom [real strength?].

"Paying homage" in this way introduced many prisoners abruptly to the power relations of S-21. It highlighted the contrast or contradiction in Khmer Rouge thinking between hidden, abject, foreign, and treasonous "facts" on the one hand and the overwhelming "truth" of the hidden but resplendent Organization on the other, and between the omnipotence of the interrogators and the powerlessness of "guilty people." This particular torture also set out the discipline of the interrogation that was to follow and forced the prisoners to identify themselves, even before they started talking, as traitors.

Some "ninety percent" of the prisoners, it seemed, began their interrogations by pluckily referring to themselves as "revolutionaries." How was this possible, the interrogators wondered, if they had been arrested? How could a genuine revolutionary be fettered, numbered, and locked up? "Paying homage" was one of a series of degradations designed to force prisoners to recognize their animal status. Their foreign masters *(me)* were depicted as animals, and only animals would pay homage to them. Once the patron–dogs' identities and the prisoners' loyalty to them had been displayed, the prisoner was divested of revolutionary and human status, and the interrogation could proceed, majestically or at a fast clip, to unearth "treacherous activities," "plans," and "strings of traitors." The prisoners by that point had become debased, unhealthy, document-producing creatures tottering on all fours toward their deaths.

To place torture at S-21 into a historical context, it seems clear that "paying homage," electric shock, immersion, suffocation, beatings and other tortures at S-21 combined the traditional "vengeance of the sovereign" with a comparatively new, disturbingly "rational," and quasi-judicial quest for documents, memories, and evidence, raw terror transmuted into history.

In this hushed and brutal ambience, counterrevolutionary actions, whether "true" or "false," needed to be brought to light, and memories had to coincide with expectations. Inevitably, however, "doing politics" often failed to motivate the interrogators or to unearth the memories that were required. Was torture any more reliable? There is no way of telling; no discussions of the issue have survived. The practice was certainly widespread. I would argue that after demonizing and dehumanizing the "enemies," routinizing violence and unleashing the interrogators' hatred, torture was doled out in substantial portions at S-21 with no thought for the pain it caused or, as far as the "truth" was concerned, its value compared to that of "doing politics."

The Interrogators' Notebook

The relation of torture to "doing politics" that the officials at S-21 desired is spelled out in a handwritten, unsigned notebook prepared at the prison between July and September 1976, with doodles dating from 1978 on the closing pages. The notebook may have been initiated by an S-21 cadre, perhaps one of those purged in 1976 or 1977, and lost or abandoned for a couple of years.[63] In the pages that relate to doing torture and doing politics, the notes stress that

> we must take the view that the question of keeping [prisoners] alive or asking for their papers or killing them is decided on for us by the Party. That is, we do whatever we can, so long as we get answers.
>
> The use of torture is a supplementary measure. Our past experience with our comrades the interrogators has been that they fell for the most part on the side of torture. They emphasized torture instead of propaganda. This is the wrong way of doing things; we must show them the proper way to do them.

The notes go on to suggest that while torture is inevitable, its use should be delayed in many cases until after a valid confession has been obtained:

> The enemies can't escape from torture; the only difference is whether they receive a little or a lot. While we consider torture to be a necessary measure, we must do politics [with them] so they will confess to us, [but] it's only when we have forced them via politics to confess that torture can be used. Only when we put maximum political pressure on them, forcing them by using politics to confess, will torture become effective. . . . Furthermore, doing politics makes the prisoners answer clearly, whether or not the use of torture follows.

The passage suggests that torture should be used and indeed became "effective" *after* confessions were obtained, seemingly acknowledging that workers were going to torture prisoners anyway and that perhaps some tortures carried out as medical experiments might best be performed after documentation was complete. The passage also implies that torturing prisoners might be a bonus for S-21 workers after a confession had been obtained. But what is meant by "effective" remains unclear. Except when prisoners died, after all, interrogators were not punished for inflicting pain. The notebook goes on to provide hints about tactics that interrogators might employ to propagandize, beguile, and disarm the prisoners without torturing them, and adds:

> One objective of doing torture is to seek answers from them, and not to make us happy. . . . It's not done out of individual anger, out of heat. Beating is done to make them fearful, but certainly not to kill them. Whenever we torture them we must examine their health beforehand, and examine the [condition of the] whip as well. Don't be greedy and try to hurry up and kill them.

The passage suggests that torturing prisoners made some interrogators "happy," while others freely acted out of "heat" or were in haste to kill the Party's "enemies." Moreover, provided that the whips were in acceptable condition, beating relatively healthy prisoners almost but not quite to the point of death was considered fair. None of this violence is surprising, given the wholesale dehumanization of prisoners and the culture of the prison, but it is chilling to see it so dispassionately written down. Almost as if its author were aware of overstepping a limit, the document then backs off and adds sanctimoniously:

> You must be aware that doing politics is very important and necessary, whereas doing torture is subsidiary to politics. Politics always takes the lead. Even when doing torture, you must also constantly engage in propaganda.

Even when "doing politics" occupied such a privileged position, torture was certain, and "doing politics" might occasionally be overlooked. It is hard to decide whether cautionary injunctions like these were sincere and systematically enforced or whether they were intended to provide bureaucratic cover for Duch and his colleagues should unwelcome excesses at the prison be discovered by the "upper brothers"[64] or an important prisoner be beaten to death prematurely out of "heat" or "greed." The notebook continues:

> Break them with propaganda or break them with torture, but don't let them die. Don't let them get so feeble that you're unable to question them. . . . Defend against the enemy. Keep [the prisoners] from dying. Don't let them overhear each other.

Two years later Chan wrote, in a similar vein:

> Take their reports, observe their expressions. Apply political pressure and then beat them until [the truth] emerges. Thinking only of torture is like walking on one leg—there must be political pressure [so that we can] walk on two legs.[65]

The passage suggests that "one-legged" interrogations (those involving lots of torture and little or no politics) were still being carried out. At about the same time, Pon was noting that "problems" at S-21 included "beatings that deprive enemies of strength" and "the problem of torture: still too heavy." He went on to criticize an interrogator specifically. "He said he beat [a prisoner] a little; in fact, he beat [him] a lot."[66]

A contradiction in Khmer Rouge thinking that affected the practice of torture at S-21 arose between the notion of "independence-mastery" extolled by the regime and the requirement that followers of the Organization succumb unthinkingly to its requirements. "Independence-mastery" supposedly meant shaking loose from deferential ties to pre-revolutionary patrons. The process led to empowerment at the price of personal independence, because of the demands of revolutionary discipline. People were liberated from dependence into the companionable solidarity of the Party. Empowered men and women became instruments of the popular will, which is to say the servants of the Party. This subtle point was lost on many young recruits, who may have seen permission to torture the Party's "enemies" or "guilty people" not merely as an assignment but as a right. In these cases the violence implicit in their empowerment overrode the constraints imposed by obedience to the often austere directives of the Party. In the heat of the revolution, however, such "left" deviations, where "enemies" were involved, were often ignored.

Crimes of Obedience

The watchword at S-21, to alter Talleyrand's famous dictum, might have been *"surtout, trop de zèle"* (above all, [display] too much zeal). As the 1976 notebook put it,

> It is necessary to avoid any question of hesitancy or half-heartedness, of not daring to torture, which makes it impossible to get answers from our enemies. . . . It is necessary to hold steadfast to a stance of not being half-hearted or hesitant. We must be absolute.

Who could decide, and what did it matter, to the interrogators at least, when being "absolute" shaded into being "excessive"?

The cruelties committed at S-21 and at its killing field at Choeung Ek fit neatly into what Kelman and Hamilton, drawing on the work of Stanley Milgram and others, have called "crimes of obedience." The interrogators at S-21 who tortured prisoners and the people charged with executing them responded, instinctively or not, to orders given by people whose authority they accepted without question, in part because questioning that authority could have led to their own deaths. Zygmunt Bauman, writing about the Holocaust, suggests that "moral inhibitions against violent atrocities tend to be eroded" when violence is authorized and routinized and when the victims are dehumanized. Tzvetan Todorov holds a similar view.[67] Moreover, when they hurt and killed people, many of the interrogators at S-21, and the executioners at

Choeung Ek, thought that they were answering to a higher level of morality and a more encompassing discipline than they had ever encountered before. Isolated, bonded, terrified, yet empowered, these young men soon became horrific weapons. The pleasures they derived from cruelty, in some cases, enhanced their satisfaction from surviving at the prison and gaining and holding their superiors' approval.

Many of them were pleased to serve the revolution as it was embodied by their superiors and the unseen "upper brothers."[68] To borrow terms from Maoist China, as they gradually became "expert," the interrogators remained entirely "red." They would probably have agreed with the Chinese Red Guard who wrote: "It is a small matter to beat someone to death, but it is very important to conduct revolution, to uproot resistance, to preserve redness."[69]

In the Cambodian case, to be sure, the revolution eventually collapsed, "resistance" sprang up everywhere, and "redness" was discredited. Years later, we are left, as the survivors are, with the echoes and shadows of "excessive violence." We encounter them as we leaf through confession dossiers or scan a stack of mug shots where people look imploringly or angrily at the people taking their pictures and, long after their own executions, imploringly or angrily at us. All these scraps of paper—photographs, memoranda, rosters, statistics, and confessions—emit images and approximations of the hubris, pain, fear, and malodorous confusion that made up the everyday culture and the everyday horror of S-21.

Images of S-21

We may get a little closer to what "really happened" when we visit the Museum of Genocidal Crime. Judy Ledgerwood, who worked at Tuol Sleng for many months on the Cornell microfilming project, has written,

> Over time, one begins to see the details. On stairway landings, for example, holes have been knocked in the wall so the stairs can be cleaned by sloshing water down the staircases. Below each of these openings on the building exterior one can still see stains of the blood that ran down the sides, as if the buildings themselves had bled.[70]

As we draw near to the prison in passages like this, brushing against its walls, we come a little closer to "reading" what happened there on a daily basis. Some of our readings bring us closer than others. Scattered phrases, an interrogator's doodle, or a prisoner's expression in a mug shot can illuminate the whole experience of the prison in a flash, although such "illuminations" vary from one person to the next. For me, it was a statement of Nhem En's that brought the routine horror of the prison suddenly to life. Talking with Douglas Niven, En was asked about his "most frightening memory" of S-21. He replied:

> What made me really scared was when I saw the trucks loaded with people and they shoved the people off the trucks and then pushed them when they hit the ground. I was still young and it scared me. These people were blind-folded and their hands were tied behind them.[71]

By contrast, when prisoners were taken off from S-21 to be killed, they were lifted one at a time onto the trucks, like pets or children. "They couldn't get onto the trucks themselves," Him Huy told Peter Maguire, "because the trucks were too high."

Nearly all the killings took place in secret and at night. In 1976, Kok Sros recalled, blindfolded prisoners were clubbed to death with iron bars in the field immediately to the west of the compound. They were buried where they fell, in shallow graves that measured only 1.5 meters deep. Although the killings were never openly discussed, the smell of decomposing bodies, mingled with the stench of feces and urine, was overwhelming.[72]

"Smashing Enemies" at Choeung Ek

During 1977, when purges intensified, the facility at S-21 filled up, and so did the impromptu cemetery nearby. At some point in 1977 a Chinese graveyard near the hamlet of Choeung Ek, fifteen kilometers southwest of the capital, was put into service as a killing field, although important prisoners continued to be executed on the prison grounds. Located near a dormitory for Chinese economic experts, the site was equipped with electric power to illuminate the executions and to allow the guards from the prison to read and sign the rosters that accompanied prisoners to the site. This was where the prisoners Nhem En saw were sent to be "smashed" or "discarded." After the site was discovered in 1980, it was transformed under Vietnamese guidance into a tourist site where even today scraps of bones and clothing can be found near the excavated burial pits.[73]

Kok Sros and Him Huy have conflicting memories about the killings. Kok Sros claims that he never went to Choeung Ek. Him Huy admits to driving trucks full of prisoners to the site on several occasions and to performing "one or two" executions there himself. According to Kok Sros and Nhem En, interviewed months apart, by 1978 Him Huy was a seasoned killer, an important figure at the prison and a key participant in the execution process. Vann Nath, shown his photograph in 1996, concurred. In 1978, according to Kok Sros, Him Huy often chose the execution teams, which were made up of "men who were able to do anything." Those without previous experience of killing prisoners were not selected, and the executioners never talked about the killings. On many occasions, Kok Sros had to bring prisoners from their cells to the assembly point just outside the prison gates. "When the prisoners heard they were to be taken away," he said, "they tried to break their locks and struggle with the guards"—to no avail. Soon they were packed into trucks and, in Kok Sros's words, taken "away to the west"—in Khmer mythology, the direction of death.

Him Huy's description of the killings at Choeung Ek, repeated with variations in several interviews, is the only firsthand account that we have so far. What follows is drawn from these interviews, which took place between 1987 and 1997.

The number of prisoners executed at Choeung Ek on a daily basis varied from a few dozen to over three hundred. The latter figure was recorded in May 1978, at the height of the purges in the Eastern Zone. Normally, "once a month, or every three weeks, two or three trucks" would go from S-21 to Choeung Ek. Each truck held three or four guards and twenty to thirty "frightened, silent" prisoners. When the trucks arrived at the site, Huy recalls, the prisoners were assembled in a small building where their names were verified against an execution list prepared beforehand by Suos Thi, the head of the documentation section. A few execution lists of this kind survive. Prisoners were then led in small groups to ditches and pits that had been dug earlier by workers stationed permanently at Choeung Ek. Him Huy continued, with an almost clinical detachment:

> They were ordered to kneel down at the edge of the hole. Their hands were tied behind them. They were beaten on the neck with an iron ox-cart axle, sometimes with one blow, sometimes with two. . . . Ho inspected the killings, and I recorded the names. We took the names back to Suos Thi. There could not be any missing names.

Him Huy remembers prisoners crying out, "Please don't kill me!" and "*Oeuy!*" (my beloved). He recalls telling one prisoner whom he knew that if he didn't kill him as ordered he would be killed himself. Asked if he felt "sadness or fear" when he was at Choeung Ek, Him Huy replied, "No, but I sometimes thought, 'I ought to run away from this, but if I ran where would I run to, and where could I go without a weapon? If I had a weapon and a vehicle to drive. . . . I thought about it a lot in those days.'"

Killing people he had worked with in S-21 was particularly difficult for him, and before they died, he said, these victims "could see how sad I was." When the prisoners were dead, he remembered on another occasion, some of their bodies were stripped of useful items of clothing. Female corpses were not stripped.

When we deal with the culture of S-21, it is tempting to rush to judgment, but it is also easy to judge the interrogators, guards, or executioners too severely. They could disobey orders only on pain of death. Without similar experiences, temptations, and pressures it is impossible for any of us to say how we might have behaved had we been interrogators ourselves, locked in a cell facing a helpless and devalued "enemy" alongside a pair of colleagues, either of whom might report us to the authorities for failing to inflict torture or for "counterrevolutionary" hesitation. Similarly, we cannot say what we would have done at Choeung Ek if a superior gave us an iron bar with which to smash the skull of a kneeling victim. Faced with so many threats and ambiguities, did the torturers and killers hesitate, barge ahead, or make choices on a case-by-case basis? No refusals to inflict torture or to execute prisoners have surfaced in the archive. Once prison personnel began to torture people, it seems, they were too callous, bonded, empowered, or terrified to stop or question what they were doing. Few constraints came from those above them, from the victims, or from others in their teams. The real horror of S-21 may lie outside the violence itself, embedded in the administrators' indifference and the indifference of the Party Center to what they were doing to other human beings. In a sense, some of the people who were tortured at Tuol Sleng may have been fortunate not to have survived, if we consider the continuous, traumatic aftereffects of torture that afflict so many of its victims and that led many survivors of the Nazi concentration camps, for example, to kill themselves long after they had been set free.[74] Similar sad endings awaited many of the people who were humiliated and attacked in the Chinese Cultural Revolution; perpetrators, as a class, seem to be more thick-skinned.

Two examples of such victims may suffice. Jean Améry, a prominent Jewish intellectual in postwar Europe and a survivor of Auschwitz, committed suicide in 1978. His friend and contemporary at Auschwitz, Primo Levi, threw himself out of his own apartment in Turin a decade later. In his eloquent short book, *At the Mind's Limits*, Améry may have foreshadowed his own death while describing torture when he wrote:

> Anyone who has been tortured remains tortured . . . anyone who has suffered torture will never again be at ease in the world; the abomination of the annihilation is never extinguished. Faith in humanity, already cracked by the first slap in the face, then demolished by torture, is never acquired again.[75]

CHAPTER SIX

Explaining S-21

Knowing what we do about a "total institution" like S-21 that poignantly embodied and fastidiously documented so much terror and history in the service of a desperate, inept regime, how can we explain what happened there in terms that might be useful to survivors, historians, and readers?

This chapter attempts to answer this question. By taking a more detached view of what happened at S-21, I do not intend to minimize the cruelties inflicted at the prison or the criminality of the Party Center. The preceding chapters have documented the crimes against humanity that occurred at S-21. But there is more to understanding S-21 than merely condemning it as evil. Trying to figure out what happened within its walls, how, and why is more fruitful, I believe, than passing judgment and moving on.

Comparisons have frequently been made between S-21 and the Nazi extermination camps in World War II. Writers who have examined the Nazi camps illuminate the culture of obedience that suffuses total institutions and the numbing dehumanization that occurs, among perpetrators and victims alike, within their walls. Studies of the Holocaust also bring us face to face with the indifference that the Nazis, like the Cambodians, showed their victims, coupled in some cases with the pleasure they derived from causing pain.[1] The same callousness toward "guilty people" and similar bursts of sadism characterized, among others, the judges in the Moscow show trials in the 1930s, the perpetrators of massacres in Indonesia in 1965 and 1966, the military torturers in Argentina, and those who organized the mass killings in Bosnia and Rwanda in the 1990s. As a twentieth-century phenomenon, S-21 was by no means unique.[2]

Even so, when we sift through the dossiers from the prison the scale of horror is overwhelming. Words fail us. A similar feeling of helplessness swept over the French historian Alain Forest when he visited the site in 1982. "It's stronger than me," he wrote, "and there's no chance of thinking or writing about it. I pull my head instinctively down into my shoulders."[3] When Boris Pasternak toured collective farms in the USSR in the 1930s, when thousands of people were dying of starvation, he recoiled also. "What I saw," he wrote, "could not be expressed in words. There was such inhuman, unimaginable misery, such a terrible disaster that it began to seem almost abstract, it would not fit within the bounds of consciousness. I fell ill."[4]

When we confront so many extinguished histories, we need to say something to make sense of S-21 and to bear witness to the victims; but, as Jonathan Spence has reminded us, coming at the issue from another angle, "It is one of the tragedies of writing about tragedy that the weight and texture of words matter unduly, for suffering needs a measure of grace to be bearable to others."[5] In a sense, Mai Lam's effort to turn S-21 into a museum was an attempt to make its raw terror "bearable to others." The map of skulls that he designed for the museum is so grotesque that it increases our distance from the prison. In the same way, the ersatz stupa that Mai Lam erected at Choeung Ek imposes a spurious Buddhist reading onto the skulls displayed inside it. Anything we say or write about S-21, or about the Holocaust, has the effect of softening and cleaning what went on. This is as true of the banal, repetitive, mean-spirited cruelty of S-21, and of Mai Lam's museum, as it is of the facilities in other times and places to which S-21 has been fruitfully compared. Words fail us also because, as Judith Shklar has written, "We talk around cruelty because we do not know how to talk about it."[6]

Why, then, do we persist? Are there advantages to getting close to the terror and intimacy of S-21? Does writing about its victims make their sufferings "bearable to others?" If so, who are the beneficiaries, besides my readers and myself? Historians are always invasive. In these pages I have been an uninvited visitor to S-21, inducing my evidence from the traces left behind by the victims and victimizers at the prison. In the process, I have been talking "around cruelty," and this is a perilous exercise, as Shklar has pointed out: "For all our wealth of historical experience, we do not know how to think about victimhood. Almost everything one might say would be unfair, self-serving, undignified, untrue, self-deluding, contradictory or dangerous. Perhaps the best intellectual response is simply to write the history of the victims and victimizers as truthfully . . . as possible."[7]

In this book I have tried my best to follow Shklar's humane suggestion, so as to bear witness to the victims, to grasp how S-21 could come to be, and to consider how similar institutions have come to life in the past and might reappear again. To perform these tasks, I have had to overcome my reluctance to move in close, my reluctance to share responsibility for what happened, and my eagerness at all costs to maintain my balance. I need to find the words that fit, and what happened at the prison continually overwhelms the words. As a historian and a student of literature I have tried, over the years, to control the data I deal with and to comprehend the writings that I read. When I have immersed myself in the S-21 archive, the terror lurking inside it has pushed me around, blunted my skills, and eroded my self-assurance. The experience at times has been akin to drowning.

Writing about state-induced violence in Argentina in the 1970s, Marcelo Suárez-Orozco has taken issue with people who were reluctant to confront and analyze the phenomenon. These timid figures, he writes, have asserted that "the materials are simply too sinister for any form of detached analysis. Any attempt at analyzing the materials would invariably do violence to an immensely complex and delicate subject. In the end, analysis simply reproduces the discourse of violence, albeit in another idiom." Suárez-Orozco argues that the analysis of horror must continue, even though the materials in question are "so unnerving that no distancing from the terror can ever be truly achieved," not because understanding what happened will allow us to pardon the perpetrators but because "terror is part of the everydayness of life."[8] By confronting terror, he suggests, we are confronting something that is not only "out there" but also inside ourselves. S-21 is closer to all of us than we would like to think. Along with trying to write the history of the place as "truthfully as possible," therefore, I have tried to penetrate the everydayness that Suárez-Orozco describes. If "S-21" in a sense is everywhere and we are all inside it, the prison becomes simultaneously harder to cope with and easier to explain.

In 1971 the British journalist Gitta Sereny spent several weeks interviewing Franz Stangl, the SS colonel who commanded the extermination camp at Treblinka, where over a million people, the vast majority of them Jews, were put to death from 1941 to 1943. Stangl was arrested in 1967 in Brazil, where he had been living under his own name. When Sereny talked to him, he had stood trial in Düsseldorf for his activities in World War II and had been sentenced to life imprisonment. He died of a heart attack in prison in 1972, after Sereny's interviews with him and before the publication of her book.

In the interviews Stangl apparently struggled to be helpful and to align what remained of his Catholic upbringing and his honor as a career policeman with what he had seen and done in World War II. Sereny was courteous with him but pulled no punches. Asked at one stage why the Nazis had exterminated the Jews, Stangl replied that it was because the Nazis "wanted their money." Sereny then asked him, "If they were going to kill them anyway, what was the point of all the humiliation, all the cruelty?" and he answered, "To condition those who actually had to carry out the policies. To make it possible for them to do what they did."

Over time, Stangl assured her, the workers at Treblinka became conditioned to performing horrible tasks, so long as the horrors were sanctioned and encouraged and so long as the victims meant nothing to them "personally" and could be thought of as outside the human race. In a similar fashion, the "ordinary men" of the SS reserve police battalion described by Christopher Browning, after some initial aversion, were able to massacre thousands of Jews in Poland in 1941.[9] For workers at S-21, a similar toughening process was hastened and intensified not only by the supposed ubiquity of "enemies" in Cambodia but also by the merciless discipline of the place. If they refused to work or worked too slowly, the guards and interrogators at S-21, unlike their Nazi counterparts, might become victims overnight. Their survival soon became a corollary of hard work. As Kok Sros has recalled, "I tried to work my hardest. If I died, so be it. If I died after I had worked very hard, it would be better than if I hadn't tried hard enough."[10]

For Kok Sros, Stangl, and perhaps Browning's "ordinary men," the importance of doing a good job eclipsed the nature of what they were doing. As the director of Treblinka, Stangl believed that he had been able to prevent worse atrocities by working hard and by adopting a conscientious, even-handed command style. "Of course, thoughts [about what was happening at Treblinka] came," he told Sereny. "But I forced them away. I made myself concentrate on work, work and again work."[11] Even so, he said, he needed several glasses of brandy every night to get to sleep.

After noting her agreement with what Stangl had just said, Sereny wrote: "To achieve the extermination of these millions of men, women and children the Nazis committed not only physical but spiritual murder: on those they killed, on those who did the killing, on those who knew the killing was being done and also, to some extent . . . on all of us, who were alive and thinking beings at the time."[12] Sereny's troubling comment suggests that to achieve the murders at Treblinka, the Nazis could count on the spiritual deadness of the world at large. In a similar sense, I suggest, we allowed S-21 to happen because most of us are indifferent to phenomena of this kind happening far away to other people. Evil, we like to think, occurs elsewhere. [13]

Browning, Sereny, and other authors, however, suggest that under extreme conditions, such as those that applied in World War II, boundaries of this kind become impossible to draw. Primo Levi has written that a "gray zone" enveloped many of the guards and prisoners at Auschwitz. Browning refers to the "zone" from the point of view of perpetrators as a "murky world of mixed motives, conflicting emotions and priorities, reluctant choices and self-serving opportunism and accommodation wedded to self-deception and denial." At S-21, in one sense, there was no such zone, because there was too little connivance among victims, perpetrators, and the outside world to construct it. Yet although prisoners at S-21 could never become interrogators or guards, workers at S-21 could become prisoners overnight. In this sense, everyone in S-21 inhabited a gray zone all the time.[14]

To complicate things further, we need to remember that the people working in the Nazi camps and at S-21 were not inherently brutal or authoritarian. Most of them appear to have been unexceptional, often poorly educated men and women who were cast in brutal roles. How much free choice, peer pressure, obedience, and ambition were involved in what they did is impossible to determine. What we know about the workers at S-21 points in most cases, as Browning's research would suggest, to their ordinariness and banality. Bonded with people like themselves and abjectly respectful of those in charge, the workers at S-21, like the prisoners, were trapped inside a merciless place and a pitiless scenario.

To be entrapped like this, and to act in this way, does not require the context of Treblinka, Auschwitz, or S-21. The process was chillingly demonstrated, under relatively genteel conditions, in Palo Alto, California, a few years before S-21 began its operations. In the so-called Zimbardo experiments in 1971, a group of Stanford University graduate students, all volunteers, were placed in a role-playing situation that sought to duplicate the culture, practices, and power relations of an American prison. As the "guards" began to relish their empowerment and the "prisoners" became fearful and dehumanized, the experiment spun out of control. It was cut short before anyone was seriously hurt.[15]

Another sequence of experiments conducted in the United States in the early 1960s by Stanley Milgram provides additional insights. Volunteers in New Haven, Connecticut, were asked by the "educational psychologist" to sit at a console and act as "teachers" (college students were expressly forbidden to take part). They were then asked to deliver what they were told were electric shocks in response to "incorrect" replies given to questions put by the "psychologist" to unseen but audible "students" in another room. In fact, there was no electricity transmitted by the buttons the teachers pressed, and the students were actors hired by Milgram. As the students' "errors" multiplied, the intensity of the shocks increased until some of the teachers were delivering what they were told were extremely painful, dangerous doses of electricity—a fact seemingly confirmed by thumps, cries, and eerie silences from the adjoining room. Over several days, only one in three of the teachers objected to what was happening or broke off the experiment. Over the next two years, several variables were introduced into the experiments, including moving them to the working-class city of Bridgeport, allowing physical contact between teachers and students, introducing a greater number of women into the teacher group, and removing the psychologist from the room. Most of the results remained consistent. With rare exceptions, the experiments showed, as Alan Elms has written, that "two-thirds of a sample of average Americans were willing to shock an innocent victim until the poor man was screaming for his life, and to go on shocking him well after he lapsed into silence."[16]

In another study of the experiments, John Darley suggests that the obedience of the teachers was keyed to the presence of the experimenters, who were asked to validate extended violence. Left to their own devices, Darley suggests, the teachers would not have administered the shocks. There is thus a gap, as he vigorously argues, between Milgram's teachers and people who commit atrocities. He adds, however, that socializing people toward greater violence might be merely a matter of time.

Alexander Hinton has argued that unquestioning obedience of the sort displayed most of the time in these experiments occupies a particularly strong position in Cambodian culture. I would agree that the destruction of "enemies" at S-21 was made easier because of the defer-ence and respect that were traditionally due in Cambodia to those in power from those "below" them. This culture of exploitation, protec-tion, obedience, and dependency had deep roots in Cambodian social practice and strengthened the grip of those in power in DK in spite or even because of the power-holders' insistence that prerevolutionary power relations had been destroyed.[17] Hierarchies, patronage, and "paying homage," so characteristic of "exploitative" society (the Cam-bodian phrase translated as "exploit," *chi choan,* literally mans "ride on and kick") had not been extinguished by the revolution. Instead, familiar, lopsided relationships involving a new set of masters and ser-vants (however much they might be deemed "empowered" and desig-nated as comrades), as well as a new set of victims, came into play. Under its discipline the population of S-21 was divided: on one side were those who commanded or put others to use *(neak prao)* and those who "listened" *(neak sdap)* and were put to use *(neak bomrao);* on the other side were their common victims. In some ways, the "new" society consisted of the same mixture as before and followed prerevolutionary patterns of authority and compliance.[18]

Although interrogators at S-21 owed allegiance to those "above" them, and although the relationship between interrogators and prison-ers in any institution is always complex, at S-21 the interrogators' over-riding advantage, as Pon remarked in his notebook, was that the pris-oners were "in [the interrogators'] hands." No constraints of law, no pressures from outside the government, and no deadlines operated in the prisoners' favor. So long as they questioned prisoners energetically and tortured them sufficiently to obtain confessions, the interrogators were free to operate as they saw fit.[19]

In a haunting fashion the power of the interrogators and the power-lessness of prisoners and the process of interrogation at S-21 call to mind La Fontaine's fable about the wolf and the lamb. In the fable, a wolf encounters a lamb and proposes to kill it because the lamb, according to the wolf, had insulted the wolf "a year ago." When the lamb replies that it had not been born a year ago, the wolf answers, "If it wasn't you, it was your brother." "I have none," says the lamb. "Then it was some relative of yours, or a shepherd, or a dog," the wolf retorts and devours the lamb.[20]

In chapter 5, we examined some precedents in Cambodia's past for the violence at S-21 and the ways in which torture at the prison fell under Foucault's rubric of the "vengeance of the sovereign." We also saw that the totality and thoroughness of S-21 drew on a range of peculiarly twentieth-century models, linked in part to Communist practice and in part to modern systems of surveillance. Models for S-21 included the Moscow show trials and purges in the 1930s and "reeducation" campaigns in Maoist China and Communist Vietnam. More distantly, S-21 drew on the notion of French "revolutionary justice." In the 1790s revolutionary justice received much of its momentum, semantically, from the neologisms *counterrevolution* and *counterrevolutionary*, which allowed its proponents enormous freedom to maneuver. The significance of these two words could change from one day to the next.[21] At S-21, the word *enemy* had the same elastic character.

From other Communist regimes, the Party Center adopted the doctrine that the leaders of a Communist Party, unfettered by a "bourgeois" legal code or a capricious judicial system, were fully entitled to punish enemies of the state. They were empowered to do so because of their privileged relationship to historical laws. From Communist China and Vietnam came the somewhat contradictory idea that at least some enemies of the state could be reeducated and reformed—a notion that had deep roots in both countries but little resonance in Cambodia. Tools for this reformation included the practices of criticism and self-criticism, embodied in self-critical, publicly presented life-stories. At S-21 prisoners redeemed themselves and were reeducated by their confessions, that is, by the same texts that condemned them all to death.

While what happened at S-21 was "Cambodian," "Communist," and "foreign" to varying degrees, the massive death toll in DK forces us to seek deeper explanations than these to account for the effects of the regime and for S-21 in particular. Ben Kiernan's suggestion that one of the "two most important themes" of the Pol Pot era was "the race question" is helpful up to a point, and so is Michael Vickery's proposal that the Cambodian revolution, far from being Marxist-Leninist, can best be described as a prolonged and largely uncontrollable outburst of peasant rage.

Kiernan's notion is helpful because the ferocity and indifference of S-21 displayed a belief that those killed were considered subhuman and therefore not of the same "race" as their assassins. Overt, anti-Vietnamese racism, shading into a sense of Khmer racial superiority, also dominated DK thinking, speeches, and behavior after 1977; in 1978, many prisoners at S-21, as enemies of the state, became for all intents and purposes Vietnamese.[22] The ways in which some prisoners were made to pay homage to pictures of Ho Chi Minh and Lyndon Johnson suggest that they were being erased from Pol Pot's Cambodia in the same fashion that Nazism's racial enemies, even before they were killed, were erased from Hitler's Europe. Although most of the victims had been born into the same "race" as their assassins, racist mechanisms came into play in their arrest, torture, and execution. Turning the victims into "others," in a racist fashion—and using words associated with animals to describe them—made them easier to mistreat and easier to kill. A similar process of distancing has been described by writers dealing with the Holocaust and the Indonesian massacres of 1965 and 1966.

In Steve Heder's view, the racism displayed by DK toward its enemies was linked to its leaders' feelings of superiority not so much over other races as over those individuals unwilling or unable to carry out a Marxist-Leninist revolution with the same uncompromising fervor as the Party Center. Those targeted as incompetent or as counterrevolutionaries were often labeled "Vietnamese." Heder writes: "Democratic Kampuchea racism was a by-product of efforts to advance an historic world view based on unexamined and unsubstantiated assumptions about the potentialities of the Cambodian nationality and 'race' to make a contribution to the modern world via rapid construction of a highly advanced socialism."[23]

It is tempting to agree with Vickery, however, that the savagery of the Cambodian revolution owed less to racism or to Marxism-Leninism than to peasant anger. Vickery argues that the Party Center was swept along, perhaps to some extent against its will, by the fervor of class hatred from "below." Vickery's argument, which proceeds by analogy with such violent non-Marxist movements as Spanish anarchism, can be applied to the purges that swept the country in mid-1975 and to the vicious treatment of "new people" by DK cadres later on, particularly in the northwest. Peasantism was indeed an ingredient of the Cambodian revolution, as it was in China, and so was the mobilization of hatred, which characterizes all revolutionary movements. Vickery's explanation is not especially helpful, however, when we face the mountain of DK documentation including theoretical journals, the leaders' speeches, and the notebooks recording self-criticism sessions. His argument breaks down further before the methodical, Communist-inspired procedures of interrogation and "confession" that were followed so fastidiously at S-21. For the argument to work, Duch, Chan, and Pon, all intellectuals, would have had to be reflecting the passions of their subordinates, rather than the reverse.[24]

At S-21, as we have seen, traditional Cambodian punitive practices and others inspired by Communist models blended with other twentieth-

century techniques of surveillance, documentation, and control discussed so eloquently in Foucault's *Discipline and Punish* and, from
another perspective, in Orwell's *1984*. The contradictory ingredients
that constituted "S-21" were tempered in turn by notions of intrinsic
Khmer superiority that pervaded the thinking of the Party Center, provided a triumphalist language for its pronouncements, and insulated its
members from reality. These notions of innate superiority, in turn, came
in part from DK readings of Cambodian history and in part from the
windfall empowerment of a small segment of Cambodia's rural poor,
whose supposedly revolutionary energies, harnessed for economic programs, found expression more frequently in flaunting newly won
power, claiming privileges, and humiliating and exterminating "class
enemies" when they were asked to do so.

S-21, therefore, like DK itself, was a Cambodian, Communist, imported, twentieth-century phenomenon. As an amalgam, it was unique.
For this reason, prolonged comparisons with facilities in other times and
places are not especially rewarding. In spite of its "Cambodian" character, a jailer from prerevolutionary Cambodia would have been baffled by
S-21. While the physical abuse, chains, fetters, poor food, and mercilessness would have been familiar to him, its inflexibility and totality, its isolation from the outside world, and the masses of documentation assembled there were without precedent. Similarly, while Prey So can be
compared with the "reeducation" facilities in China and Vietnam, the
mercilessness of S-21 is unmatched in either country, while the interrogations at S-21, so central to its operations, set the place apart from the
Nazi extermination camps to which it has often been compared.

From the sources I have examined it is impossible to say whether anyone working at S-21 or any of their superiors was ever distressed or disoriented by what they were doing. Misgivings were luxuries that workers
at the prison and the leaders of the country could not afford. Kok Sros
told Douglas Niven, however, that interrogators who hesitated to use torture were arrested, suggesting that hesitations occasionally did occur, and
in a "livelihood meeting" convened by Chan for S-21 staff in February
1976, Duch himself is recorded as saying to his colleagues:

> You must rid yourselves of the view that beating the prisoners is cruel *[kho
> khau]*. Kindness is misplaced [in such cases]. You must beat [them] for
> national reasons, class reasons, and international reasons.[25]

Interestingly, Duch's comment dated from the early months of *santebal*'s operations, at precisely the phase in which Christopher Browning

and other students of the Holocaust have recorded the highest levels of hesitation, revulsion, and alarm among those charged with executing people en masse. In the early stages of S-21's existence, a natural reluctance to torture and kill the prisoners, like the one Duch warned against, needed to be overcome. As time went on the workers at S-21, like their Nazi counterparts, insulated themselves from their own behavior, the smell of death, the woeful appearance of the prisoners, and their screams.

Insulation of this kind is understandable, but the perpetrators' indifference to the pain of others retains a capacity to shock. We wait in vain for hints that what the workers did damaged their relations with each other, jarred their calligraphy, or disturbed their sleep. To Duch and his associates, the prisoners were "less than garbage." Extracting confessions from them was crucial to protecting the revolution and was no more complicated or distressing, it seems, than hosing down a pavement or plowing up a field. The violence that the perpetrators inflicted met with indifference from their superiors or was noted with approval, and there is no way of telling when the cruelty so heavily documented in the archive became an end in itself or how much the perpetrators may have come to enjoy what they were doing. None of the former workers at the prison, in their interviews, complained of nightmares after 1979; all the surviving prisoners did.

We can only speculate on how interrogators felt when they were working at S-21 because none of them has come forward. If any of these people were ever to be brought to justice, they would probably argue that they were obeying legitimate orders under wartime conditions and that beatings and torture, however unpalatable, accelerated the discernment of the truth, protected the Party Center, and saved the nation from being swallowed up by "the contemptible Vietnamese consumers of territory." Like Adolf Eichmann, Franz Stangl, and, more recently, the Khmer Rouge defectors Ieng Sary, Nuon Chea, and Khieu Samphan, the former workers might also claim in their defense that then was then and now is now. "Let bygones be bygones," said Khieu Samphan at a press conference in December 1998, in halting English. The cruelty and violence of S-21, they might add, were by-products of the all-consuming war visited on DK from abroad by its enemies and were incidental to the fight for survival of the intrinsically innocent and victimized Cambodian "race." In keeping with this Manichean view of the world, any "mistakes" or excesses committed at the prison must have been the work of "Vietnamese agents." This is the line that Khieu Samphan took in the 1980s and that Pol Pot insisted on in his interview with Nate Thayer. The linguistic armor that encased workers at the prison and the "upper brothers" remained intact.

Excuses like those offered by Ieng Sary, Nuon Chea, and Khieu Samphan are easy to understand, perhaps, but there are limits to the contextualizing of mass killing and terror. No "context" is spacious enough to contain Son Sen, Duch, and the "upper brothers." No explanations can let the murderers of fourteen thousand people off the hook. Someone or several people acting in the name of the Party Center decided to murder the prisoners held by *santebal,* regardless of what they had done, so as to warn off potential opponents, protect the secrecy of the operation, and demonstrate the Party's infallibility. Given the way DK was organized, a decision of this magnitude probably stemmed from Pol Pot, or at least met with his approval, even though no written proof of his approval has survived. The "upper brothers" who followed S-21's operations and Son Sen and Duch, who were directly responsible for them, knew what they were doing and chose to do it. Conceivably they might have lessened the suffering of prisoners, released the hundreds of small children imprisoned with their parents, or curtailed the executions had they wished to do so. There were moments during the DK era when such choices could have been made and revolutionary justice been tempered with mercy. Indeed, many survivors of the DK era single out kindly or permissive cadres. At S-21, however, alternatives were never considered. Instead, Son Sen, Duch, and the people working under them inflicted enormous quantities of suffering on the prisoners coolly, systematically, and without remorse.

Writing about the Holocaust and modernity in the context of Milgram's work, Zygmunt Bauman made a humane but devastating statement. "The most frightening news brought about by the Holocaust and what we learned of its perpetrators," Bauman reminded us, "was not the likelihood that 'this' could be done to us, but the idea that we could do it." If the significance of S-21 (or the Holocaust, for that matter) could be reduced to a sentence, Bauman's is the one I would choose. The psychologist Robert Jay Lifton, writing about Nazi medical personnel in the camps, makes a similar point when he remarks that "ordinary people can commit demonic acts."[26]

Explanations for S-21 that place the blame for evil entirely on "evil people," which is to say on others, fail to consider that what all of us share with perpetrators of evil is not a culture, a doctrine, or an innate tendency to kill but our similarity as human beings and, in particular, our tendencies toward acculturation and obedience. Most of us, I suspect, could become accustomed to doing something (such as torturing or killing people) when people we respected told us to do it and when there were no institutional constraints on doing what we were told. For many of us the task would be made easier if the victims were branded as outsiders. Writing of his experiments, Milgram remarked: "A person is in a state of agency when he defines himself in a social situation in a manner that renders him open to regulation by a person of higher status."[27] The implication is that what is permitted, or commanded, however awful, is usually what occurs; resistance is rarer than compliance, and immorality, as Bauman cogently suggests, is often socially conditioned. Acts of defiance or uncalled-for mercy, on the other hand, stem from individual choices that run against the grain and are therefore rare. As Staub has reminded us in another context: "The courage that is required to limit violence is frequently not physical courage, the willingness to put one's life on the line, but the courage to oppose one's group and to endanger one's status in the group or one's career."[28]

Recalling Bauman's melancholy words, therefore, it seems that explanations for the cruelties of S-21, the killing fields of DK, cataclysmic occurrences like the Holocaust, and the massacres in Rwanda, Bosnia, and Indonesia need to be sought not only among those inflicting the pain and giving the orders but also at a more generalized level, as Sereny and Bauman have proposed. In *Facing the Extreme,* Tzvetan Todorov rebuts charges that Sereny was too sympathetic to Stangl. "To understand all is to pardon all, as the saying goes," Todorov writes. "Is that what we really want? Such reactions reveal the fear that one can feel in discovering that evildoers are not radically different from oneself."[29]

Explanations for phenomena like S-21 are embedded in our capacities to order and obey each other, to bond with each other against strangers, to lose ourselves inside groups, to yearn for perfection and approval, and to vent our anger and confusion, especially when we are encouraged to do so by people we respect, onto other, often helpless people. To find the source of the evil that was enacted at S-21 on a daily basis, we need look no further than ourselves.

Siet Chhe's Denial of Incest

Siet Chhe (alias Tum) had been brought into the Communist movement while still a student by his teacher, Pol Pot, and by Pol Pot's wife, Khieu Ponnary. For many years he served as an aide-de-camp for Brother Number One, accompanying him on his travels and nursing him when he was ill. Because of the positions of trust that he held, he rose inside the ranks of the CPK. By mid-1977, however, because of his links with the Eastern Zone and with intellectuals then being purged, he was brought to S-21. For several days he could not believe that he had been abandoned by Pol Pot, but by the time the interrogator Tuy questioned him in June 1977, he had been imprisoned for several weeks and severely tortured. In May, he had asked Duch's permission to commit suicide. He had not yet "broken," however, and Tuy wrote to him, masking his brutality with respect:

> Respected Tum *(lok Tum)*: Write out the story of [your] sexual activities with your own child in detail because from the standpoint of the masses, this [offense] has been clearly observed. You don't need to deny this. Don't let your body suffer more pain because of these petty matters.

Siet Chhe's eloquent reply, translated by Richard Arant, appears below. It represents a rare attempt by a prisoner at S-21 to meet a false, highly personal accusation head-on. It also gives some idea of the loyalties that bound many Cambodian revolutionaries and their family members together.

This was apparently the last memorandum Siet Chhe was allowed to address to the Organization. For the next five months, he confessed under torture to an ever-widening range of counterrevolutionary activities before being put to death. The charge of incest was never repeated, and his denial was neither contradicted nor withdrawn. The presence of his original memorandum in the archive suggests that it never left the prison, as Siet Chhe had hoped it would.

RESPECTS TO THE ORGANIZATION!

I ask to make a report to the Organization concerning the matter of my daughter (on the accusations against me).

My daughter was born in 1957, and named Seat Soupha (revolutionary name Sath). She was my first child. She is the only daughter among my four children.

I was taken with her more than the others from the time that she was small. When she was eight years old [in 1963–1964], I went into the forest. I was separated from my entire family for about seven years.

When her aunt met comrade Dam Cheng, her husband, my daughter was taken to live with her. She lived with comrade Dam Cheng and was as close to her uncle as she had been with [me]. Comrade Dam Cheng taught my daughter to sing many revolutionary songs. At twelve years of age, she still hugged her uncle closely. I met her again in late 1970, and saw her boyish character. With her three younger brothers, she was close as boys are with boys, as if she forgot she was a girl.

In 1968 [representatives of] the enemy knocked on the door and arrested her while she was asleep alone in the house. In late 1970 [after she was released] she arrived in the liberated area of Sector 22 with her aunt. When she first saw me, she embraced me in front of everybody. That evening I slept with my wife on a mat in the house of a comrade in the middle of a field. The owner of a nearby house guarded the door. My wife and all of my children slept with me on the same mat. My wife slept on one side of me, my daughter on the other, and the three boys nearby, all with deep remembrances and feelings of warmth. Later, I sent my daughter, then about 13 or 14, to [work at] the Sector 22 hospital.

Around late 1974, I brought her back to work in the sector headquarters because the exchange of letters was not so good, and I suspected the activities of some traitors (as I saw in the content of the letters), but could not identify anyone.

In late April 1976, I withdrew her from Sector 22 and sent her to Koh Uknha Tei with her aunt. While living at Koh Uknha Tei, my daughter came to Tuol Kouk [in Phnom Penh] three or four times when taking her sick aunt to the hospital or traveling with her brothers to the hospital herself (when she had pneumonia and fainting spells).

The house in Tuol Kouk northern side was normally closed up because no one was there. Only my room was opened once in a while when I was there. The other rooms were open when there were visitors, and sealed when there were none. The downstairs was used for meetings, and all the windows and doors were kept closed.

Organization, I love my daughter a little more than I love my three sons. Because she is the only girl in the family and was more responsible than her brothers.

When I went to the forest, she knew what was happening and was with her mother when the enemy agents persecuted them in my absence.

She was put in prison by the enemy when she was 12 during the events of 1968 along with her uncle (Dam Cheng) and her aunt.

This all causes me to pity her and love her the most. When I saw her during my travels, I touched her on the head or shoulders with the love and pity of a father for his child.

In the matter of sexual morality, I am certain that she is a proper child who can be trusted. From then until now, I am certain she is a virgin with no moral blemishes with me or any other man. The accusations that I took advantage of my own child are ridiculous.

I love my daughter and want her to be pure so that in the future she will meet and live her life with a revolutionary who is pure both politically and morally.

If anything I have reported here is mistaken, I request the Organization's kind forgiveness.

5/6/77

Tum

Notes

ABBREVIATIONS

The following abbreviations are used in the notes:

CMR	Cornell Microfilm Reel
DC–Cam	Documentation Center–Cambodia
FBIS	U.S. Foreign Broadcast Information Service
Heder interviews	Steve Heder, "Interviews with Kampuchean Refugees, at Thai-Cambodia Border, February–March 1980," unpublished document

CHAPTER ONE. DISCOVERING S-21

1. See Bui Tin, *Following Ho Chi Minh*, 117 ff., an eyewitness account. For background to the conflict, see Elliott, ed., *The Third Indochina Conflict*. For a contemporary overview of the campaign, see Chanda, "Cambodia: Fifteen Days."

2. The best general accounts of the Khmer Rouge period are probably three of the earliest: Becker, *When the War Was Over*; Etcheson, *The Rise and Demise of Democratic Kampuchea*; and Ponchaud, *Cambodia Year Zero*. Subsequent studies include Burgler, *The Eyes of the Pineapple*, and Kiernan, *The Pol Pot Regime*. Two collections of essays dealing with the period are Chandler and Kiernan, eds., *Revolution and Its Aftermath*, and Jackson, ed., *Cambodia 1975–1978*.

3. Author's interviews with Nhem En and with Kok Sros. These S-21 workers spent 7 January 1979 in hiding before walking out of the city the next day.

4. On the appearance of Phnom Penh in the DK era, see Becker, *When the War Was Over*, 420 ff. Becker visited the city in December 1978. See also Pilger,

Heroes, 380 ff. Pilger came to Phnom Penh in the summer of 1979 and apparently first saw S-21 a year later. When I was there in August 1981 prerevolutionary banknotes could still be picked up off the streets. The notion of "year zero," drawn from the French Revolution, was never explicitly adopted by the Khmer Rouge, who followed the Christian calendar throughout their time in power.

5. Author's interview with Chey Saphon, October 1997.

6. Chanda, "The Cambodian Holocaust," includes a photograph of a "sinister school building" and one of the pictures taken of corpses discovered there "by the invading Vietnamese forces on 8 January 1979." On the smell, see Rivero, *Infierno,* 24. For a useful history of the site, see Ledgerwood, "The Cambodian Tuol Sleng Museum."

7. The placard is shown in the 1981 East German documentary film *Die Angkar.* I am grateful to Peter Maguire for providing me with a copy of the book containing the storyboards for the film and a transcript of his 1995 interview with the filmmaker, the late Gerhard Schuemann. Maguire arranged for a showing of the film at Bard College in October 1998, which I attended. Many of the still photographs used in the film, which were found at Tuol Sleng in 1979 and 1980, have apparently disappeared.

8. These details come from People's Republic of Kampuchea, People's Revolutionary Tribunal, *The Extermination Camp of Tuol Sleng.* The original, French-language text was prepared by Ung Pech, an S-21 survivor and the first director of the Tuol Sleng Museum of Genocidal Crimes.

9. Douglas Niven's interview with Ho van Thay. Kok Sros, a former guard at S-21, recalled that "about twenty" prisoners were murdered at S-21 just before the Vietnamese invasion (author's interview). From other sources we know that by 1978 the southernmost building had become a "special prison" *(kuk pises)* where high-ranking prisoners were confined. Several confessions were transcribed on 6 January 1979, either just before or shortly after the last prisoners were killed.

10. Shawcross, *The Quality of Mercy.* Shawcross first visited the prison in 1980. On feces, see Rivero, *Infierno,* 24.

11. Some writers have assumed that "S" stood for *santebal,* but the prefix recurs in reference to other DK entities: S-71, the Party school, and S-8, the Party's logistical headquarters. See Hawk, "The Tuol Sleng Extermination Centre," in which "21" is fancifully explained by Ung Pech as representing the "Second Bureau" (intelligence) reporting to "Number One" (Pol Pot). The fact that Vietnamese prisoners of war were held and interrogated at S-21 in 1978 suggests that it was not only a counterintelligence operation aimed at internal enemies but also a military prison.

12. On Ponhea Yat, see Vickery, *Cambodia after Angkor,* 492 ff. Serge Thion, who has written widely about Cambodia, taught at the Ponhea Yat *lycée* in 1966 and 1967.

13. Chhang Youk, "The Poisonous Hill."

14. People's Republic of Kampuchea, *The Extermination Camp of Tuol Sleng,* lists these *santebal* sites as "the camp of Ta Khmau, formerly a psychiatric hospital, the former National Police headquarters south of the new market, the former Lycée Descartes, Wat Phnom in the former Navy Officers' build-

ing, the former Lycée Sangkum and the camp of Prey Sar west of Phnom Penh in Kandal province." Corroboration that *santebal* operated at these locations occurs in several S-21 confession texts and in Douglas Niven's interview with Nhem En, a photographer for *santebal*.

15. See Document N0001223, "Summary of 3 May 1976," a memorandum from Pheap of Regiment 588 to "Brother 89" (Son Sen, the DK minister of defense, in charge of military and security affairs) in the DC–Cam archive, Phnom Penh. The memorandum reports that "at the Tuol Svay Prey School a 20-man party cleaned up two levels of the facility, removed 250 tables, and cut 20 square meters of grass." When S-21 received its first prisoners is not known. On its closing days, see interviews with Kok Sros, Nhem En, and Him Huy. In late 1978 some of the functions of S-21 may have been transferred to Division 502, reflecting suspicions inside the Party Center directed at Son Sen (Steve Heder, personal communication).

16. Rivero, *Infierno*, 25. For another journalist's report from 1979, see Mate, *Genocide in Cambodia*. Rivero's final observation may have reflected wishful thinking, for no Cambodian edition of the *Little Red Book* was ever published. According to Kiernan, *The Pol Pot Regime*, 465, S-21 was introduced to nonsocialist readers by Wilfred Burchett in the *Guardian* (London), 11 May 1979.

17. Hawk, "Cambodia: A Report from Phnom Penh," *New Republic*, 15 November 1981. Mai Lam, now in his seventies, was interviewed on two occasions in Vietnam by Sara Colm and once by Peter Maguire and Chris Riley. I am grateful to them for providing transcripts of their interviews.

18. Maguire and Riley, interview with Mai Lam. Talking to Sara Colm, Mai Lam suggested that certain Cambodian cultural elements kept Cambodians from understanding what had happened to them under DK. "The Cambodian people's nature is that they want to stay in a quiet, peaceful atmosphere—Buddhist temple, rice farm, village," he said. "They are very nostalgic about the quiet times they had." Mai Lam's attitude toward the Khmer fits into what Christopher Goscha has called the "evangelistic" tendency in Vietnamese relations with Cambodia and Laos (personal communication).

19. Serge Thion, "Genocide as a Political Commodity," in Kiernan, ed., *Genocide and Democracy in Cambodia*, 184.

20. Mai Lam's interviews with Colm, Maguire, and Riley, and Ung Pech's interview with David Hawk. See also Heder interviews, 10–11 and 14 ff., with Ong Thong Hoeung, a Cambodian intellectual who worked in the S-21 archive between June and November 1979. Hoeung told Heder that "ten other Vietnamese" worked with Mai Lam at S-21 at that time. See also Ong Thong Hoeung, "Le 30 novembre j'ai quitté Phnom Penh precipitamment," in Scalabrino, ed., *Affaires cambodgiennes*, 121–28.

21. See in particular Vann Nath, *Prison Portrait*. I am grateful to Sara Colm for introducing me to Vann Nath in 1995. Another survivor, Ten Chan, was also interviewed on several occasions, as was the late Ung Pech. See also Lionel Vairon's interview with Pha Thachan, who became a typist at S-21, and DC–Cam document D-17, 4 December 1985, an interview with Ruy Nikon, who worked as a carpenter at S-21 from 1976 until the Vietnamese invasion.

22. It is impossible to determine what percentage of the total number of confession texts has survived. If every prisoner produced a confession, then as many as ten thousand texts must have disappeared, which seems unlikely. While as many as half this number of confessions may well have disappeared, it seems more probable that several thousand of the prisoners at S-21 never prepared confessions. Two key confessions that apparently have disappeared are those of Chau Seng, a leftist intellectual who served as information minister under Sihanouk, and Chea San, DK's ambassador to the USSR and Romania, whose Tuol Sleng mug shot from February 1978 appears in *Die Angkar*.

23. The Holocaust-oriented texts that have most inspired me are Améry, *At the Mind's Limits*; Bauman, *The Holocaust and Modernity*; Browning, *Ordinary Men*; Levi, *The Drowned and the Saved*; Sereny, *Into That Darkness*; Sofsky, *The Order of Terror*; and Todorov, *Facing the Extreme*. On Argentina, see Feitlowitz, *A Lexicon of Terror*, and Graziano, *Divine Violence*. The books by Sereny and Feitlowitz contain extended interviews with perpetrators. Studies on the massacres in Indonesia in 1965–1966 and on state-sponsored violence in the Cultural Revolution in China have also been useful, and my discussion of S-21 from a comparative standpoint benefits from comments by students at the University of Wisconsin in 1998 who attended my seminar on twentieth-century political killings.

24. Author's interview with Taing Kim Men. See also the confession of Seat Chhe (alias Tum), CMR 138.11, in which he writes to the prison director, Duch: "I understand that as for entering S-21, there is only one entry. As for leaving, that never happens." CMR 179.16, Tot Ry, expresses a similar idea.

25. Thayer, "Day of Reckoning." Pol Pot would have known Tuol Sleng by its code name, S-21. See Christine Chameau's interview with Ieng Sary, "Rehabilitation Completed," in which Sary said: "I said I never heard of Tuol Sleng. . . . We were always talking in code names and security was S-21." Asked who gave orders for S-21, Sary replied, "For political things like that, Khieu Samphan." There is no corroboration in the archive for this assertion.

26. Ledgerwood, "The Cambodian Tuol Sleng Museum," 90. Cambodians are still looking. See Seth Mydans, "Twenty Years On."

27. Ledgerwood, "The Cambodian Tuol Sleng Museum," 88, quoting the Ministry of Culture report. Ledgerwood adds that "the museum was open to the public every Sunday . . . [while] organized visits by foreign and local groups took place on weekdays."

28. Sara Colm interview with Mai Lam. Asked why some Cambodians preferred to blame foreigners for the atrocities of the DK period, Mai Lam added: "They don't want to open their minds. . . . They're tired, they don't want to think." As a historian, Mai Lam had no qualms about what he was doing. Moreover, without his dedication and hard work, the museum would never have existed, nor would this book have been possible. On manipulations of memory under Marxist-Leninist regimes, see Watson, ed., *Memory, History and Opposition*.

29. Hiegel and Landrac, "Les khmers rouges," 65. See also Hiegel and Landrac, "Revolution des khmers rouges," and Levi, *The Drowned and the Saved*, 36–37.

30. Ong Thong Hoeung (Heder interviews, 14) claims that in late 1979 he was asked to join committees for drafting the PRK Constitution and for writing "an official government history text": "The Vietnamese asked me to use the Vietnamese Constitution as a model for the Cambodian constitution and they also asked me to completely ignore French sources . . . and to write in such a way that the basic point was historical solidarity between Vietnam and Cambodia." On this issue, see Frings, *Allied and Equal*.

31. Lionel Vairon's interview with Pha Thachan, which begs the question of whether killing "foreigners" is acceptable. See also Bui Tin, *Following Ho Chi Minh:* "In reality [the Khmer Rouge genocidal policy] was much more cruel and lethal than that carried out by the Nazis in the Second World War. But it was beautifully cloaked under the form of communism, pure communism, the purest form of communism" (131). Drawing on Rubie Watson's work, Ledgerwood points out that the Chinese have failed to provide a satisfying "meta-narrative" for the Cultural Revolution. On this point, see also Lu Xiuyuan, "A Step toward Understanding Popular Violence."

32. Ledgerwood, "The Cambodian Tuol Sleng Museum," 91. The days of hate were celebrated on 20 May, commemorating the day in 1973 when the CPK had inaugurated collectivization in those parts of Cambodia under its control: see Heder interviews, 35.

33. See Hannum and Hawk, *The Case against the Standing Committee,* and Hawk, "The Cambodian Genocide." On the propaganda value of S-21, see Chanda, *Brother Enemy,* 382.

34. See, for example, *New York Times,* 27 April 1998. Efforts to prosecute the top Khmer Rouge came close to fruition just before Pol Pot's apparent suicide in April 1998 and gathered momentum again after Nuon Chea and Khieu Samphan defected to the Phnom Penh government in December 1998. See Richburg, "Support Grows for Trial of Khmer Rouge," and Adams, "Snatching Defeat from the Jaws of Victory." If such a trial ever takes place, documents from the S-21 archive now housed in DC–Cam are certain to be used in evidence. The concepts of justice, forgiveness, mercy, and revenge are perhaps hopelessly tangled in the minds of DK survivors. Unfortunately, this book had gone to press when I learned of Martha Minow's well-received comparative study of these issues, *Between Vengeance and Forgiveness.*

35. These young men prepared confessions, written in English, alleging that they were career CIA agents and had been paid enormous sums of money to spy on DK. They were among the last prisoners to be executed at the prison. On American prisoners, see Bryson, "Cambodia Rakes the Ashes of Her Ruin." Peter Maguire's research has revealed that the four Americans, who had known each other in high school in California, were caught off the Cambodian coast when they were heading from Singapore to Bangkok to pick up cargoes of processed marijuana that they planned to deliver to Hawaii. Because they had a high-school classmate working for U.S. intelligence services in Thailand, it is conceivable that they were taking commissioned photographs of the coastline when they were arrested.

36. The nonconfessional reels are CMR 93–103, 112–15, 187–88, and 198. The interrogators' manual, discussed in detail in chapter 5, is CMR 99.7. For a

partial translation, see Hawk, "The Tuol Sleng Extermination Centre," 27. The "Last Plan" (CMR 99.13) is translated in Jackson, *Cambodia 1975–1978,* 299–314.

37. Djilas, *Of Prisons and Ideas,* 139.

38. As Robert Moeller has suggested (personal communication), the mug shots also brought news (in the form of facial expressions, clothing, and, by implication, memories) from outside the prison. They depict the faces of people crossing into a total institution. Niven and Riley, *Killing Fields,* contains a haunting selection of the mug shots. Niven and Riley's Photo Archive Group cleaned, developed, and archived over six thousand negatives found at the museum in 1994 and 1995. Most of these photographs can be accessed on the CD-ROM prepared by the Cambodia Genocide Program at Yale University. Lindsay French, "Exhibiting Terror," discusses an exhibit of the photos at the Museum of Modern Art in New York in 1997. Vann Nath has recalled painting the torture pictures "in September 1979, when the government started to open [S-21] as a museum." Chameau, "No. 55 Delivers His Verdict."

CHAPTER TWO. S-21: A TOTAL INSTITUTION

1. Goffman, *Asylums,* 11. See also Boesche, "The Prison"; Horowitz, *Taking Lives,* 27; Foucault, *Discipline and Punish;* and Solzhenitsyn, *The Gulag Archipelago,* vol. 1, chapter 14, "Totalitarianism as a Penal Colony."

2. Goffman, *Asylums,* 22.

3. Foucault, *Discipline and Punish,* 302–3: "In its function, the power to punish is not essentially different from that of curing or educating." All three activities took place at S-21. See also Kinzie, "The 'Concentration Camp' Syndrome." Bauman, *Modernity and the Holocaust,* compares a society operating under these conditions to a "garden to be designed and kept in the planned shape by force" where "plants" are taken care of and "weeds [are] exterminated" (18).

4. Cited in Frame, *Dialectical Historicism and Terror,* 71. S-21 was arguably the most important institution in DK. According to Nhem En (author's interview), Son Sen, the man in charge of DK's national security, referred to S-21 as the "nation's breath" *(donghaom cheat).* See also CMR 99.7, interrogators' notebook from 1976: "The work of the Special Branch is class struggle work, achieving the smashing of the exploiting classes, uprooting them completely so as to defend the party, the proletariat, DK, and the line of independence-mastery. . . . No enemy agents can do things the way we do them!"

5. Ieng Sary told Steve Heder in 1996 that a "Military-Security Commission" *(kanak kammathikar yothea-santesok)* composed of Pol Pot, Nuon Chea, Son Sen, and Sao Phim, with Son Sen's wife, Yun Yat, participating on an informal basis, "oversaw arrest detention and execution at S-21" (Steve Heder, personal communication). The only corroboration of Sary's statement so far is CMR 71.10, Meas Mon (alias Keo Sithun), written in June 1978, after Sao Phim's suicide, which quotes Sao Phim in 1976 as saying, to reassure his interlocutor, that he was still a member of the "central military commission." Speaking to a journalist in 1997, Ieng Sary claimed that only "two people knew [about S-21] for certain . . . Nuon Chea, who was responsible for party security,

and Son Sen, who was responsible for state security" (Kamm, *Cambodia,* 14). It seems likely that some high-ranking military cadres in Phnom Penh also knew of the prison's existence, because delegates from S-21, so designated in the minutes, attended meetings convened by Son Sen for such people.

6. Summers, "The CPK: Secret Vanguard."

7. *Tung Padevat,* December 1977–January 1978, 16.

8. Summers, "The CPK: Secret Vanguard," 11. See also Pol Pot, "Long Live the Seventeenth Anniversary of the Communist Party of Kampuchea," speech of 29 September 1977, FBIS, 2 October 1977, which noted that "secret work was the fundamental thing. It allowed us to defend the revolution and allowed us to arouse the people."

9. CMR 99.7. The document goes on to say that "nourishing secrecy is the heart and soul of *santebal* work."

10. "The Party's Plan for 4.8.78." Uncatalogued, one-page item from S-21 archive.

11. The telephone directory is CMR 187.9. The dormitories for the interrogation and document units had their own telephone extensions. Duch had two. Communications outside the prison were maintained by radio telephone.

12. Douglas Niven's interview with Kok Sros.

13. On the Chinese automobile, author's interview with Neak Ek Bunan. On Office 100, see Chandler, *Brother Number One,* 71 ff.; CMR 42.21, Ing Cheng Im; CMR 53.27, Kheang Sim Horn; and CMR 138.11, Siet Chhe (alias Tum).

14. Jackson, *Cambodia 1975–1978,* 88 n. On "bourgeois" see CMR 134.28, Chey Suon, one of several biographical sketches of CPK figures that form a segment of the confession. Chey Suon went on to suggest that in his view Son Sen might profitably "refashion his personality . . . to make him into a worker-peasant in his speech and everyday life." After this outburst, he added, "I ask him to forgive me if this is erroneous" (trans. Steve Heder).

15. Author's interview with Nhem En, who claimed that Son Sen visited S-21 on a weekly basis; "Son Sen to Duch" memorandum of October 1977. CMR 67.25, Loeung Ly, contains a note from Son Sen to Duch. The staff of the DC–Cam archive have identified eighty-four S-21 documents—all but four of them from 1977—that bear notes in Son Sen's writing.

16. See Steve Heder, "Racism, Marxism, Labelling," 127 ff. Confessions in the S-21 archive that implicate Son Sen include CMR 20.34, Chea Samath; CMR 21.25, Chhay Kim Huor; and CMR 21.26, Chan Kim.

17. When Pol Pot was "tried" at the Khmer Rouge base in Anlong Veng in July 1997, he was charged with ordering the murder of Son Sen and sentenced to life imprisonment. In his interview with Nate Thayer three months later, Pol Pot took responsibility for killing Son Sen but regretted the deaths of the children assassinated with him. See Thayer, "Day of Reckoning."

18. Author's interviews with Neak Ek Bunan. See also Pringle, "Pol Pot's Hatchet Man"; Kiernan, *The Pol Pot Regime,* 31; and Becker, *When the War Was Over,* 272 ff. and Dunlop and Thayer, "Duch Confesses."

19. On the blackboard, Jeremy Stone's interview with Ly Sorsane, in *Fellowship of Atomic Scientists Public Interest Report* 424 (April 1989). On Chan, author's interview with Lach Vorleak Kaliyan.

20. Author's interviews with Nek Bunan and with a former Chinese student who requested anonymity and who confirmed that all but one of his colleagues who had studied in Phnom Penh in the 1960s had remained "Cambodia experts."

21. Author's interview with François Bizot. See also Swain, *River of Time,* 258–61, and Vickery, *Cambodia 1975–1982,* 152. Le Carré, *The Secret Pilgrim,* 255 ff., gives a fictional rendering of Bizot's captivity. Two years later Duch surfaced at a meeting for "intellectuals" in the Special Zone; a visitor noted at the time that he appeared "thin and ill" (Carney, ed., *Communist Party Power in Kampuchea,* 12). Duch's wife, Rom, whom he had married in Amleang, was then in charge of a "clothes making shop."

22. Kiernan, *How Pol Pot Came to Power,* 331–35. See also Chandler, *Tragedy,* 359 n. 77, and Heder interviews, 25–27.

23. For Duch annotations, see, for example, CMR 53.13, Koy Suon; CMR 90.23, Oum Soeun; CMR 117.112, Prum Khoeun; and CMR 139.9, Sman Sles. An uncatalogued item from DC–Cam, dated 20 January 1976, refers to "M-21," where "M" presumably stands for *munthi,* or "office," and lists Duch as chairman. I am grateful to Steve Heder for this reference.

24. On the Ta Khmau location, CMR 24.11, Duong Khoeurn.

25. Data based on interviews by author, Ben Kiernan, and Peter Maguire with him, and Alexander Hinton's interview with Khieu Lohr. Duch's self-criticisms are contained in notes from a "livelihood meeting" in Mam Nay's script dated 18 February 1976 (uncatalogued item, S-21 archive), in which Duch admitted that he was "disorganized," relied too much on his own efforts, neglected the "collectivity," and occasionally "lost mastery and felt despair." Kok Sros, who was interviewed about S-21 for the first time in 1997, harbors memories of Duch that seem to be unaffected by the demonization of the man in Phnom Penh since 1979; in his interview, he said that Duch was relatively "easygoing."

26. CMR 99.13. For an English translation, see Jackson, *Cambodia 1975–1978,* 299–314.

27. On Duch's departure, author's interviews with Him Huy, Nhem En, and Vann Nath and Ben Kiernan's interview with Him Huy. In 1998, Nhem En stated categorically that Duch was dead. On Duch's dramatic reappearance in 1999, see Dunlop and Thayer, "Duch Confesses" and Seth Mydans, "70s Torturer in Cambodia 'Now Doing God's Work.'"

28. Author's interview with Kok Sros. The former document worker Suos Thi told Seth Mydans in 1996: "I was very afraid of Ho. I was afraid even to look at his face, In my dreams, he was like a tiger" (Mydans, "Cambodian Killers' Careful Records"). Him Huy told Douglas Niven and Peter Maguire that on one occasion after Ho had cursed him, "I sat by myself and cried. I wanted to shoot myself."

29. On Peng, Alexander Hinton's interview with Khieu Lohr, Ben Kiernan's interview with Him Huy, Youk Chhang's interview with Him Huy, and Sara Colm's interview with Vann Nath. See also Item D-15, DC–Cam archive, an interview with Him Huy dated 1987. An uncatalogued document from DC–Cam dated 30 May 1978 contains the names of eighteen prisoners, some

as young as nine, annotated by Duch: "Uncle Peng: Discard [kill] every last one."

30. Kiernan, *The Pol Pot Regime,* 315. Interrogations of Vietnamese in Chan's writing, all in CMR 18, are numbered 1, 2, 4, 22–24, 29–31, 35, 37–44, 51–57, 64–67, 74–75, 78–99, 102–6, and 110–14. Nhem En said that Chan interrogated "all the Vietnamese prisoners" (author's interview, February 1997), and an untitled notebook containing Chan's thumbnail biographies of several Vietnamese prisoners has survived in Box 13, DC–Cam. In 1990 Nate Thayer watched him interrogating supposedly Vietnamese prisoners on the Thai-Cambodian border (personal communication). On the 1996 sighting, Christophe Peschoux (personal communication).

31. See "Chivavoas padevat reboh mit Pon" (Comrade Pon's revolutionary outlook), uncatalogued 21-page document in DC–Cam archive, 7–12 December 1976. In the document, Pon regarded his repeated use of force against prisoners as a "shortcoming," but no reprimands for this behavior surfaced in the archive. In Chan's notebook entry for 26 December 1977, probably after another self-criticism session, Pon is praised for "scrupulously following the wishes of the Higher Organization."

32. Tuy-Pon notebook, uncatalogued item in DC–Cam archive, entry for 9 September 1978.

33. See Suos Thi's self-critical autobiography, dated 6 June 1977, in DC–Cam archive; Chris Riley and Peter Maguire's interview with him in 1996; and Mydans, "Cambodian Killers' Careful Records."

34. Peter Maguire's interview with Suos Thi.

35. Sara Colm's interview with Vann Nath, author's interview with Him Huy, Douglas Niven and Peter Maguire's interview with Vann Nath, author's interviews with Nhem En, and document D-15, DC–Cam archive, dated 1987. See also Nath, *Prison Portrait* (110), Him Huy's self-critical autobiography, uncatalogued in DC–Cam archive, and Molly O'Kane, "The Eradication of Year Zero," *Guardian Weekend,* 26 July 1997. I am grateful to Victoria Smith for drawing my attention to this article.

36. "Rice-field" Huy's confession is at CMR 83.2. On study sessions, CMR 97.2, Lon Kim Ay's political notebook from 1976. Huy's wife's self-critical autobiography is Document 96 ST, DC–Cam archive; her confession has not survived. Kok Sros stated that only high-ranking cadres such as Duch, Ho, and Chan were allowed to house their families near the compound (author's interview).

37. *Kach* group: CMR 87.2, Nop Nuon. *Slout:* cf. 1067 DC–Cam, 1 June 1977. On the prohibition of *slout* interrogators to torture, CMR 92.11, Ouch Orn. On *trocheak* group, CMR 159.2, Sok Ngim; confession of Chhim Chhun BBK-Kh 418 (not microfilmed) in DC–Cam; and uncatalogued lists of prisoners from DC–Cam dated 30 March and 27 May 1978. *Angkhiem* and *trocheak* groups are identified in several loose, uncatalogued sheets from the DC–Cam archive dated 2 June 1978. Prisoners interrogated by the "chewing" group were often middle-ranking cadres from the zones. In February 1978, fifty-one prisoners were being questioned by this group; a month later, the group was dealing with fourteen. For *kdau,* see uncatalogued DC–Cam document dated 2 June

1978 and uncatalogued items from DC–Cam archive from February and 30 March 1978. Seybolt, "Terror and Conformity," mentions "soft" and "hard" interrogation groups in Yan'an in 1943.

38. Document 96 TS in DC–Cam archive. CMR 45.2, the confession of Kun, the wife of a senior cadre, is signed by two female interrogators named Ny and Li. The latter's name appears in the telephone directory. For Ung Pech's testimony, see Pringle, "Pol Pot's Hatchet Man." Vann Nath claimed that there had been a female interrogator at S-21 in 1978, but "she went crazy" (interview with author). Nath added that females were sometimes asked to witness interrogations of female prisoners to forestall sexual assaults. Seth Mydans, "A Cambodian Woman's Tale," is based on Mydans's interview with a former female guard from S-21, Neang Kin, who, like Him Huy, was imprisoned briefly by the Vietnamese for committing atrocities at the prison. She confessed to these at the time but now denies them.

39. CMR 69.30.

40. See, for example, CMR 86.25, Neou Puch.

41. Confessions of documentation workers include CMR 3.24, Buth Heng; CMR 46.15, Keo Ly Thong; and CMR 106.11, Peng Leng Huoy.

42. The negatives have been cleaned, processed, and catalogued by the Photo Archive Group, a nongovernmental organization set up in 1994 by the American photojournalists Douglas Niven and Chris Riley. See Niven and Riley, *The Killing Fields.* The photography unit also took snapshots of employees at the prison, according to Nhem En. Some of these snapshots, displayed in the East German documentary *Die Angkar,* have since disappeared, as have many of the photographs of dead prisoners shown in the film.

43. Interviews by author and Douglas Niven with Nhem En. See also McDowell, "Photographer Recalls Days behind Lens at Tuol Sleng." For a reference to the "bad photographs," see Chan notebook, uncatalogued DC–Cam document, entry for 26 December 1977.

44. See CMR 99.8, "Ompi viney kapea khmang" (On the rules for guarding enemies). See also uncatalogued document from S-21 archive, dated 2 August 1976 (another set of rules), and author's interviews with Him Huy, Vann Nath, and Kok Sros.

45. Author's interview with Kok Sros.

46. CMR 98.8 lists thirty rules for guards. DC–Cam Document 1064, dated 31 October 1976, sets out some slightly different regulations. The rule about guards not observing interrogations is in an uncatalogued DC–Cam text dated 4 August 1976.

47. For example, CMR 29.3, Eam Ron. According to Vann Nath, prisoners were sometimes beaten at random in the open spaces between buildings. See also Chameau, "No. 55 Delivers His Verdict," and Todorov, *Facing the Extreme,* 141. Todorov's assertion that moral goodness was widespread among victims in the camps he writes about is impossible to document in S-21. With so few survivors, no inducements that prisoners could offer the staff, and poor material conditions nationwide, there is no evidence of bribery, special privileges, or friendships between prisoners and staff, and no S-21 workers ever confessed to such "offenses."

48. Document D-1063, DC–Cam archive, dated 15 October 1976. The document closes by mentioning that only 258 prisoners were held at S-21 at the time. No confessions survive from any of the prisoners named in the text. Steve Heder suggests that procedures may have been tightened in the wake of Keo Meas's incarceration in September 1976 (personal communication). The uniqueness of the document, clearly of a type that was prepared on a nightly basis, suggests that masses of documentary material prepared at S-21 have disappeared.

49. CMR 17.24, Chey Pang, and CMR 29.3, Eam Ron, who confessed to depriving prisoners of food and beating some of them, for which they were made to carry excrement. For an example of a prisoner transferred to S-21 from Prey So, see CMR 20.4, Chhoeun Chek.

50. On the economic support unit, see uncatalogued item in DC–Cam archive dated 18 July 1977. Duch's report is CMR 99.10. The ducks and chickens, unlike the people, were of economic use.

51. Uncatalogued item from Prey So in DC–Cam archive, dated 27 November 1977. See also CMR 80.28, Mam Bol, who was recaptured three days after escaping from Prey So, where he had been sent for deserting his military unit.

52. See DC–Cam document 1116 TS, 7 March 1976, signed by Chan, listing "many" prisoners as seriously ill. See also the 1977 political notebook titled "Lothi Mak Lenin" (Marx-Leninism), uncatalogued item in S-21 archive, 38. See as well Chan notebook, 26 December 1977, for the accusation of Pheng Try. CMR 183. Va Sreng, a paramedic at S-21, confessed to taking a two-week course in microscopy before coming to work at S-21.

53. CMR 106. 3, Phoung Damrei. See uncatalogued document from S-21 dated 2 March 1977: "4 people executed by taking blood." Kiernan, *The Pol Pot Regime,* 439, refers to a "tiny rectangular notebook . . . entitled 'Human Experiments *(pisaot monus)'*" found near S-21 in 1979. Pages of the booklet are reproduced in *Die Angkar,* along with testimony from former S-21 workers that prisoners were occasionally bled to death. On other surgical experiments, Richard Arant (personal communication) cited an interview he conducted with a former Khmer Rouge cadre in 1996.

54. The class categories assigned to rural people in DK ("rich peasant"; two divisions of "middle peasant" and three divisions of "poor peasant") had been borrowed from China via Vietnam without much regard for Cambodian conditions. See Carney, "The Organization of Power," 99–100.

55. Mao's comment was made first in 1956. See Starr and Dyer, comps., *Post-Liberation Works of Mao Zedong,* 173, and Moody, *Opposition and Dissen,* 62. See also Bauman, *Modernity and the Holocaust,* writing in another context: "The combination of malleability and helplessness constitutes an attraction which few self-confident adventurous visionaries [can] resist. It also constitutes a situation in which they cannot be resisted" (114).

56. CMR 47.14, Kang Lean. The paragraph also draws on author's interviews with Suong Soriya, Sieu Chheng Y, and Mouth Sophea, who were teenagers during the DK era.

57. Talking to Alexander Hinton, the former guard Khieu Lohr noted that "Young people were often attached to cadres from the civil war when they were

very young [*touch,* literally 'small']. The cadre remained their patron *(me)* afterwards and brought the kids along to help [them] at the prison."

58. See Gourevitch, "Letter from Rwanda," 78–95, and his poignant and vivid book, *We Wish to Inform You That Tomorrow We Will Be Killed with Our Families.* Mollica has worked extensively with Cambodian refugees in the United States. See also Ponchaud, "Social Change in the Vortex of Revolution," which suggests that "Khmer revolutionaries modified what was at the core of Khmer society" (169). For a chilling study of U.S. Marines of the same age, see Solis, *Son Thang.*

59. Minutes of Second Ministerial Meeting, 31 May 1976, document 705 in DC–Cam archive, 29. Pol Pot went on to say that young cadres in hospitals sometimes administered the wrong medicines because they were unable to read. He closed the meeting on an upbeat note, saying that "in three to five years we will be so powerful that enemies will be unable to do anything to us. We will have become a model for the world." See also Document 1127, DC–Cam archive, undated youth meeting at S-21, which notes that young people at the prison are often lazy "and take advantage of meetings and study sessions to 'enjoy themselves'" (literally "play," *lenh*).

60. Quoted in Shawcross, *The Quality of Mercy,* 334.

61. See Chandler, *Tragedy,* 218–19, and Gibson, "Training People to Inflict Pain," 72–87. The sorts of discipline and bonding that Gibson's investigations revealed among military personnel in Greece in the 1970s are similar to those experienced by interrogators at S-21.

62. Ben Kiernan's interview with Him Huy. On Khieu Samphan, see Heder, *Pol Pot and Khieu Samphan,* and Thayer, "Day of Reckoning."

63. Douglas Niven's interview with Nhem En.

64. Douglas Niven's interview with Nhem En, who said that the numbering system for prisoners in 1976–1977 was based on daily intakes, beginning with one at midnight every day. Several photographs show prisoners with tags numbered higher than 300. Starting in December 1978, prisoners were photographed with boards giving their names, the date of the photograph, and a number that placed them in a sequence begun each month.

65. Note from Huy to Duch, December 1978, uncatalogued item in S-21 archive. See also document 1180, DC–Cam, listing twenty-four prisoners confined in the "special prison" in November and December 1978. Him Huy, talking to Peter Maguire, remembered that S-21 was to a large extent "cleared out" by the end of 1978. It is unclear from Ruy Nikon's account whether all the "craftsmen" he mentions, who also figure in Nath's memoir, were prisoners like himself or people brought in from outside the prison.

66. See Locard, "Le Goulag des khmers rouges." The large number of military prisoners accused of (or admitting to) petty offenses suggests that errant members of DK's armed forces were held at S-21, a military facility, rather than in provincial prisons.

67. Confessions of women enjoying high status in DK include those of CMR 26.3, Dim Saroeun; CMR 27.3, Ear Hong; CMR 41.8, Im Ly; CMR 61.25, Leng Son Hak; CMR 67.21, Lach Vary; CMR 116.20, Prun Ohal; CMR 165.11, Yaay Kon; and CMR 167.4, Tep Sam.

68. Two of these, Von Vet and Sao Phim, had been deputy prime ministers of DK, the latter serving concurrently as secretary of the Eastern Zone. On the sequence of purges in DK, see chapter 3.

69. Douglas Niven's interview with Kok Sros. References to the "special prison" in the archive all date from 1978, but the photograph of Koy Thuon, a high-ranking cadre imprisoned in 1977, shows him chained to a metal bed (see photographs).

70. Sofsky, *The Order of Terror*, 153.

71. Hawk, "The Tuol Sleng Extermination Centre," 26.

72. Execution schedule for 2 June 1977, uncatalogued item from S-21 archive. For instances of sexual assaults on prisoners by prison staff, see CMR 17.3, Chea May; CMR 153.1, Sok Ra; and CMR 183.27, Vong Samath. Although documentation of sexual assaults on prisoners is rare, the dehumanization of the prisoners and the monastic conditions imposed on the staff would suggest that assaults were frequent.

73. Foucault, *Discipline and Punish*, 237.

74. Sara Colm's interview with Vann Nath. See also Chameau, "No. 55 Delivers His Verdict," which quotes Vann Nath: "During my first night I had some hope, but all my hope had gone away by the time morning came."

75. See People's Republic of Kampuchea, *The Extermination Camp of Tuol Sleng*.

76. Sara Colm's interview with Vann Nath.

77. CMR 22.8, Sun Heng; CMR 156.11, Suas Phon; CMR 169.17, Thai Peng; and CMR 174.6, Ton Tith. See also CMR 48.13, Khieu Son, in which Chan, after questioning, recommends further confinement but not execution. Kok Sros told Douglas Niven that "when the prison was at Ta Khmau, prisoners were sometimes released when they told the truth. Regulations were more relaxed then." In *Die Angkar*, a document is cited that lists one prisoner, Duk Chheam, as "released" in 1976. I have been unable to locate this text in the archive.

78. Ashley's interview with Vann Nath. The mock-up has not survived. The idea that Pol Pot should be depicted carrying a book of "revolutionary works" is ironic, since his speeches are almost devoid of references to written sources and were themselves never collected into a volume. The aim of the statue seems to have been to demonstrate the resemblances between Pol Pot and his revolutionary forebears, Mao Zedong and Kim Il Sung.

CHAPTER THREE. CHOOSING THE ENEMIES

1. On Mao's idea of permanent revolution, see Meisner, *Mao's China and After*, 206–16. See also Walder, "Cultural Revolution Radicalism." Walder suggests that the values of the Cultural Revolution were "expressed in the framework of [a] conspiracy theory" (43). See also Starr and Dyer, *Post-Liberation Works of Mao Zedong*. "Enemies" at 120–22 is cross-referenced to "accomplices, agents, alien class elements, bad elements, bandits, degenerates, lackeys, opponents, traitors to Marxism." "Friends" is cross-referenced only to "contradictions," 72.

2. Locard, *Petit livre rouge,* 133. Vann Nath told Alexander Hinton: "That one word 'enemy' had great power. . . . Upon hearing the word 'enemy' everyone became nervous." Hinton, "Why Did You Kill?" 113. The Cambodian verb *boh somat,* like the English word "clean," has no negative connotations in ordinary speech and can refer simply to cleaning house.

3. For the text of the speech as it was delivered in 1957, see MacFarquhar et al., eds., *Secret Speeches,* 131–89. Pol Pot probably referred to the milder, authorized version when he mentioned the speech in his eulogy on Mao (FBIS, 20 September 1976). In the transcript of the speech (142–43), Mao admitted that in the *sufan* campaigns in 1950–1952, "We killed 700,000. . . . If they had not been killed, the people would not have been able to raise their heads. . . . The people demanded those killings in order to liberate their productive forces." The last sentence could probably have served the Party Center in Cambodia as a justification for the massacres of "class enemies" in 1975, but not for the existence of S-21.

4. Pol Pot, "Long Live the Seventeenth Anniversary of the Communist Party of Kampuchea," FBIS, 4 October 1977. See also *Tung Padevat,* special issue, December 1975–January 1976, 41, which refers to "opportunists, accidental [revolutionaries] and those with . . . unclear biographies." *Tung Padevat,* March 1978, translated in Jackson, *Cambodia 1975–1978,* speaks of "savage [reactionaries] who cannot be reeducated" (297). See also "Lothi Mak-Lenin," undated notebook from S-21 archive: "The exploiting classes that were scattered and smashed in 1975 need to be scattered and smashed again" (59). For two stimulating discussions of political violence and the manufacture of enemies, see Merkl, ed., *Political Violence and Terror,* 28–29, and Apter, ed., *The Legitimation of Violence,* 1–20.

5. See Tucker, *The Soviet Political Mind, 55,* which quotes Stalin in 1928 as saying, "We have internal enemies. We have external enemies. This, comrades, must not be forgotten for a single moment." I am grateful to Steve Heder for providing this reference.

6. "CIA Plan," uncatalogued document in Mam Nay's handwriting from S-21 archive, dated 3 March 1976. The document asserts that "Son Ngoc Thanh's [pro-American] forces and the Viet Cong have been allied for many years."

7. Document 1090, DC–Cam archive, "Essence of Interrogations of Soldiers Coming from the U.S."

8. Summers, "The CPK: Secret Vanguard," 30. Pol Pot shared this fantastic view of the world. Speaking to Western journalists in December 1978, he informed them that only "NATO" could stop the planned invasion of Cambodia by troops affiliated with the "Warsaw Pact." Becker, *When the War Was Over,* 433–36. Similarly, according to the "Last Plan," in Jackson, *Cambodia 1975–1978,* "the US used the Vietnamese [after 1975] with Soviet co-operation because the US had no troops to fight in Kampuchea" (312).

9. Locard, *Petit livre rouge,* 166. See also Dittmer, "Thought Reform and Cultural Revolution," which gives a Chinese quotation: "The enemies without guns are more hidden, cunning, sinister and vicious than the enemies with guns" (75).

10. Author's interview with Seng Kan, a "new person" who was imprisoned for two years in Svay Rieng. See also Locard, "Le Goulag des khmers rouges," and Etcheson, "Centralized Terror in Democratic Kampuchea."

11. Kiernan, *The Pol Pot Regime, 55–59*, has a detailed discussion of this meeting, based on his interviews with participants.

12. *Tung Padevat,* December 1975–January 1976, 41 (trans. Steve Heder). See also "Sharpen the Consciousness of the Proletarian Class," *Tung Padevat,* September–October 1976, translated in Jackson, *Cambodia 1975–1978:* "The feudalists and the capitalist classes are . . . overthrown but their specific traits of contradiction . . . still exist in policy, in consciousness, in standpoint and class rage" (270).

13. "Pay Attention to Sweeping out the Concealed Enemies," *Tung Padevat,* July 1978, 9–10. The passage schematically opposes an open, enlightened, wakeful, and resplendent CPK to the closed, dark, hidden, and burrowing forces arrayed against it. Some listeners may have been reminded fleetingly of the Buddha's struggle with the evil forces of Mara.

14. Summers, "The CPK: Secret Vanguard," 27.

15. "Sharpen the Consciousness," 273. See also "Abbreviated Lesson on the History of the Kampuchean Revolutionary Movement" in Chandler, Kiernan, and Boua, *Pol Pot Plans the Future:* "Contradictions between classes still exist . . . as standpoints, as attitudes, as self-interest" (222); and CMR 55.5, Kae San: "What can we see that's weak about the revolution? It's weak in that ideologically individualism is not yet gone. There's still factionalism. There's an ideology of unit, of organizationism. There's an ideology of one's own sector, there's an ideology of one's own zone, and simply of oneself." These views are echoed in Zhang Chunqiao, "On Exercising All-Round Dictatorship over the Bourgeoisie," an important article published in China in April 1975. See also Ling Hsaio, "Keep on Criticizing the Bourgeoisie." Ironically, Stalin, Mao, and Pol Pot, atheists all, seem to have been drawn toward a doctrine that resembled the Roman Catholic dogma of original sin. At a more worldly level, if the struggle against enemies was permanent, so was the need for the enlightened leadership of the Party. When the people were still surrounded by enemies, how could the state wither away?

16. Locard, *Petit livre rouge,* 175. The slogan was probably inherited from Vietnam. See Vo Nhan Tri, *Vietnam's Economic Policy,* 2–7, citing Vo Nguyen Giap from 1956. I am grateful to Steve Heder for this reference. The adage begs the question of how or by whom anyone's innocence or guilt could be determined. Ironically, the ratio of "innocent" to "guilty" people executed at Tuol Sleng may well have reached ten to one. In Locard's anthology, the saying appears alongside one that was frequently addressed to "new people" and is recalled by many survivors of DK: "Keeping [you] is no gain; losing [you] is no loss."

17. On strategies, see "The Last Plan" in Jackson, *Cambodia 1975–1978:* "Pol Pot wanted to have everyone to be clean *(s'aat)* and pure *(borisut).* People who weren't clean and pure were killed" (305). See also Pha Thachan's interview with Lionel Vairon. On enemies as quintessential outsiders, see Giddens, *The Nation-State and Violence,* 117. I am grateful to Zara Kivi Kinnunen for this reference. See also Kapferer, *Legends of People,* which argues that the Tamils in Sri Lanka, like "unbelievers" *(thmil)* in Cambodia, represent a subdued, demonic antithesis to the more widely accepted Theravada Buddhist "order."

18. For a translation of this speech, see Chandler, Kiernan, and Boua, *Pol Pot Plans the Future,* 183. See also Suárez-Orozco, "A Grammar of Terror," 239, which cites an Argentine admiral in the 1970s who referred to death squads as "antibodies" combating the "germs" of radical dissent. *Tung Padevat,* April 1978, 39, has another microbe reference, and *Tung Padevat,* July 1976, "Whip up a Movement to Constantly Study the Party Statutes," asserts: "The CIA attacks the revolution by injecting drugs into its veins" (51).

19. CMR 12.25 (trans. Steve Heder). See also Ponchaud, *Cambodia Year Zero,* 40 ff. In 1988 Pol Pot told cadres that former Lon Nol personnel had been "smashed . . . because they represented imperialist strata" (Roger Normand, personal communication). See also Heder interviews: "[The former Lon Nol officers] were asked to go and meet the Organization . . . and offered forgiveness but then were just taken away and executed" (46). Although there is abundant anecdotal evidence of these executions (see, e.g., Quinn, "Pattern and Scope of Violence," 185 ff.), few documents recording the killings have survived. On propaganda encouraging the executions, see Ponchaud, *Cambodia Year Zero,* 50–51. On the government's curtailing the killings when they got out of hand, see Kiernan, *The Pol Pot Regime,* 92. Mouth Sophea recalls a similar order reaching Khmer Rouge cadres in June 1975 in Battambang (author's interview, February 1998). See also Vickery, "Democratic Kampuchea," 109–10. In his "History of the Struggle Movement" (1997), Nuon Chea denied centralized responsibility. "As for the killing," he wrote, "we didn't know anything about it *[ot dung teng oh te].* It was the people lower down *[puok khang krom]* who behaved stupidly *[pdeh pdah].*" There is no record of any of these culprits being punished.

20. Chomsky and Hermann, *After the Cataclysm,* 38–39 and 149. See also Aron, *L'histoire de l'épuration,* 3 vols. (Paris, 1967–1975), and Marguerite Duras's mordant vignette "Albert du Capitale." The so-called White Terror in France in 1795–1796 and the 1965–1966 massacres of suspected Communists in Indonesia offer additional parallels. See Cribb, ed., *The Indonesian Killings,* 1–43.

21. On the Hanoi Khmer, see Kiernan, *How Pol Pot Came to Power,* 319–21 and 358 ff., and Heder interviews, in which a former Khmer Rouge cadre recalled that in 1974 "it was said that all of those people who came from the North would . . . allow the Vietnamese to come back and control the country" (44). "The Last Plan" referred to them as "100 percent Vietnamese [who] had nothing left as Khmers" (Jackson, *Cambodia 1975–1978,* 301). Other prisoners at S-21 documented from this period included malingerers, thieves, deserters, and foreigners who strayed onto Cambodian territory. People in these categories continued to be brought into S-21 until the collapse of the regime. Few of the earlier prisoners put a counterrevolutionary "spin" on their behavior.

22. Becker, *When the War Was Over,* 274, and Arendt, *Totalitarianism,* 120.

23. On the Siem Reap explosion, see Kiernan, *The Pol Pot Regime,* 316–19, and Vickery, *Cambodia 1975–1982,* 128. Intriguingly, the S-21 document "CIA Plan," prepared a week later (see n. 6 above), failed to mention it, and a telegram to Son Sen from the acting secretary of the Northern Zone, Ke Pauk,

dated 4 April 1976 (uncatalogued item in the DC–Cam archive), reported no unrest in the Zone. CMR 12.25, Cho Chan (alias Sreng), parroting the Party line, suggested in March 1977 that the explosion reflected "the angry fury of American imperialism, which had never [before] lost to any country in the world." Steve Heder (personal communication) has suggested that Thai military aircraft might well have been involved.

24. Writing such a history was my original goal when I started working on the S-21 archive in 1994. Because of the nature of the S-21 texts, the task soon became impossible. See chapter 1, n. 2, for a list of historical syntheses of the Khmer Rouge period. Only Becker's *When the War Was Over* makes extended use of the S-21 archive.

25. On using the confession texts as evidence, see Heder, "Khmer Rouge Opposition to Pol Pot": "In principle, you have to assume that every word may either be a falsehood forced upon a terrified writer . . . or a falsehood concocted by the writer to save his or her life by denying what is true. . . . And yet long before one is through the first thousand pages, it becomes obvious to the reader that some things are undoubtedly true" (11). Heder suggests (private communication) that the "truest" parts of confessions are often those dealing with events prior to 1970.

26. See, for example, my own faulty assessment in Chandler, Kiernan, and Boua, *Pol Pot Plans the Future,* xviii.

27. Published translations of DK documents into English include Becker, *When the War Was Over* (appendixes); Carney, *Communist Party Power in Kampuchea,* 251–314; and Chandler, Kiernan, and Boua, *Pol Pot Plans the Future.* Heder has translated several key articles from *Tung Padevat* and *Revolutionary Youth* and over a thousand pages of confessions from S-21. None of these invaluable translations, aside from some passages from confessions in the appendixes to Becker's book, has yet been published in full. With Heder's permission, I have used several of them in this book.

28. In 1995–1997, additional DK documents were turned over to the CGP and DC–Cam by the Cambodian Ministry of the Interior and other sources. On DK archives in Vietnam, see Engelbert and Goscha, *Falling out of Touch,* xv–xvii. Cooperatives kept extensive records in DK, which have for the most part disappeared (Steve Heder, personal communication). Additional archives from the DK period were assembled in the 1980s by the historical commission of the People's Revolutionary Party of Kampuchea (PRPK). These are known to have survived but are not accessible to outsiders. I am grateful to Richard Arant for this information.

29. Heder, conversations with the author, 1995–1996.

30. See Central Committee of the CPSU, *History of the Communist Party.* According to author's interview with Pierre Brocheux, French Communist Party members in the early 1950s, who would have included Pol Pot, Son Sen, and Ieng Sary, diligently studied this text. On its popularity at Yan'an during the 1940s, see Apter and Saich, *Revolutionary Discourse,* 275. On CPK notions of history, see Chandler, "Seeing Red," and the Party histories translated in Jackson, *Cambodia 1975–1978,* 251–68, and in Chandler, Kiernan, and Boua, *Pol Pot Plans the Future,* 213–26.

31. Engels to Marx, 4 September 1870; see also also Juan Corradi, Patricia Weiss Fagen, and Manuel Antonio Garreton, "Fear: A Cultural and Political Construct," in Corradi, Fagen, et al., eds., *Fear at the Edge*, 1–10.

32. D. Spence, *Narrative Truth and Historical Truth*, and Malcolm, *The Purloined Clinic*, 31–47, a review of Spence's book. See also Ignatieff, *The Warrior's Honor*, 98–99, which speaks of "narratives of explanation" and "moral narratives" that shape our views and color our behavior. In a recent book David Apter compares what he commends as "historians' history" with "'fictive history,' the stories and myths people use to 'order' the events of their lives and circumstances" (*The Legitimation of Violence*, 20).

33. "Decisions of the Central Committee on a Variety of Questions," in Chandler, Kiernan, and Boua, *Pol Pot Plans the Future*, 1–9.

34. See uncatalogued item in DC–Cam archive, dated 12 April 1976. Duch's note is attached to a brief, unmicrofilmed confession by Yim Sombat, a soldier in Division 170, who admitted throwing the grenade, egged on by fellow soldiers. His company commander, Sok Chhan (CMR 145.13), had confessed earlier to ordering the "attack." Duch's covering note on Yim Sombat's confession mentions a two-sided tape recording, one side devoted to questions and the other to Sombat's replies, and observes that Sombat "lost consciousness" at several points in the course of his interrogation.

35. For a list of Division 170 prisoners, see CMR 103.2, "Division 170." Exactly what happened on 2 April remains unclear. Scattered evidence suggests the existence of antigovernment feeling centered in the military in the capital and extending into the Eastern Zone. See Heder interviews, in which a former DK cadre said that "around April 1976 artillery was set up around Chbar Ampeou to bombard Pol Pot's headquarters. . . . The Center found out about the plan and suppressed it before it could be carried out" (45). Again, it is unclear whether the cadre was drawing on his own memories or on what he was told at Party meetings after the event.

36. Chan Chakrei's 849-page confession is CMR 11.7. On his career, see Heder interviews, 44 ff.; Burgler, *Eyes of the Pineapple*, 108–9; and Kiernan, *How Pol Pot Came to Power*, 257. According to Heder (personal communication, drawing on interviews), Chan Chakrei had been hired by Sihanouk's police to infiltrate the CPK but had instead drawn some of his handlers into the CPK. Quinn, "The Pattern and Scope of Violence," 195 ff., quotes Cambodian refugees on Chakrei, who may have been told by cadres about Chakrei's alleged offenses, using information drawn from his confession. See also Chandler, Kiernan, and Boua, *Pol Pot Plans the Future*, in which Hu Nim confesses that Chan Chakrei had told him, "I know how to disguise myself misleadingly. Whenever I went to a new place I would adopt a new name. No one knows my real history" (299). Kampuchea Démocratique, *Livre noir*, states that Chakrei "intended to murder the leaders of the CPK."

37. I am grateful to Richard Arant for pointing out this passage to me and for providing this deft translation. On the timing of Chhouk's arrest, see CMR 123.2, Phuong, November 1978: "Upon Phim's return from abroad, he arrested Chhouk and sent him to the Organization in accordance with the dossier [from] the Organization."

38. On acclimatizing cadres to the Plan, see Chandler, Kiernan, and Boua, *Pol Pot Plans the Future,* 9–35, a relatively upbeat June 1976 speech by a "party spokesman" in the Western Zone. See also CMR 50.14, Keo Meas; CMR 80.36, Ney Saran; CMR 13.28, Chey Suon. A fourth veteran, Keo Moni (Number XVI, CMR 49.15) was a "Hanoi Khmer" arrested in late October 1976. Chhouk's deputy in Sector 24, Pot Oun (CMR 106.28), was not arrested until mid-1977. Two other senior figures linked to the anti-French resistance were Sao Phim and Nhem Ros, the secretaries of the East and Northwest Zones, who in April 1976 became first and second vice presidents of the DK National Presidium under Khieu Samphan. Their names began cropping up in confessions in mid-1976, but Nhem Ros was not arrested until 1978, and Sao Phim committed suicide in May 1978. Meas Mon, arrested after Sao Phim's suicide, suggested in his confession that a full-scale conspiracy was under way in the east in 1976. The Party Center's tardiness in acting on such a conspiracy suggests that it did not exist, that the Center was not confident enough to attack high-ranking cadres in the zone, or that Keo Samnang was backdating the Center's 1978 suspicions of the east to 1976, to enhance its record of clairvoyance. All three possibilities probably were at work.

39. On the foundation of the WPK, see Kiernan, *How Pol Pot Came to Power,* 190–93, and Chandler, *Brother Number One,* 79. The notion that the WPK was a "rival" party is a clear case of the Center and S-21 fabricating or inducing "evidence" consonant with its altered versions of history and the Party Center's habit of giving its opponents multiple labels. Interestingly, many prisoners who confessed to membership in the WPK gave it the three-man cell structure of the CPK, often "remembering" only two other members. Attacks on the "rival party" persisted for the lifetime of DK. On 25 July 1978, for example, the Tuy-Pon notebook carried the notation: "Our task: locate the leading apparatus *(kbal masin)* of the Kampuchean Workers' Party (Vietnamese slave)." By then, Sao Phim, long suspected of filling this position, had already killed himself.

40. CMR 124.17, trans. Steve Heder. CMR 71.10, Meas Mon, for example, confessed that the WPK had been established in 1976 and had five members. Senior cadres often confessed to crimes and memberships that they could well have learned about in study sessions before they were arrested. See also "The Last Plan," 313: "The enemies admitted many names, such as the new CP, the CP of Revolutionary Cambodia, the Workers' Party, the People's Party, the Socialist Party." Once the prisoners had become traitors, by being arrested, the names of the "parties" they had belonged to were of marginal interest—although the admission of membership was crucial.

41. The speech and the plan itself are translated in Chandler, Kiernan, and Boua, *Pol Pot Plans the Future,* 119–63 and 36–118. Willmott, "Analytical Errors," analyzes the conceptual framework of the Four-Year Plan and other CPK initiatives. The announcement of the Party's existence was delayed until September 1977, and the Four-Year Plan was never formally launched.

42. Heder interviews, 61.

43. At the 18 September ceremonies, Pol Pot delivered two eulogies to the Chinese leader (FBIS, 29 September 1976). For Sun Hao's remarks, see FBIS, 21

September 1978. A dutiful DK attack on Deng Xiao Ping, broadcast by Phnom Penh Radio on 1 October, was soon eclipsed by the arrest of the Gang of Four, and on 22 October 1976, after Pol Pot had publicly resumed work as DK's prime minister, he sent a telegram to Beijing condemning the Gang of Four. According to a former Chinese diplomat, the key personnel of the Chinese Embassy in Phnom Penh, all Cambodia experts, remained unchanged (author's interview).

44. On the resignation, FBIS, 30 September 1976. On Ta Mok's and Nuon Chea's reactions to it, Nate Thayer (personal communication). The fact that Ieng Sary recalled the incident clearly in his interview with Steve Heder suggests that the "resignation" may have had something to do with foreign affairs; perhaps, for example, it was done so that Pol Pot could avoid meeting an unwelcome foreign guest. No corroboration for such a hypothesis is available, however.

45. For a translation of these notes, see Chandler, Kiernan, and Boua, *Pol Pot Plans the Future*, 164–76.

46. Chandler, Kiernan, and Boua, *Pol Pot Plans the Future*, 171.

47. CMR 80.36. The pages that survive in Ney Saran's writing are almost illegible, and his full confession, if it ever existed, may have been passed along to the "upper brothers," whose archive has disappeared. A substantial text may have existed at some point, however, for Ney Saran's former bodyguard, interviewed in Ratanakiri by Sara Colm in 1996 on condition of anonymity, recalled Khieu Samphan reading aloud from Saran's confession "for three hours" at a Party meeting (Colm, personal communication). On the other hand, Duch's and Pon's notes to the partial confession that survives suggest that Ney Saran was a very stubborn prisoner whom the Party Center wanted swiftly out of the way. He may well have been killed without providing a detailed confession. See also Kampuchea Démocratique, *Livre noir*, 57 n., which claims that Ney Saran was "a double agent, working both for the Vietnamese and the CIA" to destroy DK.

48. CMR 50.14, in eight sections, dated 25 September–10 October 1976.

49. CMR 50.14, the 27-page document in Keo Meas's handwriting, "Speaking Clearly about the Contradiction in Hanoi about Whether to Fix the Party's Birthday in 1951 or 1960."

50. Chandler, Kiernan, and Boua, *Pol Pot Plans the Future*, 4. Steve Heder (personal communication) has suggested that the CPK's birthday was also discussed at the CPK Party Congress earlier in the year. Keo Meas, under surveillance much of the time, would not have been privy to these discussions.

51. See Steve Heder's unpublished interview with Tiounn Mumm, 4 August 1980: "[In 1973] we took 1951 as the Party's foundation date, but notice that no day or month from 1951 is referred to. Instead we took the day and month of the 1960 Congress." I am grateful to Heder for providing a copy of this interview.

52. FBIS (Vietnam Service), 31 October 1978, before the Vietnamese had access to the S-21 archives. The defector went on to report a massive purge in April 1977. No copies of the circular invalidating CPK membership before 1960 have come to light.

53. *Tung Padevat*, special issue, September–October 1976, 4, following on *Revolutionary Youth*, September 1976, 3. See also Chandler, "Revising the Past in Democratic Kampuchea."

54. CMR 13.28. On Non Suon's arrest, see Heder interviews, 29. The anonymous speaker, a former courier for Non Suon, told Heder that news of Suon's arrest in 1976 had baffled him because "I never heard [Suon] expressing any dissatisfaction with the Party's line either in terms of national construction or . . . national defense." Non Suon's 394-page confession includes biographical sketches of Pol Pot, Nuon Chea, Ieng Sary, Sao Phim, Ta Mok, and Son Sen. The sketches accused Ta Mok, the secretary of the Southwestern Zone, of "individualism and nepotism" and of having an "obdurate and boastful personality"—a reputation that has endured into the 1990s. Non Suon also noted the "rich peasant" backgrounds of Nuon Chea and Ieng Sary and the "landlord" background of Son Sen. It is unclear why these criticisms were solicited or volunteered. They survive only in a handwritten, original text and may never have been forwarded to the Party Center.

55. The December speech urged Cambodians to "make long-term preparations for guerrilla war." Chandler, Kiernan, and Boua, *Pol Pot Plans the Future,* 191. See also Kiernan, *The Pol Pot Regime,* 357 ff. DK hostility toward Vietnam may well have been fueled by the decision taken at the Fourth Congress of the Vietnamese Workers' Party in December 1976 to forge ahead with establishing "special relationships" with Laos and Cambodia. The CPK does not seem to have been consulted about this decision: see Chen, *China's War with Vietnam,* 33 ff. Vairon's magisterial "Du Parti Indochinois" provides informed speculation about this crucial period, drawing on interviews with Khmer and Vietnamese participants.

56. CMR 139.15, Sean An, and CMR 35.10, Hak Seang Lay Ni. See also CMR 35.28, Hak Padet, confession of Hak Seang Lay Ni's wife, and CMR 174.14, Touch Kamdoeun, a DK diplomat who had studied in France and confessed that "students in France learned to be happy like Europeans and hence how to oppress people." Kamdoeun, the brother of the senior DK official Touch Phoeun, "died of illness" in S-21. Picq, *Au-delà du ciel,* 99–100, recounts a study session presided over by Ieng Sary in early 1977 in which these offenders were lumped together with Koy Thuon, Sua Va Si, and Touch Phoeun, who were incarcerated in S-21 at the time. See also Picq, "I Remember What Ieng Sary Did."

57. Jackson, *Cambodia 1975–1978,* 307. When he was brought to Phnom Penh in early 1976, Koy Thuon was grilled at first about his sexual transgressions. CMR 140.12, Sbauv Hin, the former secretary of (northern) Division 310, names twenty women who had "immoral encounters" with Koy Thuon, and in Thuon's wife's confession (CMR 162.18, Yun) she refers to him as "the contemptible Thuon" *(a-Thuon)* and complains of his infidelities.

58. "The Last Plan," in Jackson, *Cambodia 1975–1978,* 307. The insults suggest that Koy Thuon may have inspired genuine affection among his followers.

59. As microfilmed, Koy Thuon's confession (CMR 50.19) covers only 34 pages, drawn from three interrogation sessions in early March 1977. The text held as items 916–20 at DC–Cam, on the other hand, is over 600 pages, drawn from 45 interrogation sessions from February to April 1977. The DC–Cam copy, which includes the material microfilmed by Cornell, has copious notations by Duch and Son Sen. The confession text from S-21 has been severely

culled. Even so, the longer text in DC–Cam may still be incomplete, for several pages of retyped material, obtained from a confidential source in 1997, that purported to come from a Koy Thuon confession text held in yet another archive, do not duplicate material in the DC–Cam copy.

60. Heder, "Racism, Marxism, Labelling," 126 ff., argues this case in detail. So-called "democracy activists" not mentioned already included Mau Khem Nuon (alias Phom), secretary of S-71, the CPK school, Phok Chhay (alias Toch), who worked in Office 870, and Siet Chhe (alias Tum), who had been the secretary of Sector 22 in the Eastern Zone and later worked under Son Sen in the military general staff.

61. On these uprisings, see Paul, "Plot Details Filter Through"; Burgler, *Eyes of the Pineapple,* 118–19; Kiernan, *The Pol Pot Regime,* 342 ff.; and Quinn, "The Pattern and Scope of Violence," 200 ff. It is possible that refugees interviewed by Paul in 1978 recalled accusations made in cadre study sessions. See also DC–Cam document L0001414, a memorandum from Office 401 summarizing purges in the Northern Zone in 1977.

62. The latter group included the nationalist intellectual Han Tun Hak, who had attended the Lycée Sisowath with Koy Thuon and became prime minister of the Lon Nol government in 1972. According to one of his parliamentary colleagues, Hak had been active in pro-Chinese circles, alongside Hu Nim, Phok Chay, and Koy Thuon, in the 1960s (author's interview with Keuky Lim). As prime minister, he had tried to open negotiations with the Khmer Rouge using these pre-1970 connections. At S-21 his rebuffed initiatives became acts of betrayal set in motion by Koy Thuon.

63. Tuy-Pon notebook entry for 25 July 1978.

64. See "The Last Plan" in Jackson, *Cambodia 1975–1978,* 309: "Koy Thuon was uncovered, dismissed and replaced by another traitor."

65. Heder, *Pol Pot and Khieu Samphan,* suggests that Samphan was the driving force behind the 1977 purges of "democracy activists" whose life stories resembled his own. By 15 April 1977, indeed, Samphan was speaking of the necessity to "suppress all stripes of enemies at all times" (Barnett, Kiernan, and Boua, "Bureaucracy of Death," 669). Samphan defected to the Phnom Penh government in December 1998.

66. See Chandler, Kiernan, and Boua, *Pol Pot Plans the Future,* 227–318. The Cambodian text is CMR 34.19. Hu Nim's cell at S-21 is the only one identified with a particular prisoner at the Museum of Genocidal Crimes.

67. Kiernan, *The Pol Pot Regime,* 351.

68. Burgler, *Eyes of the Pineapple,* 120 ff.; Chandler, Kiernan, and Boua, *Pol Pot Plans the Future,* 291.

69. Chandler, Kiernan, and Boua, *Pol Pot Plans the Future,* 293. Hu Nim's wife, Yar Law (CMR 185.8), arrested with him, asked the CPK to spare her small child, "who is still unable to read," and offered the child to the Party.

70. I am grateful to Richard Arant for pointing out this segment of Siet Chhe's confession and for providing a draft translation. Siet Chhe's wife, Pun Sothea (CMR 121.2), was arrested in early 1978. For Siet Chhe's confession, see appendix.

71. Heder, *Pol Pot and Khieu Samphan,* 17.

72. See for example CMR 12.4, Chim Chun, who "allowed cattle to eat rice": CMR 16.15, Chan Oeun, who confessed to burning and flooding rice fields, killing five hundred cows, ruining six hundred hectares of rice land, and allowing people to flee to Thailand; and CMR 127.12, Roeun Run, who "didn't allow people to grow rice."

73. See the discussions in Vickery, "Democratic Kampuchea," 116–22, and Kiernan, *The Pol Pot Regime,* 216–50. On Samlaut, see Chandler, *Tragedy,* 163–67, and the detailed account in Kiernan and Boua, *Peasants and Politics,* 166–205.

74. On Khek Pen, see CMR 48.20 and Kiernan, *The Pol Pot Regime,* 245. *Tung Padevat,* October–November 1977, 4. In "The Last Plan," Khek Pen was castigated for using "new people" who were "all CIA agents" to "run various technical services, control mobile units, etc. In so doing, they tried to establish a treacherous state administration . . . or to create a state within a state." Jackson, *Cambodia 1975–1978,* 312.

75. Nhem Ros's confession (CMR 78.21) in the archive is only thirty pages long and may well have been culled after 1979. Nhem Ros had worked with his fellow northwesterners Sieu Heng and Nuon Chea in the northwest in the first Indochina war and visited communist cadres in Office 100 in 1964.

76. Vickery, *Cambodia 1975–1982,* 121.

77. Chandler, Kiernan, and Boua, *Pol Pot Plans the Future,* 56. As Kiernan points out (*Pol Pot Regime,* 246), the Northwest Zone was expected to produce the bulk of the nation's rice under the Four-Year Plan. Unlike the other zones, however, it was not allocated a quota of its harvests for local consumption.

78. Becker, *When the War Was Over,* 246–47.

79. CMR 118.11, trans. Steve Heder. See also *Tung Padevat,* July 1978, "Pay Attention to Purging the Hidden Enemies Boring from Within": "[Enemies] have starved the people and made them thirsty, caused them to have nothing to wear and no place to stay. They wreck water, seed rice, compost, draft animals, plows and harrows, digging tools, spoons, plates and pots, wreck everything . . . as long as doing so makes our people hunger" (13). See also CMR 124.17, Von Vet, speaking of industrial cadres: "Some of the time [the workers] could be provoked to work too hard and this made them sick and tired of the collective regime." In Sector 4, in the Northwest Zone, people who complained about inadequate food were accused of being "free" (CMR 37.2, Hang Bun).

80. On purges in the Northwest Zone in 1977 and 1978, see Jackson, *Cambodia 1975–1978,* 105–7.

81. See, for example, Kamm, "Cambodian Refugees"; Kamm, *Cambodia,* 130 ff.; and Kramer, "Cambodia's Communist Regime."

82. Burchett, *The China, Cambodia, Vietnam Triangle,* 160.

83. FBIS, 4 October 1977. Interestingly, only two other members of the Party Center, Nuon Chea and Khieu Samphan, were named in the speech. Heder, "Racism, Marxism, Labelling," 139, 142. The September attacks, proposed by Sao Phim and Ta Mok, had been approved by the Party Center and arguably backfired when the Vietnamese launched a larger and better-coordinated counteroffensive in November. See also Chanda, *Brother Enemy,* 84 ff.

84. CMR 96.20, a seventeen-page leaflet dated 3 January 1978, titled "How to Defeat the Vietnamese." The target of Vietnamese to be killed was also broadcast over Phnom Penh radio: Kiernan, *The Pol Pot Regime,* 393–94. See also CMR 96.10, a shorter leaflet from Office 870 offering a general amnesty in an effort to gain support for the war. The first leaflet is discussed in Kiernan, *The Pol Pot Regime,* 387–88. Tuy-Pon notebook, entry for 21 May 1978, discussing the 1977–1978 campaign, notes that Khmer "who sacrificed their lives" (*poli,* a respectful term, favored by DK) were outnumbered ten to one by Vietnamese "heads" (*kbal,* a classifier usually reserved for animals) who had "croaked" (*n'goap,* a slang word rarely used for human deaths).

85. Tuy-Pon notebook, entry for 3 June 1978, referring to an earlier document.

86. Kiernan, *The Pol Pot Regime,* 386–90; Heder, "Racism, Marxism, Labelling," 138 ff. and *Kampuchea Dossier* I. See also Richard Arant's interview with Lay Samon, a "Hanoi Khmer" who began training on the Cambodian border in February 1978. *Livre noir,* 75: "[The Vietnamese] were able to advance rapidly thanks to their agents in the interior of Kampuchea."

87. For a discussion of this image, see chapter 5. See also "Pay Attention to Sweeping out Concealed Enemies," *Tung Padevat,* July 1978: "The concealed enemies who were running-dog agents of the Vietnamese . . . were noxious to the uttermost and of the uttermost danger" (4).

88. Heder, *Pol Pot and Khieu Samphan,* 21, citing evidence from the confessions of Sok Thuok (alias Von Vet, CMR 124.17) and Chou Chet (CMR 12.22). See also Kampuchea Démocratique, *Livre noir,* 76–77.

89. CMR 124.17, Sok Thuok, trans. Steve Heder. See also Chandler, *Tragedy,* 296, citing survivors' memories, and Von Vet's confession (CMR 124.17) quoting Sao Phim as saying, "We must work secretly and with care to establish a Party which is the reverse of the CPK. We plan to spend money again; there will be salaries and badges of rank. There will be markets. These are our goals."

90. For a colleague's assessment of Sao Phim's psychology at this time, see Richard Arant's interview with Yi Yaun; Kiernan, "Wild Chickens," 188–89; and Kiernan, *The Pol Pot Regime,* 392 ff.

91. It is possible that Chou Chet (CMR 12.22) had been involved in plotting a military uprising in the zone. See Kiernan, *The Pol Pot Regime,* 391 ff. Different portions of his wife's confession are filed under Im Ly (CMR 39.23) and Im Nan (CMR 41.8). Proud of her years of service to the Party, she courageously praised her mentor, Keo Meas. The "string of traitors" attached to CMR 41.8 is over two hundred names long. See also "The Last Plan," which names Chou Chet as a coconspirator with Sao Phim and Nhem Ros.

92. Author's interviews with Kok Sros and Nhem En.

93. The details of Sao Phim's last days are from Kiernan, "Wild Chickens," Richard Arant's interview with Yi Yaun (an eyewitness), and Kiernan, *The Pol Pot Regime,* 400.

94. Kiernan, *The Pol Pot Regime,* 405 ff., and Kiernan, *Cambodia: The Eastern Zone Massacres.* See also Heder's interpretation of these events in "Racism, Marxism, Labelling," 149–51. Because the Eastern Zone cadres "were skeptical about the wisdom and humanity of building socialism at a

breakneck pace," Heder argues, they were also, in the eyes of the Party Center, "objectively" Vietnamese, and, in Heder's phrasing, "laxly organized, traitorously led and wrongly indoctrinated."

95. Confessions implicating Son Sen (all from late 1978) include CMR 21.25, Chhay Kim Hor; CMR 43.10, In Nat; CMR 159.11, Sun Ty; CMR 159.16, Soeung Kun; and CMR 165.17, Yang Kon. See also Heder, "Racism, Marxism, Labelling."

96. "Learning from Important Experiences in Fulfilling the Party's First Semester 1978 Tasks," *Tung Padevat*, special issue, May–June 1978, 17–33, and "Guidelines from the Central Committee of the CPK 20 June 1978," uncatalogued item in S-21 archive. See also Vickery, *Cambodia 1975–1982*, 141.

97. Steve Heder's interview with Mey Mann.

98. David Ashley's translation of the tape-recorded trial of Pol Pot at Anlong Veng, 25 July 1997. I am grateful to Ashley for this text. For a description of the trial, see Thayer, "Brother Number Zero."

99. CMR 161.3, Yann. Similarly, CMR 56.3, Ky Chin, another former interrogator, noted: "Interrogations need not be clear because if they are the Organization will catch everybody." In 1980 a survivor of the regime told Heder that the logic of the system would eventually have killed everyone in Cambodia except Pol Pot. For a Chinese parallel, see Stephen Averill, "The Origins of the Futian Incident," in Saich and Van de Ven, eds., *New Perspectives*, 79–115. In passing Averill notes the "remarkable compatibility of moral purpose and mindless persecution" in the Chinese Cultural Revolution (109). Averill's phrase applies nicely to *santebal*'s operations.

CHAPTER FOUR. FRAMING THE QUESTIONS

1. Vann Nath's interview with Sara Colm. See also CMR 27.1, Em Yan, in which the interrogator notes, "He says he doesn't know why he was arrested," and CMR 33.14, Hang Nguon, in which the interrogator "asked him why the Organization had arrested him." For similar formulations, see CMR 42.11, Im Som Ol; CMR 59.7, Keo Kun; CMR 62.12, Ly Hok Bay; CMR 150.13, Sim Yet; and CMR 151.35, Sok Sareth. CMR 59.16, Krin Lean, has Mam Nay's notes under "reasons for arrest": two of these suggestions are preceded by "perhaps."

2. For other Communist examples, see Solzhenitsyn, *Gulag Archipelago* I, 137 ff., and Shentalinsky, *Arrested Voices*, 24, which recounts Isaac Babel being asked in 1939: "How can you reconcile [your] declaration of innocence with the fact of your arrest?" See also Gilboa, *Confess! Confess!* 128 ff., which describes Gilboa's interrogator saying in 1941: "Cut the foolishness! The NKVD never makes mistakes. If you are here, that means that everything is known. . . . We know, but nevertheless you will say it; you will talk." See also Rittenberg and Bennett, *The Man Who Stayed Behind*, 392: "[In 1968 in Beijing] I was visited by a team of investigators [who] gave no clue about the charges against me. They simply admonished me to think about my guilt." Similarly, Picq, *Au delà du ciel*, 123, recalls the DK foreign minister, Ieng Sary, addressing a meeting of cadres: "As for the last traitor, it's for you to find him!" Mouth Sophea (personal communication) has recalled "livelihood meetings" in Battambang between 1976 and

1978 in which cadres would periodically single someone out and say, "The Organization knows all about your guilt. All you have to do is to tell the Organization about it." See also Ofshe, "Coerced Confessions," 1–15.

3. Gay, *Freud,* 172, 321. Gay calls Freud a "Schliemann of the mind" (326). See also Schorske, "Freud." Irina Paperno kindly provided this reference.

4. For a discussion of these issues see Spence, *Narrative Truth,* 81 ff.; Crews, *The Memory Wars,* and Ofshe and Watters, *Making Monsters.* When Crews writes that "the therapist's and the patient's joint biographical artifact becomes, as it were, the perfect crime—but with the patient also serving as victim of her own concoction" (26), he might have been speaking about interrogations at S-21.

5. Ofshe and Watters, 40; Kotkin, *Magnetic Mountain,* 336.

6. CMR 157.9.

7. Trans. Steve Heder. Sbauv Hin's wife, Prum Nhar (CMR 119.20), who had worked with him in Division 310, was arrested a month later. See also CMR 17.24, Chey Peng, who had worked before his arrest in the economic support unit of S-21. Told by the interrogator that if he told the truth he would be released, he knew the interrogator was lying and wrote, "I have no hope . . . with these fetters on, I'm as good as dead."

8. CMR 140.12. The full passage reads, "With regard to the accusations of betrayal of the Party and the revolution, I do not concur. Even if I am going to die, I will die as someone who was loyal to the Party and the revolution. If I am to die, I ask the Party to seek justice for me. Only the Party knows my biography."

9. Kundera, *The Art of the Novel,* 84. The process described by Kundera ends with the "criminal" eager for punishment. Kundera is commenting on Kafka, remarking that "the court [in *The Trial*] is impervious to proof." By implication Kundera is dealing with post–1949 Czechoslovakian police procedures.

10. Horowitz, *Taking Lives,* 185, citing Solzhenitsyn. Chan notebook, entry for 21 January 1978. See also Tuy-Pon notebook, entry for 18 September 1978: "We must trick [the enemy] so as to conceal our intentions, but we must know how to be inquisitive, and when questioning we must dig and claw from beginning to end."

11. CMR 53.2. In a passage composed a month later, But adds: "As long as I was asked [about Son Sen] I was going to reply, because to conceal this [material] was very dangerous." See also CMR 24.27, Duk Sambo, held for twenty-seven days in Battambang, where he gave security officers the names of his coconspirators before he was sent on to S-21.

12. CMR 182.13. By 1977, however, the code name was already known to a few outsiders. Uon Sokho, rummaging in his memory for an offense, confessed to telling someone else the location of S-21.

13. Chandler, Kiernan, and Boua, *Pol Pot Plans the Future,* 312. Hu Nim cited the case of a colleague, Prom Samar, who had said at a self-criticism meeting: "I am an enemy whom the Party must smash." Hu Nim continued: "The group that took part in the session concluded: 'Prom Sam Ar is an enemy.' Prom Sam Ar was then reported to the Organization and Brother Haem (Khieu Samphan) ordered further surveillance." The culprit committed suicide before he could be arrested.

14. See Locard, "Le Goulag des khmers rouges," an excellent summary of research so far. In 1978, Pol Pot told Belgian visitors: "We have no prisons and we

do not even use the word 'prison'" (FBIS, 26 September 1978); technically he was correct, in that prerevolutionary jails were not used by DK. See also Etcheson, "Centralized Terror in Democratic Kampuchea"; Locard and Moeung Son, *Prisonnier de l'Angkar;* and Kiernan, *The Pol Pot Regime,* 346 ff. On the transmission of supplementary documents, see CMR 81.7, Nam Dul, whose interrogation from Sector 505 accompanied him to S-21, and document D-123, DC–Cam, 20 May 1977, a letter from Office 401 in Sector 32 to the Organization, transmitting fourteen serious offenders and listing thirty-five less serious ones being held back for "education." DC–Cam items 1066–68 transmit prisoners from Division 502; 1120 sends along three suspects from Kompong Thom, and N0001880 transmits some preliminary interrogations from Sector 21. The dossiers of CMR 87.37, Nuon, and CMR 166.13, Yos Thoeurn, include data forwarded to S-21 by the security office of Division 310, to which both men had belonged. CMR 80.30, Meas Em, and CMR 4.25, Buy Boeun, describe *santebal* operations in the Northwestern Zone. See also DC–Cam document L0045, in which Met, a cadre of Division 402, reports to Son Sen that he has sent "more than fifty no-goods *[puok min l'oo]* to S-21"—a rare reference to the prison in a document produced outside its walls.

15. Steve Heder's transcribed conversation in 1985 about S-21 with David Hawk. I am grateful to Hawk for providing me with a copy of the transcript.

16. CMR 43.11.

17. CMR 120.4.

18. CMR 126.20.

19. On sustained fatigue and suggestibility in interrogations, see Feldman, *Formations of Violence.* Regarding the prisoner telling lies, the parallel with psychoanalysis, although fortuitous, is interesting, for, as Janet Malcolm has remarked in *The Purloined Clinic,* "Lies are of the deepest interest to analysts. They are like dreams. They lead somewhere. . . . Mistrust is the analyst's stock in trade, an attitude from which he can never relent" (41). See also G. Gudjonsson, "The Application of Interrogative Suggestibility to Police Interviewing," in Schumaker, ed., *Human Suggestibility,* 280–88.

20. CMR 99.7. See also CMR 87.11, Nong Chan, in which the interrogator lists "what was already asked" before he came to S-21: "Biography; why did the Organization arrest him; is he an enemy or not; has he had political training?" See also an uncatalogued notebook from S-21, dated 1976 and 1977, in which a proposed sequence of questions for interrogators reads: "Are you a traitor? A traitor since when? Background and age? Activities over the years? Why are you a traitor?"

21. Author's interview with Kok Sros; Lionel Vairon's interview with Pha Thachan. See also Tuy-Pon notebook, entry for 8 October 1978, which notes that workers at the prison were still being encouraged to "insult the prisoners and press them hard; then the questions will become easier."

22. Moise, *Land Reform in China and Vietnam,* 246. Although it seems likely that many Cambodians were trained in such methods by the Vietnamese in the 1950s and 1960s, when the two parties were close, no documentation for this training has come to light.

23. CMR 174.2, Thong Vann, wrote later: "I know that the Organization is quick-witted and just. Respected Party Organization! I am living in total dark-

ness and have lost mastery." For another vivid example of Communist interrogation techniques, including both questions and answers, see Brankov, "János Kádar," drawn from a tape recording.

24. CMR 138.11, trans. Richard Aran. Using the Khmer text, I have slightly altered the translation.

25. CMR 118.20, trans. Richard Arant. See also item N0001880 in DC–Cam archive, reflecting two sessions with Chaom Savat in Sector 21 on 4–5 June 1976. These implicate numerous personnel from the sector as well as Keo Meas, Ney Sarann, Chhouk, Koy Thuon, and Tiv Ol. In CMR 67.13, Loeung Souk, 96 of the 170 people named in the "string of traitors" had already been arrested.

26. Tuy-Pon notebook, entry for 18 December 1977. The same aphorism is found in the unsigned notebook from the period "Lothi Mak-Lenin," 73.

27. CMR 99.7. CMR 99.14, "The New Plan," probably from 1977, gives S-21's motto as: "Make storming attacks as mightily as possible so as to serve the movement, the masses, and the splendid great leap forward." The text seems to echo CMR 96.4, "Building and Expanding the Party in Accordance with Certain Marxist-Leninist Teachings," undated, but pre-1975. The four "laws" of dialectical materialism discussed in CMR 96.4 were that everything is interrelated, everything changes, everything undergoes transformation, and everything is contradictory. Mouth Sophea has pointed out (personal communication) that the first two "laws" resembled well-known Buddhist teachings and employ Buddhist philosophical terms.

28. CMR 141.20.

29. Steve Heder's unpublished interview, cited in Burgler, *The Eyes of the Pineapple,* 160.

30. Son Sen's memorandum is an uncatalogued item in DC–Cam archive. See Tuy-Pon notebook, entry for 20 April 1978: "If a prisoner's answer implicates a very important person, prepare a summary and submit it to [the administrators] for an opinion." No such summaries have survived. See also Tuy-Pon notebook, entry for 18 December 1977: "If we overvalue the enemies, they will lead us into pessimism. We will see the Party as black, the army as black, the people as black. If, on the other hand, we undervalue the enemies, we will lose our revolutionary vigilance and they will be able to destroy us."

31. Untitled cover page in an uncatalogued, undated cadre notebook, DC–Cam archive. The previous pages in the notebook have been torn out. Subsequent ones, in Tuy's handwriting, date from 1978. The passage adds that when enemies are discovered, the "self-confidence of the masses will rise and the revolution will prosper." See also document 1128, DC–Cam, minutes of a Communist Youth meeting at the prison: "Guards are lazy, fearful of difficulties, and shy *(khmas)* toward their superiors *(bong)*."

32. Douglas Niven interview with Kok Sros.

33. Heder interviews, 59. See also Rittersporn, "The State against Itself," which refers to "the unpredictable, incomprehensible and treacherous daily reality of the [Soviet] system" (95).

34. See CMR 88.17, Ngin Toi; CMR 104.17, Ou Yan; CMR 154.31, Sao Say; and CMR 159.5, Soeum Peou. The term "discard," along with "smash" *(komtec),* was used to signify execution at S-21.

35. See, for example, CMR 62.1, Leang Chan Hen (328 pp.); CMR 64.7, Ly Vay (366 pp.); and CMR 65.7, Lam Samreth (304 pp.), among many.

36. See CMR 137.9, Sar Ngon, and CMR 140.11, Sar Phon; both date from October 1975.

37. Tuy-Pon notebook, entry for 26 April 1978. The confessions held in the DC–Cam archive probably constitute half of those sent to the "upper brothers" and were probably those handled by Son Sen. When the confessions were transmitted to DC–Cam by Cambodian authorities in 1997, they came mingled with material from the DK era related to defense matters, that is, those for which Son Sen was responsible.

38. For Soviet parallels, see Conquest, *The Great Terror,* and Khlevnyuk, "The Objectives of the Great Terror."

39. Document from Interrogation Group 5, uncatalogued item in DC–Cam archive, 14 December 1976. See also CMR 151.35, Sok Sarith, which carries the notation "questions to be asked."

40. It seems likely that these forms have survived by accident and that similar ones, destroyed on a daily basis, guided the interrogators' work for hundreds of other prisoners.

41. On the genre, see Rossi, *A Communist Party in Action,* and *Tung Padevat,* special issue, December 1975–January 1976, 40–41. Burgler suggests astutely that "the [self-critical] biography . . . abolishes time as all elements of the past are reinterpreted in the light of the necessities of the present" (*The Eyes of the Pineapple,* 114).

42. Apter and Saich, *Revolutionary Discourse,* 264. DK did not follow the Chinese and Soviet practice of circulating biographies of revolutionary heroes, let alone those of the men and women in the Party Center. At S-21, the prisoners' life stories, as well as their bodies, were under constant surveillance and subject to filing and revision. In *Discipline and Punish* Foucault speculates on the simultaneity of interest in biography as a genre and the development of modern punitive systems (319–20 n. 14).

43. Document 1129 from DC–Cam archive records a self-criticism session of Communist Youth Group workers held at S-21 on 14 February 1977, in which several interrogators assess their "strong points" and "shortcomings" in their own handwriting. As the text was passed around the group, people could probably read what their predecessors had written. Knowing the "shortcomings" of one's colleagues enabled one to accuse them of these faults at other meetings. Faults, unlike strong points, were considered cumulatively, so in criticizing themselves people had to tread carefully between making their shortcomings too trivial and too severe.

44. Apter and Saich, *Revolutionary Discourse,* 293. Similar procedures, of course, are employed by many secret societies.

45. Author's interviews with Kok Sros and Nhem En.

46. On Ratanakiri, see Locard, "Le Goulag des khmers rouges," 148; *Tung Padevat,* special issue, December 1975–January 1976, 8. See *also Tung Padevat,* March 1978, 37–53, translated in Jackson, *Cambodia 1975–1978,* 296: "Scrutinize autobiographies meticulously." For Pol Pot's statement, see Chandler, Kiernan, and Boua, *Pol Pot Plans the Future,* 203. On the

importance of biographies in DK, see Someth May, *Cambodian Witness*, 195–97.

47. CMR 13.28, trans. Steve Heder.

48. See "Chea Kak's Life Story," with notes by Mam Nay, 24 April 1977 (uncatalogued item in DC–Cam archive), which uses the dimensions of his parents' house and land, the number of livestock, and the style of roofing to determine his class status. Him Huy told Peter Maguire that he had to alter his biography once cadres had verified that his parents' house had a tile roof. Although Pol Pot claimed in 1977 that most Cambodians were poor peasants, those in the "middle peasant" category probably accounted for the largest portion of the population, according to Delvert, *Le paysan cambodgien*, 490 ff. See also Willmott, "Analytical Errors." DK class categories are listed with commentaries in Jackson, *Cambodia 1975–1978*, 99–100, drawing in part on the tables in Summers, "The CPK: Secret Vanguard," 15.

49. CMR 129.3, Sary Chheang, however, confesses to having rich parents and mentions the number of cattle, water buffaloes, and elephants that his parents owned.

50. For a discussion of these categories, which were used by villagers themselves, see May Ebihara, "Revolution and Reformulation in Kampuchean Village Culture," in Ablin and Hood, eds., *The Cambodian Agony*, 20. Ebihara (personal communication) has suggested that no connection existed between wealth and power at the village level. See also Hinton, "Why Did You Kill?" 99–100.

51. See "A Short Guide to the Application of Party Statutes," in Carney, *Communist Party Power*, 56 ff. See also CMR 21.25, Chhay Keum Hor, who confessed that when he was recruited into the CIA in 1962 by Son Sen, CIA and CPK statutes were both discussed at study sessions. CMR 26.3, Dim Saroeun, recalls "saluting the CIA flag, though I forget now what it looked like"; CMR 87.8, Nuth Kap, locates the initiation ceremony in the U.S. Embassy in Phnom Penh, and CMR 136.14, Son Hoeun, claimed to have saluted a flag "with the image of a star." In early 1976, mimeographed questionnaires prepared at S-21 traced several prisoners' employment history, wages, and sponsors inside the CIA. See CMR 2.16, Chou By; CMR 173.5, Tan Pheng; and CMR 184.11, Va Heng. The form was scrapped after a few months.

52. DC–Cam Document 60–84, from security office, Northern Zone, 22 June 1976. The American's name transliterates as Zhombu Douvinh. I'm grateful to Chhang Youk of DC–Cam for bringing this document to my attention.

53. For Khieu Thirith reference, see CMR 64.12, Lauk Chhot. CMR 173.13, Liang Kiny, who had studied in West Germany, claimed to have been recruited as a spy in 1967 at Kep by an American named Vikeri, and CMR 78.12, Men Tul, a "Hanoi Khmer," claimed that he had been brought into the CIA in Hanoi in 1956 by an American "tourist." See also CMR 131.3, Sok Knol, who claimed that his CIA recruiter was "Johnson." Sok Knol also quoted a colleague, who had not seen his wife for a year, as saying: "That was why we are looking for a road to happiness . . . namely the CIA," while CMS 178.20, Truong Sin, stated that "the CIA has prestige and an extravagant lifestyle." CMR 166.28, Yusip Ganthy, a DK diplomat, claimed that he was recruited first by an agent named "Anderson" and again while a diplomat in Stockholm in

1971 by "Johnson." Ganthy then described a Soviet "plan" to airlift tanks to Phnom Penh and to invade Cambodia.

54. CMR 161.4, Yin Ron, and CMR 184.11, Va Heng. See also CMR 127.5, Penh Sopheap, Von Vet's daughter.

55. Heder conversation with Hawk. For the Chinese reference, see Dittmer and Ruoxi, *Ethics and Rhetoric*, 44. CMR 188.36, an administrative document from S-21, contains an organizational chart of the "CIA" under Lon Nol that seems to be coterminous with the regime. Duch's obsession with the "CIA" led him to authorize a translation into Khmer of a global directory of CIA agents, published in English in East Berlin in the 1960s. Both texts are uncatalogued items in the S-21 archive. See also Tuy-Pon notebook, entry for 16 July 1978, which claims that the "CIA" in Cambodia split in 1954 into those treacherous agents sent north to Hanoi and those who remained behind.

56. White, *Policies of Chaos*. For examples of this and an interesting discussion, see Lu Xiuyuan, "A Step toward Understanding Popular Violence," 533–62.

57. "Involvement with foreign intelligence services" was a mantra so deeply embedded in Soviet thought that Khrushchev used it in his "secret speech" in 1956 when he accused Lavrenty Beria, Stalin's hanging judge in the 1930s, of working for (unnamed) foreign intelligence agencies. See Ali, ed., *The Stalinist Legacy*, 258. See also CMR 174.15, Touch Phoeun, a senior DK figure, who claimed that the anti-Communist massacres in Indonesia in 1965 and 1966, which he refers to as a coup d'état, had been caused by CIA agents "burrowing inside" the Indonesian Communist Party.

58. CMR 99.19 gives the text of the speech.

59. Thayer, "Day of Reckoning." Once Pol Pot had been shunted aside by his colleagues in 1997, the man who replaced him, Ta Mok (probably "Brother Number Three" for much of the DK era), called his former mentor a "Vietnamese agent." Interestingly, the notion that Pol Pot was always in some way working for Vietnamese interests (which is to say, against those of the Cambodian people) is widespread among survivors of the regime (Judy Ledgerwood, personal communication).

60. CMR 141.3, Sam Hean, described six "faults" *(komho)* that had led to his arrest. Similarly, CMR 160.15, Yen Kun, names sexual encounters as his "weak points." See also Locard, *Petit livre rouge:* "A comrade with many shortcomings equals an enemy" (145).

61. CMR 166.13, Yos Thoeurn; CMR 36.16, Huy Savorn; and CMR 88.3, Neou Kantha, an interrogator who claimed that he had been asked to pull a plow "just like a prisoner," cited in Vickery, *Cambodia 1975–1982*, 344 n. 45. On "trusties," see Levi, *The Drowned and the Saved*, 22–51, and Sofsky, *The Order of Terror*, 130 ff. For staff assertions of discomfort, see CMR 20.19, Chon Chhay; CMR 22.23, Chau Kut; and CMR 46.6, Khleang Hu.

62. On religion, CMR 47.17, Korm Ron; CMR 160.25, You Phon; and CMR 173.16, Tan Doeun; on rank, see *pravatt'rup* of Chea Kak, uncatalogued item in DC–Cam archive, in which this S-21 guard remarked that he had joined the revolution in part "because I wanted a reputation and I wanted others to admire me."

63. CMR 87.2 and CMR 58.4.

64. CMR 107.16 and CMR 56.28, Khuth Boeurn. See also CMR 144.1, Sok Hak : "I encouraged people to be corrupt, to drink liquor, to overeat, to chase women, to do anything that made them happy"; and CMR 169.13, Tong Chun: "I can't survive in the revolution; it gives me no pleasure." CMR 105.28, Ou Sou Neng, remarked that "we can't figure out what's going on in the revolution or where it's going." Has Saran (CMR 33.5) lamented that "all my relationships are personal, disorganized, and lack the Party's permission." While pursuing policies that promised rapid elevations in status, improved material welfare, and a more ascetic life style, the CPK's intolerance of "happiness" contributed to its unpopularity. For a sympathetic view of Communist asceticism, however, see CMR 119.23, Pou Labine, a female Party member, who confessed proudly: "I have been in the revolution for five years. I have built myself by reducing freedom-ism, family-ism, factionalism, and meritism."

65. Interestingly, landless people on the margins of prerevolutionary rural life—gamblers, cattle thieves, and drunkards—had frequently been recruited into the anti-French resistance (Thong Thel and Sok Pirun, personal communications). In this regard, see Wise, "Eradicating the Old Dandruff," in which a former Cambodian schoolteacher, then a refugee in Thailand, is quoted: "M'sieur, Cambodia is governed by drunkards, thieves, savages, barbarians and classless illiterates." May Ebihara (personal communication) notes that the litany reflected clichéd views of "bad characters" in prerevolutionary, rural Cambodia.

66. See Chhin Chhum confession, BBK-Kh 418 in DC–Cam archive.

67. CMR 19.10.

68. CMR 24.8.

69. CMR 183.18.

70. CMR 88.2. See also CMR 48.8, Khom Khan: "In Vietnam, there are markets, women, and alcohol, as well as motorcycles to ride. No one is ordered around." These statements were presumably allowed to stand because they provided evidence of the pro-Vietnamese bias of those who made them.

71. CMR 23.13.

72. CMR 55.5. CMR 26.32, E Che, a woman enrolled in the CPK by Son Sen's wife, also played on the contrast between "rest" and "storming attacks."

73. CMR 56.24.

74. CMR 56.14. See also CMR 55.5, Kae San: "Chhin said that having things the way they are means lots of hardship. His wife was in Phnom Penh and he was in Kompong Chhnang. What sort of happiness was there in going to see her once a year?" (trans. Steve Heder); CMR 141.20, Sav Kang, a veteran revolutionary who reported another party member saying that the separation of husbands from their wives was "very extreme" and that resistance to the policy might "lead to a second revolution."

75. Scott, *Domination and the Arts of Resistance.* But see the adages quoted by CMR 108.2, Pech Ny, in 1978, as "current in Mondulkiri": "The Vietnamese have taken all our land already, but the Organization says we're winning," and "Work all day, work all night, where does the strength to do the work come from?"

76. CMR 123.26. This confession is only two pages long.

77. CMR 35.2, 37. In the confession, Ho also attacked the collectivization of private property.

78. CMR 84.27.

79. CMR 173.16. See also CMR 128.9 for Srey Daung's astute assessment: "The Party is moving too quickly to the left. I've stopped believing in it, I want to fight against it so it won't go so fast."

80. Douglas Niven's interview with Nhem En.

81. CMR 39.25. The relatively frank biographical sketches prepared by Non Suon (CMR 13.28), while uncritical of Brothers Number One and Two, are exceptions to this rule.

82. CMR 123.2, as quoted in Steve Heder, *Pol Pot and Khieu Samphan*, 22. Phuong went on to speak of the people's "unbearable pain and burning sorrow" and to describe DK as a "black and stultifying state."

83. CMR 12.22 (trans. Steve Heder). See also CMR 76.16, Mau Khem Nuon, a high-ranking cadre who quoted a colleague as saying, "Those who are discontented with the new arrangements amount to . . . more than half the population, a formidable force."

84. Author's interview with Vann Nath; Pha Thachan's interview with Lionel Vairon.

85. Memorandum from Roeun of Division 801 to Brother 89 (Son Sen), 15 November 1976. Uncatalogued item in DC–Cam archive. See also CMR 99.19, "Summary of the Organization's Views," an undated speech, probably from late 1977, in which Pol Pot complained that "traitors [in the countryside] have destroyed fuel, machines, husked rice, clothes, coconut trees, and jackfruit. They have transplanted rice with the roots sticking up in the air." In "The Last Plan," in Jackson, *Cambodia 1975–1978*, Duch suggests that "banditry, vices, pacifism [and] rumor-spreading were encouraged so as to create feelings of insecurity among the people."

86. CMR 174.9. Tuy-Pon notebook, entry for 19 July 1978, continues: "If we can catch the hidden Vietnamese, that would be a great victory. If we catch the traitors who are hiding them, that would be a small victory. However, if we catch lots of traitors who are concealing Vietnamese, that would amount to a large victory." See also CMR 16.4, Chea Sin, which lists the Vietnamese hidden in Sector 20 by name; presumably these were real people who could be rounded up. The fears of hidden Vietnamese outlasted the DK regime. In 1992 a Cambodian official told Serge Thion that "the Vietnamese are most dangerous when they are invisible."

87. For examples of prisoners who confessed to concealing Vietnamese, see CMR 57.28, Kim Sok; CMR 58.3, Kong Phoeur; CMR 67.22, Leng Chhang; CMR 67.24, Lot Sophon; CMR 166.11, Yin Yum; and CMR 184.27, Ven Vean, a low-ranking medical official who "planned" not only to carry out a coup d'état but also to "conceal Vietnamese, to conceal Thais, and to conceal medicine." Tuy-Pon notebook, entry for 18 June 1978.

88. CMR 164.13.

89. CMR 84.8. See also CMR 144.3, Sam Huoy (alias Meas Tal; trans. Steve Heder): "We must have destructive stratagems, such as shooting revolu-

tionary cadres, surreptitiously throwing grenades and placing mines surreptitiously firing pistols or using poison in various forms. Cadres at any level must be killed if they don't belong to us."

90. CMR 104.23; CMR 79.19; CMR 107.14. See also CMR 24.5, Dong Kin, who confessed to "trading cloth and firing a single shot for fun," and CMR 34.18, Hul Kim Huat, who "encouraged immorality and cooked in private."

91. Confession contained in DC–Cam 846 BBK-Kh (not microfilmed).

92. CMR 56.21, Khim Yu; CMR 7.14, An Huot; CMR 26.4, Chhuon.

93. Forty seven summaries of confessions, divided by those from military units, government offices, and sectors and zones, are contained in CMR 102, 103, 113, and 114. Some of these texts list all the names that appear in confessions from a targeted unit or region. Most of the summaries run to less than forty pages, but the one dealing with Division 310, purged in 1976, is over a thousand pages long.

94. On Cambodian historiography, see Chandler, *Facing the Cambodian Past,* 189–204; Claude Jacques, "Nouvelles orientations pour l'étude de l'histoire du pays khmer," *Asie du sud-est et monde insulindien* XIII, 1–4 (1982): 39–57, and Vickery, *Cambodia after Angkor.* For Soviet parallels, see also Tucker, "Stalin, Bukharin, and History as Conspiracy," in his *Soviet Political Mind.*

95. CMR 99.14, undated but probably from 1977.

96. For examples of Party histories, see Jackson, *Cambodia 1975–1979,* 251–68. For discussions, see Chandler, "Seeing Red," and Liu Chao Ch'i, "Liquidation of Menshevik Thought in the Party," in Compton, *Mao's China,* 267: "The history of the Party is the history of the struggle with [Menshevism] and its subjugation and annihilation." See also Saich, "Where Does Correct Party History Come From?" Saich's title, of course, echoes Mao's essay, "Where Do Correct Ideas Come From?" in which Mao equates "correct" ideas with those that have successful outcomes.

97. Spence, *Narrative Truth,* 263–78, deals interestingly with Freud's notion of "archaeology" and its relation to what Spence, a psychiatrist, calls "narrative truth." For Freud's notions, see chapter 3. Spence writes, "A life story is often so loosely constituted that almost any datum can find a home" (268). See also Ofshe and Watters, *Making Monsters,* especially 15–44 and 289–304, passages that deal with the vexed question of "recovered" memories of sexual abuse.

98. Quoted in Crews, *Memory Wars,* 209, citing Freud, *Collected Writings,* Standard Edition, Volume 2, 279–80. The passage could easily have been written by an official at S-21. So could another passage cited by Crews: "We must not be led astray by initial denials. . . . We shall in the end conquer any resistance by emphasizing the unshakable nature of our convictions" (116 n. 8). See also Taussig, "Culture of Terror": "It is also clear that the victimizer needs the victim for the purpose of making truth, objectifying the victimizer's fantasies in the discourse of the other." Tucker and Cohen, eds., *The Great Purge Trial,* characterize forced confessions in the Stalin period as "vehicles for the acting out of . . . a paranoid delusional system complete with a central theme (the great conspiracy) and a malevolent pseudo-community" (xxii). See also Hanson, "Torture and

Truth in Renaissance England." Catholic critics of Protestant-administered torture, Hanson argues, claimed that instead of looking for hidden truth the torturers were forcing prisoners to invent the truth the torturers wanted.

99. CMR 99.7. An interrogator's notes to a confession (CMR 105.4, Oum Chhan) state that "when there were points he didn't mention I beat him, according to the weaknesses in his story." Another interrogator notes (on CMR 126.20, Re Sim), "I tortured him some more, concentrating on hidden stories. If he was hiding small stories, he must be hiding large ones as well."

100. For a stimulating survey of the phenomenon of surveillance in nineteenth-century Europe, see Holquist, "Information is the Alpha and Omega.'"

101. See Chandler, *Brother Number One,* 187; the second quotation was given to me by David Ashley. The idea that "learning to walk" might entail the unwarranted deaths of uncalculated numbers of innocent people calls to mind the arrogance of Mao's inscribing "beautiful lines" onto people who were "poor and blank." In his 1997 interview with Nate Thayer, Pol Pot admitted some "mistakes," but blamed major disasters on outside "agents" and on the Vietnamese.

CHAPTER FIVE. FORCING THE ANSWERS

1. Sofsky, *The Order of Terror,* 224. See also Todorov, *Facing the Extreme,* 179–93 ("The Enjoyment of Power").

2. CMR 57.24. For another sequence of tortures, see CMR 122.9, Pol Piseth, in which the interrogator claims to have beaten the prisoner, used electric shock, and force-fed him *(chrok bobong),* after which the prisoner "stammered" his confession.

3. Foucault, *Discipline and Punish.* 23. On Foucault's attitudes to torture, see Miller, *The Passion of Michel Foucault,* 165–207, and Foucault, "Why Study Power," especially 220–21, on violence. See also "Sexual Choice, Sexual Act," an interview in which Foucault compares sadomasochism to a "chess game in the sense that one can win and the other can lose. The master can lose . . . if he finds he is unable to respond to the needs of his victim. Conversely the servant can lose if he fails to act or can't stand meeting the challenge thrown at him by the master." See also Zulaika and Douglass, *Terror and Taboo,* 190 ff.

4. CMR 105.4, Oum Chhan. See also Levi, *The Drowned and the Saved,* 77–78.

5. On the lack of a universally valid definition of torture, see Mollica and Caspi-Yavin, "Assessing Torture," 582. For one definition of the practice, see U.S. Senate Committee on Foreign Relations, *Convention against Torture.* On "unspeakability," see Améry, *At the Mind's Limits,* 24 and 33. For theoretical perspectives, see Daniel, *Charred Lullabies,* 135–53; Rejali, *Torture and Modernity,* 160–76; Scarry, *The Body in Pain,* 27–59; and Certeau, "Corps torturés, paroles capturées." He writes: "Torture is the technical process whereby tyrannical power obtains that impalpable primary material which it has itself destroyed and which it lacks: authority or, if one prefers, a capacity to make itself believed" (65). Appalled by French tortures in the Algerian war, Certeau

was writing about genuine opponents of those administering the torture; not all the prisoners at S-21 can be classified in this way. See also Mellor, *La torture*.

6. Author's interview with Him Huy, January 1997. Huy has also been interviewed by Ben Kiernan, Peter Maguire, Youk Chhang, and Douglas Niven. The S-21 interrogators quoted briefly in the 1981 documentary *Die Angkar* have not been located since. See also Mydans, "A Tale of a Cambodian Woman." On the paucity of perpetrators' testimony, Goldhagen muses in *Hitler's Willing Executioners:* "It is remarkable how little is known about the perpetrators of other genocides [than the Holocaust]. A review of the literature reveals little about their identities, the character of their lives or their motivations" (596 n. 78). When one considers how few perpetrators outside Germany and, more recently, Rwanda have ever been brought to trial, how most have spent their lives in hiding, and how risky it would be for them to reveal themselves, Goldhagen's observation is absurd. Moreover, "truth commissions" in such countries as South Africa and El Salvador, and amnesties in such nations as Argentina, have encouraged former perpetrators to talk freely, further undermining Goldhagen's assertion that we know little about them. For valuable testimony by perpetrators, see Feitlowitz, *Lexicon of Terror*, 193–256, and Huggins, "Brazilian Political Violence."

7. Browning, *Ordinary Men;* Goldhagen, *Hitler's Willing Executioners;* Raul Hilberg, "Perpetrators, Victims, Bystanders"; J. Timerman, *Prisoner without a Name;* Levi, *The Drowned and the Saved;* Sereny, *Into That Darkness;* and Solzhenitsyn, *The Gulag Archipelago.* See also Michael Taussig, "Terror as Usual: Walter Benjamin's Theory of History as a State of Siege," in *The Nervous System,* 11–35. Authors working in Latin America have been able to draw heavily on perpetrators' testimony. See Corradi, Fagen, et al., *Fear at the Edge,* 39–120; Huggins, "Brazilian Political Violence," which includes extensive interviews with former torturers; and Feitlowitz, *Lexicon of Terror.* For information on a Greek torturer, see Gibson and Harotos-Fatouros, "The Education of a Torturer."

8. On the notion of "rehumanizing" victims of DK, see Hinton, "Agents of Death," and Daniel, *Charred Lullabies,* 194–212.

9. Rejali, *Torture and Modernity,* 176; Zulaika and Douglass, *Terror and Taboo,* 193. See also Bauman, *Modernity and the Holocaust,* and Gregory and Timerman, "Rituals of the Modern State." These authors all argue that torturers are "ritual specialists" and that torture sessions resemble rites of passage. Bauman writes: "Violence has been turned into a technique. Like all techniques, it is free from emotions and purely rational" (98). Certeau sees torture as "a collusion between the technician's rationality and the violence of power," with power seeking assent to its peculiar "language" at all costs ("Corps torturés, paroles capturées," 64).

10. On permission needed to beat, CMR 22.33, Chau Kut; CMR 49.2, Khun Khom; and CMR 99.7 (the interrogators' notebook), 68. The prisoners who were not beaten were CMR 36.10, Hin Sinan; CMR 54.13, Kenh Yim; CMR 57.32, Keo Phat; CMR 67.27, Liv Chheam; CMR 68.30, May Len; CMR 80.22, Mok Khon; CMR 157.29, Seng Sopheat; and CMR 171.3, Tep Meng.

11. See CMR 86.1, Ngel Kong.

12. CMR 99.7, the interrogators' manual, is partially translated in Hawk, "The Tuol Sleng Extermination Center," and the same translation is included in Peters, *Torture*, 270–72. In the quotations that follow I draw on the Khmer original. The second quotation is from Tuy-Pon notebook, entry for 20 May 1978.

13. Sofsky, *The Order of Terror*, 226.

14. Peter Maguire and Chris Riley's interview with Ten Chan. See also People's Republic of Kampuchea, *The Extermination Camp of Tuol Sleng*, 6, quoting Ten Chan.

15. DC–Cam, BBK-Kh 675, not microfilmed by Cornell. The cover sheet bears a notation from Duch: "This is the one who beat Bun Than to death." Bun Than's incomplete confession is CMR 3.10.

16. Collins, "Three Faces of Evil."

17. Note from Pon to Duch, 27 September 1976, uncatalogued item in DC–Cam archive.

18. Institut Bouddhique, *Dictionnaire cambodgien* (Phnom Penh: 1967), 422. This text formed the basis for Robert K. Headley Jr., *Cambodian-English Dictionary*, 2 vols. (Washington, D.C.: Catholic University of America, 1977); Headley's entry for *tearunikam* is at 380. See also Wit Thiengburanathan, *Thai-English Dictionary* (Bangkok: n.p., 1992), 583 and 615. Ian Mabbett informs me that Sanskrit has a wide range of words for torture and that judicial torture was widely practiced in classical India. The Cambodian compound verb translatable as "to harm" *(tvoeu bap)* means literally to "perform demerit."

19. On interrogations and confessions in premodern China, see Susan Naquin, "True Confessions," MacCormack, *Traditional Chinese Penal Law*, and Dutton, *Policing and Punishment in China*. Peters, *Torture*, 93, briefly discusses judicial torture in Japan. Physical torture for evidentiary purposes, rare for years in Maoist China (it was not used, for example, on United Nations prisoners of war in the Korean conflict) was revived during the Cultural Revolution (Michael Schoenhals, personal communication). The Vietnamese term for interrogation contains no undertones of violence (Ton-that Quynh-Du, personal communication).

20. Peters, *Torture*, 66; Asad, "Notes on Body Pain," 305. See also Millett, *The Politics of Cruelty*, 296 ff., and Hanson, "Torture and Truth." Allen Feldman, writing about interrogations and torture in the 1980s in Northern Ireland, suggests that "the past act of transgression and a knowledge of the past are defined by interrogators as an absence hidden by the presence of the body within its own depths and recesses. . . . The body is unfolded in order to expose the past" *(Formations of Violence,* 136). Feldman adds, "The confession text signifies the erasure of the body."

21. On the bas-reliefs at Angkor Wat, see Eleanor Mannika, *Angkor Wat: Time, Space and Kingship* (Honolulu: University of Hawaii Press, 1996), 155–60. The concepts of heaven and hell came to Angkorean Cambodia from Buddhist cosmology; see Coedes and Archaimbault, *Les trois mondes*. On the guide's comments in 1981, Gough, "Roots of the Pol Pot Regime," 155–56. Interestingly, bas-reliefs on the gateway to Wat Promruot in the city of Siem Reap, erected in 1990, depict the Buddha being tempted by evil forces dressed in Khmer Rouge military costume.

22. Author's interview with Vann Nath, December 1995. On the Theravada notion of "unbelievers" *(thmil),* see Kapferer, *Legends of People,* and Southwold, "Buddhism and Evil." See also Ulmonen, "Responses to Revolutionary Change," 36, in which villagers in the 1990s call the Khmer Rouge *thmil.* Demonization and dehumanization went hand in hand; for medieval European examples, see Bauman, *Modernity and the Holocaust,* 40 ff. A similar process was at work in the Indonesian massacres of suspected Communists in 1965–1966, discussed in Fein, "Revolutionary and Anti-revolutionary Genocides." See also Staub, "The Psychology and Culture of Torture and Torturers," in Suedfeld, ed., *Psychology and Torture,* 52 ff. The final quotation from Pol Pot is from FBIS, October 4, 1977, H 28.

23. See, for example, Ivan Turgenev, "The Execution of Tropman" (1871), reprinted in Lopate, ed., *The Art of the Personal Essay.* See also Spierenburg, *The Spectacle of Suffering,* 188 ff. Public executions were staged occasionally in Cambodia under Sihanouk in the 1960s. In a twentieth-century twist, the killings were replayed as newsreels for several weeks.

24. Leclère, trans., *Les codes cambodgiens,* vol. 1, 234–36. See also Imbert, *Histoire des institutions khmeres,* 112 ff.

25. See Som, *Tum Taev,* 130–31. See also Uk Samet, *Suksa katha Tum Taev* (A brief study of Tum Taev). In Thai-administered Battambang in the early twentieth century, public executions were frequent and brutal. In the DK era, the wives and children of several important prisoners were executed with them to foreclose revenge. The murder of Son Sen and fourteen dependents, including small children, in June 1997 at Pol Pot's behest and the murders of over fifty opponents of Prime Minister Hun Sen a month later indicate the endurance of this tradition. For Thai parallels, see Reynolds, "Sedition in Thai History."

26. Foucault, *Discipline and Punish,* 87. See also Miller, *The Passion of Michel Foucault,* 208 ff. Punitive torture and "modern" penology went hand-in-hand in Argentina in the 1970s, although the documentation that characterizes S-21 was lacking. See Gregory and Timerman, "Rituals of the Modern State," 68.

27. On the links between torture and secrecy, see Améry, *At the Mind's Limits,* 23–24. For a discussion of twentieth-century judicial torture, see Peters, *Torture,* 116 ff.

28. See Chandler, "The Constitution of Democratic Kampuchea." Mass condemnation of class enemies, of the sort practiced by "people's courts" in revolutionary China and Vietnam, never seems to have taken hold in DK, although the establishment of something similar for the show trial of Pol Pot in 1997 suggests that such courts had occasionally been convened in the DK era.

29. See Locard, "Le Goulag des khmers rouges."

30. Sara Colm's interview with Vann Nath; CMR 118.20, Baen Chhae; and CMR 66.18, Long Muy, who described having been tortured at Wat Phnom before being taken across the city to Tuol Sleng.

31. Alexander Hinton's interview with Vann Nath.

32. Quoted in Todorov, *Facing the Extreme,* 159. See also DC–Cam document N0001880, a memorandum from the security office in sector 21 in the Eastern Zone, which uses the classifier "head" *(kbal)* for the noun "traitor"

(kbot); the classifier is normally applied to animals. The same demeaning classifiers were also used for prisoners under the post-DK regime (Judy Ledgerwood, personal communication).

33. On these social categories, see Jackson, *Cambodia 1975–1978,* 84. On dehumanization, see Kelman and Hamilton, *Crimes of Obedience,* 19 ff. (the book deals in depth with the My Lai massacre); Solis, *Son Thang;* and Gregory and Timerman, "Rituals of the Modern State," 66 ff., who label as *cosificación* the process by which the inmates of Argentine prisons became things.

34. A good introduction to the copious literature about the show trials is Leites and Bernaut, *Ritual of Liquidation.* See also Beck and Godin, *Russian Purge;* Khlevnyuk, "The Objectives of the Great Terror"; and Nikita Khrushchev, "Secret Report to the 20th Party Congress of the CPSU," in Ali, *The Stalinist Legacy,* 243 ff. On torture, Solzhenitsyn argues that physical torture was widely used in the 1930s in the USSR but was kept secret (*The Gulag Archipelago,* I, 102 ff.). Conquest concurs (*The Great Terror,* 120 ff.). These methods of interrogation, dubbed "brainwashing" in the West in the 1950s, were adapted and improved by Western police forces and came to be known as KGB methods. See Shallice, "The Ulster Depth Interrogation Techniques."

35. See Hodos, *Show Trials;* Leites and Bernaut, *Ritual of Liquidation,* 351–82; and Steve Heder's 1997 interview with Mey Mann, a Khmer who studied in Paris. Moloney, "Psychic Self-Abandon," 53–60, contains an interesting interview with the U.S. businessman Robert Vogeler, who was accused of spying in Czechoslovakia in the early 1950s and was groomed by his interrogators to make a full-scale confession in the manner of the show trials.

36. On the Chinese purges, see Compton, ed., *Mao's China;* Teiwes, *Politics and Purges in China;* Seybolt, "Terror and Conformity"; and Dai Qing, *Wang Shiwei and the "Wild Lilies."* May Ebihara has suggested (personal communication) that in prerevolutionary Cambodia a former offender, having apologized in some fashion and having learned to "behave," could on occasion be reintegrated into the ruling strata of society. The 1997 "defection" of Ieng Sary, who had been condemned to death in 1979, is a case in point, although in Ieng Sary's case no reeducation was called for or undertaken.

37. Berger and Luckmann, *The Social Construction of Reality.* See also Clark, "Revolutionary Ritual." On Vietnam, see Moise, *Land Reform in China and Vietnam,* and Boudarel, *Cent fleurs eclosés,* 145–231.

38. For the amnesty, see CMR 96.10, "Guidance from the CPK Party Center On the Policies of the Party toward Confused People."

39. CMR 60.3, Kim Chen.

40. Chan notebook, entry for 23 July 1978. Confessions that refer to S-21 as a *sala kay pray* are CMR 17.5, Chey Rong; CMR 36.10, Hin Sinan; and CMR 67.27, Liv Chhem—all from 1978. The Tuy-Pon notebook entry for 8 October 1978 discusses the name change, which also involved gentler methods of interrogation.

41. On K'ang Sheng, see Apter and Saich, *Revolutionary Discourse,* 280 ff; Byron and Pack, *The Claws of the Dragon;* MacFarquhar, *Origins of the Cultural Revolution,* 3:291–94; and Faligot and Kauffer, *The Chinese Secret Service,* which claims, without citing a source, that Pol Pot "took training courses

with K'ang Sheng's special services in 1965 *(sic)* and 1969" (410). See also Hu Yao-ping, "Problems Concerning the Purge of K'ang Sheng," and Schoenhls "Mao's Great Inquisition: The Central Case Examination Group, 1966–1979," *Chinese Law and Government,* May–June 1996. The CCEG, which functioned throughout the DK period, may have provided some inspiration for S-21. Until his death in 1975, K'ang Sheng was closely associated with it.

42. On Pol Pot's friendship with K'ang Sheng, author's interview with a former Chinese official, speaking on condition of anonymity. According to the official, Pol Pot's 1971 visit to China was kept secret from Sihanouk (who was in Beijing at the time) until films of the visit were shown to the prince in Phnom Penh in 1976. The Chinese official's story is difficult to corroborate and fits as neatly into the demonization of K'ang Sheng after 1976 as it does into the eagerness of many (myself included) to seek some of the origins of the Khmer Rouge outside Indochina.

43. Memories of people's cries under torture crop up in Douglas Niven's interviews with Nhem En and Kok Sros, Alexander Hinton's with Khieu Lohr, and Lionel Vairon's with Pha Tachan. See also Terzani, "I Still Hear Screams in the Night." Terzani's title derives from his interview with Ung Pech, who told him: "I think those screams will make me deaf." Vann Nath, interviewed by David Hawk in 1983, said, "You heard screams all the time: screams of terror, screams of fear and screams of asphyxiation, near death." The recurrence of these memories suggests not only that torture at S-21 was far more widespread than the scattered archival references to it might imply but also that it was the feature of life at S-21 that burned itself most deeply into people's minds.

44. Tuy-Pon notebook, entry for 11 August 1978.

45. Aristotle, *The Art of Rhetoric,* I.xv, 26: "Those under compulsion are as likely to give false evidence as true, some being ready to endure everything rather than tell the truth while others are equally ready to make false charges against others, in the hope of being released sooner from torture." Mellor, discussing this passage and other classical references to torture, points out that no classical authors expressed *moral* objections to the practice (*La torture,* 65).

46. Sofsky, *The Order of Terror,* 228. See also Gibson, "Training People to Inflict Pain," and David Hawk's interview with Steve Heder, September 1982. See also CMR 99.14, "Summary from *santebal,*" May 1977 (a self-criticism session): "A shortcoming: we fail to grasp the collective spirit of the proletariat. For example: we torture prisoners without grasping their activities, or their health. . . . the bad thing is that prisoners keep dying. Fourteen have done so in the last three months" (5).

47. CMR 69.30, Ma Meang Keng. See also CMR 88.3, Neo Kanha, a former interrogator who declared in his confession that the modus operandi of his unit was to "ask when the enemies joined the CIA, and then to beat them for a couple of months." Similarly, the interrogator's notebook from 1976 (CMR 99.7, 65) admits in notes from a self-criticism session that "we go on the offensive but we see torture as more significant than doing politics. . . . Our questions consist of screaming and yelling at the enemies."

48. For Chinese parallels, see Lin Jing, *The Red Guards' Path to Violence;* Walder and Gong Xiaoxia, *Chinese Sociology and Anthropology;* and Dittmer,

"Thought Reform and Cultural Revolution." The proportion of prisoners executed in China probably never reached that in the USSR under Stalin or in DK. MacFarquhar makes this point persuasively (*Origins of the Cultural Revolution*, 3:473).

49. For a discussion of this confession, see chapter 3 and Duch to Ney Saran (alias Ya) memorandum, uncatalogued document dated 30 September 1976 in DC–Cam archive. Two days later, Duch wrote Pon: "With this Ya you can use the hot method for prolonged periods. Even if you slip and it kills him this won't be a violation of the Organization's discipline." Pon notes in the margin: "Show to Ya so he can think it over" (trans. Steve Heder).

50. CMR 159.11.

51. *Die Angkar*. In Vann Nath's interview with the author he mentioned that some prisoners at S-21 were placed in a wooden bathtub and shocked electrically while submerged.

52. CMR 3.24, Buth Heng. Heng's wife, Chhay Phoeun, was a twenty-seven-year-old full-rights member of the CPK who was probably executed with him. Her personnel record sheet has survived.

53. Chan notebook, entry for 3 March 1978. "Pinching" may be a euphemism for sexual harrassment. For an example of sexual transgression by an interrogator, see CMR 183.27, Vong Samath, who confessed to inserting a piece of wood in female prisoner's vagina during an interrogation, and CMR 17.13, Chea May, who confessed to having sex with a female prisoner and suggested that his superiors in the unit often did the same.

54. David Hawk's interview with Ung Pech.

55. *Die Angkar*, frame 217.

56. Vann Nath in Niven and Riley, *Killing Fields*, 96. See also People's Republic of Kampuchea, *The Extermination Camp of Tuol Sleng*: "They used either electromagnetic devices with high tension but weak intensity or the domestic current of 380 volts. The electric wires were attached either to the foot or the tongue of the prisoner, or to his ears, fingers or to his sex" (4). In his interview with David Hawk, Nath said that he was "given shock by electric wire for a period of several hours." CMR 13.5, Cheak Om, was also given repeated shocks. On the admonition to prisoners, *Die Angkar*, frame 273. Ten Chan, another survivor who received electric shock, told Chris Riley and Peter Maguire in 1994: "Sometimes they electrocuted me. That's why to this day I feel something abnormal in my brain."

57. CMR 46.5, Keth Chau; CMR 37.15, Hun Som Paun; CMR 64.5, Ly Phen; Duch notation to CMR 35.4, Heng Sauy; and CMR 179.8, Tae Hut. See also CMR 24, Sy Yan, with a note by Chan: "Torture her heavily until she stops saying that she went to Vietnam."

58. Author's interview with Vann Nath, December 1995. Nath's memory is corroborated in CMR 105.39, Pal Lak Pheng, in which the interrogator writes that he showed the prisoner "the picture of a dog's body with a man's face." See also CMR 87.16, Ngin Ing. Rittenberg and Bennett, *The Man Who Stayed Behind*, recalls a slogan used with prisoners in China in the Cultural Revolution: "Bow your dog's head down" (340). See also Zhang Zhiyang, "Walls," in *China's Cultural Revolution: Not a Dinner Party*, ed. Michael Schoenhals

(Armonk, N.Y.: M. E. Sharpe, 1996), 340–54, which notes that the Chinese character for "prisoner" contains a radical that means "dog."

59. See Marston, *Cambodia 1991–1994,* 84 ff. On the similar practice in Thailand, see D. Insor (pseud.), *Thailand: A Political, Social and Economic Analysis* (New York: Praeger, 1963), 68–69.

60. CMR 77.21, Moeung Doeur, and CMR 87.16, Ngin Ing.

61. CMR 158.26. Svang Kum was the wife of Chhe Samauk (alias Pang), a high-ranking CPK member and protégé of Pol Pot arrrested in 1978. By that point, Ho Chi Minh had been dead for nine years, and Lyndon Johnson had been out of office for a decade. See also CMR 33. 11, Heang Srun; CMR 58.19, Kot Prum; and CMR 88.44, Nhem Vann.

62. On 11 August 1978, the Tuy-Pon notebook suggested that interrogators should not inflict torture when they are angry, because if interrogators "forget themselves" the prisoners will produce "unclear answers"; CMR 99.7.

63. CMR 99.7. The translations that follow are drawn from pages 70–76.

64. I am reminded here of Gunther Lewy, *America in Vietnam* (New York: Oxford University Press, 1978), quoting rules for U.S. participants in the Phoenix program in the Vietnam War, which aimed to "neutralize" the enemy's infrastructure: "[Personnel] are specifically unauthorized to engage in assassinations" (283). The same sort of "control" applied to U.S. Marines' behavior in Vietnam. See Solis, *Son Thang,* passim.

65. Chan notebook, entry for 10 February 1978.

66. CMR 99.10.

67. Bauman, *Modernity and the Holocaust,* 21; Todorov, *Facing the Extreme,* 158–78.

68. Kelman and Hamilton, *Crimes of Obedience.* See also Herbert C. Kelman, "Violence without Moral Restraint," *Journal of Social Issues* 29 (1973): 29–61; Bauman, *Modernity and the Holocaust,* 151–69; and Valentino, "Final Solutions." Profiting from his reading of Milgram, Valentino argues that permission to kill, coming from people worthy of obedience, is the sine qua non of modern state-sponsored genocides.

69. Gordon A. Bennett and Ronald N. Montaperto, *Red Guard: the Political Biography of Dai Hsiao-ai* (Garden City, N.Y.: Doubleday, 1971), 28. See also Sutton, "(Dis)embodying Revolution," in which a person who had committed ritualized cannibalism is recorded as saying, "Am I supposed to be afraid his ghost will get me? ha! ha! I am a revolutionary, my heart is red! Didn't Chairman Mao teach us, 'If we don't kill them, they'll kill us?'" (165 n.). "Redness" in these contexts may mean little more than loyalty to members of their group. The Marxism-Leninism of the workers at S-21 seems rarely to have extended beyond a facility with revolutionary jargon.

70. Ledgerwood, "The Cambodian Tuol Sleng Museum," 85.

71. Douglas Niven's interview with Nhem En. Ten Chan had a similar memory (interview with Peter Maguire and Chris Riley). See also Levi, *The Drowned and the Saved,* 24, describing the choreographed arrival rituals at Auschwitz, and Mydans, "A Cambodian Woman's Tale."

72. Author's interview with Kok Sros.

73. On the discovery of Choeung Ek in 1980, interviews by Sara Colm and Peter Maguire with Mai Lam. For vivid description of Choeung Ek as a tourist destination in the 1990s, see Kaplan, *The Ends of the Earth,* 403–4.

74. See Mollica and Caspi-Yavin, "Assessing Torture."

75. Améry, *At the Mind's Limits,* 27. Primo Levi, writing about Améry's suicide eight years later and a year before his own, noted that the act permitted "a cloud of explanations" (*The Drowned and the Saved,*136). See also Paperno, *Suicide as a Cultural Institution,* and Cover, "Violence and the Word": "The deliberate infliction of pain in order to destroy the victim's normative world and capacity to create shared realities we call torture. . . . The torturer and the victim end up creating their own terrible 'world' but this world derives its meaning from being imposed on the ashes of another. The logic of that world is complete destruction though the objective may not be realized" (98).

CHAPTER SIX. EXPLAINING S-21

1. In writing this chapter, I have benefited from conversations with Tom Cushman, Eleanor Hancock, and Eric Weitz. Benn, "Wickedness," citing Schopenhauer, refers to "that delight in the suffering of others which does not spring from mere egoism but is disinterested and which constitutes wickedness proper, rising to the pitch of cruelty" (797). Some of Duch's and Pon's annotations and Tuy's letter to Siet Chhe (alias Tum), accusing him of incest, fit neatly into this category. John Kekes speaks of "people habitually [causing] undeserved harm" (*Facing Evil,* 7)—a choice of words that seems to fit Son Sen, Duch, and Pon as they worked proactively to obey the Party Center. See also Copjec, ed., *Radical Evil,* and Dunn, *Riffs and Reciprocities,* 22.

2. For stimulating discussions of these issues, see Gourevitch, *We Wish to Inform You;* A. Rosenbaum, ed., *Is the Holocaust Unique?;* Horowitz, *Taking Lives;* Harff and Gurr, "Toward an Empirical Theory of Genocides and Politicides"; and Valentino, "Final Solutions." See also Nagengast's helpful essay, "Violence, Terror, and the Crisis of the State," and John M. Darley's two stimulating papers, "Social Organization for the Production of Evil" and "Constructive and Destructive Obedience: a Taxonomy of Principal-Agent Relations." The chapter also benefits from discussions with students in my seminar on state-sponsored terror at the University of Wisconsin, Madison, in 1998.

3. Corrèze and Forest, *Cambodge à deux voix,* 72.

4. Cited in Tucker, *Stalinism,* 212.

5. J. Spence, "In China's Gulag." The difficulty of writing about large emotional experiences, especially those experienced at first hand, is taken up by Rosaldo in "Grief and the Headhunter's Rage."

6. Shklar, *Ordinary Vices,* 44.

7. Shklar, *Ordinary Vices,* 22. See also LaCapra, *History and Memory,* 182 n.: "Empathy itself . . . raises knotty perplexities, for it is difficult to see how one may be empathetic without intrusively arrogating to oneself the victim's experience or undergoing . . . surrogate victimage," a sentence that seems to suggest that indifference or hostility are less problematic. For a subtle analysis

of the problems that interviewers encounter with perpetrators and victims, see Robben, "The Politics of Truth and Emotion among Victims and Perpetrators of Violence."

8. Suárez-Orozco, "A Grammar of Terror." See also Suárez-Orozco, "Speaking of the Unspeakable"; Taussig, *The Nervous System;* and Robben and Nordstrom, "Introduction" to *Fieldwork under Fire,* which also speaks of the quotidian nature of violence.

9. Browning, *Ordinary Men.* See also Christopher Browning, "Ordinary Men or Ordinary Germans," and Milgram, *Obedience to Authority,* 10: "Tyrannies are perpetuated by diffident men."

10. Douglas Niven's interview with Kok Sros. Talking to Seth Mydans in 1999, the former S-21 guard Neang Kin said: "They trained us to follow the path of the revolution correctly. If you didn't believe, they killed you." Mydans, "A Cambodian Woman's Tale."

11. Sereny, *Into That Darkness,* 200. See also Todorov, *Facing the Extreme,* 158–78, a chapter titled "Fragmentation."

12. Sereny, *Into That Darkness,* 101. Stangl told her, "The only way I could live was by compartmentalizing my thinking" (64)—a process described by several former employees of S-21. See the insightful discussion of Sereny's book in Todorov, *Facing the Extreme,* 278–82.

13. See Joffe, "Goldhagen in Germany": "Central to [Goldhagen's] book . . . is the sense that trembling and terror are necessary to the perception of a morally comprehensible universe. This is the evil that was done; this is who did it; here is why they did it and how they felt." A differently labeled Manichean model prevailed in DK at the official level. See the 1978 speech titled "The Need to Distinguish between Patriotism and Treason": "Without a clear line between ourselves and other people, little by little the enemy's ideology will seep into your minds and make you lose all sense of distinction between ourselves and the enemy. This is very dangerous." Cited by Stubbings, "Rationality, Closure and the Monopoly of Power."

14. Levi, *The Drowned and the Saved,* 77, and Sofsky, *The Order of Power,* 130–44, discuss the issue of "frontiers." Browning, "Ordinary Men," 67.

15. See Zimbardo, Haney et al., "The Psychology of Imprisonment"; Zimbardo, "The Mind is a Formidable Jailer"; and Haney et al., "Interpersonal Dynamics." Sofsky, *The Order of Terror,* makes the point succinctly: "The guards flogged, tormented and killed prisoners—not because they had to, but because they were allowed to, no holds barred" (115). Whether the orders were "legal" or not, a point made in defining war crimes or crimes against humanity, seems not to have occurred to many perpetrators at S-21.

16. See Milgram, *Obedience to Authority,* which draws analogies between his experiments and the behavior of personnel in the Nazi death camps and the My Lai massacre in Vietnam in 1968. Milgram's findings were both praised and criticized at the time, but most of them seem to have weathered well. See A. Miller, *The Obedience Experiments,* and A. Miller et al., *Perspectives on Obedience to Authority.*

17. Hinton, "Why Did You Kill?" and *Cambodia's Shadow.* Hinton argues that various cultural pressures worked on Cambodians to make them peculiarly

prone to obedience (and, for that matter, to giving orders). As Sofsky suggests, "Servility and obedience leave total power untouched" (*The Order of Terror*, 139). See also Tannenbaum, *Who Can Compete against the World?* a perceptive reassessment of the vexed concept of patronage in mainland Southeast Asia. Marston, *Cambodia 1991–1994*, especially chapter 4, deftly places the phenomenon of hierarchy in a contemporary Cambodian setting.

18. The verb *sdap*, often translated as "to listen" or "to hear," has strong overtones of "to understand" and "to obey," while the participle *bomrao*, usually translated as "serve," is better translated by "commanded." Hinton, *Cambodia's Shadow*, passim; Hinton, "Why Did You Kill?" 99; and Chandler, "Normative Poems *(Chbab)* and Pre-Colonial Cambodian Society," in *Facing the Cambodian Past*, 45–60. As Milgram puts it: "Obedience arises out of the perceived inequalities of human relationships" (*Obedience to Authority*, 207). Significantly, Son Sen, Duch, Chan, and Pon had all been trained as teachers and were accustomed less to listening or sharing than to giving orders, demanding compliance, setting agendas and, in a nutshell, being heard.

19. See Zimbardo, "The Psychology of Police Confessions."

20. La Fontaine, *The Complete Fables*, 22–23. La Fontaine used the fable to illustrate the adage "Le raison le plus fort est toujours le meilleur" (the strongest argument is always best), which might have served as a motto for S-21. Ironically, the Party Center justified its treatment of its "enemies" in part as a defense against what it perceived as the wolf-like behavior of the Vietnamese toward the lamb-like, sinned-against Khmer.

21. See Chu, "The Counter-Revolution"; Dispot, *La machine à terreur*; and Baker, ed., *The French Revolution*. See also Griffin, *The Chinese Communist Treatment of Counter-Revolutionaries*, quoting a Chinese revolutionary from the 1930s: "Law develops in accord with the needs of the revolution and whatever benefits the revolution is law" (141). One is reminded of Mao's essay, "Where Do Correct Ideas Come From?" in which he asserts that "correct" ideas, by and large, are the ones that succeed.

22. See the annexes to CMR 57.3, Ke Nanh (May 1978), which supply the names of soldiers in Division 280 in the Eastern Zone alleged to have Vietnamese blood, who were to be purged. Kiernan, *The Pol Pot Regime*, argues that racist policies rather than misreadings of socialist ideas were central to DK (26). His argument is weakened but not contradicted by the fact that the vast majority of people executed in the DK era were ethnic Khmer. Certain Buddhist ideas related to "unbelievers," millenarian privileges that accrue to rebels, and echoes of monastic discipline (as these affected workers at the prison) may have well have played a part in reading prisoners out of the Cambodian "race." See Southwold, "Buddhism and Evil," Ponchaud, "Social Change in the Vortex of Revolution," and Keyes, "Communist Revolution and the Buddhist Past," 43–74. In the Indonesian massacres of 1965 and 1966, the supposed Communists who were killed in such large numbers were also seen as quintessential "others," easily whited out.

23. Heder, "Racism, Marxism, Labelling," 152.

24. Vickery, *Cambodia 1975–1982*, concluding chapter. See also Vickery, "Violence in Democratic Kampuchea," and the essays by Anthony Barnett and

Serge Thion in Chandler and Kiernan, *Revolution and Its Aftermath,* with Barnett arguing for a greater amount of centralized control (and more Marxism-Leninism) and Thion for less. Vickery's overall argument rests on the assumption that genuine Marxist-Leninists would not have acted as savagely and ineptly as the Khmer Rouge did and on the notion that the voracious nationalism of the Khmer Rouge was at odds with the internationalist thrust of Marxism-Leninism. Neither issue is discussed in any detail in Kiernan, *The Pol Pot Regime.* See Ashley, "The Voice of the Khmer Rouge," 27 ff., for a judicious summary of Vickery's arguments. Ironically, the Khmer Rouge movement probably became most purely peasantist in the 1990s, when Ta Mok became its effective leader. Pol Pot's July 1997 trial, seen from this perspective, was a ritual enactment of peasant rage. I would argue that peasant rage was an important ingredient of DK ideology but not the regime's moving force. See also Hinton, "A Head for an Eye," which stresses the importance of revenge in Cambodian culture.

25. Uncatalogued item from S-21 archive, 18 February 1976.

26. Bauman, *Modernity and the Holocaust,* 152. Lifton, *The Nazi Doctors,* 5. See also Lane Gerber, "We Must Hear Each Other's Cry: Lessons from Pol Pot Survivors," in Strozier and Flynn, eds., *Genocide, War, and Human Survival,* 297–305.

27. Milgram, *Obedience to Authority,* 134, cited in Darley, "Social Organization," 207. Darley argues here and in "Constructive and Destructive Obedience" that what Milgram assumed was a sudden shift or acquiescence more frequently takes the form of a slow acculturation or toughening of the sort described by Sereny, Browning, and Hinton. We are quite far here from Elias Canetti's romantic notion of the "sting of command" as an instigation for disobedience and (commendable) rebellion. Darley notes that "within organizations that members perceive as legitimate, the forces leading to obedience are multiple, mutually enforcing, and very strong" ("Social Organization," 208). Darley suggests that people like those in Lt. Calley's platoon at My Lai in the Vietnam war are socialized into committing evil deeds, a finding echoed in Solis, *Son Thang,* which deals with a smaller-scale massacre of civilians by U.S. Marines in north-central Vietnam in 1969.

28. Staub, "The Psychology of Perpetrators and Bystanders," 66 n. Goldfield, Mollica et al., "The Physical and Psychological Sequelae of Torture."

29. Todorov, *Facing the Extreme,* 279.

Bibliography

ARCHIVAL MATERIALS

The book has been based largely on the archive of S-21 in Phnom Penh, microfilmed by Cornell University and the Cambodian Ministry of Culture in 1992 and1993. Materials from S-21 that have come to light since the microfilming was completed have also been consulted, as have materials that originated in S-21 but were held elsewhere and were not available for microfilming. The newly collected materials and a set of the films are now held in the Documentation Center–Cambodia (DC–Cam) in Phnom Penh, a facility affiliated with the Cambodia Genocide Program administered by Yale University.

AUTHOR'S INTERVIEWS

François Bizot, Pierre Brocheux, Chey Saphon (2), Chey Sophea, Chey Sopheara, Chim Heng, David Hawk, Him Huy, Ith Sarin, Keuky Lim, Kham Kuon, Khieu Samon, Kok Sros, Kun Khea, Lach Vorleak Kaliyan, Leang Kon, Henri Locard, Mouth Sophea, Neak-ek Bunan (3), Nhem En (2), Nou Beng, Pen An, Rath Leng, Rithi Phan, Seng Kan, Seng Korn, Sieng Hay Nang, Sieu Chheng Y, Sok Pirun, Sua Samorn, Suong Soriya, Vann Nath.

INTERVIEWS BY OTHERS

Richard Arant's interviews with Lay Samon, Mao Phouk, and Yi Yaun
David Ashley's interview with Vann Nath
Youk Chhang's interviews with Him Huy, Ke Kep, and Ngem Sokhan
Sara Colm's interviews with B.G., Mai Lam, and Vann Nath
David Hawk's interviews with Ung Pech, Steve Heder, and Vann Nath
Steve Heder's interviews with Ieng Sary, Mey Mann, and Ung Pech
Alexander Hinton's interviews with Khieu Lohr and Vann Nath
Ben Kiernan's interviews with Hum Huy, Uch Ben, and Vann Nath
Peter Maguire's interviews with Him Huy and Gerhard Schuemann
Peter Maguire and Doug Niven's interviews with Nhem En and Vann Nath
Peter Maguire and Chris Riley's interviews with Chey Sopheara, Vann Nath,
    Mai Lam, and Ten Chan
Douglas Niven's interviews with Ho van Tay, Kok Sros, and Nhem En
Nate Thayer's interviews with Pol Pot and Kang Kech Ieu (Duch)
Lionel Vairon's interview with Pha Thachan

PRINTED SOURCES

Ablin, David, and Marlowe Hood, eds. *The Cambodian Agony.* Armonk, N.Y.:
    M. E. Sharpe, 1989.
Adams, Brad. "Snatching Defeat from the Jaws of Victory." *Phnom Penh Post,*
    22 January–4 February 1999.
Adelman, Jonathan R., ed. *Terror and Communist Politics: The Role of Secret
    Police in Communist States.* Boulder: Westview Press, 1984.
Alford, C. Fred. "The Organization of Evil." *Political Psychology* 11, no. 1
    (1990): 5–38.
Ali, Tariq, ed. *The Stalinist Legacy.* Harmondsworth: Penguin Books, 1984.
Améry, Jean. *At the Mind's Limits.* Trans. Sydney Rosenfeld and Stella P. Rosen-
    feld. Bloomington: Indiana University Press, 1980.
Amnesty International. *Kampuchea: Political Imprisonment and Torture.* Lon-
    don: Amnesty International, 1987.
Amungama, Sarath, and Eric Meyer. "Remarques sur la violence dans l'idéolo-
    gie bouddhique: La pratique sociale a Sri Langka (Ceylan)." *Études rurales*
    July–December 1984: 47–62.
An Outline History of the Viet Nam Workers' Party. Hanoi: Foreign Languages
    Press, 1970.
Anderson, Benedict. *Imagined Communities.* London: Verso, 1995.
———. *Language and Power.* Ithaca: Cornell University Press, 1990.
Andreopoulos, George J., ed. *Genocide: Conceptual and Historical Dimen-
    sions.* Philadelphia: University of Pennsylvania Press.
Apter, David E., ed. *The Legitimation of Violence.* London: Macmillan, 1997.
Apter, David E., and Tony Saich. *Revolutionary Discourse in Mao's Republic.*
    Cambridge: Harvard University Press, 1994.
Arendt, Hannah. *On Violence.* New York: Harcourt Brace, 1969.
———. *The Origins of Totalitarianism.* London: Allen and Unwin, 1967.

————. *Eichmann in Jerusalem: A Report on the Banality of Evil.* New York: Viking, 1964.

Aristotle. *The Art of Rhetoric.* translated by J. H. Freese. London: Heinemann, 1926.

Aron, Robert. *L'histoire de l'épuration.* 3 vols. Paris: Fayard, 1967–1975.

Asad, Talal. "Notes on Body Pain and Truth in Medieval Christian Ritual." *Economy and Society* 12 (1983): 287–27.

Ashley, David. "The Voice of the Khmer Rouge: A Study of Revolutionary Political Thought." B.A. thesis, Cambridge University, 1990.

Baker, Keith Michael, ed. *The French Revolution and the Creation of Modern Political Culture.* Volume 4, *The Terror.* New York: Elsevier, 1994.

Bandura, A., et al. "Disinhibition of Aggression through Diffusion of Responsibility and Dehumanization of Victims." *Journal of Research in Personality* 9 (1975): 253–69.

Bardach, Janusz, and Kathleen Gleeson. *Man Is Wolf to Man: Surviving the Gulag.* Berkeley: University of California Press, 1998.

Barnett, Anthony, Ben Kiernan, and Chanthou Boua. "Bureaucracy of Death." *New Statesman,* May 2, 1980: 668–76.

Basoglu, M., ed. *Torture and Its Consequences.* Cambridge: Cambridge University Press, 1992.

Bauer, Raymond. "Brainwashing: Psychology or Demonology?" *Journal of Social Issues,* special issue 3 (1957).

Bauman, Zygmunt. *Modernity and the Holocaust.* Ithaca: Cornell University Press, 1989.

Beck, F., and W. Godin. *Russian Purge and the Extraction of Confession.* New York: Viking, 1951.

Becker, Elizabeth. *When the War Was Over: The Voices of Cambodia's Revolution and Its People.* New York: Simon and Schuster, 1986.

Becker, Jasper. *Hungry Ghosts.* London: John Murray, 1996.

Bem, D. J. "Inducing Belief in False Confessions." *Journal of Personal and Social Psychology* 3 (1966): 707–10.

Benjamin, Walter. "Critique of Violence" and "The Destructive Character." In Walter Benjamin, *Reflections,* ed. Peter Demetz, 277–302. New York: Harcourt Brace Jovanovich, 1979.

Benn, Stanley I. "Wickedness." *Ethics* 95 (1985): 795–810.

Berger, Peter, and Thomas Luckmann. *The Social Construction of Reality.* Harmondsworth: Penguin Books, 1966.

Besteman, Catherine. "Violent Politics and the Politics of Violence." *American Ethnolologist* 23, no. 3 (1996): 579–96.

Biderman, A. D. "Social-Political Needs and 'Involuntary' Behavior as Illustrated by Compliance In Interrogation." *Sociometry* 23 (1960): 120–47.

Billeter, Jean François. "The System of 'Class Status.'" In *The Scope of State Politics in China,* ed. Stuart Schram, 127–69. London: School of Oriental and African Studies, 1985.

Boesche, R. "The Prison: Tocqueville's Model for Despotism." *Western Political Quarterly* 33, no. 4 (1980): 550–63.

Boudarel, Georges. *Cent fleurs eclosés dans la nuit du Vietnam: Communisme et dissidence, 1954–1956.* Paris: Jacques Bertoin, 1991.

Boyer, Paul and Stephen Nissenbaum. *Salem Possessed: The Social Origins of Witchcraft*. Cambridge: Harvard University Press, 1974.

Branigan, William. "Khmer Prison Still Haunts Nation." *Washington Post*, August 12, 1981.

Brankov, Lazare. "János Kádar et l'interrogation de Lászlo Rajk." *Communisme* 32–34 (1992–1993): 189–208.

Braun, Julia, and Janine Puget. "State Terrorism and Psychoanalysis." *International Journal of Mental Health* 18 (1989): 98–112.

Brecht, Bertold. *The Measures Taken*. Trans. Carl Mueller. London: Methuen, 1977.

Breton, Albert, and R. Wintrobe. "The Bureaucracy of Murder Revisited." *Journal of Political Economy* 94 (1986): 905–26.

Browning, Christopher. "Ordinary Men or Ordinary Germans." In Robert R. Shandley, ed. *Unwilling Germans? The Goldhagen Debate*. Minneapolis: University of Minnesota Press, 1998, 55–74.

———. "German Memory, Judicial Interrogation and Historical Reconstruction: Writing Perpetrator History from Postwar Testimony." In *Probing the Limits of Representation: Nazism and the "Final Solution,"* ed. Saul Friedlander, 22–36. Cambridge: Harvard University Press, 1992.

———. *Ordinary Men: Reserve Police Batallion 101 and the Final Solution in Poland*. New York: Harper Collins, 1992.

Bryson, John. "Cambodia Rakes the Ashes of Her Ruin." *Life*, March 1980, 44–50.

Brzezinski, Zbigniew. *The Permanent Purge: Politics in Soviet Totalitarianism*. Cambridge: Harvard University Press, 1956.

Bui Tin. *Following Ho Chi Minh: Memoirs of a Vietnamese Colonel*. London: Hart, 1995.

Burchett, Wilfred. *The China–Cambodia–Vietnam Triangle*. London: Zed Press, 1980.

Burgler, R. A. *The Eyes of the Pineapple: Revolutionary Intellectuals and Terror in Pol Pot's Kampuchea*. Saarbrucken: Verlag Breitenback, 1990.

Buruma, Ian. *The Wages of Guilt: Memories of War in Germany and Japan*. New York: Farrar Straus and Giroux, 1994.

Bushnell, P. Timothy, Vladimir Shlapentokh, Christopher K. Vanderpool, and Jeyaratnam Sundram, eds. *State Organized Terror: The Case of Violent Internal Repression*. Boulder: Westview Press, 1991.

Byron, John, and Robert Pack. *The Claws of the Dragon*. New York: Simon and Schuster, 1992.

Candland, Christopher, ed. *The Spirit of Violence: An Interdisciplinary Bibliography of Religion and Violence*. New York: Harry Frank Guggenheim Foundation, 1992.

Carmichael, Joel. *Stalin's Masterpiece: The Show Trials and Purges of the 30s*. London: Weidenfeld and Nicolson, 1976.

Carney, Timothy. "The Unexpected Victory." In *Cambodia 1975–1978: Rendezvous with Death,* ed. Karl Jackson, 13–36. Princeton: Princeton University Press, 1989.

———. "The Organization of Power." In *Cambodia 1975–1978: Rendezvous with Death,* ed. Karl Jackson, 79–198. Princeton: Princeton University Press, 1989.

———. *Communist Party Power in Kampuchea (Cambodia): Documents and Discussion.* Ithaca: Cornell Southeast Asia Program Data Paper 106, 1977.

Certeau, Michel de. "Corps torturés, paroles capturées." *Cahiers pour un temps,* special issue, ed. Luce Giard, 1987: 19–70.

Chalk, Frank and Kurt Jonnason, eds. *The History and Sociology of Genocide: Analyses and Case Studies.* New Haven: Yale University Press, 1990.

Chameau, Christine. "No. 55 Delivers His Verdict." *Phnom Penh Post,* 7–20 November 1997.

———. "Rehabilitation Completed." *Phnom Penh Post,* 7–20 November 1997.

Chanda, Nayan. *Brother Enemy.* New York: Harcourt Brace, 1986.

———. "The Cambodian Holocaust." *Far Eastern Economic Review,* 20 July 1979.

———. "Cambodia: Fifteen Days that Shook Asia." *Far Eastern Economic Review,* 19 January 1979.

Chandler, David. *Facing the Cambodian Past: Selected Essays, 1972–1994.* Sydney: Allen and Unwin, 1996.

———. "Facing Death: Photographs from S-21." *Photographers International,* April 1995, 12–21.

———. *Brother Number One: A Political Biography of Pol Pot.* Boulder: Westview Press, 1992.

———. *The Tragedy of Cambodian History: Politics, War and Revolution since 1945.* New Haven: Yale University Press, 1991.

———. "Seeing Red: Perceptions of Cambodian History in Democratic Kampuchea," in *Revolution and Its Aftermath in Kampuchea,* ed. David Chandler and Ben Kiernan. New Haven: Yale University Southeast Asia Studies Monograph 25, 1983.

———. "Revising the Past in Democratic Kampuchea: When Was the Birthday of the Party?" *Pacific Affairs* 56, no. 2 (Summer 1983): 283–300.

———. "The Constitution of Democratic Kampuchea: The Semantics of Revoltionary Change." *Pacific Affairs* 49, no. 3 (Fall 1976): 506–15.

Chandler, David, and Ben Kiernan, eds. *Revolution and Its Aftermath in Kampuchea: Eight Essays.* New Haven: Yale University Southeast Asia Studies Monograph 25, 1983.

Chandler, David, Ben Kiernan, and Chanthou Boua, eds. and tr. *Pol Pot Plans the Future: Confidential Leadership Documents from Democratic Kampuchea, 1976–1977.* New Haven: Yale University Southeast Asian Studies Monograph 33, 1988.

Chang, Anita. "Dispelling Misconceptions about the Red Guard Movement." *Journal of Contemporary China* Fall 1992, 61–85.

———. *Children of Mao: Personality Development and Political Activism in the Red Guard Generation.* Berkeley: University of California Press, 1985.

Chang, Anita, et al., eds. *On Socialist Democracy and the Chinese Legal System: The Li Yizhe Debates.* Armonk, N.Y.: M. E. Sharpe, 1980.

Chang, Parris. "The Rise of Wang Tung-hsing, Head of China's Secret Police." *China Quarterly* 73 (March 1978): 122–37.

Charny, I. W., ed. *Genocide: A Critical Bibliographic Review.* New York: Facts on File, 1988.

Chen, King C. *China's War with Vietnam.* Stanford: Stanford University Press, 1987.

Chhang Youk. "The Poisonous Hill that is Tuol Sleng." *Phnom Penh Post,* 3–15 May 1997.

Chirot, Daniel. *Modern Tyrants.* New York: Free Press, 1994.

Chomsky, Noam, and Edward S. Hermann. *After the Cataclysm: Postwar Indochina and the Reconstruction of Imperial Ideology.* Boston: South End Press, 1979.

Chu, Yuan-Horng. "The Counter-Revolution—A Family of Crimes: Chinese Communist Revolutionary Rhetoric, 1928–1989." In *The Web of Violence,* ed. Jennifer Turpin and Lester R. Kuritz, 69–89. Urbana: University of Illinois Press, 1997.

Chun-Chieh Huang and E. Zurcher, eds. *Norms and the State in China.* Leiden: Brill, 1994.

Clark, Andrew. "The Nightmare at the End of a Voyage of a Lifetime." *Sunday Times Magazine,* 11 May 1980.

Clark, Ernest. "Revolutionary Ritual: A Comparative Analysis of Thought Reform and the Show Trial." *Studies in Comparative Communism* 9 (1976): 226–43.

Coedes, G., and C. Archaimbault. *Les trois mondes.* Paris: École Française de l'Extrême Orient, 1973.

Collins, Randall. "Three Faces of Evil: Toward a Comparative Sociology of Evil." *Theory and Society* 1 (1974): 415–40.

Communist Party of the Soviet Union, Central Committee. *History of the Communist Party of the Soviet Union (Bolshevik).* Moscow, 1939.

Compton, Boyd, ed. *Mao's China: Party Reform Documents, 1942–1944.* Seattle: University of Washington Press, 1966.

Conquest, Robert. *The Great Terror: A Reassessment.* New York: Oxford University Press, 1990.

Copjec, Joan, ed. *Radical Evil.* London: Verso, 1996.

Corben, Ron. "Red Tank Massacre Revealed." *The Australian,* 22 August 1994.

Coronil, E., and J. Skurski. "Dismembering and Remembering the Nation: The Semantics of Political Violence in Venezuela." *Comparative Studies in Society and History* 33 (1991): 288–337.

Corradi, Juan. "The Culture of Fear in Civil Society." In *From Military Rule to Liberal Democracy in Argentina,* ed. Monica Peralta-Ramos and Carlos Waisman. Boulder: Westview Press, 1986.

Corradi, Juan, Patricia Weiss Fagen et al., eds. *Fear at the Edge: State Terror and Resistance in Latin America.* Berkeley: University of California Press, 1992.

Corrèze, Françoise, and Alain Forest. *Cambodge à deux voix.* Paris: L'Harmattan, 1984.

Cover, Robert M. "Violence and the Word." *Yale Law Journal* 95 (July 1980): 1301–29.

Crews, Frederick. *The Memory Wars: Freud's Legacy in Dispute.* New York: New York Review Books, 1995.

Cribb, Robert, ed. *The Indonesian Killings, 1965–1966 : Studies from Java and Bali.* Clayton, Australia: Monash University Centre of Southeast Asian Studies, Papers on Southeast Asia 21, 1991.

Dai Qing. *Wang Shiwei and "Wild Lilies": Rectification and Purges in the Chinese Communist Party, 1942–1944.* Armonk, N.Y.: M. E. Sharpe, 1994.

Dallin, A., and G. Breslauer. *Political Terror in Communist Systems.* Stanford: Stanford University Press, 1970.

D'Amato, Anthony. "Torture as *raison d'état.*" *Criminal Justice and Ethics* 18 (1991): 98–108.

Daniel, E. Valentine. *Charred Lullabies: Chapters in an Anthropography of Violence.* Princeton: Princeton University Press, 1996.

Darley, John M. "Constructive and Destructive Obedience: A Taxonomy of Principal-Agent Relationships." *Journal of Social Issues* 51, no. 3 (Fall 1995): 125–51.

———. "Social Organization for the Production of Evil." *Psychological Inquiry* 3, no. 2 (1992). 199–218.

Davis, David Brion. *Revolutions.* Cambridge: Harvard University Press, 1990.

Delvert, Jean. *Le paysan cambodgien.* Paris: Mouton, 1961.

Demos, John. "Accusers, Victims, Bystanders: The Innerlife Dimension." In *Entertaining Witchcraft* (1982), reprinted in *Psycho/history,* ed. Geoffrey Cocks and Travis Crosby, 254–66. New Haven: Yale University Press, 1987.

Dimsdale, Joel E., ed. *Survivors, Victims and Perpetrators: Essays on the Nazi Holocaust.* New York: Hemisphere, 1980.

Dispot, Laurent. *La machine à terreur.* Paris: Grasset, 1978.

Dittmer, Lowell. "Rectification and Purges in Chinese Politics." *Pacific Affairs* 53 (1980): 509–14.

———. "Bases of Power in Chinese Politics." *World Politics* 31 (1978): 26–60.

———. "Thought Reform and Cultural Revolution: An Analysis of the Symbolism of Chinese Polemics." *American Political Science Review* 71, no. 1 (1977): 67–85.

Dittmer, Lowell, and Chen Ruoxi. *Ethics and Rhetoric of the Chinese Cultural Revolution.* Berkeley: University of California Center for Chinese Studies, 1981.

Djilas, Milovan. *Of Prisons and Ideas.* New York: Harcourt Brace Jovanovich, 1986.

Driver. E. D. "Confessions and the Social Psychology of Coercion." *Harvard Law Review* 82 (1968): 42–61.

DuBois, Page. *Torture and Truth.* New York: Routledge, 1991.

Dunlop, Nic, and Nate Thayer. "Duch Confesses." *Far Eastern Economic Review,* 6 May 1999.

Dunn, Stephen. *Riffs and Reciprocities: Prose Pairs.* New York: Norton, 1998.

Duras, Marguerite. "Albert du Capitale." In *La douleur.* Paris: Presses Universitaires de France, 1985, 133–62.

Dutton, Michael R. *Policing and Punishment in China: From Patriarchy to "The People."* Cambridge: Cambridge University Press, 1992.

Ebihara, May. "Societal Organization in Sixteenth and Seventeenth Century Cambodia." *Journal of Southeast Asian Studies* 15, no. 2 (September 1984): 280–95.

Ebihara, May, Carol A. Mortland, and Judy Ledgerwood, eds. *Cambodian Culture since 1975: Homeland and Exile.* Ithaca: Cornell University Press, 1994.

Elliott, David, ed. *The Third Indochina Conflict.* Boulder: Westview Press, 1981.

Elms, A. C. "Obedience in Retrospect." *Journal of Social Issues* 51, no. 3 (Fall 1995): 21–32.

Elms, A. C., and S. Milgram. "Personality Characteristics Associated with Obedience and Defiance toward Authoritative Command." *Journal of Experimental Research in Personality* 2 (1966): 282–89.

Engelbert, Thomas, and Christopher E. Goscha. *Falling out of Touch : A Study on Vietnamese Communist Policy towards an Emerging Cambodian Communist Movement, 1930–1975.* Clayton, Australia : Centre of Southeast Asian Studies, Monash University, 1995.

Erlanger, Steven. "Phnom Penh Journal: A Museum for the Things Too Painful to Forget." *New York Times,* 30 December 1988.

Etcheson, Craig. "Terror in the East: Phases of Repression in Region 23 of Democratic Kampuchea." Unpublished paper, 1997.

———. "Centralized Terror in Democratic Kampuchea." Paper delivered at Association for Asian Studies Annual Meeting. Chicago, 1997.

———. *The Rise and Demise of Democratic Kampuchea.* Boulder: Westview Press, 1987.

Faligot, Roger, and Remi Kauffer. *The Chinese Secret Service.* London: Headline, 1989.

Farber, I. E., H. F. Harlow, and L. West. "Brainwashing, Conditioning and DDD (Debility, Dependency and Dread)." *Sociometry* (1957): 27–85.

Fayard, J.-F. *La justice revolutionnaire: Chronique de la Terreur.* Paris: Hachette, 1987.

Fein, Helen. "Revolutionary and Anti-revolutionary Genocides: A Comparison of State Murders in Democratic Kampuchea, 1975 to 1979, and in Indonesia, 1965 to 1966." *Comparative Studies in Society and History* 35, no. 4 (October 1993): 796–823.

———. *Genocide: A Sociological Perspective.* London: Sage, 1990.

Feitlowitz, Marguerite. *A Lexicon of Terror: Argentina and the Legacies of Torture.* New York: Oxford University Press, 1998.

Feldman, Allen. *Formations of Violence: The Narrative of the Body and Political Terror in Northern Ireland.* Chicago: University of Chicago Press, 1991.

Finkelstein, Norman. "Daniel Jonah Goldhagen's 'Crazy' Thesis." *New Left Review* 224 (July–August 1997): 39–88.

Forrest, Duncan, ed. *A Glimpse of Hell: Report on Torture Worldwide.* New York: New York University Press, 1996.

Foucault, Michel. "Why Study Power: The Question of the Subject." In *Michel Foucault: Beyond Structuralism and Hermeneutics,* ed. Hubert Dreyfus and Paul Rabinow. Chicago: University of Chicago Press, 1982.

————. *Discipline and Punish*. New York: Vintage Books, 1979.

————. "La grand colère des faits." In *Faut-il brûler les nouveaux philosophes?* ed. Silvie Boucasse and Denis Bourgeois. Paris: Nouvelles Éditions Oswald, 1978, 63–79.

Frame, William V. *Dialectical Historicism and Terror in Chinese Communism.* Ann Arbor: University Microfilms, 1970.

French, Lindsay. "Exhibiting Terror." Paper delivered at the annual meeting of the Association for Asian Studies, Washington, D.C., 1998.

Friedlander, Saul, ed. *Probing the Limits of Representation: Nazism and the "Final Solution."* Cambridge: Harvard University Press, 1992.

Friedman, Edward. *National Identity and Democratic Prospects in Socialist China.* Armonk, N.Y.: M. E. Sharpe, 1995.

————. "After Mao: Maoism and Post-Mao China." *Telos* (1986): 23–46.

Frieson, Kate. "The Political Nature of Democratic Kampuchea." *Pacific Affairs* 61 (Fall 1988): 405–27.

Frings, Viviane. *Allied and Equal: The Kampuchean People's Revolutionary Party's Historiography and Its Relations with Vietnam.* Clayton, Australia: Monash University Centre of Southeast Asian Studies, Working Paper 90, 1994.

Furet, François, ed. *Unanswered Questions: Nazi Germany and the Jews.* New York: Schocken, 1989.

Furet, François, and Ernst Nolte. *Fascisme et Communisme.* Paris: Plon, 1998.

Fyfield, John. *Re-educating Chinese Anti-Communists.* New York: St. Martin's Press, 1983.

Gao Yu. *Born Red.* Stanford: Stanford University Press, 1986.

Garfinkel, H. "Conditions of Successful Degradation Ceremonies." *American Journal of Sociology* 61 (1956): 420–24.

Gay, Peter. *Freud: A Life for Our Time.* New York: Norton, 1988.

————. *Freud for Historians.* New York: Oxford University Press, 1985.

Geertz, Clifford. *Local Knowledge.* New York: Basic Books, 1983.

Getty, J. Arch. *Origins of the Great Purges: The Soviet Communist Party Reconsidered, 1933–1939.* Cambridge: Cambridge University Press, 1985.

Getty, J. Arch, and Roberta T. Manning, eds. *Stalinist Terror: New Perspectives.* Cambridge: Cambridge University Press, 1993.

Getty, J. Arch, Gabor T. Rittersporn, and V. N. Zemskov. "Victims of the Soviet Penal System in the Pre-War Years: A First Approach on the Basis of Archival Evidence." *American Historical Review* 98, no. 4 (October 1993): 1017–48.

Gibson, Janice T. "Training People to Inflict Pain: State Terror and Social Learning." *Journal of Humanistic Psychology* 31, no. 2 (1991): 72–87.

Gibson, Janice, and Mika Harotos-Fatouros. "The Education of a Torturer." *Psychology Today* 20 (1986): 50–58.

Giddens, Anthony. *A Contemporary Critique of Historical Materialism.* Vol. 2: *The Nation-State and Violence.* Berkeley: University of California Press, 1985.

Gilboa, Yehoshue A. *Confess! Confess! Eight Years in Soviet Prisons.* Boston: Little, Brown, 1968.

Ginzburg, Carlo. "Killing a Chinese Mandarin: The Moral Implications of Distance." In *Historical Change and Human Rights,* ed. Olwen Hufton. New York: Basic Books, 1995.

———. *Myths, Emblems, Clues.* London: Hutchinson, 1990.

Goffman, Erving. *Asylums: Essays on the Social Situation of Mental Patients and Other Inmates.* Garden City, N.Y.: Doubleday, 1961.

Goldfield, Anne, Richard Mollica, et al. "The Physical and Psychological Sequelae of Torture." *Journal of the American Medical Association* 259, no. 18 (1988), 2725–29.

Goldhagen, Daniel. *Hitler's Willing Executioners: Ordinary Germans and the Holocaust.* New York: Alfred A. Knopf, 1996.

Gough, Kathleen. "Roots of the Pol Pot Regime in Cambodia." In *Themes in Ethnology and History: Essays in Honor of David E. Aberle,* ed. Donald Leland. Meerut, India: Archana Publications, 1987, 125–74.

Gourevitch, Philip. *We Wish to Inform You That Tomorrow We Will Be Killed with Our Families.* New York: Farrar, Straus, 1998.

———. "Letter from Rwanda: After the Genocide." *New Yorker,* 18 December 1995, 78–95.

Graziano, Frank. *Divine Violence: Spectacle, Psychosexuality and Radical Christianity in the Argentine "Dirty War."* Boulder: Westview Press, 1992.

Greenfeld, Liah. "Formation of the Russian National Identity: The Role of Status Insecurity and *Ressentiment.*" *Comparative Studies in Society and History* 32, no. 3 (July 1990): 549–91.

Gregory, Stephen, and Daniel Timerman. "Rituals of the Modern State: The Case of Torture in Argentina." *Dialectical Anthropology* 11, no. 1 (1986): 63–72.

Griffin, Patricia. *The Chinese Communist Treatment of Counter-Revolutionaries, 1924–1949.* Princeton: Princeton University Press, 1976.

Gudjonsson, Gisli. *The Psychology of Interrogations, Confessions and Testimony.* Chichester: John Wiley, 1992.

———. "The Application of Interrogative Suggestibility to Police Interviewing." In *Human Suggestibility,* ed. John F. Schumacher, 279–88. New York: Routledge, 1991.

Guo, Mobo C. F. "Maoist Discourse and a Critique of the Present Assessments of the Cultural Revolution." *Bulletin of Concerned Asian Scholars* 26, no. 3 (July–September 1994): 13–32.

Gurta, M., et al. "Torture and Related Behavior." *Psychohistorical Review* 18 (1990): 219–27.

Han, Harry H., ed. *Terrorism and Political Violence.* New York: Oceana, 1993.

Haney, Craig, Curtis Banks, et al. "Interpersonal Dynamics in a Simulated Prison." *International Journal of Criminology and Penology* 1 (1973): 69–97.

Hannum, Hurst, and David Hawk. *The Case against the Standing Committee of the Communist Party of Kampuchea.* New York: Cambodia Documentation Commission, September 1986.

Hansen, Anne R., and Bounthay Phath. "Understanding Suffering in the Context of Khmer Buddhism." Unpublished paper, Harvard University, 1988.

Hanson, Elizabeth. "Torture and Truth in Renaissance England." *Representations* 34 (1991): 53–84.

Harff, Barbara, and Ted Gurr. "Toward an Empirical Theory of Genocides and Politicides: Identification and Measurement of Cases since 1945." *International Studies Quarterly* 32 (1988): 359–71.

Haritos-Fatouros, M. "The Official Torturer: A Learning Model for Obedience to the Authority of Violence." *Journal of Applied Social Psychology* 18 (October 1988): 1107–20.

Harrison, Judy. "Wrongful Treatment of Prisoners: A Case Study in Ch'ing Legal Procedure." *Journal of Asian Studies* 23 (1964): 227–44.

Haslam, J. "Political Opposition to Stalin and the Origins of Terror in Russia, 1932–1936." *Historical Journal* 29 (1986): 395–418.

Hawk, David. "International Law and Cambodian Genocide: The Sounds of Silence." *Human Rights Quarterly* 11 (1989): 82–138.

———. "The Photographic Record." In *Cambodia 1975–1978: Rendezvous with Death,* ed. Karl Jackson. Princeton: Princeton University Press, 1989, 209–14.

———. "The Cambodian Genocide." In *Genocide: A Critical Bibliographic Review,* ed. Israel Charny. New York: Facts on File, 1988, 137–53.

———. "The Tuol Sleng Extermination Center (Cambodia)." *Index on Censorship* 15, no. 1 (January 1986): 25–31.

———. "Pol Pot's Cambodia: Was It Genocide?" In *Toward the Understanding and Prevention of Genocide,* ed. Joel Charny. Boulder: Westview Press, 1984.

———. "The Killing of Cambodia." *New Republic,* November 19, 1982, 17–21.

Haynal, André, Miklos Mólnar, and Gerard de Puymège. *Fanaticism: A Historical and Psychoanalytical Study.* New York: Schocken, 1983.

Heaslet, Juliana P. "The Red Guards: Instruments of Destruction in the Cultural Revolution." *Asian Survey* 19 (1972): 1932–47.

Heder, Steve. "Racism, Marxism, Labelling and Genocide in Ben Kiernan's *The Pol Pot Regime.*" *Southeast Asian Research* 5, no. 2 (1997): 101–53.

———. *Pol Pot and Khieu Samphan.* Clayton, Australia: Monash University Centre of Southeast Asian Studies Working Paper 70, 1991.

———. "Khmer Rouge Opposition to Pol Pot: 'Pro-Vietnamese' or 'Pro-Chinese.'" Unpublished paper, Australian National University, 28 August 1990.

Heder, Steve, and Judy Ledgerwood, eds. *Propaganda, Politics and Violence in Cambodia.* Armonk, N.Y.: M. E. Sharpe, 1996.

Heder, Steve, and Masoto Matsushita. "Interviews with Kampuchean Refugees at Thai-Cambodian Border." Unpublished paper, 1980.

Hepworth, Mike, and Bryan Turner. *Confession: Studies in Dominance and Religion.* London: Routledge, 1982.

Heryanto, Ariel. "Discourse and State Terrorism: A Case Study of Political Trials in New Order Indonesia, 1988–1990." Ph.D. diss., Monash University, 1992.

Heuveline, Patrick. "Between One and Three Million: Towards the Demographic Reconstruction of a Decade of Cambodian History (1970–1979)." *Population Studies* 52 (1998): 49–65.

Hiegel, Jean-Pierre, and Colette Landrac. "Les khmers rouges: Orthodoxie et paradoxe." *Les temps modernes* 525 (1992): 62–90.

———. "Revolution des khmers rouges et pathologie mentale." *Les temps modernes* 523 (February 1990): 23–49.

Hilberg, Raul. "Perpetrators, Victims, Bystanders: The Jewish Catastrophe, 1933–1945." Unpublished paper, 1992.

Hinkle, Lawrence, and H. G. Wolff. "Communist Interrogation and Indoctrination of 'Enemies of the State.'" *Archives of Neurology and Psychiatry* (1956): 115–74.

Hinton, Alexander Laban. "A Head for an Eye: Revenge in the Cambodian Genocide." *American Ethnologist* 25, no. 3 (1998): 352–77.

———. "Why Did You Kill? The Cambodian Genocide and the Dark Side of Face and Honor." *Journal of Asian Studies* 57, no. 1 (February 1998): 93–122.

———. *Cambodia's Shadow: An Examination of the Cultural Origins of Genocide*. Ann Arbor: University Microfilms, 1998.

———. "Agents of Death: Explaining the Cambodian Genocide in Terms of Psychosocial Dissonance." *American Anthropologist* 98, no. 4 (1996): 818–31.

Hirsch, Herbert. *Genocide and the Politics of Memory*. Chapel Hill: University of North Carolina Press, 1995.

Hochschild, Adam. *King Leopold's Ghost: A Story of Greed, Terror, and Heroism in Colonial Africa*. Boston: Houghton Mifflin, 1998.

Hodos, George. *Show Trials: Stalinist Purges in Eastern Europe, 1948–1954*. New York: Praeger, 1987.

Hoffer, Eric. *The True Believer*. New York: Harper and Row, 1951.

Hoffman, Jan. "Police Refine Methods So Potent, Even the Innocent Have Confessed." *New York Times,* 30 March 1998.

Holquist, Peter. "'Information is the Alpha and Omega of Our Work': Bolshevik Surveillance in Its Pan-European Context." *Journal of Modern History* 69 (September 1997): 415–50.

Horowitz, Irving Louis. *Taking Lives*. New Brunswick: Transaction Books, 1997.

Hou Youn. "The Peasantry of Kampuchea: Colonialism and Modernization." In Ben Kiernan and Chanthou Boua, *Peasants and Politics in Kampuchea, 1942–1981*, 34–68. Armonk, N.Y.: M. E. Sharpe, 1982.

Hu Yao-ping. "Problems Concerning the Purge of K'ang Sheng." *Issues and Studies* (June 1980): 74–100.

Huggins, Martha T. "Brazilian Political Violence: Legacies of Authoritarianism in Police Professionalism, a Study of Torturers and Murders." Unpublished paper, April 1998.

Ignatieff, Michael. *The Warrior's Honor*. New York: Henry Holt, 1997.

Imbert, Jean. *Histoire des institutions khmeres*. Phnom Penh: Portail, 1961.

Inbau, F. E. *Criminal Interrogation and Confessions*. Baltimore: Williams and Wilkins, 1986.

Ith Sarin. "Regrets of the Khmer Soul." In *Communist Party Power in Kampuchea (Cambodia): Documents and Discussion,* ed. Timothy Carney. Ithaca: Cornell University Southeast Asia Program Data Paper 106, 1977.

Jackson, Karl, ed. *Cambodia 1975–1978: Rendezvous with Death*. Princeton: Princeton University Press, 1989.

Jacques, Claude. "Nouvelles orientations pour l'étude de l'histoire du pays khmer." *Asie du sud-est et monde insulindien* 13 (1–4, 1982): 39–57.

James, Gene G. "Brainwashing: The Myth and the Actuality." *Thought*, June 1986, 241–57.

Joffe, Josef. "Goldhagen in Germany." *New York Review of Books*, 28 November 1996.

Jonasson, Kurt. "The Consequences of Ideological Genocides and Their Role in Genocide Prevention." *Armenian Review* 42 (1989): 1–16.

Joravsky, David. "Comrade Stalin and His Party." In Joravsky, *Russian Psychology: A Critical History*. Oxford: Blackwell, 1989, 311–34.

Jordens, Justin. *A 1991 State of Cambodia Political Education Text: Exposition and Analysis*. Clayton, Australia: Monash University Centre of Southeast Asian Studies Working Paper 71, 1993.

Joseph, William. *The Critique of Ultraleftism in China, 1958–1981*. Stanford: Stanford University Press, 1984.

Joseph, William, et al., eds. *New Perspectives on the Cultural Revolution*. Cambridge: Harvard University Press, 1991.

———. "A Tragedy of Good Intentions: Post-Mao Views of the Great Leap Forward." *Modern China* 19, no. 4 (October 1986): 419–57.

Kafka, Franz. *The Trial*. Trans. Edwin and Wilma Muir. New York: Schocken Books, 1956.

Kamm, Henry. *Cambodia: Report from a Stricken Land*. New York: Arcade Publishing, 1998.

Kampuchea Dossier, 3 vols. Hanoi: Vietnam Courier, 1978–1979.

———. "Cambodian Refugees Depict Growing Famine and Hunger." *New York Times*, 13 May 1978.

Kampuchea Démocratique, Ministère des Affaires Étrangères. *Livre noir: Faits et preuves des actes d'aggression et d'annexation du Vietnam contre le Kampuchea (septembre 1978)*. Paris: Éditions du Centenaire, 1979.

Kapferer, Bruce. *Legends of People, Myths of State: Violence, Intolerance and Political Culture in Sri Lanka and Australia*. Washington, D.C.: Smithsonian Institution Press, 1988.

Kaplan, Robert D. *The Ends of the Earth*. Boston: Houghton Mifflin, 1996.

Karklins, Rasma. "The Organization of Power in Soviet Labor Camps." *Soviet Studies* 41, no. 2 (April 1989): 276–97.

Kekes, John. *Facing Evil*. Princeton: Princeton University Press, 1990.

Kelman, Herbert C. "Violence without Moral Restraint." *Journal of Social Issues* 29 (1973): 29–61.

Kelman, Herbert C., and V. Lee Hamilton. *Crimes of Obedience*. New Haven: Yale University Press, 1989.

Keng Pao. "Report on the Situation in the Indochinese Peninsula, January 1979." *Issues and Studies* (January 1981): 78–96.

Keo Norin. "La mobilisation des ressources nationales pour une développement autonome du Kampuchea Democratique (1975–1978)." *Asie du sud-est et monde insulindien* 15, nos. 1–4, 1984: 331–49.

Kernig, C. D., ed. *Marxism, Communism and Western Society.* 8 vols. New York: Herder and Herder, 1973.

Keyes, Charles F. "Communist Revolution and the Buddhist Past in Cambodia." In *Asian Visions of Authority,* ed. Charles F. Keyes, Laurel Kendall, and Helen Hardacre, 43–74. Honolulu: University of Hawaii Press, 1993.

Khlevnyuk, Oleg. "The Objectives of the Great Terror, 1937–1938." In *Soviet History 1919–1953 : Essays in Honour of R. W. Davies,* ed. Julian Cooper, Maureen Perrie, and E. A. Rees, 158–75. London: St. Martin's Press, 1995.

Kiernan, Ben. *The Pol Pot Regime: Politics, Race and Genocide in Cambodia under the Khmer Rouge, 1975–1979.* New Haven: Yale University Press, 1996.

———, ed. *Genocide and Democracy in Cambodia.* New Haven: Yale University Southeast Asian Studies Monograph 41, 1993.

———. *Cambodia: The Eastern Zone Massacres.* Documentation Series, No. 1. New York: Columbia University Center for the Study of Human Rights, 1986.

———. *How Pol Pot Came to Power.* London: Verso, 1985.

———. "Wild Chickens, Farm Chickens and Cormorants: Kampuchea's Eastern Zone under Pol Pot." In *Revolution and Its Aftermath in Kampuchea: Eight Essays,* ed. David Chandler and Ben Kiernan, 136–211. New Haven: Yale University Southeast Asia Studies Monograph 25, 1983.

Kiernan, Ben, and Chanthou Boua. *Peasants and Politics in Kampuchea, 1942–1981.* Armonk, N.Y.: M. E. Sharpe, 1982.

Kiljunnen, Kimmo, ed. *Kampuchea: Decade of the Genocide.* London: Zed Books, 1984.

Kinzie, J. D. "The 'Concentration Camp Syndrome' among Cambodian Refugees." In *The Cambodian Agony,* ed. David Ablin and Marlowe Hood, 332–52. Armonk, N.Y.: M. E. Sharpe, 1989.

Klor de Alva, J. J. "Raconter des vies: L'autobiographie confessionelle et la reconstruction de l'être nahua." *Archive des sciences sociales et religions* 77 (1992): 19–35.

Koestler, Arthur. *Darkness at Noon.* New York: Macmillan, 1948.

———. *Scum of the Earth.* New York: Macmillan, 1941.

Kotkin, Stephen. *Magnetic Mountain: Stalinism as a Civilization.* Stanford: Stanford University Press, 1995.

Kramer, Barry. "Cambodia's Communist Regime Begins to Purge Its Own Ranks." *Wall Street Journal,* 19 October 1977.

Kraus, Richard Curt. *Class Conflict in Chinese Socialism.* New York: Columbia University Press, 1981.

———. "Class Conflict and the Vocabulary of Social Analysis in China." *China Quarterly* 69 (1977): 54–74.

Krohn Hansen, Christian. "The Anthropology of Violent Interaction." *Journal of Anthropological Research* (1994): 368–81.

Kubis, J. F. "Instrumental, Chemical and Psychological Aids in The Interrogation of Witnesses." *Journal of Social Issues* 13, no. 2 (1957): 40–49.

Kuhn, Philip A. *Soulstealers: The Chinese Sorcery Scare of 1968.* Cambridge: Harvard University Press, 1990.

————. "Chinese Views of Social Classification." In *Class and Stratification in Post-Revolution China*, ed. James L. Watson. Cambridge: Cambridge University Press, 1983.

Kundera, Milan. *The Art of the Novel*. New York: Grove Press, 1986.

Kuper, Leo. *Genocide: Its Political Use in the Twentieth Century*. New Haven: Yale University Press, 1981.

Labedz, L. "Holocaust." *Survey* 30 (1980): 240–63.

LaCapra, Dominick. *History and Memory after Auschwitz*. Ithaca: Cornell University Press, 1998.

La Fontaine, Jean de. *The Complete Fables*. Translated by Norman Spector. Evanston, IL: Northwestern University Press, 1988.

Lahusen, Thomas, Veronique Garros, and Natalia Korenevskaya, eds. *Intimacy and Terror: Soviet Diaries of the 1930s*. New York: New Press, 1995.

Lampert, Nick, and G. Rittersporn, eds. *Stalinism: Its Nature and Aftermath*. Armonk, N.Y.: M. E. Sharpe, 1992.

Langbein, John H. *Torture and the Law of Proof*. Chicago: University of Chicago Press, 1977.

Le Carré, John. *The Secret Pilgrim*. New York: Bantam Books, 1990.

Leclère, Adhémard, trans. *Les codes cambodgiens*. 2 vols. Paris: Leroux, 1898.

Ledgerwood, Judy. "The Cambodian Tuol Sleng Museum of Genocidal Crimes: National Narrative." *Museum Anthroplogy* 21, no. 1 (Spring–Summer 1997): 83–98.

LeGoff, Jacques. *History and Memory*. Trans. Steven Rendall and Elizabeth Claman. New York: Columbia University Press, 1992.

Leites, Nathan. *Psychopolitical Analysis: Selected Writings*. Ed. E. W. Marvick. New York: John Wiley, 1977.

Leites, Nathan, and Elsa Bernaut. *Ritual of Liquidation: The Case of the Moscow Trials*. Glencoe, Ill.: Free Press, 1954.

Lev, Daniel, and Ruth McVey, eds. *Making Indonesia*. Ithaca: Cornell University Southeast Asia Program, 1996.

Levi, Primo. *Survival in Auschwitz*. Trans. Stuart Woolf. New York: Touchstone, 1996.

————. *The Drowned and the Saved*. Trans. R. Rosenthal. New York: Summit, 1988.

Lewis, John Wilson, ed. *Peasant Rebellion and Communist Revolution in Asia*. Stanford: Stanford University Press, 1974.

————, ed. *Party Leadership and Revolutionary Power in China*. Cambridge: Cambridge University Press, 1970.

Lewy, Guenther. *America in Vietnam*. New York: Oxford University Press, 1979.

Lewytzkyj, B. *Stalinist Terror in the Nineteen Thirties: Documentation from the Soviet Press*. Stanford: Hoover Institution Press, 1974.

Lifton, Robert Jay. *The Nazi Doctors: Medical Killing and the Psychology of Genocide*. New York: Basic Books, 1986.

————. *Revolutionary Immortality: Mao Tse-tung and the Chinese Revolution*. New York: Random House, 1968.

————. *Thought Reform and the Psychology of Totalism: A Study of "Brain-washing" in China.* New York: Norton, 1963.

Lifton, Robert Jay, and Eric Markusen. *The Genocidal Mentality.* New York: Basic Books, 1990.

Lin Jing. *The Red Guards' Path to Violence: Political, Educational and Psychological Factors.* New York: Praeger, 1991.

Ling Hsaio. "Keep on Criticizing the Bourgeoisie." *Peking Review,* 23 May 1975.

Lipman, Jonathan, and Stevan Harrell, eds. *Violence in China.* Buffalo: SUNY Press, 1992.

Liu Shaoqi. "How to Be a Good Communist." *Selected Works,* vol. 1, 194–98. Beijing: Foreign Languages Press, 1982.

Locard, Henri. *Le petit livre rouge de Pol Pot, ou les paroles de l'Angkar.* Paris: L'Harmattan, 1996.

————. "Le Goulag des khmers rouges." *Communisme* (1996): 127–64.

Locard, Henri, and Moeung Sonn. *Prisonnier de l'Angkar.* Paris: Fayard, 1993.

London, Artur. *The Confession.* London: Macdonald, 1971.

Lopate, Philip, ed. *The Art of the Personal Essay.* New York: Random House, 1986.

Lopez, George A., and David Pion-Berlin. "Of Victims and Executioners: Argentine State Terror, 1975–1979." *International Studies Quarterly* 35 (1987): 63–86.

Lu Xiuyuan. "A Step toward Understanding Popular Violence in China's Cultural Revolution." *Pacific Affairs* 67, no. 4 (Winter 1994–1995): 533–62.

Luhrmann, T. M. "The Magic of Secrecy." *Ethos* 17 (1989): 131–65.

Ma Bo. *Blood Red Sunset: A Memoir of China's Cultural Revolution.* New York: Viking, 1995.

MacCormack, Gavan. "The Kampuchean Revolution, 1975–1978: The Problem of Knowing the Truth." *Bulletin of Concerned Asian Scholars* 10, nos. 1–2 (1980): 75–118.

MacCormack, Geoffrey, ed. *Traditional Chinese Penal Law.* Edinburgh: Edinburgh University Press, 1990.

MacFarquhar, Roderick. *The Origins of the Cultural Revolution.* 3 vols. Oxford: Oxford University Press, 1986–1997.

MacFarquhar, Roderick, et al., eds. *The Secret Speeches of Chairman Mao.* Cambridge: Harvard University Press, 1989.

Malcolm, Janet. *The Purloined Clinic: Selected Writings.* New York: Alfred A. Knopf, 1992.

Markusen, Eric. "Comprehending the Cambodian Genocide: An Application of R. J. Lifton's Model of Genocidal Killing." *Psychohistory Review* 20 (1993): 149–69.

Marston, John. *Cambodia 1991–1994: Hierarchy, Neutrality and Etiquettes of Discourse.* Ann Arbor: University Microfilms, 1998.

————. "Metaphors of the Khmer Rouge." In *Cambodian Culture since 1975: Homeland and Exile,* ed. May Ebihara, Judy Ledgerwood, and Carol Mortland, 105–18. Ithaca: Cornell University Press, 1994.

————. "Language Reform in Democratic Kampuchea." M.A. thesis, University of Minnesota, 1984.

Martin, Marie Alexandrine. *Le mal cambodgien*. Paris: Hachette, 1989.

Masson, Jeffrey, ed. *The Complete Letters of Sigmund Freud to Wilhelm Fleiss, 1987–1904*. Cambridge: Harvard University Press, 1985.

Mate, Georges. *Genocide in Cambodia*. Budapest: Conseil Hongrois de la Paix, 1979.

May, William F. "Terrorism as Strategy and Ecstasy." *Social Research* (Summer 1974): 277–98.

McDowell, Robin. "Photographer Recalls Days behind Lens at Tuol Sleng." *Cambodia Daily*, 4 February 1997.

McIntyre, Angus. "The Training of Australian Communist Cadres in China." *Studies in Comparative Communism* 11, no. 4 (Winter 1978): 410–23.

McIntyre, Kevin. "Geography as Destiny: Cities, Villages and Khmer Rouge Orientalism." *Comparative Studies in Society and History* 35, no. 4 (October 1996): 730–58.

Meeus, W. H. J., and Q. A. W. Raaijinakers. "Obedience in Modern Society: The Utrecht Studies." *Journal of Social Issues* 52, no. 3 (Fall 1995): 155–75.

Meisner, Maurice. *Mao's China and After*. New York: Free Press, 1986.

———. *Marxism, Maoism and Utopianism*. Madison: University of Wisconsin Press, 1982.

Mele, Alfred. "Recent Work on Self-Deception." *American Philosophical Quarterly* 24, no. 1 (1987): 1–17.

Mellor, Alec. *La torture*. Paris: Horizons Littéraires, 1949.

Merkl, Peter H., ed. *Political Violence and Terror: Motifs and Motivations*. Berkeley: University of California Press, 1986.

Merleau-Ponty, Maurice. *Humanism and Terror*. Boston: Beacon Press, 1969.

Metzl, Jamie, *Western Responses to Human Rights Abuses in Cambodia, 1975–1980*. Oxford: St. Antony's College, 1996.

Milgram, Stanley. *Obedience to Authority: An Experimental View*. New York: Harper and Row, 1974.

Miller, Arthur G. *The Obedience Experiments: A Case of Controversy in the Social Sciences*. New York: Praeger, 1986.

Miller, Arthur G., Barry Collins, and Diane Brief, eds. *Perspectives on Obedience to Authority: The Legacy of the Milgram Experiment. Journal of Social Issues*, special issue, Fall 1995.

Miller, James. *The Passion of Michel Foucault*. New York: Simon and Schuster, 1993.

Millett, Kate. *The Politics of Cruelty : An Essay on The Literature of Political Imprisonment*. New York: Norton, 1994.

Mills, Charles W. "The Moral Epistemology of Stalinism." *Politics and Society* 22, no. 1 (March 1994): 31–58.

Milosz, Czeslaw. *The Captive Mind*. Harmondsworth: Penguin, 1980.

Minow, Martha. *Between Vengeance and Forgiveness: Facing History after Genocide and Mass Violence*. Boston: Beacon Press, 1998.

Moise, Edwin. "Classism in North Vietnam, 1953–1956." In *Vietnamese Communism in Comparative Perspective*, ed. William Turley, 91–196. Boulder: Westview Press, 1980.

———. "Land Reform and Land Reform Errors in North Vietnam." *Pacific Affairs* 9, no. 1 (Spring 1976): 70–92.

Mollica, Richard, and Yael Caspi-Yavin. "Assessing Torture and Torture-Related Symptoms." *Psychological Assessment* 3, no. 4 (1991): 581–87.

Montaigne, Michel de. "On Cruelty." In *The Complete Works of Montaigne,* ed. Donald Frame, 306–18. Stanford: Stanford University Press, 1957.

Moody, Peter A. *Opposition and Dissent in Contemporary China.* Stanford: Hoover Institution Press, 1977.

Moore, Barrington. *Inequality: The Social Bases of Obedience and Revolt.* White Plains, N.Y.: M. E. Sharpe, 1978.

Mydans, Seth. "70s Torturer in Cambodia 'Now Doing God's Work.'" *New York Times,* 2 May 1999.

———. "A Cambodian Woman's Tale: Assigning the Guilt for Genocide." *New York Times,* 21 January 1999.

———. "Twenty Years on, Anger Ignites against Khmer Rouge." *New York Times,* 10 January 1999.

———. "Come and Meet the Non-existent Khmer Rouge." *New York Times,* 24 July 1998.

———. "Cambodian Killer's Careful Records Used against Him." *New York Times,* 7 June 1996.

Nagengast, Carol. "Violence, Terror and the Crisis of the State." *Annual Review of Anthropology* 23 (1994): 109–36.

Naquin, Susan. "True Confessions: Criminal Investigations as Sources for Ch'ing History." *National Palace Museum Bulletin* (Taipei) 11, no. 1 (March–April 1976): 1–17.

Niven, Douglas, and Chris Riley, eds. *The Killing Fields.* Santa Fe: Twin Palms Press, 1996.

Nordstrom, Carolyn, and JoAnn Martin, eds. *The Paths to Domination, Resistance and Terror.* Berkeley: University of California Press, 1992.

Nordstrom, Carolyn, and Antonius C. G. M. Robben, eds. *Fieldwork under Fire: Contemporary Studies of Violence and Survival.* Berkeley: University of California Press, 1995.

Norodom Sihanouk. *Prisonnier des khmers rouges.* Paris: Hachette, 1986.

Nuon Chea. "History of the Revolutionary Movement." Translated by David Ashley. Unpublished manuscript, 1997.

———. "Statement of the CPK to the CWP of Denmark, July 1978." *Journal of Communist Studies* 3, no. 1 (March 1987): 20–30.

Ofshe, Richard. "Coerced Confessions: The Logic of Seemingly Irrational Action." *Cultic Studies Journal* 6 (1989): 1–15.

Ofshe, Richard, and Ethan Watters. *Making Monsters: False Memories, Psychotherapy and Sexual Hysteria.* New York: Charles Scribner's Sons, 1994.

O'Kane, Molly. "The Eradication of Year Zero." *Guardian Weekend,* 26 July 1997.

Ong Thong Hoeung. "Le 30 novembre j'ai quitté Phnom Penh precipitamment." In *Affaires cambodgiennes 1979–1989,* ed. C. Scalabrino, 121–28. Paris: L'Harmattan, 1989.

Orwell, George. *Nineteen Eighty Four.* New York: Harcourt Brace, 1949.

Pacy, James S., and Alan Wertheimer. *Perspectives on the Holocaust: Essays in Honor of Raul Hilberg.* Boulder: Westview Press, 1994.

Paden, R. "Surveillance and Torture: Foucault and Orwell on the Methods of Discipline." *Social Theory and Practice* 10 (Fall 1984): 29–71.

Paperno, Irina. *Suicide as a Cultural Institution in Dostoevsky's Russia.* Ithaca: Cornell University Press, 1997.

Patson, David. "Did Pol Pot Know that Mao Zedong's Great Leap Forward Had Failed?" B.A. Honours thesis, Monash University, 1990.

Pasqualini, J. "Glimpses Inside China's Gulag." *China Quarterly* (Winter 1993): 253–357.

Passerini, Louisa, ed. *Memory and Totalitarianism.* Oxford: Oxford University Press, 1992.

Paul, Anthony. "Plot Details Filter Through." *Far Eastern Economic Review,* May 19, 1978.

Pelikan, Jiři, ed. *The Czechoslovak Political Trials, 1950–1954.* Stanford: Stanford University Press, 1991.

People's Republic of Kampuchea. People's Revolutionary Tribunal . . . for the Trial of the Genocide Crime of the Pol Pot–Ieng Sary Clique. *The Extermination Camp of Tuol Sleng.* Document 2.4.10. Phnom Penh, 1979.

Perdue, William D. *Terrorism and the State: A Critique of Domination through Fear.* New York: Praeger, 1989.

Perrot, Michel, ed. *L'impossible prison.* Paris: Seuil, 1980.

Perry, Elizabeth J., and Li Xun. "Revolutionary Rudeness: The Language of Red Guards and Rebel Workers in China's Cultural Revolution." Bloomington: University of Indiana East Asian Studies Center, Working Paper No. 2, 1993.

Peschoux, Christophe. *Les nouveaux khmers rouges: Essai de débrouillage.* Paris: L'Harmattan, 1993.

Peters, Edward. *Torture.* Updated edition. Philadelphia: University of Pennsylvania Press, 1996.

Picq, Laurence. "I Remember What Ieng Sary Did." *Far Eastern Economic Review,* 10 October 1996.

———. *Au delà du ciel: Cinq ans chez les khmers rouges.* Paris: Barrault, 1984.

———. "De la réforme linguistique et de l'usage des mots khmers rouges." *Asie du sud-est et monde insulindien* 15, 1–4 (1984): 351–57.

Pilger, John. *Heroes.* London: Jonathan Cape, 1986.

Pin Yathay. *L'Utopie meurtrière.* Paris: Laffont, 1979.

Ponchaud, François. "Social Change in the Vortex of Revolution." In *Cambodia 1975–1978: Rendezvous with Death,* ed. Karl Jackson, 151–78. Princeton: Princeton University Press, 1989.

———. *Cambodia Year Zero.* New York: Henry Holt, 1977.

Price, E. H. "The Strategy and Tactics of Revolutionary Terrorism." *Comparative Studies in Society and History* 19 (1977): 52–63.

Pringle, James. "Pol Pot's Hatchet Man." *Newsweek,* September 8, 1980.

Quinn, Kenneth. "The Pattern and Scope of Violence." In *Cambodia 1975–1978: Rendezvous with Death,* ed. Karl Jackson. Princeton: Princeton University Press, 1989.

———. *The Origins and Development of Radical Cambodian Communism.* Ann Arbor: University Microfilms, 1982.

Raben, Edward. "Briton Executed at Massacre Camp." *Now,* 11 January 1980, 48 ff.

Rejali, Darius M. *Torture and Modernity: Self, Society and State in Modern Iran.* Boulder: Westview Press, 1993.

Reynolds, Craig J. "Sedition In Thai History: A Nineteenth Century Poem and Its Critics." In *Thai Constructions of Knowledge,* ed. Manas Chitakasem and Andrew Turton. London: University of London: School of Oriental and African Studies, 1991, 15–36.

Richard, Guy, ed. *L'histoire inhumaine: Massacres et genocides des origines à nos jours.* Paris: Armand Colin, 1993.

Richburg, Keith. "Support Grows for Trial of Khmer Rouge." *Washington Post,* 7 February 1999.

Riches, D., ed. *The Anthropology of Violence.* Oxford: Basil Blackwell, 1986.

Rickett, Allyn, and Rickett, Adele. *Prisoners of Liberation.* New York: Anchor Books, 1973.

Rittenberg, Stanley, and Amanda Bennett. *The Man Who Stayed Behind.* New York: Simon & Schuster, 1993.

Rittersporn, Gabor T. *Stalinist Simplifications and Soviet Complications.* Chur, Switzerland: Harwood Academic Publishers, 1991.

———. "The State against Itself: Socialist Tensions and Political Conflict in the USSR, 1936–1938." *Telos* 41 (Fall 1979): 87–104.

Rivero, Miguel. *Infierno y amanecer en Kampuchea.* Havana: Ediciones Especiales, 1979.

Robben, Antonius C. G. M. "Ethnographic Seduction, Transference and Resistance in Dialogue about Terror and Violence in Argentina." *Ethos* 24, no. 1 (1996): 71–106.

Robins, Robert S., and Jerrold Post. *Political Paranoia: The Psychopolitics of Hatred.* New Haven: Yale University Press, 1997.

Rogge, O. John. *Why Men Confess.* New York: Nelson, 1959.

Rosaldo, Renato. "Grief and the Headhunter's Rage: On the Cultural Force of Emotions." In *Text, Play and Story: The Construction and Reconstruction of Self and Society,* ed. Edward Bruner, 178–95. Washington, D.C.: Smithsonian Institution Press, 1984.

Rosenbaum, Alan, ed. *Is the Holocaust Unique?* Boulder: Westview Press, 1996.

Rosenbaum, M. *Compliant Behavior: Beyond Obedience to Authority.* New York: Human Sciences Press, 1983.

Rosenberg, Tina. *The Haunted Land: Facing Europe's Ghosts after Communism.* New York: Random House, 1995.

Rossi, A. *A Communist Party in Action: An Account of the Organization and Operations in France.* Trans. W. Kendall. New Haven: Yale University Press, 1949.

Rouquet, F. "L'épuration administrative en France après la libération." *Vingtième Siècle* 1992, 106–95.

Rubenstein, Richard. "The Bureaucratization of Torture." *Journal of Social Philosophy* 13 (1982): 31–51.

———. *The Cunning of History.* New York: Harper, 1978.

Rubin, Zick, ed. *Doing unto Others.* Englewood Cliffs, N.J.: Prentice-Hall, 1974.

Rummell, R. J. "Democracy, Power, Genocide and Mass Murder." *Journal of Conflict Resolution* 39, no. 1 (March 1995): 3–26.

———. *Death by Government: Genocide and Mass Murder since 1900.* New Brunswick, N.J.: Transaction Books, 1994.

Ruthven, Malise. *Torture: The Grand Conspiracy.* London: Weidenfeld and Nicolson, 1978.

Saich, Tony. "Where Does Correct Party History Come From? The Construction of a Maoist Party History." In *Norms and the State in China,* ed. Chun-Chieh Huang and E. Zurcher, 296–336. Leiden: Brill, 1994.

Saich, Tony, and Hans van de Ven, eds. *New Perspectives on the Chinese Communist Revolution.* Armonk, N.Y.: M. E. Sharpe, 1994.

Sargant, William. *Battle for the Mind: A Physiology of Conversion and Brain-Washing.* London: Heinemann, 1957.

Sat Sutsakhan. *The Khmer Republic at War and the Final Collapse.* Washington, D.C.: U.S. Army Center of Military History, 1980.

Saunders, Kate. *Eighteen Layers of Hell: Stories from the Chinese Gulag.* London: Cassell, 1996.

Scarry, Elaine. *The Body in Pain: The Making and Unmaking of the World.* New York: Oxford University Press, 1985.

Scheff, Thomas J. *Bloody Revenge: Emotions, Nationalism and War.* Boulder: Westview Press, 1994.

———. *Emotions and Violence: Shame and Rage in Destructive Conflicts.* Lexington, Mass.: Lexington Books, 1991.

Schein, Edgar H., et al. *Coercive Persuasion: A Social-Psychological Analysis of "Brainwashing" of American Civilian Prisoners by the Chinese Communists.* New York: W. W. Norton, 1961.

Schell, Orville. "Dragons and Dungeons: A Review Article." *China Quarterly* 139 (September 1994): 782–93.

Schoenhals, Michael, ed. *China's Cultural Revolution, 1966–1969: Not a Dinner Party.* Armonk, N.Y.: M. E. Sharpe, 1996.

———, ed. *Mao's Great Inquisition: The Central Case Examination Group, 1966–1979. Chinese Law and Government,* special issue, May–June 1996.

———. "The Central Case Examination Group (1966–1979)." *China Quarterly* March 1996, 87–110.

———. *Saltationist Socialism: Mao Zedong and the Great Leap Forward.* Stockholm: Skreifter utrgivnsa Foreningen for Orientaliska Studier, 19, 1987.

———. "Original Contradictions: On the Unrevised Text of Mao Zedong's 'On the Correct Handling of Contradictions among the People.'" *Australian Journal of Chinese Affairs* 16 (1986): 93–112.

Schorske, Carl E. "Freud: The Psychoarchaeology of Civilizations." In *The Cambridge Companion to Freud,* ed. Jerome Neu, 8–24. Cambridge: 1991.

Schumaker, John F., ed. *Human Suggestibility: Advances in Theory, Research, and Application.* New York: Routledge, 1991.

Schwarcz, Vera. *The Time for Telling the Truth is Running Out.* New Haven: Yale University Press, 1992.

Schwartz, Stephen. *Pavlov's Heirs.* Sydney: Angus and Robertson, 1987.

Scott, D. "The Demonology of Nationalism: On the Anthropology of Ethnicity and Violence in Sri Lanka." *Economy and Society* 19 (1990): 491–510.

Scott, James C. *Seeing Like a State: How Certain Schemes to Improve the Human Condition Have Failed.* New Haven: Yale University Press, 1998.

———. *Domination and the Arts of Resistance: Hidden Transcripts.* New Haven: Yale University Press, 1992.

———. *Weapons of the Weak.* New Haven: Yale University Press, 1985.

Sederberg, Peter C. *Fires Within: Political Violence and Revolutionary Change.* New York: Harper Collins, 1994.

Selden, Mark. *China in Revolution: The Yenan Way Revisited.* Armonk, N.Y.: M. E. Sharpe, 1994.

Sereny, Gitta. *Into That Darkness: From Mercy Killing to Mass Murder.* London: Andre Deutsch, 1974.

"Sexual Choice, Sexual Act: An Interview with Michel Foucault." *Salamagundi* (Fall 1982–Winter 1983): 19–24.

Seybolt, Peter. "Terror and Conformity: Counter-Espionage Campaigns, Rectification, and Mass Movements." *Modern China* 19, no. 1 (January 1986): 35–74.

———, ed. *The Rustication of Urban Youth in China: A Social Experiment.* White Plains, N.Y.: M. E. Sharpe, 1977.

Shallice, T. "The Ulster Depth Interrogation Techniques and Their Relation to Sensory Deprivation Research." *Cognition* 1, no. 4 (1977): 385–405.

Shalom, Stephen R. *Deaths in China Due to Communism.* Tempe: Arizona State University, 1984.

Shandley, Robert R. *Unwillling Germans? The Goldhagen Debate.* Minneapolis: University of Minnesota Press, 1998.

Shawcross, William. *The Quality of Mercy.* New York: Simon and Schuster, 1984.

Shentalinsky, Vitaly. *Arrested Voices: Resurrecting the Disappeared Writers of the Soviet Regime.* New York: Free Press, 1996.

Shernock, Stanley K. "The Refractory Aspect of Terror in Movement-Regimes." In *State Organized Terror: The Case of Violent Internal Repression,* ed. P. Timothy Bushnell, Vladimir Shlapentokh, Christopher K. Vanderpool, and Jeyaratnam Sundram, 169–206. Boulder: Westview Press, 1991.

Shklar, Judith N. *Ordinary Vices.* Cambridge: Harvard University Press, 1986.

Shue, Henry. "Torture." *Philosophy and Public Affairs* 7 (Winter 1978): 124–43.

Shue, Vivienne. *The Reach of the State: Sketches in the Chinese Body Politic.* Stanford: Stanford University Press, 1988.

Sliwinski, Marek. *Une analyse démographique du génocide des khmers rouges.* Paris: L'Harmattan, 1994.

Smith, L. B. "English Treason Trials and Confessions in the Sixteenth Century." *Journal of the History of Ideas* 15 (1954): 471–98.

Smith, Tony. *Thinking Like a Communist: State and Legitimacy in the Soviet Union, China and Cuba.* New York: W. W. Norton, 1987.

Sofsky, Wolfgang. *The Order of Terror: The Concentration Camp.* Princeton: Princeton University Press, 1996.

Solis, Gary D. *Son Thang: An American War Crime.* New York: Bantam Books, 1998.

Solzhenitsyn, Aleksandr. *The Gulag Archipelago, 1918–1956: An Experiment in Literary Investigation.* 3 vols. New York: Harper and Row, 1974.

Som. *Tum Taev.* Phnom Penh: Institut Bouddhique, 1960.

Someth May. *Cambodian Witness: The Autobiography of Someth May.* London: Faber, 1986.

Southwold, Martin. "Buddhism and Evil." In *The Anthropology of Evil,* ed. David Parkin, 198–41. Oxford: Basil Blackwell, 1985.

Spence, Donald P. *Narrative Truth and Historical Truth: Meaning and Interpretation in Psychoanalysis.* New York: Norton, 1982.

Spence, Jonathan D. "In China's Gulag." *New York Review of Books,* 10 August 1995.

Spierenberg, Pieter. *The Spectacle of Suffering.* Cambridge: Cambridge University Press, 1984.

Starr, John Bryan. *Continuing the Revolution: Political Thought of Mao Zedong.* Princeton: Princeton University Press, 1979.

Starr, John Bryan, and Nancy Dyer, eds. *Post Liberation Works of Mao Zedong: Bibliography and Index.* Berkeley: Center for Chinese Studies, 1976.

Staub, Ervin. *The Roots of Evil: The Origins of Genocide and Other Group Violence.* Cambridge: Cambridge University Press, 1989.

———. "The Psychology of Perpetrators and Bystanders." *Political Psychology* 6 (1985): 61–86.

Steinhoff, Patricia. "Portrait of a Terrorist: An Interview with Kozo Okamoto." *Asian Survey* 19, no. 9 (September 1976): 830–46.

Stohl, Michael, and George A. Lopez, eds. *Government Violence and Repression: An Agenda for Research.* Westport, Conn.: Greenwood Press, 1986.

Storr, Anthony. *Human Aggression.* London: Allen Lane, 1968.

Stover, Eric, and Elena Nightingale. *The Breaking of Bodies and Minds: Torture, Psychiatric Abuse, and the Health Professions.* New York: W. H. Freeman, 1985.

Strozier, Charles B., and Michael Flynn, eds. *Genocide, War, and Human Survival.* Lanham, Md.: Rowman & Littlefield, 1996.

Stubbings, Demelza. "Rationality, Closure and the Monopoly of Power in Democratic Kampuchea." M.Sc. thesis, University of London, 1993.

Suárez-Orozco, Marcelo. "A Grammar of Terror: Psychocultural Responses to State Terrorism in Dirty War and Post–Dirty War Argentina." In *The Paths to Domination, Resistance and Terror,* ed. Carolyn Nordstrom and JoAnn Martin, 219–59. Berkeley: University of California Press, 1992.

———. "Speaking of the Unspeakable: Toward a Psychological Understanding of Responses to Terror." *Ethos* 18 (1990): 353–83.

Suedfeld, Peter, ed. *Psychology and Torture.* New York: Hemisphere, 1990.

Summers, Laura. "The CPK: Secret Vanguard of Pol Pot's Revolution." *Journal of Communist Studies* 3, no. 1 (March 1987): 8–30.

Sutton, Donald. "(Dis)embodying Revolution: The Ritual and Culture of Cannibalism in Wuxuan, Guiangxi (May to July 1968)." *Comparative Studies in Society and History* 37 (1995): 136–71.

Swain, Jon. *River of Time*. London: Minerva, 1996.

Tannenbaum, Nicola. *Who Can Compete against the World? Power Protection and Buddhism in the Shan World-View*. Ann Arbor: Association for Asian Studies, 1995.

Taussig, Michael. *The Nervous System*. New York: Routledge, 1992.

———. "Culture of Terror, Space of Death: Roger Casement's Putumayo Report and the Explanation of Torture." *Comparative Studies in Society and History* 26 (1984): 466–97.

Teiwes, F. C. *Politics and Purges in China*. 2d ed. Armonk, N.Y.: M. E. Sharpe, 1993.

———. "The Origins of Rectification: Inner Party Purges and Education before Liberation." *China Quarterly* 65 (January 1976): 15–53.

Terzani, Tiziano. "I Still Hear Screams in the Night." *Der Spiegel,* 11 April 1980, translated in FBIS, 18 April 1980.

Thayer, Nate. "Death in Detail." *Far Eastern Economic Review,* 13 May 1999.

———. "Day of Reckoning." *Far Eastern Economic Review,* 27 October 1997.

———. "Brother Number Zero." *Far Eastern Economic Review,* 17 July 1997.

Thion, Serge. *Watching Cambodia*. Bangkok: White Lotus, 1993.

Thion, Serge, and Ben Kiernan. *Khmers rouges!* Paris: Albin Michel, 1982.

Thurston, Robert W. *Life and Terror in Stalin's Russia*. New Haven: Yale University Press, 1996.

Timerman, Jacobo. *Prisoner without a Name, Cell without a Number*. New York: Alfred A. Knopf, 1981.

Todorov, Tzvetan, *Facing the Extreme: Moral Life in the Concentration Camps*. New York: Henry Holt, 1996.

Totten, Samuel, William Parsons, and Israel Charney, eds. *Genocide in the Twentieth Century*. New York: Garland, 1995.

Tucker, Robert C., ed. *Stalinism: Essays in Historical Interpretation*. New York: W. W. Norton, 1977.

———. *The Soviet Political Mind: Stalinism and Post-Stalin Change*. London: Allen and Unwin, 1971.

Tucker, Robert C., and Stephen F. Cohen, eds. *The Great Purge Trial*. New York: Grosset and Dunlap, 1965.

Turley, William, ed. *Vietnamese Communism in Comparative Perspective*. Boulder: Westview Press, 1980.

Ulmonen, Paula. "Responses to Revolutionary Change: A Study of Social Memory in a Khmer Village." M.A. thesis, University of Stockholm, 1994.

Uk Samet. *Soksa katha Tum Taev (A Study of Tum Taev)*. Phnom Penh: Apsara, 1966.

Um, Khataraya. *Brotherhood of the Pure: Nationalism and Communism in Democratic Kampuchea*. Ann Arbor: University Microfilms, 1990.

U.S. Department of the Army. *Communist Interrogation, Indoctrination, and Exploitation of Prisoners of War*. Department of the Army Pamphlet 30–101. Washington, D.C., 1956.

U.S. Foreign Broadcast Information Service, Asia and the Pacific. *Daily Reports,* 1975–1981.

U.S. Senate Committee on Foreign Relations. *Convention against Torture (Hearings January 30, 1990)*. Washington, D.C.: U.S. Government Printing Office, 1990.

Vairon, Lionel. "Du Parti Communiste Indochinois à la 'Triple Alliance Indochinoise' (1975–1979)." Ph.D. diss., Institut Nationale des Langues Orientales, 1998.

Valentino, Benjamin. "Final Solutions: The Causes of Mass Killings and Genocide." Unpublished paper, February 1998.

Vann Nath. *A Cambodian Prison Portrait: One Year in the Khmer Rouge's S-21*. Trans. Moeun Chhan Nariddh. Bangkok: White Lotus, 1998.

Vickery, Michael. "How Many Died in Pol Pot's Cambodia?" *Bulletin of Concerned Asian Scholars* (1988): 377–385.

———. "Violence in Democratic Kampuchea: Some Problems of Explanation." Unpublished paper, University of Adelaide, 1984.

———. *Cambodia 1975–1982*. Boston: South End Press, 1983.

———. "Democratic Kampuchea: Themes and Variations." In *Revolution and Its Aftermath in Kampuchea: Eight Essays,* ed. David Chandler and Ben Kiernan. New Haven: Yale University Southeast Asia Studies Monograph 25, 1983.

———. *Cambodia after Angkor: The Chronicular Evidence from the Fourteenth to the Sixteenth Century*. Ann Arbor: University Microfilms, 1978.

Vo Nhan Tri. *Vietnam's Economic Policy since 1975*. Singapore: Institute for Southeast Asian Studies, 1990.

Vu Can. *La sanglante experience*. Phnom Penh: Maison des Éditions "Culture," 1984.

Walder, Andrew G. "Cultural Revolutionary Radicalism: Variations on a Stalinist Theme." In *New Perspectives on the Cultural Revolution*, ed. William Joseph et al., 41–62. Cambridge: Harvard University Press, 1990.

———. "Actually Existing Maoism." *Australian Journal of Chinese Studies* 18 (July 1987): 155–62.

Walder, Andrew G. and Gong Xiaoxia, eds. *Violence in the Cultural Revolution. Chinese Sociology and Anthropology,* special issue, January 1994.

Walliman, Isidor, and Michael N. Dobkowski. *Genocide in Our Time: An Annotated Bibliography with Analytical Introductions*. Ann Arbor: Pierian Press, 1992.

———, eds. *Genocide and the Modern Age: Etiology and Case Studies of Mass Death*. New York: Greenwood Press, 1987.

Walter, Eugene V. *Terror and Resistance: A Study of Political Violence*. New York: Oxford University Press, 1969.

Watson, Rubie, ed. *Memory, History and Opposition under State Socialism*. Santa Fe: School of American Research Press, 1995.

White, Lynn T. *Policies of Chaos: The Organizational Causes of Violence in China's Cultural Revolution*. Princeton: Princeton University Press, 1989.

White, Peter T. "Kampuchea Wakens from a Nightmare." *National Geographic,* May 1982, 590–623.

Whyte, Martin King. "Inequality and Stratification in China." *China Quarterly* 64 (December 1975): 684–711.

————. *Small Groups and Political Rituals in China.* Berkeley: University of California Press, 1974.

————. "Corrective Labor Camp Inmates and Political Rituals in China." *Asian Survey* 13, no. 3 (March 1973): 253–70.

Wi Jingsheng. "Q-1, a Twentieth Century Bastille." In *Seeds of Fire: Chinese Voices of Conscience,* ed. Geriemie Barme and John Metford. New York: Hill and Wang, 1988, 111–21.

Willmott, William E. "Analytical Errors of the Kampuchean Communist Party." *Pacific Affairs* 45, no. 2 (Summer 1981): 209–27.

Wise, Robert. "Eradicating the Old Dandruff." *Far Eastern Economic Review,* 21 September 1977.

Wolgast, Elizabeth. "Intolerable Wrong and Punishment." *Philosophy* 60 (1985): 161–74.

Wolff, K. "For a Sociology of Evil." *Journal of Social Issues* 25 (1969): 111–25.

Wright, Robert. *The Moral Animal: Why We Are the Way We Are.* New York: Vintage, 1994.

Y Phandara. *Retour à Phnom Penh.* Paris: E. Metaille, 1982.

Young, Graham, and Dennis Woodward. "From Contradictions among the People and Class Struggle to Theories of Uninterrupted Revolution and Continuous Revolution." *Asian Survey* 18, no. 9 (September 1978): 912–33.

Zhang Chunqiao. "On Exercising All-Round Dictatorship over the Bourgeoisie." *Peking Review,* April 4, 1975.

Zhang Zhiyang. *In Celebration of Blasphemy.* Ed. Michael Schoenhals. *Chinese Studies in Philososphy,* special issue, Spring 1994.

Zheng Yi. *Scarlet Memorial: Tales of Cannibalism in Mao's China.* Boulder: Westview Press, 1996.

Zimbardo, Philip G. "The Mind is a Formidable Jailer: A Pirandellian Prison." *New York Times Magazine,* 8 April 1973, 38–60.

————. "The Psychology of Police Confessions." *Psychology Today,* July 1969, 17–20.

Zimbardo, Philip G., Craig Haney, W. Curtis Banks, and David Jaffe. "The Psychology of Imprisonment: Privation, Power and Pathology." In *Doing unto Others,* ed. Zick Rubin, 61–73. Englewood Cliffs, N.J.: Prentice-Hall, 1974.

Zulaika, Joseba, and William A. Douglass. *Terror and Taboo: The Follies, Fables and Faces of Terrorism.* London: Routledge, 1996.

Zweig, David. *Agrarian Radicalism in China, 1968–1981.* Cambridge: Harvard University Press, 1991.

Index

adolescent participants in Cambodian revolution, 29, 33–34, 172n59
agriculture, failure of, under DK, 68–70
Alice in Wonderland (Carroll), 48, 123
American prisoners at S-21, 165n35
Amery, Jean, 111, 141
angkar. See Organization, the
Angkor Wat, 118–19, 123, 197n21
Angleton, James Jesus, 22
An Hot, 105
Anlong Veng, 76
Apter, David, 90
Arant, Richard, 157
archive at S-21: microfilming of, 11; rationale for, 49, 50
Argentina, "dirty war" in, 7, 38, 143
Asad, Talal, 117
Ashley, David, 40
At the Mind's Limits (Amery), 142
Auschwitz, 5, 122, 141, 147; "gray zone" at, 147
autobiographies, as ideological tools, 89–90, 189n41

Baen Chae (alias Chhaon Savath), 85, 121
Battambang, 68, 77, 121
Bauman, Zygmunt, 137, 154–55
Becker, Elizabeth, 46, 69
Berger, Peter, 124
Bizot, François, 21
Bosnia, 144, 155

Brother 89. *See* Son Sen
Brother Number One. *See* Pol Pot
Brother Number Two. *See* Nuon Chea
Browning, Christopher, 146–47, 152–53
Buddhism, 95, 106, 188n27, 197n21; and evil, 205n22
Buddhist Institute Dictionary, 116
Bun Than, 115
Burgler, R. A., 64
Buth Heng, 131

Cambodia Genocide Program, 49
Carney, Timothy, 106
Case Examination Committee (Chinese security agency), 127; named changed to Central Case Examination Group, 15, 127
Central Intelligence Agency (CIA), in S-21 confessions, 92–93, 190–91nn51,52,55
Chamraon Vichea School, 65
Chan (Mam Nay), 12, 20, 23–24, 28 133, 136, 152
Chan Chakrei, 52–53, 121, 178n36
"Characteristics of the CPK" (CPK pamphlet), 106
Chea Mai, 17
Chea Sim, 48
Cheng An, 74
Chey Saphon, 2, 4
Chhim Chhun, 96
Chhim Peou, 104

Text: 10/13 Sabon
Display: Sabon
Composition: Impressions Book and Journal Services, Inc.
Printing and binding: Thomson-Shore, Inc.

FOSTERING CHANGES

MYTH, MEANING & MAGIC BULLETS IN ATTACHMENT THEORY

Richard J. Delaney, PhD

Contents

FOREWORD

Fostering Changes. And it has! The lives of many professionals and parents alike have been impacted in significant ways by the previous editions of this book. It is known by students and professors as a "great little primer" on attachment issues, by clinicians as a wonderful resource for professional skills and parent referral, and to foster and adoptive parents as the guide that explains and addresses many issues that plague their troubled children.

Much has changed in the last 15 years. Not only in our brazen, somewhat out-of-control little world, but definitely in the world of attachment theory and its application. The world of attachment is full of opinions, theories, speculations, treatment strategies—some researched, some not—and a division among the ranks coming from the passionate beliefs of those who are desperately seeking to do what is best for their children, clients, and families.

Dr. Delaney has been a steady, consistent, and enduring force in this mixed-up chaos. His many years of experience allow for a calm voice, able to synthesize the best in theory, treatment, and parenting skills to help bring about positive change. Steadfast and clear thinking, he has navigated the occasional chaos of the attachment world—which is enough to push even the best to a new level of frustration—to "shake the tree" of attachment and sort the "leaves" of change that result in a better place for treatment and care to occur.

The goal of this book is not only to leave in place all the strong educational attributes and the insightful training from the previous editions, but to review some of the changes, some of the flaws in thinking, and the ever-changing dynamics of today's attachment climate.

David Wood
Publisher
Wood 'N' Barnes Publishing

PREFACE

I have written this book primarily for today's parents, caseworkers, therapists, psychologists, psychiatrists, and other helping professionals who find themselves caring for—and trying to cope with—emotionally disturbed foster, kinship, and adoptive children. Drawing heavily from attachment theory and research, *Fostering Changes* outlines a way for helping professionals to consult with and teach foster and adoptive parents to better understand and help their children. This book does not describe a psychotherapeutic approach to working with children in group or individual counseling. Instead, it provides a resource for offering mental health consultation and parent training to foster, kinship, and adoptive families.

There are well over 500,000 children in foster care in the United States (non-relative and kinship care combined). Another 1.5 million children live with grandparent-headed households nationwide. Up to half of these grandchildren are drug exposed or fetal alcohol exposed (Task Force on Permanency Planning, 1990). The scourge of drug and alcohol abuse has contributed to the marked rise in out-of-home placements; in some parts of the United States the crisis of methamphetamine use by parents has resulted in huge increases in placements of children and infants. Consensus among veteran caseworkers and foster parents—along with the increase in children requiring out-of-home placement—points to an upsurge in foster children with significant psychological problems. Statistically, 50% to 85% of foster children have significant emotional, behavioral, or developmental problems (American Academy of Child and Adolescent Psychiatry, 2002). As many as one-third of these children carry three or more psychiatric diagnoses (dosReis, Zito, Safer, & Soeken, 2001). Previously these children had been treated only in inpatient settings, e.g., on psychiatric wards or in residential child care facilities. Now, many of them are diverted into regular (also called "basic") foster homes, relatives' homes, or therapeutic or treatment foster homes, which are deemed to be the "least restrictive alternative," i.e., the most humane residence for young children.

Since the emphasis on permanency following the passage of ASFA in 1997, there's been a dramatic increase in adoptions throughout the country, including special needs adoptions (e.g., older children, some of whom have significant emotional and/or behavioral problems). Children adopted from the foster care system often have physical, cognitive, or emotional problems and have high rates of diagnoses such as ADHD and depression (Benson, Sharma, & Roehlkepartain, 1994). In clinical practice, special needs adopted children who have been seen by various mental health therapists often simultaneously carry several diagnoses, notably, ADHD, ODD, PTSD, bipolar, depression, RAD, OCD, PDD, CD, and Autistic Spectrum Disorder. Many of these children are on one or more psychotropic drugs for these diagnoses.

Large numbers of foster, kinship, and adopted children exhibit behavior problems which include aggression, destructiveness, sexual acting out, disruptive behavior, anxiety, and low self-esteem (Benson, Sharma, & Roehlkepartain, 1994) as well as assaultiveness, suicide attempts, drug/alcohol dependency, running away, truancy, fire-setting, and law violations (Chamberlain & Reid, 1991). Other problems include wetting or soiling, stealing, serious eating problems, promiscuity, and vandalism (Partridge, Hornby, & McDonald, 1986). Younger children with disrupted backgrounds may show ongoing problems with hoarding food, stereotypic behaviors such as rocking and head-banging, and sleep problems (Cirttenden & Claussen, 2000; Friedrich, 2002). In clinical practice, foster and adoptive parents report problems that their children have with anger outbursts, lying, stealing, noncompliance, resistance, self-harm, cruelty to animals, aggression toward other children, and behavior problems at school, among other presenting complaints.

Disturbed foster and adopted children have often (read: almost always) been the victims of child abuse, neglect, sexual exploitation and/or abandonment. Indeed, virtually every foster child has suffered some loss, disruption, and trauma prior to placement in foster care. Many have experienced severe, repeated, chronic maltreatment at the hands of their birth parents, relatives, or other caregivers. Many of these maltreated children are thought to develop attachment patterns early in life—overarching strategies for connecting with caregivers—which are either insecure or disorganized (Crittenden & Claussen, 2000). How these attachment patterns relate to and perhaps explain ongoing emotional and behavioral problems of foster and adopted children is extremely important. In fact, a central focus of this book is to make connections between attachment patterns and the persistent behavioral, emotional, and relational problems of disturbed foster, kinship, and adopted children. We will look to attachment theory for concepts and data which can help us understand these problems.

Children who experience adverse conditions early in life (e.g., disadvantaged youngsters from our nation and deprived adopted children from foreign orphanages) predictably show significant needs and complex problems. Unfortunately, ever-increasing recognition of their needs and problems has not been matched by remedies. Articles, books, and Web sites on purported attachment-related disorders are plentiful while factual, evidence-based, empirical writing on the subject is sparse (O'Connor & Zeanah, 2003). In fact, the diagnosis of the increasingly ubiquitous RAD (Reactive Attachment Disorder) is shrouded in myth and clouded by inaccuracy. Reactive Attachment Disorder is increasingly given as a diagnosis, although it may often be used erroneously. As we will emphasize in this book, there are currently no proven treatments for RAD, though many unjustified claims are made about certain attachment therapies. It is no surprise that beleaguered, well-intentioned foster and adoptive parents hope for a "magic bullet" (i.e., an answer to what ails their child). These parents are joined by mental health therapists, caseworkers, psychiatrists, and other helpers who feel perplexed by the serious, complex, and intractable problems shown by their young patients who have come from maltreatment, trauma, and disruption. These children seem fairly unresponsive to the individual, nondirective, client-centered approaches that work well with less troubled youngsters.

Commonly, by the time foster, kinship, and adoptive parents become involved with these troubled children, tremendous psychological damage has already been done. Though these children have been, by then, removed from the source of abuse and neglect, they take with them the invisible, internal scars of early maltreatment. More accurately, the child's development has been set on a pathway that is off course. It becomes the task of the foster and adoptive parents not only to provide a safe home but also to provide a therapeutic environment for these foster children to help them to get back on course. On the surface, that might appear to be a fairly straightforward job: to provide physically and psychologically for hapless, dependent, young human beings. However, many foster and adoptive families soon find themselves faced with a task more challenging than they ever dreamed. In fact, the dream of helping an abused child can often turn into a nightmare. These parents, bewildered by the child's severe, confusing, and sometimes alarming emotional and behavioral problems, find themselves asking, "Where did our plans for helping this child go wrong?" or "How did we get ourselves into this mess, and how can we get out of it?"

Likewise, caseworkers, mental health professionals, and others involved in helping the child can also become caught up in this bad dream. The mental health professional, often entering the picture too late, may find himself under pressure to treat the child and foster or adoptive family quickly lest the placement disrupt. He might question why the foster or adoptive parents describe the child so differently from how he would. He might wonder, "Is this foster family causing disturbance in this child?" (Note: Clearly, foster and adoptive parents are not responsible for the initial development of attachment disorders; however, how they impact the disorder after placement is unknown [O'Connor & Zeanah, 2003].) The caseworker also may find himself under the gun, confronted by the foster or adoptive parents who ask, "Why didn't anyone tell us how disturbed this child was?" or "Can you move this child to a new placement as soon as possible?" When foster, kinship, and adoptive parents come to the worker at this point, they often appear quite exasperated and detached, the appearance of which might be misinterpreted as the cause of the child's disturbance rather than its effect (Delaney & Kunstal, 1997; O'Connor & Zeanah).

PUTTING A HUMAN FACE ON THE SUBJECT

What follows is a brief description of a case of a young adopted girl with significant behavioral problems. The adopted mother and father are at wit's end with her and likely have run out of ideas and approaches to help her.

Five-year-old Tilly was brought in for psychological help by her parents who adopted her at 5 months of age. Tilly was never conclusively determined to have been prenatally exposed to drugs or alcohol, though neglect was rampant during the first months of her life.

The adoptive mother described Tilly as having been difficult from "day one." She had (and still has) problems with eye contact, she was colicky and rigid as an infant, and she has become increasingly defiant, stubborn, and angry as she has developed.

The adoptive mom stated that currently Tilly yells at her and screams that she is the "boss." When the two of them are alone, Tilly is extremely clingy. When others are present, Tilly is exceptionally needy, disruptive, and noncompliant. If sent to her room for a time-out, she destroys it. She is often in time-out because she has been mean to her baby sister, biting, punching, and kicking her. One year ago, the couple adopted this baby girl, who has serious medical issues. Both adoptive mother and father expressed concern about whether the baby is safe around Tilly, as she has screamed during rage attacks that she will stab the baby. Once she was found putting a rope around the baby's neck.

The adoptive mom admitted that she was an extremely attentive, or perhaps overly attentive, first-time mother to Tilly. She was eager to "bond" with this child and also assumed that stepped-up involvement would help Tilly overcome the early neglect. As Tilly got older and grew insatiably needy, the adoptive mother sought to correct what she assumed had been a mistake on her part, i.e., the "mistake" of overdoing it. Tilly responded with defiance and increased demands on the mother's time. With the arrival of the baby sister, the situation deteriorated rapidly. At present the adoptive father has concluded that Tilly is a defiant, angry child who has RAD. "She sounds just like the kids with that disorder. She has no guilt about hurting her baby sister, she has poor eye contact with us, and she is insatiably needy and demanding. Furthermore, she wants to be the boss and would like to be in control of the house. What is wrong with our daughter?"

ATTACHMENT THEORY MAY PROVIDE SOME ANSWERS AND BETTER QUESTIONS

Although there typically is no magic bullet in cases like Tilly's, help can be found in "attachment theory," a theory which stresses the importance of early caregiving for later psychological health. In a nutshell, attachment theory has proposed that disruption in reliable caregiving of young children results in defective or disordered attachment, i.e., the emotional bond linking caregiver and child (Bowlby, 1969). Defective attachments, in turn, beget psychological problems in the child that may span a lifetime. Unfortunately, though research abounds concerning attachment, few guidelines are offered to foster and adoptive parents, caseworkers, and mental health professionals for their crucial work with children having significant attachment issues. Sadly, since the DSM-III included "disorders of attachment" in its nosology 25 years ago, there has still been no agreement on the definition of RAD, and/or how it should be evaluated, managed, or treated (O'Connor & Zeanah, 2003). Indeed, the amount of confusion, disinformation, and laxity in describing AD or the more pandemic RAD diagnosis may undermine the credibility of attachment theory (O'Connor & Zeanah).

This book translates information from attachment theory and research to the day-to-day work with and parenting of attachment-disordered foster, kinship, and adopted children. Attachment theory and research can inform parents and those who consult with, advise, and train them. It can guide caseworkers and mental health professionals in helping parents raise their challenging children.

THE NEED FOR PARENT TRAINING AND MENTAL HEALTH CONSULTATION

Foster, kinship, and adoptive parents currently seek help for their children at unprecedented levels. Many of them feel ill-prepared for the challenges they encounter with their troubled youngsters, who may have special needs that include significant emotional or behavioral disorders. Parents, at first, typically fall back on parenting approaches from raising less troubled children, if they've been lucky enough to have that bit of prior training. When their "tried and true" methods prove ineffective, they use a shotgun approach and over time they devolve into a scattered trial-and-error approach, often to no avail.

Even if parents have had pre-service training, there seems to be no foolproof way to prepare them thoroughly for the realities of raising a troubled, formerly maltreated child. Ongoing, post-placement supports (e.g., respite care, in-service training, support groups, and mental health services) increase the chances of successful placement outcomes. However, the indisputable fact is that today's foster and adoptive parents need specialized, in-depth training and ongoing, relevant mental health consultation if they are to have the best chance of helping their troubled kids.

OVERVIEW OF THE BOOK

Chapter one begins with a historical overview and definition of attachment theory. It explains the survival value of attachment and describes normal infant and child attachment behaviors. Discussion then turns to the parent's role in attachment formation, the stages of normal and secure attachment formation in children (with special emphasis on the "partnership" stage), and an examination of the child's "internal working model" (or expectations), which develops during the earliest years. The chapter concludes with a description of the characteristic reaction of children to disruption in their attachment relationships.

Chapter two focuses on the various patterns of attachment that children develop. The relationship between early exposure to maltreatment and the formation of insecure patterns of attachment is discussed. This is followed by an explanation of the "negative working model," which the child develops in response to unfavorable early attachment experiences. Lastly, this chapter explains how some children fail to learn to negotiate the meeting of their needs within the parent-child relationship.

Chapter three addresses the wide range of mental health issues (and related behavior problems) evidenced by foster, kinship, and adopted children. It also describes the official diagnosis and symptoms of Reactive Attachment Disorder of Infancy and Young Childhood (RAD). Next, the "unofficial" symptoms of Reactive Attachment Disorder promulgated by therapists out of the mainstream of attachment research are listed. Discussion then turns to research on the relationship between attachment and conduct problems. The chapter concludes with a brief synopsis of diagnoses whose use would be more accurate than the RAD (unofficial) diagnosis which is (too) often given to foster, kinship, and adopted children.

Chapter four outlines the aberrant developmental pathways that many foster and adoptive children take due to earlier disruption in attachment. It describes "reenactment" (in the foster or adoptive home) of problematic relationships learned by the maltreated child prior to placement. This chapter explains how the child's negative working model correlates to reenactment and conduct problems. Next, it explains hallmark functions of conduct problems and describes the relationship between attachment patterns and functions.

Chapter five addresses the overall foster and adoptive parent response to their troubled child. It describes how foster and adoptive parents are impacted by the troubled child's past. It also addresses how foster and adoptive parents' own attachment issues may affect the ways they respond to their troubled child. Lastly, we turn to an explanation of the common, if unexpected, emotional responses parents feel toward their troubled foster or adopted child.

Chapter six focuses on parent training and mental health consultation. It covers teaching parents how to reinterpret conduct problems by considering the attachment functions. It also describes how parents can be trained about social learning approaches. Next is an explanation of the importance of training and consultation to the foster and adoptive parents concerning eliciting vocalization of emotion from and negotiating with their children. The chapter then emphasizes training parents about how to increase positive encounters with their troubled children. And, lastly, it discusses teaching parents about their own attachment issues and parenting styles, which may impact or interact with the child's issues and conduct problems.

Chapter seven moves to a discussion of the controversy surrounding the RAD diagnosis and a subset of controversial, coercive attachment therapies. It discusses the proliferation of the RAD (unofficial) diagnosis. It also summarizes the many pronouncements against the use of holding therapies. The chapter concludes with a description of the "disconnect" between the subset of controversial attachment therapies and attachment research; a brief discussion of promising treatment approaches; and comments on the difficult struggles foster and adoptive parents face with emotionally disturbed children.

A word about the case examples in this book: In the interests of protecting confidentiality and concealing identities of the many foster, kinship, and adopted children and families I have worked with over the years, I have scrupulously developed "psychological composites," which present the flavor of typical and bona fide cases without revealing actual names, places, histories, outcomes, and other details of the original children and families treated. Thus, any resemblance of these cases or the names used herein to actual children and families is due either to mere coincidence or to the sad fact that the traumatic histories and common symptoms of maltreated children form a familiar, recognizable mosaic.

ACKNOWLEDGMENTS

Finally, I would like to express my deepest gratitude to a number of individuals who were vital to the completion of this book. They are Caesar Pacifici, Ph.D.; Frank R. Kunstal, Ed.D.; James Wm. Browning, M.D.; Mike DeWitt; Elisabeth Braun; Enita Kearns; Lee Phillips; and Margaret Delaney. I would like to thank them, my good friends and colleagues, who have tirelessly read and reread the manuscript which became this book. While their frank reflections and suggestions have added immeasurably to the quality of the finished product, I am solely responsible for any remaining problems with the book's contents. In addition, I must pay my respects to the luminaries in research on attachment theory: John Bowlby, Mary Salter-Ainsworth, Dante Cicchetti, Patricia Crittenden, Angelika Claussen, Jay Belsky, Mary Main, Robert Marvin, Charles Zeanah, Matthew Speltz, Inge Bretherton, Alan Sroufe, Mary Dozier, and Mark Greenberg. While I have drawn heavily from their notions regarding attachment, the finished product of this book is in no way meant to summarize or reflect their thinking. The work of these researchers has provided a springboard to my own thinking, as has also the work of T. Berry Brazelton, Selma Frailberg, Margaret Mahler, Erik Erikson, Melitta Sperling, Jerome Kagan, Vera Colburn-Fahlberg, Victor Bernstein, and Norman Polansky.

Fruita, Colorado
Richard J. Delaney
May 2006

*"Suffering deserves a voice,
and attachment theory, by its very subject matter,
is supremely suited to the task,
whether it is for a child whose hope is dying,
a mother whose hope died years ago,
or a whole culture struggling with persistent threat.
At the same time,
we must acknowledge the uncertainty
of knowing what we see."*

—CRITTENDEN & CLAUSSEN

1 BRIEF INTRODUCTION TO ATTACHMENT THEORY

Attachment is the cornerstone of human social development. How we connect with our fellow human beings and how we interrelate may be shaped in the initial personal experiences of the infant and young child. The earliest meaningful relationships that children of tender years form set the stage for they interact with others. This chapter will discuss what attachment is and what attachment theory has to offer us in our understanding of troubled foster, kinship, and adopted children. It will address how the earliest relationships to others contribute to and shape the way these children form attachments, how they perceive themselves and others, and what they learn about relating to others and partnering socially with them.

This chapter will cover the following topics:

1. Historical Overview of Attachment Theory

2. Definition of Attachment

3. Survival Value of Attachment

4. Normal Infant/Child Attachment Behaviors

5. Parent or Caregiver's Role in Attachment Formation

6. Stages of Normal Attachment Formation

7. The Securely Attached Child and the "Internal Working Model"

8. Reaction to Disruption in the Attachment Relationship

Before launching into a discussion about attachment theory, consider this specific case. If you are a foster or adoptive parent, a caseworker, or psychotherapist who works with maltreated children, you may find this story quite familiar.

———

Candy, a wisp of a Caucasian girl, had lived in nine different foster homes by her present age of 6. She was a suspected drug-affected baby, though her mother denied drug abuse during the

*pregnancy. Horribly malnourished as an infant, Candy was diag-
nosed as "failure to thrive" by a doctor at the health department.
A neglected and delayed child, she was too weak to hold her head
up at 6 months of age. Candy crawled at 14 months and finally
walked and talked (in garbled, one-word utterances) at age 2.
Following reports of neglect, unsanitary living conditions, and
abandonment by the mother, Candy was placed in foster care
on several occasions by the local welfare agency. By her third
birthday this child had spent 75% of her life in foster care. During
her brief stays with the biological mother—between foster placements—Candy was often left for days in the care of the maternal
grandmother, neighbors, and numerous baby-sitters while the
mother disappeared with the violent, drug-abusing men she was
dating. When the birth mother was present with Candy, it was
usually between boyfriends when she was depressed, drank heavily, and slept on the couch day and night, leaving Candy to fend
for herself.*

*To compound the problem, when Candy was removed from the
mother's care, she was placed (due to an unfortunate set of circumstances) in four different foster homes. In her fourth placement, Candy was described by the foster parents as "unlikable,"
"unrewarding," "unattached," and a RAD (Reactive Attachment
Disorder) kid. They mentioned that she called them "Daddy"
and "Mommy" immediately after meeting them, but they felt
that even after 6 months in their home, she would walk off with
any stranger. Following this half-year placement, Candy was returned to her birth mother for one last try. Once again, Candy,
nearly 4 years old, was left with a host of surrogate parent figures
when her mother disappeared for days and sometimes weeks.
A psychological evaluation of the birth mother at this time described her as an inadequate, passive woman who showed little or
no emotion toward her child. This mother viewed her life with a
sense of "apathy and futility." Reports of neglect prompted caseworkers to remove Candy once and for all. By this time, Candy,
now in her fifth foster home, seemed much more disturbed and
started showing a number of behavior problems. She lied, stole
food, and urinated in the corner of her bedroom. The foster
family described her as "withdrawn," "fakey," and as "not a real
child—a phony." They portrayed her as sometimes depressed
and rejecting of them and at other times very dependent, needy,
and draining.*

Eventually, a psychologist was called in to do a thorough evaluation and found Candy to suffer from a "sense of powerlessness, underlying insecurities, and lack of empathy for others." She was also depicted as "seeing the world as a dangerous place" and as having "problems with attachment." Psychotherapy was recommended and started for Candy, but it was too late to save the foster placement and the two others that followed in quick succession. At this point, Candy seemed to be "blowing out" placements as quickly as she arrived in the homes. On her sixth birthday, Candy was placed in her ninth foster home—a therapeutic foster home with parents specially trained to work with attachment-disordered children.

———

Candy's tragic case is representative of many foster, kinship, and adopted children. These children may have been drug- or alcohol-exposed infants who were chronically neglected. They may have genetic predispositions that affect their temperaments. Earliest interactions with their caregivers may have been non-rewarding and may have failed to address their needs for a sense of safety and security. They may also have been physically and sexually abused along the way. Many of these children have witnessed domestic violence as well. Overall, their early lives might be described as chaotic and unstable with exposure to many moves, losses, and separations from caregivers. They have received substandard caregiving from birth parents. Following removal from their abusive situations by the child protection system, they may have been placed in a succession of foster/kinship homes and/or reunited unsuccessfully and repeatedly with the birth parent. By the time these children are finally placed in an adoptive family or with a caring relative, they may have significant issues which seem to thwart successful life in their present home.

The purpose of this chapter is to set the stage for later discussion on parenting and treating troubled foster, kinship, or adopted children—children a lot like Candy. To understand troubled foster and adopted children, an understanding of attachment theory is highly useful. It's especially helpful to understand what can happen when attachment goes awry. With that in mind, this chapter provides a quick historical overview of attachment theory, a definition of attachment, and examples of normal attachment behaviors in children and their caregivers. It examines the four stages of attachment formation along with the characteristics of the child who has successfully passed through these stages.

The focus then shifts to the abnormal attachments young children develop in response to chronic disruptions in the attachment process.

HISTORICAL OVERVIEW OF ATTACHMENT THEORY

By 1958 John Bowlby, the founding father of attachment theory, had developed and applied his theory of attachment to an understanding of the child's relationship to the mother. In his survey of existing research, Bowlby (1969) reported two revolutionary, albeit simple, findings: (1) the infant's need for his parent resembles his need for food, and (2) significant separation from or loss of the parent results in psychological trauma to the child. Bowlby's overarching conclusion about attachment is that an unbroken, uninterrupted, mutually satisfying connection between mother and child promotes mental health (Bowlby, 2004). Research has documented the fact that children who suffer chronic separations, without intervention, may be placed on a pathway toward serious problems and unfortunate outcomes (Johnson-Reid & Barth, 2000). As discussed in later chapters, the trauma to the child of separation and/or loss may range from minor, short-term, emotional insecurities to major, long-lasting aberrations in the ability to relate to other human beings. Research has pointed out that children who experienced early deprivation in orphanage care, for instance, are likely to show vestiges of insecure attachment years after placement in a caring adoptive home (O'Connor & Zeanah, 2003).

Drawing heavily from "instinct theory" and its notions about "imprinting," Bowlby's (1969) work culminated in a detailed account of the infant's growing connection, i.e., attachment, to his caregiver. His innovative notions about infant attachment spurred others to examine attachment in the laboratory setting, in the delivery room, in the pediatric clinic, and in the psychotherapist's office[1]. Today, Bowlby's thoughts are tremendously useful in the understanding and treatment of abused and neglected foster, kinship, and/or adopted children whose attachments to others have been severely affected by repeated exposure to separation from and loss of parents or through mistreatment, rejection, and abandonment by insensitive, unreliable parent figures.

---

[1] Ainsworth, Blehar, Walters, & Wall, 1978; Belsky & Nezworski, 1998; Brazelton & Cramer, 1990; Chisholm, 2000; Fahlberg, 1979; Greenberg, Cicchetti, Cummings, 1990; Pound, 1982

DEFINITION OF ATTACHMENT

Bowlby (1982) described attachment as the child's tendency to "seek proximity to and contact with a specific figure" when afraid, sick, or tired. More broadly speaking, attachment may be defined as a "lasting psychological connectedness between human beings." In the psychological study of children, more specifically, attachment is the emotional bond which grows between the child and parent and vice versa. Despite a tender, almost magical quality ascribed to attachment, it remains a hypothetical construct. That is, attachment is essentially an abstraction—an unseen internal state in the child and parent (Ainsworth et al., 1978; Bowlby, 1969; Mahler, Pine, & Bergman, 1975). It is important to acknowledge that with the tumultuous backgrounds of many troubled children the attachment relationships that have been formed may differ in quality from the healthy attachments of children with more fortunate histories.

SURVIVAL VALUE OF ATTACHMENT

In humans, as with other mammals, offspring attachment to their caregivers (e.g., mothers) improves the chances for survival (Bowlby, 1973). Attachment relates to survival-of-the-fittest principle; those infants and children who stick by protective adults have a greater chance of survival (Dozier & Albus, 2000). By keeping the immature, helpless infant/child close, the caregiver reduces risks to the child's health and safety. In turn, by encouraging the caregiver to remain close by, the infant/child contributes to his own survival. The normally attached child, for example, by remaining relatively close to his caregiver, escapes many hazards which beset attachment-disordered children, such as running into busy streets, walking off with strangers, and the like. The most obvious function of attachment is, then, protection from danger of all sorts (Crittenden & Claussen, 2000). Further, the crux of attachment theory is that any child who is endangered should attempt to remain close to primary caregivers and thereby reduce threats and increase protection. As discussed later, many children who have formed unusual attachment patterns or relationships in their earliest years show unique problems related to remaining close to primary caregivers. In addition, they often show unusual strategies for interrelating to caregivers.

In addition to physical survival, the child's psychological well-being is predicated on secure attachment formation. When children feel safe

and reassured by the availability of their caregiver, they are able to explore—a hallmark sign of confidence. To the contrary, children who lack
secure attachment may evidence behavioral and emotional problems
of various levels of severity. Healthy attachment, as Bowlby observed,
promotes mental health. As discussed later in this book, traumatized
foster, kinship, and adopted children often suffer from abnormal, unhealthy, insecure attachments, out of which spring a variety of complex
emotional and behavioral problems. (We should remember here that
not all foster or adopted children's emotional and behavioral problems
stem from insecure attachments. A host of other factors, e.g., genetic
predispositions, basic temperament, and neurological problems can
account for difficulties as well [Dozier & Albus, 2000].)

Attachment behaviors in the normal child emerge very clearly and
almost on cue in specific critical situations, such as when the child is
sick, tired, or injured; in the presence of a stranger or in strange sur-
roundings; and when the child is left alone (i.e., separated from the
parent). We've all seen the young child hiding behind his mother's
skirts when a stranger approaches. Or we've seen the increased clinging to the parent of a sickly child, thumb in mouth and security blan-
ket in hand. (See Table 1.1 for a summary of critical situations which
elicit attachment behaviors in the infant/child.) To reiterate, increases
in the normal child's attachment behaviors in critical situations serve
a survival value, keeping the parent and child closest when the child
is most vulnerable. These situations of vulnerability evoke a strong
feeling of anxiety in the child, who reacts by increasing attachment
behaviors, such as crying or seeking out the parent for comfort or protection. Importantly, in children with severe attachment issues there
can be a suppression or distortion of the normal tendency to seek
proximity to the parent.

As discussed later in this book, troubled foster and adopted children
do not always act as expected in critical situations. Some avoid the
caregiver; many of them do not come to the foster parent (or any
other caregiver) when they are sick, injured, or frightened. In fact,
these disturbed children often avoid or rebuff caregivers in critical
situations, preferring to handle the crises themselves. Undoubtedly related to their history of mistreatment by adults, these children
learn to fend for themselves. Their behaviors at time appear "feral,"
the learned pattern of self-parenting in a child who has been sorely,
habitually neglected or deprived. In effect, the child has developed
behavior strategies based on predictions about how caregivers have
responded or not responded to them. If their history of interactions

with caregivers involves maltreatment, strategies emerge in response to insensitive and/or unreliable caregiving. The child adapts but not in positive ways (Dozier & Albus, 2000)[2]. Ultimately the child's conclusion about parents is that they don't help, don't protect, and don't increase safety and security.

CRITICAL SITUATIONS THAT ELICIT ATTACHMENT BEHAVIORS
• Illness
• Unavailability of Caregiver
• Presence of Stranger
• Aloneness
• Darkness
• Novel Settings
• Injury
• Danger, Hunger, Fatigue
Bowlby, 1973
TABLE 1.1

NORMAL INFANT/CHILD ATTACHMENT BEHAVIORS

Child attachment behaviors are observable actions that point to underlying attachment. We cannot see or touch "attachment," but we can observe attachment behaviors. Attachment behaviors in the child serve to keep the caregiver close by, in physical contact with, and/or otherwise connected to the child. The proximity or connection function of these behaviors is important to keep in mind. Typical behaviors of the infant/child toward the caregiver change with age, but include the following: making eye contact with, smiling at, crying, pouting, protesting angrily, searching after, following, reaching for, signaling to, clinging or holding onto, seeking to be picked up, and sitting with. (See Table 1.2 for infant attachment behaviors.) These behaviors from the child serve to promote and sustain contact with or proximity to the parent (Ainsworth et al., 1978). Their purpose is, in effect, to invite the parent to stay close and to censure the parent for

---

[2] It should be pointed out that attachment problems may not explain all cases where the child fails to seek out adults. Similar interactional difficulties between parent and infant/child are also seen, for example, when children have been drug-exposed prenatally (Dozier & Albus, 2000).

moving away. As the child becomes more verbal, speech and other more sophisticated approaches increasingly replace some of these earlier primitive, physical forms of engagement between parent and offspring (Mahler et al., 1975).

As we will discuss in later chapters, the conduct problems of disturbed foster and adopted children may function as attachment behaviors. These behavior problems may be upsetting to foster and adoptive parents, and they may even be dangerous to the child or others. But, at their root, they may be directed at engagement with parent figures or others. Though these conduct problems might be misguided and counterproductive to the process of improving attachment relationships or, for that matter, securing safety, the child has learned from past relationships that they are at least partly effective in maintaining contact with caregivers.

INFANT/CHILD ATTACHMENT BEHAVIOR
• Eye Contact
• Smiling
• Pouting
• Protesting Separation
• Following
• Searching
• Reaching
• Signaling or Calling
• Holding or Clinging
• Seeking to Be Picked Up
• Sitting With
TABLE 1.2

PARENT OR CAREGIVER'S ROLE IN ATTACHMENT FORMATION

The child's attachment cannot be understood outside the context of his relationship to attachment figures, i.e., his parents or chief caregivers. That is, attachment is a relational phenomenon. Indeed, infant attachment develops not in a vacuum,[3] but in interaction. It is important,

---

[3] However, the infant or young child who is sorely deprived and neglected probably could be said to develop atypical attachment almost in a vacuum.

then, to consider the parent's role in attachment formation. In addition, though primary attachment figures such as mother and father typically play the central role in the developing attachment of children, others in the family system can also be key players (Sroufe, 1998).

In a nutshell, development of secure attachment in the infant is strongly influenced by two caregiver qualities: accessibility and responsiveness (see Table 1.3). Accessibility means that the parent is available, physically and emotionally, to the infant and child. That is, the attachment figure is with the infant/child throughout the period of attachment. Indeed, secure attachment requires the presence of a figure to whom one becomes attached.

TWO ESSENTIAL CAREGIVER QUALITIES

- Responsiveness
- Accessibility

TABLE 1.3

Parental responsiveness means that the caregiver sensitively, accurately, and directly addresses the child's needs. (This is also referred to as "maternal sensitivity.") The responsive or sensitive attachment figure can accurately read signals from the infant/child and can respond to or even anticipate needs based on past experiences with her young child. She successfully identifies the child's needs from cries, facial expressions, vocalizations, body language, and overt behavior. Depending upon the stage of attachment and the specific child, the parent's response differs. For example, during the "pre-attachment" stage (see Table 1.4), the parent feeds, diapers, comforts, holds, and stimulates the infant when the need is expressed. Later, during the "active attachment" stage, the caregiver remains at times more physically distant, though emotionally available to the child. During this stage, the caregiver must tolerate and encourage independence, while providing the child a "secure base" through emotional availability (Bowlby, 1969; Mahler et al., 1975).

In the tragic lives of maltreated children the parent figures may be extremely deficient and unavailable (i.e., inaccessible) or they may be unable or unwilling (i.e., unresponsive) to read signals from their child, or to comprehend their child's needs and wants. There is a lack of maternal (or parental) sensitivity. Under those circumstances, children's typical level of signaling the need for caregiving must be altered and sometimes ratcheted upwards to send a message to the parents that is hard to ignore. Children's behavior adapts to the negligent parenting to insure some modicum of engagement with the caregiver. These children adapt with so-called "strategies" for connecting with caregivers—distorted "rules of engagement" you might say. Unfortunately, while the strategies have been a necessary way of coping or adapting in a maltreating home, these strategies do not simply disappear once the child is placed in a safe, non-maltreating foster or adoptive home. Indeed, the ongoing use of learned strategies may put off subsequent caregivers and discourage them from attempts to respond to the child. In the end the child reexperiences a relative absence of caregiving, which only serves to reinforce their negative conclusions about caregivers (Dozier & Albus, 2000).

Inevitably, if the caregiver is accessible and responsive to the infant/child, attachment will form (given a normal infant/child). Even when infants are born with "difficult temperaments," such as Down Syndrome or with cerebral palsy, they can develop secure attachments if their caregivers are sensitive (Dozier & Albus, 2000). However, "responsiveness and accessibility" must span the first 3 to 5 years of the child's life for attachment to solidify.

It is important to note here that normal infants and young children usually are quite receptive to caregivers. They, figuratively speaking, "soak up" as much parenting, nurturing, and stimulation as possible. The disturbed, attachment-disordered foster or adopted child, however, is another story. This unfortunate child often rejects nurturing behavior from the accessible and reliable foster, kinship, or adoptive parents due to his past history of maltreatment from caregivers. As discussed in later chapters, the child's jaundiced view of parent figures can contaminate his relationship to the foster or adoptive parents. Indeed, beyond these views, the child has accumulated a bag of tricks, a repertoire of strategies to relate to caregivers. If foster, kinship, and adoptive parents are to successfully reach the child with sensitive, responsive parenting, they will have to get past the child's off-putting behavior strategies (Dozier & Albus, 2000).

STAGES OF NORMAL ATTACHMENT FORMATION

The birth of the child and the birth of attachment are not simultaneous (Mahler et al., 1975). While physical birth of the infant occurs with a sudden, remarkable event, attachment emerges over time and through a series of predictable stages. As shown in Table 1.4, attachment to the caregiver has been found to develop across four predictable stages during the critical period of his first 3 to 5 years of life (Ainsworth et al., 1978; Bowlby, 1973; Mahler et al., 1975).

The formation of attachment during the first years of life is critical to later psychological health. As we will see ahead, in those children who have failed to attach securely during a "window of opportunity" in the first 5 years of life, the chances for developing normal attachment relationships later in life may be diminished. However, some key researchers do not view this as a hard and fast rule, giving more credit to the child's capacity to change and improve at later stages (Sroufe, 1988; Sroufe et al., 2002). It seems strongly likely, though, that the child's "earliest relationship" with the primary attachment figure draws a "mental blueprint" or set of expectations about that figure and subsequent caregivers (Dozier & Albus, 2000).

Here is a description of the four stages of attachment:

1. In the first stage of normal attachment formation—the "pre-attachment" stage (Ainsworth et al., 1978)—the tiny infant (birth to 3 months old) is totally dependent upon the caregiver, who reacts to the child protectively. The infant, though totally dependent, is not completely inert in the attachment interaction. He orients toward the sound of the female voice; he tracks moving objects with his eyes; and he reflexively reaches out to be held. At this first stage, his smile is relatively indiscriminate and reflexive; and on the whole, he is a comparatively passive player in the attachment drama.

2. Next, in the "recognition/discrimination," stage (Ainsworth, et al., 1978, Bowlby, 1969) the infant (age 3 to 8 months) differentiates visually between his primary caregiver and others. In her presence, he vocalizes differently and cries in a distinct fashion when she leaves the room. He examines his primary caregiver enthusiastically and smiles at and "greets" her after brief separations. At this stage the child is beginning to form a "selective" attachment to a preferred caregiver, usually one who is consistently accessible and responsive. As discussed later, the absence of a steady caregiver and the lack of selective attachment relate to development of attachment disorders (O'Connor & Zeanah, 2003).

3. In the "active attachment" stage, from 8 months to 3 years of age, the child shows clear preference for the primary caregiver (Ainsworth et al., 1978; Bowlby, 1969). Correspondingly, the child shows a "stranger reaction," which indicates he clearly discriminates between his primary attachment figure and strangers. At this stage also, the child checks back to the caregiver's face, visually touching base with her. In addition, the child crawls (or walks) away from his caregiver. He becomes intoxicated by his newfound mobility and begins to explore the world outside his immediate attachment relationship, (i.e., he "practices" separating [Mahler et al., 1975]). As a toddler, he revels in exploration, independence, and locomotion, relatively unconcerned about his mother's whereabouts.

    By this stage in attachment formation, the child has become a much more active, more sophisticated player in the attachment relationship (Cicchetti, Cummings, Greenberg, & Marvin, 1990). Verbal interchanges often replace physical contact, proximity seeking, and other more primitive attachment behaviors. Certainly, as children mature they draw comfort increasingly from the psychological connection to their caregiver and are less dependent upon physical closeness (Hans, Bernstein, & Sims, 2000). As a result, strategies for engaging parents become more advanced and rely more on distance contact and verbal communication.

4. In the "partnership"[4] stage (i.e., 36 months and beyond), the child solidifies attachment relationships and becomes more proficient in the verbal communication of needs and in the verbal negotiation of differences with his caregivers (Ainsworth et al., 1978; Bowlby, 1969; Speltz, 1990).

    As we will see ahead, many disturbed foster children never reach the partnership stage, nor have they mastered the skill of communicating their needs and of negotiating conflicts and differences with caregivers. Many children have concluded that they are "in it alone" or that they can't expect that others

---

[4] Technically, this has been called "goal-corrected partnership," which suggests that the parent and the child do not always agree on goals or objectives. The mother, for example, may need to leave the child at day care, but the child has different thoughts on the subject. Or the child would like unending, exclusive time with the father, but the other children and mother interrupt his goal with father. These differing goals need to be recognized, acknowledged, negotiated, and corrected.

STAGES IN ATTACHMENT FORMATION		
AGE	STAGE	DESCRIPTION
Birth - 3 months	Pre-attachment	Infant orients toward the sound of the caregiver's voice; he tracks visually. Infant smiles reflexively.
3 - 8 months	Recognition/ Discrimination	Infant differentiates between primary caregiver and others. Smiles are based on recognition. Infant scans the caregiver's face with excitement. Infant greets caretaker and vocalizes differently to her.
8 - 36 months	Active Attachment	Stranger reaction emerges. Infant shows clear preference for the chief caregiver. He checks back to his caregiver's face. Child crawls or walks away from caregiver.
36 months +	Partnership	Attachment solidifies. Child shows increased ability to communicate needs verbally. Child negotiates differences.
TABLE 1.4		

can meet their needs. Indeed, they have never learned the mutual give and take of relationships and may presume that they cannot achieve the meeting of their needs in the context of a parent-child relationship. In cases where abuse has been present, children may have to remain mute on the subject of their goals, needs, wants, and disagreements, since expression of same might trigger parental abuse. *Overall, a grasp of the partnership phase is essential to understanding many troubled foster, kinship, and adopted children.* In truth, many of them have never really developed a sense that there is a partnership.

THE SECURELY ATTACHED CHILD AND THE "INTERNAL WORKING MODEL"

The stages of attachment formation outlined above are thought to follow sequentially, if the interrelationship between caregiver and child remains unbroken, secure, and healthy. Thus, the typical infant/child, having found his primary attachment figure both accessible and responsive to him, develops a secure attachment.

On average, by the partnership stage, the attached child has developed a positive internal working model (Bowlby, 1969), i.e., an optimistic expectation, mental representation, or blueprint regarding himself, his caregiver, and their relationship.[5] A child's mental blueprint regarding himself, caregivers, and relationships begins to form and firm up in the first year of life (Sroufe et al., 2002). By preschool, the child's views of those around him can be seen in his stories and drawings (Bretherton, Ridgeway, & Cassidy, 1990).

The child's working model is a concept, something that we infer from his behavior, statements, and drawings. The working model in attachment theory is the repository of thoughts and feelings that have developed based upon the child's early experiences with caregivers. Well formed by age 3, the working model, in effect, is an internal, mental representation of how things work at the level of important interpersonal relationships. The individual child forms internal expectations and conclusions about caregivers, himself, and the world he has experienced. The working model theoretically should help the child exist in the interpersonal world in which he finds himself. It helps him make predictions about how he will be treated by important individuals (e.g., caregivers) and how he needs to adapt to the way they act. And, of course, the child's thoughts, representations, expectations, conclusions, and predictions have related feelings attached to them (e.g., if the child expects that caregivers are sensitive and reliable, he enjoys a sense of calm; if the child concludes that parents are insensitive and inaccessible, he is plagued by a sense of insecurity). It should be pointed out that the working model is assumed to be automatic and often operating at a preconscious level.

In the normal, securely attached child, the working model would contain mostly positive images of himself and his caregivers. Table 1.5 outlines the working model of a normal, well-attached child. As you see in the table, the secure child sees himself as worthwhile, wanted, safe, and capable. He views caregivers as available, responsive, and capable of meeting his needs.

The securely attached young child has developed what has been called by others "basic trust" (Erikson, 1968), an expectation that the world

---

[5] As discussed in later chapters, the disturbed foster or adopted child often has developed a pessimistic, cynical negative working model of himself and his caregivers which interferes with his development of healthy attachment relationships in the foster or adoptive family.

THE POSITIVE WORKING MODEL

About himself:
1. I am worthwhile/wanted.
2. I am safe.
3. I am capable.

About caregivers:
1. They are available.
2. They are responsive.
3. They meet my needs.

TABLE 1.5

will be generally safe and that close relationships will be satisfying. Furthermore, he is secure in himself and in his relationships to primary attachment figures; he knows that he belongs and to whom he belongs (Bowlby, 1969). Attachment theory focuses upon the growing confidence and self-worth in the child and the expectation that he is effective in finding caregiving and a secure base when needed (Bowlby). It also focuses upon the growing capacity to achieve emotional intimacy (Sroufe et al., 2002). With that comes a sense of inner, one might say, tranquility, which permits greater independence and confidence. Relatively unconcerned about the most important relationships in his close-in, "proximate world," this child can venture out into the "distal" world at large. That is, he can become thoroughly absorbed in play, exploration, learning, and mastery of the world around him without inordinate fears about loss of his parents. The child begins to show healthy independence. (However, the foster or adopted child who at 3 years of age can cook, clean, and feed himself may have serious attachment issues, though appearing "independent."[6])

The normally attached child has a well-formed conscience, a sense of right and wrong which grows out of his desire to please attachment figures. He shows need awareness, a range of genuine emotion, and the ability to identify and express needs in a remarkably insightful fashion; he displays affection and anger freely. In all, the normally at-

---

[6] As we will see in chapter two, in cases where the disturbed foster or adopted child has not developed a "secure base" and the confidence that goes with it, the child may develop an appearance of independence, a premature sense of false autonomy, in which he or she will go off on their own without a backwards look. Or, the child may not ask for help but take matters into his own hands.

tached child relates empathically to children and adults, and he can negotiate disagreements through increasingly complex verbal inter-changes (Ainsworth et al., 1978).

REACTION TO DISRUPTION IN THE ATTACHMENT RELATIONSHIP

Although minor disruptions in the caregiver-child relationship are common and often harmless, major separations from and loss of the caregiver can impact the child's attachment in very measurable ways. Major disruptions to attachment may occur in cases of parent men-tal or physical illness and/or death; abandonment of the child by the parent; chronic abuse, neglect, or exploitation of the child; periodic rejection of the child; and in cases of prolonged substandard orphan-age care (Chisolm, 2000; Fraiberg, 1980; Main & Hesse, 1990; Main & Solomon, 1990). Child maltreatment (e.g., abuse, neglect, sexual exploitation) sets up a distorting, deleterious environment which in-creases the risk that the child will adapt socially and emotionally in unusual, dysfunctional ways (Cicchetti, 2004). Children from orphan-ages and other institutional settings, who often develop attachments later than expected, are at increased risk of developing unusual at-tachments (Chisholm, 2000). Additionally, children who are placed in multiple foster care and other out-of-home placements are at increased risk of atypical attachment formation. Multiple foster care placements have been associated with dire outcomes for children and adolescents (Jonson-Reid & Barth, 2000).

Admittedly, certain infant/child factors can also precipitate disrup-tions in the growing caregiver-child bond. For instance, temperament, prematurity, early life-threatening illnesses, and hyperactivity may negatively impact the continuity of the attachment relationship (Bates & Bayles, 1988; Brazelton & Cramer, 1990; Delaney & Kunstal, 1997). Exposure to alcohol or drugs in utero may also set the stage for dis-ruptions in the attachment process (Dozier & Albus, 2000). It also can increase the risk of development of insecure attachments perhaps due, in some measure, to the fact that drug-exposed infants may not engage in ways that caregivers find positively reinforcing or inviting (Dozier & Albus).

Research has clearly demonstrated a distinct, three-part cycle in the infant/toddler's response to disruptions in attachment during and af-ter brief separation from the mother in a laboratory setting (Ainsworth et al., 1978) or in longer periods of separation due to, for example, lengthy hospitalization of the mother (Bowlby, 1973). This cycle in infant/toddlers can be used as a prototype for understanding reactions in older foster and adopted children who have experienced significant separations and losses. The three steps in this cycle are protest, despair, and detachment.

1. The protest-despair-detachment cycle is predictable (see Table 1.6). Upon first becoming aware of his caregiver's absence, the child initially protests; that is, he cries, whines, calls to, pursues, searches after, rages, and/or otherwise makes his displeasure known.

2. Finding that his protests are lodged in vain and that his attempts to get his caregiver to return are futile, the child often despairs, i.e., becomes saddened, depressed, and lethargic. He refuses the stranger's attempts at comforting him.

3. The child eventually detaches from others in a withdrawn, somewhat cynical posture. Even if reunited with the caregiver, the child may rebuff her, fail to recognize her, and remain remarkably disinterested in becoming involved with her again.[7]

A grasp of the protest-despair-detachment cycle in normal children can foster an understanding of serious attachment problems caused by chronic separation and loss. The three-part cycle, when repeated frequently during the first 3 years of life, may result in short- and long-term aberrations in attachment formation. It seems intuitive that children who have reached the stages of despair and detachment chronically will lack security and may give up on active protest while learning other strategies for securing what they need, or an approximation thereof, from caregivers. Indeed, depending upon the chronicity and severity of caregiver-child disruptions (and perhaps upon

---

[7] Mothers and fathers of infants/toddlers/preschoolers often observe the protest-despair-detachment cycle at the baby-sitter's or at day care. When the parents come to pick up the child they are told the child cried (protest) for a half hour after they dropped him off. They are further told that the child was inconsolable (despair) for a long period of the day, retreating into himself and refusing contact with the baby-sitter or day care provider. When the parents attempt to engage the child at the end of the day, he may appear aloof, disinterested in them, and may even refuse to leave the nursery (detachment) or daycare center. Of course, the protest-despair-detachment cycle in this case could be expected and normal. With loving management children pass through the many, expected, normal cycles without lasting negative effects.

REACTION TO DISRUPTION IN ATTACHMENT

The Protest – Despair – Detachment Cycle:

Protest – Crying, distress, pursuit of the mother, searching after the mother, temper tantruming.

Despair – Depression, quiet withdrawal, refusal to be comforted by strangers, disinterest in play or exploration.

Detachment – Lack of interaction with the primary caregiver after reunion, active avoidance of the caregiver, and failure to recognize the caregiver.

TABLE 1.6

the child's innate temperament and age at the time of disruption), attachment becomes weakened, seriously damaged, and abnormal. And, as a result, the child adapts to his environment by learning or developing strategies for relating to parent figures. These strategies become entrenched, overlearned, and perhaps difficult to unlearn or change even when environments change for the better, e.g., if the child is placed in a loving, nurturing foster, kinship, or adoptive home. The child is on a developmental pathway that has been set in motion prior to coming to the present home, and the new parent figures may have a difficult time helping the child take an alternative, safer course (O'Connor & Zeanah, 2003).

CONCLUDING REMARKS

Attachment between infant and caregiver is a prerequisite to the physical survival and emotional health of the child. Typically, an infant/child marches through four predictable stages of development on the road to secure, mature attachment. When the process of attachment unfolds without significant disruptions, the child becomes normally, securely attached, as seen in his positive internal working model, conscience development, ability to empathize, sense of basic trust in the world, inner feeling of security, growing awareness of his needs, and negotiating skills. However, when significant disruptions or substandard parenting mar the attachment process, a pattern of abnormal attachment may emerge. With that comes a host of unusual strategies which the child has developed along the way to insure some modicum of parental attention and protection.

2 PATTERNS OF ATTACHMENT

There are individual differences in how children develop attachments to their caregivers. As with any developmental task, children vary in how completely they accomplish the task. Attachment research has identified four main patterns or types of attachment in children that develop as early as 12 months. Three of the four main types show insecure connection to the caregiver. Although these insecure types are not disorders of attachment per se, they may be markers of ongoing difficulties with relationships. When children develop insecure attachment patterns, along with it they develop internal working models (i.e., expectations) of the world, which reflect insecurity. In some children the working models can be quite negative, that is, the child's conclusions about himself and his expectations about caregivers are pessimistic. He does not expect sensitive, reliable caregiving. If the child concludes that he is unable to obtain caregiving from parent figures as needed, he does not develop a sense of partnership with them. The upshot may be that the child fails to learn or attempt to negotiate with caregivers for the meeting of needs.

This chapter will focus on the following topics:

1. Patterns and Sub-Patterns of Attachment

2. Maltreatment and Insecure Attachment

3. The Negative Working Model

4. Failure to Negotiate with Caregivers

Before we address these topics let's return to the case of Candy, described in chapter one. Candy had been placed in numerous foster homes before she was 6 years old. However, once placed in her ninth home—the therapeutic foster home—she stabilized somewhat, at least to the point where she was not asked to leave. Nonetheless, after a year in placement, Candy's problem behaviors still appeared intermittently. She continued to lie, steal, and hoard food, and in general she withdrew from the foster family. Interestingly, Candy never confronted her foster parents directly, though she would argue incessantly with the other children in the home. The foster mother gave an example of how overly compliant and non-assertive Candy was.

> On one occasion, Candy showed a uncharacteristic display of anger to the foster mother over using the DVD player. Candy had a passion for specific cartoons and would watch them for hours. However, other children in the home also had their favorite movies; thus, the foster parents set up a system whereby the children would take turns. The previous week, the foster mother heard the children arguing about whose turn it was, and she intervened somewhat hastily. In the process, she determined that it was another child's turn, not Candy's. In a rare instant of honest emotion, Candy protested loudly to the foster mother that is was her turn to watch her cartoons. Over her protest, the foster mother stated, "If you are going to act that way, Candy, then you'll miss your next turn." In an almost eerie transformation, Candy immediately smiled and said compliantly, "Okay, Mom, I guess you're right." After that incident, however, Candy's behavior problems suddenly resurfaced, almost to the point they were a year earlier.

With Candy any assertive self-expression, any voicing of needs or feelings in her relationship to adults was rare. Basically, she avoided any confrontation with adults, suppressed feelings of dissent, and overtly complied. Children who are this tentative around adults may be forced into secret and solitary worlds where they do what they want alone and unseen by adults. Candy's passive (or passive-aggressive) relationship to her foster mother illustrated a number of issues which will be addressed in this chapter, namely, an insecure pattern of attachment, exposure to unresponsive and inaccessable caregiving in the past, a negative conclusion about caregivers (and herself), and failure to develop a sense of true partnership with a parent (along with the capacity to negotiate with that partner).

PATTERNS AND SUB-PATTERNS OF ATTACHMENT

Most infants and young children will grow attached to those who care for them, however bad the caregiving is. The tenor or quality of that attachment ranges widely, based on the quality of the caregiving (Sroufe et al., 2002) and perhaps on child factors as well (Kagan, 1984). The phrase "pattern of attachment" refers to the quality of attachment or the overall attachment strategy in which the young child engages. The pattern, quality, or strategy of attachment does not bring with it a judgment of goodness or badness, but rather identifies the overarching approach to relating with caregivers and others (Crittenden, 2000).

Of the four main patterns (i.e., qualities or strategies) of attachment—Types A, B, C, and D—which have been identified through Ainsworth-type research in infants and young children, three are insecure patterns (Ainsworth et al., 1978). Researchers have discovered, using "separation experiments," that the NORMALLY OR SECURELY ATTACHED (TYPE B) infant, after brief periods of physical separation from his caregiver, shows clear signs of missing her; then, upon reunion with her, the Type B infant seeks and finds closeness to her and, as a result, eventually seems to be secure enough to resume play or exploration.

The three patterns of insecure attachment include the following: (1) Type A – insecure-avoidant; (2) Type C – insecure-ambivalent; and (3) Type D – disorganized/disoriented (Ainsworth et al., 1978; Main & Hesse, 1990; Main & Solomon, 1990). These patterns (see Table 2.1) first identified in infants, show some permanence as children mature into middle childhood. Some research has found that fewer older children are identified as insecure (Egeland & Sroufe, 1981); however, in clinical practice many foster and adopted children are thought to show vestiges of insecure attachment to others.

THREE PATTERNS OF ATTACHMENT
Type A – Insecure-Avoidant
Type C – Insecure-Ambivalent
Type D – Disorganized-Disoriented
TABLE 2.1

All three patterns of insecure attachment are observed in maltreated children who are subject to a great deal of disruption during attachment formation years. After placement in foster care, many of these children remain insecure or disorganized in their attachments. Children from orphanage care often develop insecure attachments to their primary caregivers (Chisholm, 2000).[1] In the worst cases, these children are highly resistant to change.

---

[1] It should be noted that the three types A, C, and D are not considered to be psychiatric diagnoses, e.g., Reactive Attachment Disorder, but rather are types of attachment observed early in life.

For clarity's sake, the three major "abnormal" attachment patterns or types as they emerge in the "separation experiments" are described in detail:

1. INSECURE-AVOIDANT (TYPE A) infants, also referred to simply as avoidant, casually avoid and nonchalantly ignore the caregiver after being reunited with her. These Type A infants/young children appear to avoid closeness to or interaction with the mother after reunion with her, although not in an extremely angry or actively rejecting way. They might merely move away, glance away, or fail to cling to their mothers, and they treat a stranger much like they treat the mother. Insecure-avoidant infants ironically may show little distress during the separation period away from the mother (Ainsworth et al., 1978).

   It should be pointed out that later studies of Type A children who came from maltreating backgrounds discovered that they develop unusual strategies or sub-patterns for dealing with caregivers, such as super-compliant behavior, squelching of negative feelings, and/or displaying false positive emotion and compulsive caregiving of the parent (Crittenden & Claussen, 2000). These children are classified as A3 (compulsive-caregiving) or A4 (compulsive-compliant) children. Foster and adoptive parents see this in children who may be overly obedient or role-inverted.

   > COMPULSIVE-COMPLIANT CHILD (A4) is one who has insecure emotional ties to his parent figures. This child has often been exposed to abusive caregiving and has attempted to reduce exposure to abuse by complying. The child avoids any expression of negative feelings around the caregiver and makes few if any demands on the caregiver, instead acting "self-reliant." Overall, this child doesn't make waves, acts obediently, and does not complain or protest to parents. This child often relies rigidly and excessively on the compliance strategy (Crittenden & Claussen, 2000).

   > COMPULSIVE-CAREGIVING CHILD (A3) is one who (similar to the compliant child) has insecure emotional ties to his parent figures. This child has often been exposed to neglectful caregiving and has attempted to increase the chances of gaining attention from the parent by suppressing his negative feelings; by putting few if any demands

on the parent; and by taking care of the parent rather than being cared for by the parent. In some ways, the child may obtain some meager parental attention in the process of attending to that parent figure. Overall, this youngster takes care of himself and makes no demands on others to care for him. This child, in role-inverted fashion, may actually become a caregiver to others. He often relies rigidly and excessively on this caregiving strategy (Crittenden & Claussen, 2000).

These children may employ these odd strategies to remain safe from abuse and to achieve some modicum of parental attention and protection. These strategies may develop in reaction to a caregiver who responds to the distressed infant or young child by rebuffing the child's needs through distracting or discounting the fact that the child is hurt, sick, or afraid (Dozier & Albus, 2000).

2. INSECURE-AMBIVALENT/RESISTANT (TYPE C) infants, also referred to as resistant, act markedly distressed during separation and upon reunion become inconsolable and obsessed with the parent, vacillating between need for closeness to and anger at the parent (Ainsworth et al., 1978; Main & Hesse, 1990). They have been described as coercing parents to attend to their needs through tantrums, poutiness, helplessness, and coyness. The resistant child's strategies amount to a carrot-and-stick approach, which combines threatening and manipulating to gain parental attention (Hans et al., 2000). These infants/young children show angry dependency mixed with active and/or passive resistance to closeness or contact with their mother. Insecure-ambivalent infants/children are very distressed during the period of separation from the mother.

The resistant child may be used to caregivers who are inconsistent in maternal sensitivity and availability and therefore has developed one or more of three strategies: (a) resisting or turning away from the parent as a way of dealing with typical unresponsive parenting; (b) hypervigilance and super-alert attention to the mother to detect those occasions when she is available; and (c) "exaggerated signals of distress" and loud entreaties which are difficult for even an unresponsive mother to ignore (Dozier & Albus, 2000). Interestingly, in the separation experiments these youngsters, though quite upset about

being separated from their mothers, could not make "full use" of their mothers when they were reunited due to either their anger or significant passivity. The ambivalence of these children seems correlated to exposure to parental unresponsiveness and results in stepped-up expression of emotion and dependence to command the caregiver's attention (Hans et al., 2000). Research has identified two variations or sub-patterns of Type C children who are extraordinarily forceful:

> COERCIVE CHILD (C3) has insecure emotional ties to his parent figures. This child has often been exposed to unpredictable, intermittent, or on-again-off-again parenting, and has attempted to increase the chances of gaining attention by showing strong negative emotion, protesting, and clamoring for attention in ways that cannot be easily ignored. Overall, this child makes forceful, angry, negative demands on caregivers for their time and attention.

> CHILD FEIGNING HELPLESSNESS (C4) also shows insecure attachment to his caregiver. This child may have been exposed to "severe threats and unpredictable outcomes" (von der Lippe & Crittenden, 2000). Like other C children, this child invests a great deal of energy in engaging and holding the caregiver's attention (Hans et al., 2000). While the C strategy in general is marked by intense, unrelenting involvement between child and caregiver, the C4 child relies on exaggerated and feigned helplessness. Emotional displays are falsified and curiously disappear once he has attained the goal of successfully engaging the caregiver. The C4 child might use simulated helplessness to disarm others and to cloak his demands in a coy, dependent, needy "veneer of childishness."[2]

Overall, Type C children seem consumed with their continuous attempts to attract and hold their caregiver's attention. They never arrive at a state of rest in that relationship, and they put an extreme amount of effort into maintaining an unbroken connection with the parent (Hans et al., 2000). Foster and adoptive parents often observe that their child or children show unrelenting, insatiable neediness reminiscent of Type C.

---

[2] What comes to mind is the young child using baby talk and infantile body language, gestures, and gait.

3. DISORGANIZED/DISORIENTED (TYPE D) infants show the most confusing, contradictory attachment behavior. When distressed around their caregivers, these infants or young children seem conflicted and wary of the very parent figure they must turn to for comfort (Dozier & Albus, 2000). Their behavior is marked by two conflicting drives: one to approach and the other to flee the caregiver. The infant may show a burst of angry behavior followed by sudden "freezing," or "dazed behavior" (Main & Solomon, 1990). This behavior might be akin to that described by Fraiberg (1980) as "frozen watchfulness" in maltreated children.

Indeed, Type D children are overrepresented among samples of abused and neglected children and among children whose biological parent figures have significant, unresolved trauma and loss histories (van IJzendoorn, 1995). These parents often are themselves both "frightened and frightening" (Dozier & Albus, 2000). As many as half of abused children show Type D attachments. In Ainsworth-style separation exercises, after being reunited, the disorganized/disoriented infant might sit on the parent's lap but with eyes averted, or he might allow the parent to hold him but with his limbs stiff. A particularly curious example of such contradictory behavior is that of the child who smiles frequently or constantly but fearfully. Other behaviors which signal disorganized/disoriented attachment in the infant are: infant goes away from or fails to seek out the caregiver when distressed or frightened; infant attempts to leave with a stranger rather than staying with the caregiver; and infant shows fright at the sight of the caregiver after reunion (Main & Solomon, 1990). It's likely that many Type D children are also highly insecure but their behaviors around caregivers are fragmented and "nonstrategic." They might be seen as sending confusing, off-the-wall, desperate signals which are then hard for parents (including foster, kinship, and adoptive parents) to interpret and respond to.[3]

---

[3] It is likely that Type D infants have experienced a great deal of trauma in the relationship to their attachment figures. They have been described as showing the most "pathology" by preschool and elementary school age (Carlson, 1998). It should be noted that while we might classify an anxious (insecure) or disorganized attachment, this is not equivalent to making a diagnosis of, for instance, Reactive Attachment Disorder or some other psychiatric disorder. In fact, there are no standardized tests for evaluating attachment disorders (O'Connor & Zeanah, 2003).

MALTREATMENT AND INSECURE ATTACHMENT

Reminding ourselves that attachment develops within a relationship, typically the caregiver-infant dyad, is crucial. This first relationship, when healthy, shows mutual satisfaction, reciprocity, and synchrony, i.e., the contribution of both caregiver and child to a secure partnership (Vizziello, Ferrero, & Musicco, 2002). When the first relationship is unhealthy, as in child maltreatment, the resultant partnership is marked by insecurity due to inadequate, hostile, or abusive caregiving (Crittenden, 1988; Speltz, 1990; Spieker & Booth, 1988).

While some maltreated children may be "invulnerable" to the effects of abuse, undoubtedly the lion's share of victimized children develop some attachment disorders of a relatively fixed nature (Anthony & Cohler, 1987; Greenberg & Speltz, 1988). They are subject to many separations from and losses of the primary caregivers. Most probably they have cycled through the protest-despair-detachment sequence innumerable times. During infancy, many of these children may form insecure, ambivalent/resistant, or disorganized/disoriented (Type A, C, or D) attachment patterns due to the insensitivity, unresponsiveness, unreliability, and unavailability of their caregivers (Bowlby, 1973; Brazleton, 1990). By the age of 2 or 3, these children may already have begun to develop strategies for engaging parents which appear to others as conduct problems, the functions of which are to reduce danger and secure caregiving at some level. What baffles both parents and researchers alike are those children who appear to discourage or punish parents for involvement with them, as in children who are avoidant or resistant (Dozier & Albus, 2000). These children may have a crying need for parental attention but cannot signal clearly due to their own mixed feelings about caregivers. (It is important to assert here that all children require comfort when distressed and upset, whether they can show this clearly to a parent or not [Dozier & Albus]). Foster, kinship, and adoptive parents must become exquisitely sensitive to the underlying distress and poorly communicated needs of children with attachment disorders. Since many troubled children send "unclear" signals, parents need to see beyond conduct problems, apparent indifference, and active resistance to detect the underlying need. If parents mistake the child's unclear signals as a pure and simple desire to alienate, they risk missing the true meaning: These kids' behavior may be a strategy for keeping some modicum of safety in a world of dangerous, unresponsive caregivers (Dozier & Albus).[4]

It is essential for professionals who work closely with foster, kinship, and adoptive parents and their children to gather information on the child's earliest and ongoing caregiving experiences. If the child was grossly and chronically neglected, for instance, a secure attachment is unlikely. Resultant strategies may have developed in which the child does not appear to need a caregiver. Foster or adoptive parents who take this child into their home must be instructed to see beyond the stiff-arming and apparent indifference of this child. Foster and adoptive parents, in effect, inherit the child's expectations about parent figures, which are none too rosy.

THE NEGATIVE WORKING MODEL

As explained in chapter one, the working model is the expectation, mental representation, or conclusion that the child forms about himself, his caregivers, and their relationship to him (Bowlby, 1969; 1973). It's a mental blueprint of relationships. This working model emerges out of myriad interactions with the caregiver(s), and by the age of 12 months infants already show clear individual differences in working models, although they cannot yet verbalize it (Schneider-Rosen, 1990). However, by 3 years of age the contents of the working model can be ascertained by analyzing children's verbalizations (Bretherton et al., 1990); and by 4 years of age, the working model may already be relatively fixed and resistant to change (Greenberg & Speltz, 1988).

Clinicians and parents may have some accurate observations about how these children view their world, caregivers, and themselves. If a young foster child states, "Mothers are the ones who leave you," we have a pretty clear impression of one of the child's expectations (i.e., internal working model). Generally speaking the working model contains overall impressions of accumulated experiences the child has had with his primary caregivers (Bretherton et al., 1990). More impressionistic than exact, the working model is an inner reflection of

---

[4] It is beyond the scope of this book to cover the range of maltreatment to which foster, kinship, and adoptive children have been exposed. However, as most professionals and substitute parents learn, children in out-of-home care have been victims of abuse, neglect, and/or sexual exploitation. Suffice it to say that children, in the extreme, may have been beaten, burned, bruised, maimed, and even tortured; they may have been starved, unstimulated, unwanted, and abandoned; and they may have been victimized sexually by parents, stepparents, or strangers. In these instances and even in less extreme cases, children's resultant attachment patterns fairly predictably become insecure.

outer realities. As previously stated, in the normal, securely attached child, the working model would contain a preponderance of positive images of self, caregivers, and their relationships.

It is important to note that a sizeable portion of the working model, once developed, appears to function at an unconscious level (Bowlby, 1969; 1973; Cicchetti et al., 1990). This may be explained by the fact that much of that mental image is formed when the child is young and pre-verbal. The unconscious functioning of the working model is especially evident in the maltreated child, who often holds highly idealized conscious notions regarding his abusive, maltreated caregivers (e.g., his birth parents). At the same time, at an unconscious level, the maltreated child has developed negative, cynical, pessimistic expectations about himself, caregivers, and the world. Consciously, for example, the foster child may hold these thoughts: "My mother loves me and looks after me," "My father is the best dad a kid could have," and "My parents will visit me while I'm in foster care, because they love me." Behavior toward the biological parents may resemble the unnaturally compliant style shown by the A3 child previously described. Simultaneously, at a preconscious level, the maltreated child holds different expectations—some too painful, confusing, or frightening for the child to deal with. For example, "My mother does not behave as if she wants me," "When my father hurts me, I feel rejected and angry."

Many disturbed foster children develop a negative working model. That is, the maltreated child's mental blueprint consists of highly negative expectations about caregivers and himself. As seen in Table 2.2 the maltreated child views himself as worthless, unsafe, and impotent to make an impact on others (Bretherton et al., 1990; Speltz, 1990). When youngsters conclude that they have little or no effect on the reactions of their adults' caregiving, they feel incompetent and impotent in the caregiver-child relationship and perhaps in any other domain that involves solving problems and taking on novel challenges (Speltz, 1990). Simultaneously, they view caregivers as unreliable, unresponsive, and dangerous. They expect intimate relationships to be thoroughly undependable and ultimately frustrating of their needs. Though perhaps operating at an unconscious level, the negative working model has a dramatic influence on the child's behavior and on the maintenance of conduct problems.[5]

---

[5] Chapter seven expands upon the negative expectations of the maltreated child.

THE NEGATIVE WORKING MODEL OF THE MALTREATED CHILD

About himself:
1. I am worthless.
2. I am unsafe.
3. I am impotent.

About caregivers:
1. They are unresponsive (insensitive).
2. They are unreliable (inaccessible).
3. They are threatening, dangerous, rejecting.

TABLE 2.2

As stated before, much of the negative working model remains at an preconscious level in the troubled foster child. Given his past, it may be less painful and/or more adaptive for the child to be unaware of the negative working model, since it might reduce potential, direct confrontation with a frightening individual. Maltreating caregivers may have used withdrawal of emotional supplies and support (Mahler et al., 1975; Masterson, 1972), ridicule (Speltz, 1990), and other models of punishment, threat, and intimidation to discourage any open display of protest from the child. Accordingly, the child concludes that caregivers will either fail to respond or will punish if he expresses anger or argument. Thus, the child suppresses the vocalization. The process may be instantaneous and preclude conscious reflection by the child. This in effect relegates the negative working model to the realm of the unconscious. From a reinforcement point of view, verbalizations and thoughts about the negative aspects to the parent have been extinguished, leaving the child unaware of the "dark side" of the negative working model (Dollard & Miller, 1950).

Importantly, representations and expectations arising out of the earliest relationships to the caregiver may transfer to other, subsequent relationships (e.g., with foster or adoptive parents). The child's working model is stubbornly resistant to change, so that if he learned to expect rejection, loss, or insensitivity in the past, he continues to expect the same in the present, even with different, sensitive, accepting, available caregivers. The negative working model becomes applied to these later relationships with adults and sometimes peers. In essence, the negative working model is unfairly superimposed upon any subsequent intimate relationships, though its relevance to the reality of the new relationship may be nonexistent. This "transference" phenomenon accounts for much trouble and disruption in the foster and adoptive homes and presents both challenges and opportunities in treatment of the maltreated foster child. Indeed, in foster or adoptive care the child's behavior reflects his negative working model and becomes a replay, a "reenactment" of the earlier, unsatisfying attachment relationships.

FAILURE TO NEGOTIATE WITH CAREGIVERS

The troubled, insecure foster, kinship, or adopted child has likely never achieved a harmonious "goal-corrected partnership" with any caregiver. Remember, the partnership stage of attachment formation has as its central theme the negotiating of differences about separation and other relationship trajectory problems (e.g., the parent wants one thing, the child another). The child's negative working model of caregivers may reflect that they are insensitive, unreliable, and immutable, and that essentially you cannot expect them to recognize and meet your needs. Negotiation is out of the question. The parent-child, goal-corrected partnership is nonexistent or dysfunctional.

As discussed later, parenting approaches which exclusively stress control of and compliance from the child may miss opportunities to alter the child's negative conclusions about negotiation and partnership. *Conformity and compliance training does not lead to negotiation and may inadvertently reinforce a rift between parent and child* (Speltz, 1990). Many maltreated children have failed to learn to clearly identify their feelings, to express them directly to their caregivers, and to negotiate differences or conflicts with them. Due to fear of the caregiver or to the expectation that his needs will not be met by her, the child fails to develop the ability to vocalize his thoughts, feelings, and needs. For him, it has been either dangerous or futile to do so in the past. In particular, it has been useless or hazardous for him to articulate his differences of opinion, his complaints, his anger, or opposing goals to his caregivers, as seen in the following case.

▬▬▬▬

The foster mother described her preschool-aged foster daughter, Barbi, as a "little homemaker." Only 4 years old, Barbi made her bed without complaint, she picked up her toys after playing with them, and she never expressed any feelings of discontent. She was a "model child" to the extreme. According to the foster mother, Barbi had been completely potty trained by 9 months of age! The

oldest of three children, Barbi had become an assistant to the bio-
logical mother, who was depressed and withdrawn. Barbi was al-
ready able to diaper the younger two children and was often placed
in charge of watching over them while the birth mother napped on
the couch. Barbi had been placed in foster care after she had been
found in front of the local grocery store at 11:00 p.m. Her biologi-
cal mother had sent her to get a pack of cigarettes. Barbi showed
no distress at being separated from her mother when she was
placed in the foster home, though she spoke of her two younger
siblings. She was extremely passive and meek with older children
in the home, as well as with the foster parents. When children took
her toys from her, she acquiesced without protest. However, Barbi
would sneak off and urinate in the corner of her bedroom when she
was apparently angry at the foster parents.

When asked how she had raised Barbi to be so well-behaved, the
birth mother stated, "You can't start young enough with kids... if
you spoil them, they'll run all over you or want to be held all the
time.... If Barbi complained (as an infant) or cried, I popped her
across the mouth—not real hard, mind you—but she got the
message. Now, all I have to do is raise my eyebrow at her and
she won't even think about it" (e.g. getting angry).

You may notice how Barbi's compliant (perhaps A4) model behavior
relates to sneaking off to urinate.[6] Barbi was not allowed to be a real
child who could ask for what she wanted, say what she felt, and express exasperation with her mother if she felt unsatisfied.

As mentioned in chapter one, attachment relationships between
parents and child move through predictable stages, if all goes right.
When separations, losses, and maltreatment interfere with the proper
unfolding of stages, children develop atypical attachment relationships to their caregivers. Children with attachment disorders, in particular, develop expectations about the treatment they will or will not
receive from caregivers, and they act accordingly. Foster and adopted
children (like Barbi) with histories of serious maltreatment often fail
to show the normal levels of direct, assertive expression of feelings,
thoughts, and needs. Feeling unsafe, unwanted, and ineffective, they
go "underground" with their desires, opinions, and complaints. They
develop hidden and unilateral, secret and solitary ways of meeting

---

[6] Barbi also shows features resembling the A3 child.

needs without involvement with the parents. Superficially complaint and pleasant and verbally unskilled at voicing needs and negotiating differences, they indirectly, behaviorally express themselves (e.g., urinating in the corner of a bedroom). As we will see in chapter six, helping children may necessitate increasing the child's capacity to verbalize feelings, opinion, disagreement, and outright frustration and anger toward caregivers. And for their part, caregivers may need to learn to tolerate or even invite such verbal expressions. Merely squelching behavior problems without providing healthier avenues for expression does not equip the child to develop partnership.

CONCLUDING REMARKS

Research on infants and young children has identified four major patterns of attachment: normal, insecure-avoidant, insecure-resistant, and disorganized/disoriented. Studies involving maltreated children have found that these youngsters often develop insecure forms of attachment due to exposure to inaccessible and unresponsive parenting. In some instances they adapt by developing specialized strategies marked by compulsive compliance, compulsive caregiving, or coerciveness. Whatever the specific pattern or sub-pattern of insecure attachment that develops, children form "negative working models," or negative expectations about themselves and caregivers. Additionally, they often fail to develop a positive, functional, "goal-corrected" partnership with their caregivers.

3 CONDUCT PROBLEMS OF FOSTER/ADOPTIVE CHILDREN

Many foster and adopted children have serious, if not severe, emotional and behavior (i.e., conduct) problems. A goodly proportion of these children receive mental health assessments and psychiatric diagnoses. One diagnosis given to an increasing number of foster and adopted youngsters is Reactive Attachment Disorder (RAD). Unfortunately, the RAD diagnosis has become misused and overused.

This chapter addresses the following topics:

1. Mental Health Issues (and related behavior problems) of Foster and Adopted Children

2. The Diagnosis and Symptoms of Reactive Attachment Disorder

3. The Unofficial Symptoms of So-Called RAD

4. A Synopsis of More Appropriate Diagnoses

5. Research on Attachment and Conduct Problems

Although we introduce and discuss RAD diagnosis in this chapter, this does not impart prominence to that diagnosis. My firm belief is that attachment theory and research show their greatest value not in diagnosing RAD, but in helping us better understand a host of conduct problems.

MENTAL HEALTH ISSUES OF FOSTER AND ADOPTED CHILDREN

A survey of the literature on foster children and special needs adopted children reveals that a disproportionate number of these children have mental health problems. The sheer volume, complexity, and severity of foster children's mental health problems have created a far greater demand for services than are available. An estimated 542,000 children were in foster care as of September 30, 2001 (AFCARS, 2003). Of those entering the system, 50% to 85% have significant emotional, behavioral, or developmental problems, a rate three to six times greater than children in the general population (American Academy of Child and Adolescent Psychiatry, 2002; Halfon, Flint, & Inkelas, 2002; Marsenich, 2002). Further, as many as one-third have three or more psychiatric disorders (dosReis et al., 2001), and over half have serious developmental delays in either language, cognition, or gross motor activity (Marsenich). There are also 888,000 children being raised by grandparents—without the parents presence (Bryson & Casper, 1999). Nationally, up to half of these children are drug exposed or fetal alcohol exposed (Task Force on Permanency Planning, 1990).

Special needs adopted children exhibit high rates of psychiatric diagnoses such as ADHD, learning disorders, depression, and chemical dependence (Benson et al., 1994; Dalby, Fox, & Haslam, 1982; Deutsch, 1990; Ingersoll, 1997). Adoptive children who are alcohol exposed prenatally are at greater risk of developing multiple psychiatric disorders (Cadoret & Riggins-Casper, 2000). Foster and adopted children most often present with externalizing behavior disorders, which may include oppositional defiance, aggression, destructiveness, impulsivity, hyperactivity, sexual acting out, and delinquent behavior (Benson et al., 1994; Delaney & Kunstal, 1997; Fanshel, Finch, & Grundy, 1990; McNamara, 1990; Partridge et al., 1986). These behaviors contribute to other social adjustment problems such as poor peer relationships and school failure. Unfortunately, disruptive behaviors also become a flashpoint in these children's relationships with caregivers, which can increase the chances of failed foster and adoptive placements. These children also frequently exhibit "internalizing" problems, such as anxiety, fear, low self-esteem, withdrawal, mistrust, and depression (Crittenden & Claussen, 2000; Delaney & Kunstal, 1997; Fahlberg, 1991; Fanshel et al., 1990; Martin & Rodeheffer, 1980; McNamara, 1990).

Let's turn to a case example of parents who struggled to raise a seriously troubled foster child. In this case the boy has both internalizing and externalizing behavior problems.

———

Jimmy, age 12, was a terribly abused and neglected boy who, due to the frequent absence of his alcoholic, methamphetamine-addicted mother from the home, had been raised by his cruel older brothers. His mother may have taken drugs and drunk heavily during the pregnancy. By second grade, Jimmy had spent more time living with foster families, of which there had been several, than with his birth family. Jimmy had problems in the present foster home with poor eye contact, mistrust of adults, lack of

positive social give and take, arguing and blaming others, vin-
dictiveness (getting even), fighting at home and school, bullying
other children, anger outbursts and irritability, failing to follow
directions and not listening, hypervigilance, concentration prob-
lems, lying, stealing, and fire setting. Jimmy refused to sleep in
his bed, often sleeping at the door of the foster parents' bedroom.
He complained frequently about stomach aches on school days,
and he seemed preoccupied with the whereabouts of the foster
mother, shadowing her in the house.

Of all Jimmy's many problems, however, it was his violence
toward the younger foster children and Barney, the dog, which
was most alarming. Whenever Jimmy was left alone with other
children, even for a moment, someone "accidentally" got hurt. A
recently placed infant foster child automatically cried whenever
Jimmy even walked into the room. The family dog, a sloe-eyed
retriever, had patiently endured minor abuse from a host of foster
children over the years. However, none of it had prepared him
for the calculated, cruel mistreatment he received from Jimmy.
On two occasions Jimmy attempted unsuccessfully to push the
harmless dog off the second-floor balcony. Several times, Jimmy
deliberately threw the tennis ball into the busy street for the dog
to fetch. Miraculously, Barney survived the balcony, speeding
traffic... and Jimmy.

The fact that Jimmy has emotional and behavioral problems is indisputable; however, the exact psychiatric diagnosis may be subject to
conjecture and debate. In Jimmy's case the diagnosis might eventually include one or more of the following prevalent conditions: ADHD,
ODD, PTSD, CD, Major Depressive Disorder, Asperger's Disorder
(note: not a likely diagnosis for Jimmy), and Separation Anxiety Disorder. Over the last decade an increasing number of mental health
professionals or caseworkers (and parents) would label Jimmy as Reactive Attachment Disorder (RAD). Indeed, there has been a remarkable, if not alarming, upsurge or proliferation in the use of the RAD
label (Hanson, 2002). Although it is beyond the scope of this book to
describe and discuss all of the prevalent disorders mentioned above
in detail, the emphasis here on attachment theory and research justifies taking a close look at Reactive Attachment Disorder.

THE DIAGNOSIS AND SYMPTOMS OF REACTIVE ATTACHMENT DISORDER

Reactive Attachment Disorder is a psychiatric or "mental disorder" described in the Diagnostic and Statistics Manual (DSM-IV, American Psychiatric Association), the bible of psychiatric diagnostics. Here's what the DSM-IV tells us about RAD:

> Children with this mental disorder—associated with care that is "grossly pathological,"—relate socially either by exhibiting markedly inhibited behavior or by indiscriminate social behavior.

Diagnostic criteria for 313.89 Reactive Attachment Disorder of Infancy or Early Childhood

A. Markedly disturbed and developmentally inappropriate social related-ness in most contexts, beginning before age 5 years, as evidenced by either (1) or (2):
    (1) persistent failure to initiate or respond in a developmentally appropriate fashion to most social interactions, as manifest by excessively inhibited, hypervigilent, or highly ambivalent and con-tradictory responses (e.g., the child may respond to caregivers with a mixture of approach, avoidance, and resistance to comforting, or may exhibit frozen watchfulness).
    (2) diffuse attachments as manifest by indiscriminate sociability with marked inability to exhibit appropriate selective attachments (e.g., excessive familiarity with relative strangers or lack of selectiv-ity in choice of attachment figures).

B. The disturbance in Criterion A is not accounted for solely by develop-mental delay (as in Mental Retardation) and does not meet criteria for a Pervasive Developmental Disorder.

C. Pathogenic care as evidenced by at least one of the following:
    (1) persistent disregard of the child's basic emotional needs for comfort, stimulation, and affection.
    (2) persistent disregard of the child's basic physical needs.
    (3) repeated changes of primary caregiver that prevent formation of stable attachments (e.g., frequent changes in foster care).

D. There is a presumption that the care in Criterion C is responsible for the disturbed behavior in Criterion A (e.g., the disturbances in Criterion A began following the pathogenic care in Criterion C).

Specify type:

Inhibited Type: if Criterion A1 predominates in the clinical presentation.
Disinhibited Type: if Criterion A2 predominates in the clinical presentation.

The official symptoms of RAD, then, are very straightforward. The child either shows "excessively inhibited, hypervigilent, or highly ambivalent and contradictory responses (e.g., the child may respond to caregivers with a mixture of approach, avoidance, and resistance to comforting, or may exhibit frozen watchfulness)" or shows "diffuse attachments as manifest by indiscriminate sociability with marked inability to exhibit appropriate selective attachments (e.g., excessive familiarity with relative strangers or lack of selectivity in choice of attachment figures)."

Looking at the criteria for the official RAD diagnosis, this is not the correct diagnosis for Jimmy. Although Jimmy has problems with eye contact, mistrust, and hypervigilance, which might suggest excessive inhibition, Jimmy's problems probably fall under a number of diagnoses. Given his age (he is not really an infant or young child) and the wide array of symptoms, other diagnoses would probably be much more accurate (e.g., Conduct Disorder, ADHD, etc.). So, why then would a large number of professionals and parents look at a child like Jimmy and arrive at the RAD diagnosis? Clearly, the proliferation of the RAD diagnosis is due to an "unofficial" RAD diagnosis which has been described on the Internet and by "attachment therapists," and it includes symptoms and criteria which, I feel, have misled many parents and professionals alike. Let's turn to the unofficial symptoms list for RAD.

THE UNOFFICAL SYMPTOMS OF SO-CALLED "RAD"

Listed below are items found on an inventory which purports to identify children with Reactive Attachment Disorder. In truth, the inventory has little or no relationship to official RAD symptoms. I would describe many children diagnosed with RAD based on the list of unofficial symptoms as a case of so-called "RAD." While the symptoms listed fail to correspond with RAD as described by the DSM-IV, they indeed include many conduct problems observed in troubled foster and adopted children. When foster and adoptive parents of a disturbed, multiproblem child discover that their youngster displays some, many, or even all of the listed, unofficial symptoms, they conclude—often erroneously—that their child has RAD.

1. Unable to give and receive love
2. Oppositional, argumentative, defiant
3. Emotionally phony, hollow, or empty

4. Manipulative or controlling
5. Frequent, intense angry outbursts
6. An angry child inside
7. Unable to cry about something sad
8. Avoids or resists physical closeness and touch
9. Cannot be trusted
10. Little or no conscience
11. Superficially engaging and charming
12. Lack of eye contact on parental terms
13. Indiscriminately affectionate
14. Not affectionate on parents' terms
15. Destructive to self, others, and property
16. More disobedient toward Mom than Dad
17. Cruel to animals
18. Steals
19. Lies about the obvious (crazy lying)
20. Impulsive or hyperactive
21. Lacks cause-and-effect thinking
22. Gorges or hoards food
23. Poor peer relationships
24. Preoccupation with fire, blood, or violence
25. Persistent, nonsensical questions or incessant chatter
26. Inappropriately demanding and clinging
27. Sexual acting out
28. Bossy with peers   (Buenning, 2005)

Let me acknowledge here that many (too many) foster and special needs adoptive children show these problems. These "symptoms" present all-too-familiar challenges to many foster and adoptive parents. Unbelievably, some parents would report that their child or children show each and every one of the unofficial symptoms of so-called "RAD." However, their child may not actually have RAD; indeed, their child's problems may be related to multiple diagnoses, such as Conduct Disorder (CD), Post Traumatic Stress Disorder (PTSD), Separation Anxiety Disorder (SAD), Attention Deficit Hyperactivity Disorder (ADHD), and Oppositional Defiant Disorder (ODD). The unofficial RAD list can be misleading to parents as it captures so many of the problems they encounter with their children. At present, no research

The Unofficial Symptoms of RAD and More Appropriate Diagnoses

Unoffical Symptoms	Relevant Diagnosis
1. Unable to give and receive love	A, RAD, PTSD
2. Oppositional, argumentative, defiant	ODD
3. Emotionally phony, hollow or empty	
4. Manipulative or controlling	CD
5. Frequent, intense angry outbursts	CD, ODD, D, ADHD, PTSD
6. An angry child inside	CD, ODD, D, ADHD, PTSD
7. Unable to cry about something sad	A, PTSD
8. Avoids or resists physical closeness and touch	A, RAD
9. Cannot be trusted	CD
10. Little or no conscience	
11. Superficially engaging and charming	RAD
12. Lack of eye contact on parental terms	A
13. Indiscriminately affectionate	RAD
14. Not affectionate on parents' terms	A
15. Destructive to self, others, and property	CD, ADHD
16. More disobedient toward Mom than Dad	
17. Cruel to animals	CD
18. Steals	CD
19. Lies about the obvious (crazy lying)	CD
20. Impulsive or hyperactive	ADHD
21. Lacks cause-and-effect thinking	
22. Gorges or hoards food	
23. Poor peer relationships	A, CD
24. Preoccupation with fire, blood, or violence	
25. Persistent, nonsensical questions or incessant chatter	ADHD
26. Inappropriately demanding and clinging	SAD
27. Sexual acting out	CD
28. Bossy with peers	CD

Key: Conduct Disorder (CD), Post Traumatic Stress Disorder (PTSD), Separation Anxiety Disorder (SAD), Asberger's Disorder (A), Attention Deficit Hyperactivity Disorder (ADHD), and Oppositional Defiant Disorder (ODD).

Table 3.1

supports using the list in the assessment of RAD. Additionally, the unofficial symptom list has no support from serious researchers on attachment (see chapter six for further information).

A SYNOPSIS OF MORE APPROPRIATE DIAGNOSES

Admittedly many foster and adoptive children show symptoms on the unofficial RAD list. But more appropriate, relevant diagnoses explain the conduct problems on the unofficial list. Importantly, many of these more appropriate diagnoses have evidence-based treatments which have been developed to address the issues the child and parents contend with.

In the left-hand column of Table 3.1 is the unofficial symptoms list of so-called "RAD." In the right-hand column are the alternative, appropriate, and arguably more accurate diagnoses related to the symptoms. In some instances two or three diagnostic categories might be related to the symptom. Notice that only numbers 1, 8, 11, and 13 appear to be related to the official RAD diagnosis. Also, for numbers 3, 10, 16, 21, 22, and 24 no specific or alternative diagnosis is given, though these symptoms may suggest antisocial traits, histrionic features, pervasive developmental disorder, severe learning disabilities, bulimia, and obsessive-compulsive disorder (OCD).

RESEARCH ON ATTACHMENT AND CONDUCT PROBLEMS

Attachment theory (and research) can contribute greatly to our understanding of conduct problems. Attachment researchers have studied the relationship between attachment patterns and behavior and conduct problems (i.e., symptoms) such as noncompliance, aggression, out-of-control behavior (Speltz, 1990), hitting others, temper tantrums, frequent accidents, food refusal or overeating, running away, and destroying objects belonging to the parent figure. Other behavior problems considered by attachment theorists in these studies include rocking, lying, stealing, fears, destructive behavior, fighting, indiscriminate behavior, depression, sleep problems, and withdrawing behavior (Crittenden & Claussen, 2000). Chisholm (2000) describes clinical cases of orphans with attachment issues who deliberately injure themselves. Most research on conduct problems points to the relationship between behavior problems and a mix of factors such as attachment, genes, and present and historic environmental effects (APSAC).[1]

---

[1] Interestingly, most research on attachment avoids the use of clinical diagnoses, notably RAD, and focuses on the relationship between attachment patterns and disruptive behavior and other conduct problems (Speltz, 1990).

CONCLUDING REMARKS

Clearly, formerly maltreated foster and adoptive children exhibit more conduct problems and symptoms than their peers. While the behavior problems seem undeniable, the correct diagnosis or diagnoses for these children are more problematic. RAD has become a popular but overused and misused diagnosis due, in part, to the dissemination of the unofficial symptoms of so-called "RAD." These symptoms, while all too common, may have little or no relationship to the circumscribed, straightforward symptoms of official (i.e., DSM-IV) RAD. The controversy swirling around the unofficial RAD diagnosis and the dubious treatments for it will be comprehensively addressed in chapter seven.

4 REENACTMENT

Many foster, kinship, and adoptive parents feel trapped in déjà vu—unwitting prisoners of their foster child's past. To them it feels like they have become reluctant actors in a recurring drama written during the child's earliest years and replayed in their home. These foster parents undeservedly fall heir to their foster child's negative expectations—to his ongoing attachment issues.

Without alteration, the child's cynical picture of the world and his dysfunctional strategies might continue unabated and prompt him to isolate himself from those who might help him. The child would likely continue on a developmental pathway set in motion by negative, traumatic conditions and relationships. Without major changes in how he views himself and caregivers, the child is "programmed" to confirm and reconfirm his negative conclusions about himself and caregivers, to evidence familiar conduct problems, and to repeat past strategies for engaging caregivers—i.e., to reenact.

This chapter discusses the following topics:

1. Developmental Pathways
2. Reenactment in Foster Care
3. The Negative Working Model, Reenactment, and Conduct Problems
4. The Attachment Function of Conduct Problems
5. The Relationship Between Attachment Patterns and Functions

DEVELOPMENTAL PATHWAYS

Children who have been maltreated often display a development gone astray; they have taken a "maladaptive pathway" (O'Connor & Zeanah, 2003). The associated psychopathology that they often demonstrate is an indication of how far astray their development has gone and how maladaptive it is. While some of the behavior problems may have helped the child cope with or adapt to harsh, unhealthy earlier relationships, their continuation in a good foster, kinship, or adoptive family can be seen as maladaptive. The attachment patterns and, in some instances, full-blown psychopathology are an indication of development that has taken a misguided course. The pathway stretches ahead but, without a mid-course correction, the path may lead to nowhere positive. Let's look at a case that illustrates what we're talking about.

——

Jimmy, age 4, runs off to strangers when in public with his grand-mother who is raising him. He has no "stranger fear," and his grandmother feels he would go off with anybody and that he has no sense of to whom he should turn. Jimmy pushes away from his grandmother and shows no distress at living apart from his birth mother. Grandmother reported that Jimmy had been horri-bly undernourished and unloved as an infant and that he received almost no attention from his mother as a young child. Additionally, she reported that Jimmy had lived in several non-relative foster homes by the time she stepped in to care for him.

——

Early neglect and multiple caregivers may have rendered Jimmy indis-criminately attached. Even though his grandmother wants to offer him nurturance and attention, Jimmy runs off to strangers. Jimmy's run-ning off to strangers may endanger him while at the same time it may be rewarding to him. Severely neglected and ignored in the past, he may have reduced anxiety by seeking interaction with complete strang-ers. Development has gone in a maladaptive direction, and it has steered him away from a secure relationship to a primary caregiver, namely, his grandmother.

REENACTMENT IN FOSTER CARE

Every child makes his unique adaptation to his world. Behavior problems that are misunderstood or merely difficult to comprehend make sense when we look at the probable pattern of attachment the child developed (i.e., the attachment strategies the child has learned earlier in life). Many of the ways children adapt to their world be-come patterned and sometimes used again and again in a compulsive, unbending way. They can lead the child to isolate himself or alienate others repeatedly and to avoid the intensity of emotional and social relationships (Sroufe, 1988). In the earlier edition of this book we ap-plied the term "reenactment" to describe how a troubled child can have a powerful influence over shaping his new family environment into a familiar world.[1] That is, the child's acquired mode of interacting with initial caregivers can spread to other figures (e.g., foster and adoptive parents, peers, teachers). In essence, the child's negative working model, pattern of attachment, related conduct problems, and corresponding foster or adoptive parent responses combine to form, in our terms, a reenactment.

Infants and young children who come into foster care after extreme trauma to and disruption of their development of attachment can behave in ways that are off-putting to foster parents. Case in point, there are young children who, when hurt or sick, reject parental attempts to comfort them. These children may be unused to receiving comfort from caregivers and send the message that they don't want or need help from their new parents. These children push their new parents away and the parents may react by giving the infant or child the "space" they request. Caregivers read and respond to signs that the children do not want or need parental attention or contact. Unfortunately, the pullback on the parent's part leaves things at status quo, with a remaining rift or distance between parents and children (Dozier, 2003). Reenactment—this unhealthy recreation or reproduction— signals the presence of the underlying, negative working model of the maltreated child. The notion of reenactment gives meaning to the plethora of seemingly disjointed, at times confusing, conduct problems of the disturbed foster child. In short, conduct problems are merely familiar scenes from a recurrent drama.

With reenactment there is a "compulsive repetition" of history and transference of learning and feelings about relationships. That is, many troubled foster, kinship, or adopted children almost inevitably reenact the issues and conflicts stemming from their earlier years. (Reenactment also occurs in adoptive, residential, and hospital placements.) Sadly, maltreated, attachment-disordered children, through reenactment, replay history in the present living situation with new individuals, to whom they assign old roles and expectations. Foster, kinship, and adoptive parents can unwittingly fall into those roles if they

---

[1] Reenactment, simply speaking, is defined as the repetition or recreation of old relationships with new people (Pearson, 1968). Disturbed foster children often participate—directly or indirectly, consciously or subconsciously—in the recreation of destructive and unwanted relationships in the foster or adoptive home; these relationships are often based upon dysfunctional earlier interactions with inaccessible, insensitive, maltreating caregivers (Delaney & Kunstal, 1997).

do not understand the dynamics, the function of behavior problems, and the effect of history on their present world. Often, inexperienced families are unprepared for the fact that the child, once removed from maltreatment, doesn't simply rebound into healthier relationships. It might be expected that conduct problems, the bane of parents, should simply disappear when the child is placed into a good home. However, that may not occur. Typically, foster and adoptive parents expect compliance and correct, age-appropriate behavior and rush to eliminate noncompliance and other misbehavior without understanding the function of the conduct problems, the child's developmental pathway, and the predictability of reenactment, etc. The distorted perceptions and conclusions (i.e., working models) and the ongoing conduct problems are familiar and, perhaps, comforting to these disturbed children, as seen in the following case example:

After a brief, 2-week honeymoon, Steve, age 7, started in with full-scale problem behaviors at school and in the foster home. Steve defied his foster parents and disobeyed most of their rules. He refused to pick up his things and destroyed objects belonging to other children in the home. The foster mother stated, "He is a master of negative-attention seeking. He knows how to keep us focused on him all the time. It's too bad the focus is always negative. We don't like it, but we seem to always be forced into punishing him."

In this case, Steve reenacted his earlier experiences of abandonment and rejection. He fully expected to be ignored and rejected by his present foster home, as he had by many homes before. He also expected that he could not obtain positive parental attention. At some level he may have learned to prefer negative attention, something he could depend on from parent figures in his past. Ironically, the offer of a home, a family, and a sense of belonging (and positive attention) may have been more unfamiliar than comforting to him. That is, he may not want what he needs most (Dozier, 2003). Indeed, the intimacy offered by a foster or adoptive family is, to some disturbed children, a threat to an accustomed, cynical world view in which there is neither hope nor disappointment. Steve's conduct problems are reminiscent of the C3 pattern of attachment, in which the child coerces the caregiver to attend. See Table 4.1 for a summary of reenactment.

- Recreates old relationships with new people.
- Gives meaning to disjointed conduct problems.
- Signals an underlying negative working model.
- Presents barriers to attachment formation.
- May result in sabotage to the foster or adoptive home.

TABLE 4.1

THE NEGATIVE WORKING MODEL, REENACTMENT, AND CONDUCT PROBLEMS

We turn now to a discussion of the cyclical interrelationship between the negative working model, reenactment, and conduct problems. Table 4.2 presents a diagram of this relationship.

The negative working model contains bleak, cynical, and anxiety-ridden expectations about the world. As mentioned earlier, the general premises of the negative working model are that caregivers are unresponsive, unreliable, and rejecting and that the self is worthless, unwanted, unsafe, and impotent to do anything about it. Two conditions hold the child back from adopting revised views of the world and from testing new strategies in new homes (i.e., in their foster, kinship, or adoptive home). The first is that of exposure to danger, in other words, the greater the danger a child has lived through, coped with, and adapted to, the more rigid the child holds onto old strategies for reducing danger (Crittenden & Claussen, 2000). When the child perceives danger, stimulus-response sequence results in a knee-jerk, self-protective strategy which, due to its speed, prevents the child from learning whether the situation really merited a protective reaction. The second condition is the unpredictable nature of danger. More to the point, if the child has been historically unable to detect or predict danger clearly, if parenting has been unpredictable, or if danger emerges like a lightening bolt from the blue, the child will be reluctant to modify previous views of the world and caregivers.

As the diagram indicates, conduct problems emerge out of general negative premises or conclusions about the world. If the child has concluded that caregivers are not only unresponsive, but dangerous, he may avoid letting them know what he wants, needs, likes or dislikes.

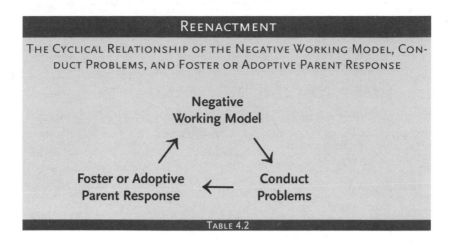

REENACTMENT

THE CYCLICAL RELATIONSHIP OF THE NEGATIVE WORKING MODEL, CONDUCT PROBLEMS, AND FOSTER OR ADOPTIVE PARENT RESPONSE

Negative
Working Model

Foster or Adoptive
Parent Response

Conduct
Problems

TABLE 4.2

Instead, he might (for example) go off in secret and solitary fashion and steal what he wants. Case in point is the formerly feral child who may continue to steal and hoard food many months or years after placement in a nurturing, providing foster, kinship, or adoptive home. The child's past survival may have necessitated "self-parenting" approaches, such as when the child had to forage for food to survive. The child may cling to this historical conduct problem and fail to permit the present caregivers to prove they can and will meet his needs.

Whether the conduct problems are totally disjointed and "random" in appearance, or predictably patterned, the net effect over time is that the child has begun to reenact his part of an earlier drama involving himself and his earlier, maltreating caregivers. Even when the family environment changes, earlier conduct problems, now obsolete and maladaptive, persist. It does not automatically follow that the child, living in a greatly improved family environment, will unlearn or give up the older conduct problems (Crittenden & Claussen, 2000). As you might expect, the child's reenactment of his side of earlier dysfunctional relationships often draws the foster or adoptive parents into a response very, perhaps hauntingly, similar to that of the maltreating parents. If the child persists in stealing food, foster or adoptive parents often respond by locking the pantry, freezer, or refrigerator. In so doing, they might inadvertently communicate to the child: "We are unresponsive." The child's negative conclusions may then be reinforced. (We will discuss foster and adoptive parents' response in detail in chapter five.) Thus, a cyclical process or reenactment develops here. The foster child's negative working model generates conduct problems; conduct problems invite negative responses from the foster or adoptive parents; and the negative responses confirm the child's negative working model. Then, the process repeats itself.

THE ATTACHMENT FUNCTION OF CONDUCT PROBLEMS

In chapter three, we discussed conduct problems—especially those shown by troubled foster and adoptive children. We also listed conduct problems specifically associated with official and unofficial symptoms of RAD. Now, we will turn to an important and often overlooked aspect of conduct problems: their attachment function. In general, the functions of attachment behaviors (and conduct problems) include such things as preparing for and responding to danger. These functions are the organizing principles around which self-protection strategies are built and organized (Crittenden & Claussen, 2000).

Function is defined as the purpose for which something is designed and the purpose that something serves. When examining the function of conduct problems, therefore, we search for how a conduct problem serves a purpose or purposes. Study of the function of behavior problems has a body of research attached to it that focuses upon the suspected "causal relations between behavior and its environment" (Jones & Ervin, 1999). Functional assessment organizes the process of understanding a child's behavior and focuses upon the antecedents and consequences related to the behavior or conduct. (Jones & Ervin). In the case of a child, for example, who becomes involved in self-harm, the function of the self-harm may be that it serves to reduce anxiety or that it expresses the child's anger over family discord. Of course, the correlates to conduct problems are variegated and multiple. The possibilities include categories of functions such as: 1) communication of need, in other words, what the child is trying to say through the behavior; 2) how the behavior relates to distorted thoughts; 3) anxiety; 4) poor self-concept (Miller, Tansy, & Hughes, 1998); 5) family issues; 6) developmental disabilities; and 7) other physiological issues.

It is beyond the scope of this book to address all possible functions related to conduct problems. We will underscore only the possible, if not probable, functions of conduct vis-á-vis attachment. From an attachment theory point of view, conduct problems serve several perhaps overlapping and interrelating functions. These include

1. Controlling proximity to the caregiver (Speltz, 1990).

2. Reinstating contact with and interventions from caregivers after interruptions (Speltz, 1990). Conduct problems may serve to engage parents who have turned attention elsewhere or who have been absent. Children, for example, often act out when their caregivers are busy.

3. Decreasing feelings of insecurity and reducing separation anxiety (Lieberman & Pawl, 1988). The older child who shadows a parent constantly may do so to diminish apprehension related to past losses.

4. Communicating caregiving needs (Speltz, 1990). Children who misbehave may do so to provide a general "wake-up call" to parent figures that they need to be reassured. Rather than asking for this directly in words, however, they let behavior do the talking.

5. Regulating the caregiver's behavior to fall in line with the child's goals (Marvin & Stewart, 1990). If the child acts up at bedtime, this may serve to keep the caregiver close at a time when she would like to pull back and let the child sleep alone.

6. Providing self with protection normally provided by caregivers (Liberman & Pawl, 1988). The child who may resist efforts by caregivers to keep him close and safe may have learned self-protection in past relationships where closeness and safety were not provided by parent figures.

7. Reducing danger and increasing safety (Crittenden & Claussen, 2000; Speltz, 1990). A child who shadows foster or adoptive parents, remaining underfoot constantly (see function 3), may have learned this behavior kept him measurably safer in the past.

8. Venting pent-up frustration/anger safely (Crittenden & Claussen, 2000). A child who directs anger toward other children may be displacing anger generated in the unfulfilling parent-child relationship onto less "powerful" people.

9. Improving the chances for self-survival (Bowlby, 1969).

10. Coercing caregiver interactions, though they are likely to be negative and potentially dangerous interactions, e.g., harsh punishment or abuse (Speltz, 1990). A young child who constantly misbehaves in the foster or adoptive home may have learned in the past that negative-attention seeking resulted in some level of interaction with caregivers.

11. Eliciting protection from caregivers (Ainsworth et al., 1978). The child who whines and cries excessively may have learned that only by extreme entreaties can protection by a caregiver be obtained.

12. Reducing the chances of evoking physical abuse from the parent (Crittenden & Claussen, 2000). Overly compliant children who inhibit any expression of negative emotion may have learned that they reduced the chances of physical abuse with smiling obedience.

13. Increasing the chances of obtaining attention from the parent (Crittenden & Claussen, 2000). A child who shows "parental" behavior toward other children or even toward the foster or adoptive parents may have learned that this premature or role-inverted caregiving behavior increased the chances of winning attention and approval from parent figures.

Conduct problems may be related to one or more of the functions listed above. Ironically, ongoing conduct problems often result in a decrease in caregiver sensitivity and nurturance, while requiring an increase in supervision and engagement with the child. In a nutshell, the parent is close physically and engaged reactively (i.e., negatively), but not addressing and impacting the true issues the child conceals (Speltz, 1990). As a result, the child may need love but instead elicits discipline. In essence, parents are constantly forced to put out fires without dealing with what fuels the fires.

The behavior that highly ambivalent children emit is confusing in that it serves simultaneously to bring the parent figure close and to keep him distant. This is not very satisfying for foster, kinship, or adoptive parents or, for that matter, for the child. In effect, the disturbed child emotionally "handcuffs" the foster parents with mixed messages. Chisholm (2000) describes a clinical case of a child who talks nonstop, asking silly questions over and over, or rambling aimlessly about "nothing." This rambling chatter served a function, however, as it kept the parent close-but-not-close. In some sense, the chatter placed the parent at a comfortable—from the child's point of view—distance.

Sadly, if a child's conduct problems cannot be replaced by positive, acceptable behaviors, parents remain locked in a role of constant correcting, supervising, disciplining, and punishing the child. In the end, the parent feels confused and discouraged and may withdraw. Without a sense of competence or potency as a parent, the adult may be hard-pressed to feel warmth, let alone build attachment toward the child. It's extremely challenging to love a child who fails to respond favorably to discipline, overtures, and love.

THE RELATIONSHIP BETWEEN ATTACHMENT PATTERNS AND FUNCTIONS

Attachment patterns, sub-patterns, and functions are related. The young child who acts in a role-reversed fashion toward her mother by fawning over her displays the A3 pattern—"compulsive-caregiving." This serves two functions simultaneously: increasing the chances of obtaining attention from the parent figure (function 13) and reducing danger and increasing safety (function 7). This child attends to the mother, deriving some meager parental attention and maintaining proximity to the caregiver that might increase the child's safety. Of course, the burden of maintaining proximity to and interaction with the caregiver remains squarely on the child.

A child who pinches himself or injures himself in some other deliberate way through head-banging, biting himself, hitting himself, etc. may employ a sub-pattern (C3) which addresses one or more attachment functions (Lieberman & Pawl, 1990). The child's self-injury, for instance, may allow for: 1) venting emotion, and 2) increasing caregiving. More specifically, this behavior may offer a way of venting anger which cannot be directed toward a powerful and perhaps dangerous caregiver (Crittenden & Claussen, 2000). This behavior may also invite sympathy or more positive involvement from the caregiver, who does not have to abuse the child but must rather stop him from abusing himself.

When attachment patterns and concomitant behavior problems developed in the context of maltreatment, they may have been truly adaptive early on. However, once the child has been placed in a safe foster, kinship, or adoptive home, these unchanging patterns would be considered maladaptive; further, their persistence results in the caregiver's feeling forced into more disciplinarian, rejecting, angry parental behaviors or even into withdrawal from and rejection of the child. Indeed, conduct problems may render the child virtually unmanageable, increasingly unlovable, and a target for more abuse.

CONCLUDING REMARKS

In this chapter we have discussed the common finding that troubled foster or adopted children may be on a maladaptive pathway. How attachment relationships have developed, in particular, may be quite atypical and unhealthy. Once placed in a foster or adoptive home these children do not automatically change course and proceed onto an adaptive, "normal" pathway. Indeed, many children rigidly hold onto what they've learned about relationships and engage new care-givers in ways that promote reenactment, i.e., a repetition of the past. Of course, reenactment relates to both the child's negative working model and ongoing conduct problems. Further, the negative working model, conduct problems, and corresponding foster parent response forms a cyclical relationship, i.e., reenactment. This chapter closed with a discussion of the definable functions of conduct problems and with an explanation of the relationship between attachment patterns and functions.

Ignore negative (nondestructive) behaviour and over praise, reward good behaviour. ★ Reverse the pattern.

5 THE FOSTER AND ADOPTIVE PARENT RESPONSE

In chapter five, discussion turns to foster and adoptive parent responses to the troubled child. From an attachment theory point of view, how parents respond, emotionally and behaviorally, is related, among other things, to the foster or adopted child's negative working model, predominant attachment strategy (i.e., pattern) and conduct problems; and to the foster or adoptive parents' own working model and attachment strategy.

Foster and adoptive parents are typically not trained to examine their own predominant attachment strategy (i.e., pattern), although attachment theory and research logically support such training. Further, these parents are not prepared for how their attachment pattern may collide with the child's negative working model, attachment pattern, and conduct problems.

This chapter discusses the following topics:

1. The Impact of the Troubled Child's Past on the Foster and Adoptive Parents

2. How Foster and Adoptive Parents' Own Attachment Issues Affect Their Response to the Troubled Child

3. Common Emotional Responses Parents Feel Toward Their Troubled Foster or Adopted Child

4. Significant Anger or Abusive Impulses Toward the Child

5. Emotional Withdrawal/Feeling Rejected by the Child

6. Feelings of Impotence and Incompetence

Children who have survived the most significant maltreatment can evoke the harshest, least positive responses from others. Ironically, they have a way of inviting punishing and negative reactions from others, thereby making themselves difficult to feel close to and to take care of (O'Connor & Zeanah, 2003).

As some authors have aptly pointed out, the cause of the foster or adopted child's conduct problems or outright disturbances antedates the foster placement or adoption, yet the current caregivers become caught up in the pessimistic and negative expectations the child has developed about caregivers based on past abuse or substandard parenting (Lieberman, 2003). Sadly, mental health professionals, caseworkers, school personnel, and others often blame the foster or adoptive parents for the child's ongoing, recalcitrant problems (Casey Family Services, 2003; Kunstal & Delaney, 1997; O'Connor & Zeanah, 2003).

Foster and adoptive parents who are essentially competent, sensitive, and responsive to "normal" children feel beyond their depth and ill-equipped to deal with their child's "pervasive emotional distance, refusal to be comforted, seeming lack of appreciation and preference for them, sudden mood shifts, indiscriminate sociability... defiance, noncompliance and aggression." This can fail to provide emotional satisfaction of a mutual, give-and-take relationship and foster feelings of hopelessness and helplessness. Parents can come to fear that the child has a fundamental, endemic, untreatable ability to form a healthy attachment to them (Lieberman, 2003).

THE IMPACT OF THE TROUBLED CHILD'S PAST ON THE FOSTER AND ADOPTIVE PARENTS

The troubled foster child with attachment issues is a product, in good measure, of his initial, significant parent-child dyad. Attachment research has focused, for instance, upon high-risk dyads where the chief caregiver (e.g., mother) has been "incompetent, insensitive, disengaged, intrusive, uninvolved, and/or emotionally flat." The caregiver's own emotional demeanor corresponds to his/her offspring's psychiatric symptoms, poor emotional control, distress, and even "gaze avoidance" (Polansky, Gaudin, Ammons, & Davis, 1985; Titi, 2002). Interestingly, it is the initial caregiver's attachment pattern and working model regarding attachment relationships that propels her incompetence, insensitivity, disengagement, intrusiveness, noninvolvement, and/or emotional flatness with her child. We can trace a three-stage, intergenerational transmission of attachment issues by first examining the 1) initial caregiver's attachment pattern and how it impacts 2) her child's resultant attachment pattern. In turn, we can see, at least clinically, 3) how the child's attachment pattern accompanies him into the foster or adoptive home and impacts the subsequent formation of attachment relationships to the foster or adoptive caregivers. Here are the three stages in brief:

1. Initial Caregiver Attachment Pattern

Four patterns of caregiver attachment relationships have been identified not only by nonverbal behavior but also by thought and language, mined for information on the caregiver's working model (George, Kaplan, & Main, 1985). Research on the caregiver's (e.g., birth mother) expectations and conclusions about attachment relationships—as measured by the Adult Attachment Interview (AAI)—has pinpointed the following four patterns:

  A. Secure
  B. Dismissing
  C. Enmeshed
  D. Disorganized/Disoriented

The SECURE pattern is essentially a healthy, balanced view of attachment relationships wherein certain attachment figures are acknowledged as significant and "influential" and are portrayed realistically and coherently without over-idealization, oversimplification, or ongoing, unresolved anger. (From clinical experience, I would expect few biological parents of troubled, maltreated foster children to evidence the secure pattern.)

The DISMISSING pattern devalues the impact of attachment relationships and past exposure on the adult's development. These caregivers lean toward overidealizing their own parents and failing to come up with specifics to back their conclusions that they had a wonderfully secure relationships to their caregivers during the formative years. (An example of the dismissing pattern may be indicated in a birth father who described his battering, alcoholic, child-abusing father—who ultimately left the family— as "your average father type who was the outdoor kind of guy. He kind of taught me everything I know about surviving in the wild." In actuality, only one instance of a father-son hunting trip was recalled.)

The PREOCCUPIED/ENMESHED pattern is marked by the inability to articulate a history of attachments in a cogent, objective way. These caregivers remain embroiled in family relationships and have anemic sense of their own identity and independence. (An example of the enmeshed pattern may be indicated in the case of a biological mother who, at 40 years of age, attends to her aging mother's psychosomatic illnesses without complaint. This biological mother has never separated from her own mother psychologically, and, even during adolescence, never once disagreed with her. She remarked, "We pretty much all think like Mom. We try not to upset her in any way, because it could make her sickness get much worse.")

The DISORIENTED /DISORGANIZED pattern relates to a history of terrifying, traumatic, anxiety-producing, loss-riddled experiences. Caregivers with this pattern remain unresolved about the significant, if painful, past relationships which continue to influence them (Soares, Fremmer-Bombik, Grossman, & Silva, 2000). An example of the disoriented/disorganized pattern may be found in the birth mother who was physically and sexually abused by a series of her own mother's "boyfriends," who also battered that woman in front of the children. This birth mother was also, as a child, sexually abused by her older brothers. Later, she also paired up with men who beat her and fathered her children. She commented, "I think Jimmy—my middle child—is the spittin' image of his father who raped me."

2. THE CHILD'S RESULTANT ATTACHMENT PATTERN

The child's attachment pattern develops, at least partly, in response to his caregiver's attachment pattern. Here are some illustrations of how the child's pattern corresponds to his primary caregiver's:

> If the child's pattern is insecure/avoidant (A), it's likely that his initial, primary caregiver's attachment classification was the dismissing type.

> If the child's pattern is insecure/resistant (C), it's likely that his initial, primary caregiver's attachment classification was the preoccupied/enmeshed type.

> If the child's pattern is disorganized (D), it's likely that his initial, primary caregiver's attachment classification was the disoriented type (Soares et al., 2000).

Whether or not the child develops precisely these attachment patterns in response to his caregiver's attachment pattern, the child's predominant attachment pattern has a great deal to do with the historic parent-child interactions (Main & Hess, 1990).

As described in chapter two, in addition to the three patterns described above, the child's attachment pattern might be more exactly classified as a subtype, such as A3 (compulsive-compliant), A4 (compulsive-caregiving), C3 (coercive), or C4 (feigned helplessness). Many older, troubled foster and adopted children appear to be compulsive-compliant, compulsive-caregiving, coercive, or helpless.

3. The Subsequent Formation of Attachment Relationships to the Foster or Adoptive Caregivers

Commonly, the foster or adoptive parent inherits the child's expectations (negative working model) about the parent-child relationship. Additionally, the foster or adoptive parent also encounters a child with a developed, sometimes entrenched, attachment pattern. Take the case of a child whose attachment strategy (i.e., pattern) is compulsive-caregiving, complete with "parentified" or "parental" behavior toward other children and perhaps even toward the foster or adoptive caregiver. This child, even after encouraged and instructed by the foster or adoptive parents to cease and desist in the caregiving role, cannot or will not stop. Or consider the case of a compulsive-compliant adopted child who never shows negative affect around the adoptive mother or father. His adopted parents are eventually put off by the child's lack of genuine emotional expression. And then, there is the coercive child who presses his foster or adoptive parent into the thankless role of providing nearly constant negative attention, or the child with the feigned helplessness pattern who exhausts and exasperates his foster or adoptive parent with infantile neediness, a strategy he overlearned with his initial caregivers.

In all of these cases, the attachment relationship which forms between foster or adopted child and his new parents can, in great measure, be predetermined or highly influenced by past attachment relationships.

HOW FOSTER AND ADOPTIVE PARENTS' OWN ATTACHMENT ISSUES AFFECT THEIR RESPONSE TO THE TROUBLED CHILD

As parents or as adults, all individuals could theoretically be classified as to their attachment. Some of us would be classified as secure and autonomous, the most balanced and healthy. A goodly percentage of parents would fall into the three remaining categories: dismissing, enmeshed, or disoriented/disorganized. In parallel fashion, all foster and adoptive parents could be classified as to predominant attachment pattern. While many would receive a secure designation, undoubtedly some would be typified as dismissing, enmeshed, or disoriented/disorganized. How foster and adoptive parents undertake caregiving in general would undoubtedly correlate with their attachment pattern as would the way in which they interrelate specifically as caregivers with troubled children. Let's turn our focus to four examples of predictable mismatches:

1. A foster or adoptive parent might have an attachment pattern that resembles the dismissing pattern, perhaps living "in denial" and flatly unaware of the frustration and disappointment felt toward her own caregivers in her early (and adult) life. This parent might, say unconsciously, seek inordinate satisfaction in the relationship to her foster or adoptive child. If this child has a D attachment pattern, unbridled emotional advances by the foster mother may cause the child to recoil and withdraw anxiously. The parent, in turn, might more desperately pursue the relationship, which prompts more withdrawal (and perhaps conduct problems) from the child in an effort to distance the caregiver.

2. A foster or adoptive parent might have an enmeshed pattern of attachment, perhaps non-insightful about a compulsive-compliant role she took on in her family of origin. If this mother was subtly and/or obviously punished for independence of thought and rewarded for conforming to the "party line," she might expect her children to conform and may misinterpret conduct problems, for example, as noncompliance. If she is raising a child with a C3 pattern, she might misperceive his coercive approaches to her as "naughty" behavior. She also might find herself increasingly frustrated with the child, but equally unable to vent the anger building in the relationship. It can be very upsetting for compulsively compliant parents who have not allowed themselves to express negative affect in relationships to deal with the child's negative affect and their own suppressed and welling anger.

3. Another foster or adoptive parent who has a mixture of enmeshed and dismissing patterns and has a history of compulsive caregiving dating to her own childhood may be offended by or competitive with a child who is "parental" or "parentified" (compulsive-caregiving). The child feels rebuffed by the foster or adoptive mother's refusal to accept her ministrations; the mother feels rebuffed similarly.

4. The foster or adoptive parent who has a disoriented/disorganized pattern of attachment, formed in relationship to trau-

matic losses or to a history of physical or sexual abuse, may exacerbate the condition of a child who himself has a type D attachment pattern. If this foster or adoptive parent interacts with a young child, say, in frightened or frightening ways (e.g., through abrupt and invasive movements and/or through a startling, abrasive tone of voice), this often alarms the child. Since the type D child already views caregivers as both the source of and the solution to alarm, erratic communication from and behavior by a disoriented foster or adoptive parent only confirms or exacerbates the child's state of disorganization.

Foster, kinship, and adoptive parents' own expectations about relationships can influence how they relate to their children's conduct problems (Dozier & Albus, 2000). If a foster or adoptive mother, for instance, expects that her children will meet all their needs through her and that they should look to her for, say, food, she may be offended by the self-parenting, feral child who steals and eats food solitarily. This conflicts with her expectations about how a child should need and turn to his mother. If the foster or adoptive parent has a strong need to be needed by her children, she may be sorely offended by the child who conveys that he does not need caregiving.

COMMON EMOTIONAL RESPONSES PARENTS FEEL TOWARD THEIR TROUBLED FOSTER OR ADOPTED CHILD

In Lieberman's (2003) work with foster and adoptive parents and children with attachment issues, she found that parents expressed distress about their child's behavior problems. Many felt guilt about their own perceived failure and incompetence. They also often reported anger at the child for the child's lack of positive (and grateful) response to their love. Other parents acknowledged strongly ambivalent feelings about the child, varying from very positive feelings to wanting to get rid of the child and regretting that they adopted the child in the first place.

Though they might not be immediately aware of the realities of "reenactment," foster and adoptive parents report a variety of negative, bewildering, and foreign reactions after the placement of their troubled child. Their expectations of how a child will respond to them are frequently in opposition to the actual responses of the child (Dozier & Albus, 2000). From an attachment point of view, these are predictable responses to a child's confusing signals. For example, if a drug-exposed infant or toddler fusses irritably when the parent holds him, the parent may deduce that they should interact less with him or withdraw from the child. However, that may result in a pattern of interaction which does not help the young child develop properly (Dozier & Albus). Table 5.1 summarizes some of the common foster and adoptive parent reactions to placement of the significantly disturbed foster or adopted child.

FOSTER OR ADOPTIVE PARENT RESPONSES OR COUNTERTRANSFERENCE
• Feelings of impotence and incompetence • Urge to reject the child or to give the child up • Significant anger or even abusive feelings toward the child • Emotional withdrawal/feeling rejected by the child
TABLE 5.1

Once the child has developed a negative working model of the world and conduct problems, the child becomes a potent agent in the parent/child dyad. For example, if the child clings to a view of parents as dangerous or unreliable and a view of himself as impotent to make his needs known, and to have his needs met within a parent-child relationship, then conduct problems may emerge. The mere act of being removed from abuse and placed in a good foster, kinship, or adoptive home is often insufficient to alter or obliterate the child's expectations. In fact, the pull of those expectations and the impact of the behavior problems which derive from those views can be felt by the foster and adoptive parents in ways that surprise and alarm them (Sroufe, 1988). Foster and adoptive parents feel, for example, unsettling levels of rage, depression, frustration, anxiety, ambivalence, confusion, inadequacy, sexual attraction, revulsion, and/or withdrawal. They often wonder if they are going crazy and they might even fear they would abuse the child. In addition, dormant, unresolved issues from their own past may be re-awakened by the presence of the disturbed child in their midst. Indeed, there can be a collision of the parent's attachment issues and the child's (Delaney, 2003).

Frequently, foster parents of children with attachment issues report that they feel ineffective, unneeded, and perhaps somewhat useless. Many feel discouraged about the child's stubborn refusal to allow intimacy to form. These reactions confirm the potency of the child's effect on the parent. That is, the child seeks out, produces, shapes, and translates situations around him. The child's history and view of the world predisposes him to misinterpretations. He may see harmless activities as hazardous, friendly gestures as hostile, and he then responds accordingly. This often serves to elicit responses from others that merely prove to the child that his pessimistic views were correct in the first place (Sroufe, 1988).

Foster and adoptive parents point to the constant, negative behaviors (including conduct problems) which force them into the thankless role of unrelenting disciplinarian. One author described a parent who adopted two Russian orphans with serious emotional issues. The single mother spent relentless time in discipline which seemed ineffective and which interfered with her capacity to be a nurturing caregiver. Parents who feel impotent and incompetent as parents often reflexively recoil from the child (Chisholm, 2000). At some level they find themselves responding in uncharacteristic and perhaps even frightening ways. One foster mother put it this way: "I never felt that I could give this child what he needed. He would not let me be me... to care for him or give him something. As a matter of fact, I felt that he wanted me to be mean to him."

Even experienced foster and adoptive parents may be appalled, somewhat disoriented, and/or mortified by the depth of their negative reactions to the child with ongoing attachment issues. Without an understanding of these reactions and some tools to handle them, a foster or adoptive parent might hastily give up the child, i.e., have the child removed from the home. In order to reduce the destructive impact of reenactment and the foster or adoptive parents' reactions, it is important that foster or adoptive parents (and caseworkers and mental health workers who assist them) first identify what some typical reactions might be. Early recognition of budding reactions allows time to gain understanding and to establish counter measures.[1] Here are four such typical reactions.

SIGNIFICANT ANGER OR ABUSIVE IMPULSES TOWARD THE CHILD

Foster and adoptive parents are often totally perplexed by the feelings

---

[1] It should be mentioned here that not only foster, kinship, and adoptive parents find themselves reacting to maltreated children with attachment issues. School personnel have been found to use more overt control and direction with children who have come from histories which produce attachment issues (Sroufe, 1988).

of anger evoked in them by children with attachment issues. As mentioned earlier, foster children often poorly identify and negotiate their own wants, needs, and feelings. Rather than dealing verbally with the frustration and anger rising interpersonally (especially with caregivers), they resort to behavioral expression. That is, they ventilate anger in oblique fashion. Oftentimes, passive-aggressive behavior is directed toward the parent, who predictably reacts with anger. In clinical practice, it appears as if the foster or adoptive parent expresses the anger which the disturbed child finds to be unutterable. The depth and frequency of these angry feelings appall foster and adoptive parents, many of whom may have been drawn to this work by a desire to express love, affection, and concern for less fortunate, dependent individuals. If parents feel overwhelmed with anger, they should report this at a support group or to their child's therapist, family therapist, or caseworker. Such sentiments of exasperation and frustration are typical in work with attachment-disordered children (O'Connor & Zeanah, 2003). The following is an example.

Mrs. R., a treatment foster mother with her first attachment-disordered child, looked drawn and haggard. Although she was unable to voice her true feelings for several sessions, finally Mrs. R. admitted to violent nightmares about Bobby. She seemed deeply distressed about having these murderous dreams, and she feared losing her temper during the day. The intensity of the anger was foreign to her.

In my later private conversation with Mr. R., he revealed his fear that his wife was beginning to lose her mind.

Mrs. R.'s feelings of anger at her foster child, as might be expected, were very disturbing to her. A very kind, gentle woman by nature, she had never experienced anything like this before. In previous work with handicapped and mentally retarded foster children, Mrs. R. had been a very poised, competent mother figure. Imagine her surprise—and that of her husband and caseworker—when she voiced abusive fantasies concerning Bobby.

As in the case of Mr. and Mrs. R. and Bobby, successful intervention often includes the following: didactic information on conduct problems, reenactment, and usual foster and adoptive parent responses; support from other experienced foster and adoptive parents; increased supports in case management and respite care; and psychotherapy with the child and family. In this case, Mrs. R. benefitted from an understanding of how her expectations and past history conflicted with Bobby's.

———

Mrs. R. seemed notably relieved after the confession of her homicidal fantasies. As she grew more comfortable with articulating her feelings, she felt less controlled by the anger. Also, as she understood and accepted her own deep feelings, she became much more effective in helping Bobby express his repressed emotion.

In individual consultation sessions with me, Mrs. R. spoke of her own repressive family background, which had poorly prepared her for the likes of Bobby. Raised in a family which was close-knit but nonverbal, Mrs. R. had never witnessed open confrontation, and did not recall any deeply felt anger toward her parents, even during her adolescence. Mrs. R. was a woman who desired closeness and felt little anger. For his part, Bobby was a child who feared yet seethed with anger. Not surprisingly, Mrs. R.'s successful, tender-loving-care approach seemed doomed to fail with Bobby.

Bobby reenacted his own early history with Mrs. R., much to her chagrin. A boy who had been sorely neglected and repeatedly abused, Bobby perceived parent figures as fearsome and non-giving. A secretly angry boy, Bobby had learned to express his frustration/ rage indirectly toward the dangerous adults around him. Indeed, he may have derived some satisfaction in evoking anger in parents.[2]

As Mrs. R. adopted a more clinical, dispassionate (but not rejecting) perspective toward Bobby, and as she reduced her need (i.e., expectation) to give and receive to a more modest level, she grew less vulnerable to Bobby's rejection of her offers. Correspondingly, it made her less threatening to Bobby, who had become phobic of the requirements of intimacy. Bobby's temporary improvement in foster placement was at least in part due to growth in the foster mother—to her increased understanding of her emotional response to Bobby's negative expectations and attempts to reenact. (See chapter six for more information on working with foster or adoptive parent issues.)

———

[2] Bobby's pattern of engagment with caregivers is reminiscent of the C3 child.

EMOTIONAL WITHDRAWAL/FEELING REJECTED BY THE CHILD

Many foster and adoptive parents feel rejected by their child and withdraw. The natural, expectable parent response to rebuff from an infant or child is to take the child's cues at face value and keep one's distance. Dozier (2003) instructs foster and adoptive parents to "see that children need them even though they may not appear to need them." Without support parents can pull back, withdraw, and appear detached from the child, which "may be mistaken as a source of the child's disturbance rather than a result of it" (O'Connor & Zeanah, 2003). To some extent most parents, not irrationally, need positive feedback from their children. This need not be glowing accolades and effusive gratitude but simple reactions to the parent's caregiving efforts. Without that feedback, emotional withdrawal is highly likely and amounts to "the reverse effect" of the child upon caregivers (Delaney & Kunstal, 1997). Behaviors that are off-putting need to be reinterpreted or reframed as the vestiges of survival behaviors learned in the problem-riddled parent-child relationships the child has come from (Dozier & Ablus, 2000).

FEELINGS OF IMPOTENCE AND INCOMPETENCE

Foster and adoptive parents often feel impotent and incompetent when raising troubled children with attachment issues. This is expected given the confusing signals or "pushing away" that permeates the child's interactions with the parents (Dozier, 2003). When parents' interventions with a child chronically meet with either no response or worsening behaviors, these caregivers feel like they are ineffectual (i.e., impotent) and have no impact on the child. Typically such parents doubt their parenting methods and perhaps even themselves (i.e., incompetence). O'Connor and Zeanah (2003) portray these foster and adoptive parents as feeling "de-skilled" and perceiving their parent-child relationship as a coexistence rather than a relationship. In essence, parents are responding to the lack of partnership with a child whose pattern of attachment and expectations about caregivers is deeply pessimistic.

It may help for foster, kinship, and adoptive parents to reframe how they think about their children's responses to them. If they keep in mind, as difficult as this may be, that the child's history has shaped them to reject caregivers, it may allow parents to remain a bit more objective and to take the rejection less personally.

CONCLUDING REMARKS

Foster and adoptive parents' emotional (and perhaps behavioral) responses to troubled foster and adoptive children often relate to the child's past and resultant attachment pattern and to the parents' own attachment issues. If foster and adoptive parents are not instructed to modify and/or attune their parenting to the needs (and strategies) of the troubled child, his past may negatively impact the current parent-child relationship. When unprepared foster and adoptive parents meet with troubled children, they often experience a range of negative (and foreign) emotions, including guilt, distress, anger, withdrawal, impotence, and incompetence. These parents are sometimes swept up in negative and punitive parenting and frequently misinterpret or overlook "attachment cues" which might, if identified correctly, coax them to parent their child in a more sensitive, attuned fashion.

6 Parent Training and Consultation

Although no forms of psychotherapy have been proven effective for children with attachment disorders (O'Connor & Zeanah, 2003), mental health professionals can play a part in helping foster and adoptive children and especially in assisting the parents to help them. As noted earlier, there is little agreement about what attachment disorder is and how it should be tested for or diagnosed. Further, not only are there no "accepted" treatments for children with RAD, but we are also uncertain about the prognosis. Behavior associated with attachment disorder endures for years following placement into caring homes (O'Connor & Zeanah).

Chapter six outlines an approach to mental health training[1] of and consultation to foster and adoptive parents. This approach is informed, in part, by concepts and findings gleaned from attachment theory and research. Teaching parents about the attachment concepts that can be helpful in raising troubled children and consulting with them about their children's issues has shown promise in indirect treatment of children with problems ranging from anxiety disorders to ADHD, from conduct problems in young children to aggression and other antisocial behaviors in older children (Kazdin & Weisz, 2003). In practice, clinicians are teaching, training, and consulting continually with parents. Much of the training is ad hoc and is not manualized. (Approaches taught to parents and outlined in this chapter shun any coercive approaches by parents or the mental health professional.)

This chapter will cover the following topics:

1. An Overview of Parent Training and the Consultation Approach

2. Teaching Parents How to Reinterpret Conduct Problems

3. Teaching Parents About Social Learning Approaches

---

[1] Training does not necessarily imply workshops or formal, didactic coursework. Training in the context of a therapist's office is informal, on going, and interactive, though it can involve homework, bibliotherapy, and even visits to relevant Web sites.

4. Teaching Parents to Increase Their Child's Verbalizations and Negotiation Skills

5. Teaching Parents How to Increase Positive Encounters with Their Child

6. Teaching Parents About Their Own Attachment Issues and Parenting Styles

AN OVERVIEW OF THE PARENTING APPROACH

It has long been the belief of this author and others that the most impacting, radical therapeutic relationship for troubled foster and adoptive children is the foster or adoptive family itself (Delaney, 1998; Delaney & Kunstal, 1997; Sroufe, 1988). Parent training and consultation can enhance or maximize the positive impact of foster and adoptive families on children who show many serious emotional and disruptive conduct problems (Chamberlain & Smith, 2003; Speltz, 1990). As described earlier, these conduct problems can include behaviors such as antisocial behavior, aggression, chronic noncompliance, hitting, temper tantrums, running away, injury, eating problems, destruction of property, and taking objects belonging to others (stealing). They might also include problems such as risk taking, compulsive caregiving (of parent), and suppression of negative affect (Crittenden & Claussen, 2000) associated with the A3 and A4 child (see chapter two). The approach described in this chapter is suggested by years of clinical work with foster and adoptive parents and involves the integration of evidence-based approaches, such as teaching parents the basics of operant and social learning theory (Chamberlain & Reid, 1991) and cognitive behavioral approaches (Lochman, Barry, & Pardini, 2003), as well as teaching parents the fundamentals of attachment theory and how to interpret children's conduct problems (Speltz). The mental health consultation and training approach that we focus upon here is, then, caregiver (e.g., foster or adoptive parent) focused. While the exact role of foster, kinship, and adoptive parents in treatment of troubled children is unclear or secondary in other approaches, in our approach the parents' roles are preeminent. Mental health professionals should always be assessing how the foster or adoptive parents can promote healthier development, changes in the pathway, alterations in the child's strategies, and formation of attachments in relationships (O'Connor & Zeanah, 2003). As seen in Table 6.1, the parenting approaches we explore and encourage are composed of five central components. While these individual components have been found effective, their use individually and collectively in the clinic setting with attachment disorders has not yet been studied. The components that we emphasize in training and consultation follow[2]:

1. Teach parents how to reinterpret conduct problems by considering the child's underlying negative working model and function; and teach parents sensitivity to cues, clues, and signals from the child.

2. Teach parents about social learning approaches.

3. Teach parents to increase the child's verbalization of the underlying negative working model. Teach parents to foster the child's communication of views, needs, and feelings; instruct parents on how to negotiate differences between themselves and the child; teach parents to build a partnership (see chapter one).

4. Teach parents how to increase positive encounters between themselves and the child.

5. Consult with the parents about their issues, including their parenting styles and the parents' own working models related to family and the parent-child relationship, which impact or interact with the child's issues and conduct problems.

---

[2] While all components of parent training and mental health consultation are important, we do not always use every component in each case; sometimes, certain components seem to take on more importance in particular cases.

Although these components can be fruitful, they are not necessarily sufficient to treating troubled foster and adoptive children. When we are dealing with children who have complicated and multiple diagnoses (typically ADHD/ODD, mood disorders, conduct disorders, pervasive developmental disorders, posttraumatic stress disorders, etc.), the mental health professional needs to collaborate with the child's psychiatrist or family doctor about medical/psychiatric issues related to the conduct problems.

Evidence-based treatments may be somewhat confining in the real world of clinical practice. Many evidence-based practice approaches have been validated for use with single diagnoses or circumscribed conduct problems, whereas in clinical practice with troubled foster and adoptive children, multiple diagnoses and plentiful, co-occurring conduct problems are the order of the day. In such real-world cases, an eclectic approach informed by EBP approaches may be helpful.

COMPONENTS OF POSITIVE PARENTING APPROACHES
1. Teaching parents to reinterpret conduct problems.
2. Teaching parents about social learning approaches.
3. Teaching parents to increase the child's verbalization and negotiation skills; build a goal-corrected partnership.
4. Increase positive encounters between parents and child.
5. Explore parenting issues, including the parent's style.
TABLE 6.1

Let's turn to a case study to illustrate how mental health consultation and parent training occur:

> Maggie, an adopted 8-year-old girl, showed a number of significant conduct problems. She lied and related to the adoptive parents in a "fakey" manner, smiling constantly and agreeing to their faces with everything they said. She was a people-pleaser around adults, though at certain times, she did not make good eye contact. Maggie could not entertain herself and would run off on her own. She acted aggressively toward younger children if they did not obey her. Accordingly, the parents restricted (e.g., grounded) Maggie from play with all children.

> She would dillydally at bedtime. If the foster mom shut off the light precipitously, Maggie cried. She could not seem to let go at the end of the day and would drag things out by not getting ready for bed. Interestingly, during the daytime Maggie could not entertain herself, had little imagination, and was constantly underfoot, shadowing the adoptive mother.

> Stealing was another concern. Maggie sneaked things from home to school and vice versa, so mom had to frisk her. She stockpiled food that she took from the pantry in her room.

> Maggie also tried to care-give the adoptive mom. The adoptive mother lamented, "Maggie tries to take care of me. She acts like the parent, not the child. I wish she were more like her older brother."

While Maggie's behavior problems are moderate compared to those of some foster or adopted children, they reflect common presenting complaints from foster and adoptive parents. We next will address the case of Maggie as it relates to the five parent training components, starting with reinterpreting conduct problems.

REINTERPRETING CONDUCT PROBLEMS

Training or teaching parents how to reinterpret conduct problems via knowledge of attachment theory and research is central to our approach. It can be broken into three parts which focus on:

1. Underlying negative working model, which we often describe to parents as being the child's "mental blueprint;" they are often given a written description of the mental blueprint taken from Troubled Transplants (Delaney & Kunstal, 1991) and informed how children can misperceive caregiver actions and intentions and may have distorted perceptions about themselves, parents, and relationships;

2. Sample attachment patterns (e.g., A3, A4, C3, C4, and D) which illustrate for parents how children have developed historic, overarching strategies for relating to caregivers. We often give parents a brief written description of those five patterns with an explanation that they are samples only and that they are not diagnoses; and

3. The function of conduct problems in terms of attachment theory; and the need for increased parent sensitivity to cues and signals from the child. We explain that children's negative or off-putting behavior may be maladaptive but explainable forms of attachment behavior. It is the third part, the function of conduct problems, that we will focus upon here in more detail.

It is understandable that foster and adoptive parents frequently seek out mental health professionals to eliminate the conduct problems their children show. As with Maggie, these conduct problems are readily apparent and obviously unacceptable. While it is tempting for the mental health professional to launch into addressing these problem behaviors posthaste, it's usually prudent to get a sense of the function (i.e., the purpose served) of the conduct problem (see chapter four) first.

Overall, foster and adoptive parents need to be provided with introductory level information about attachment theory and research and how they relate to the maltreated child.[3] It's particularly important for parents to know that traumatic early histories can render the child insecurely attached and can impact his expectations and strategies.

Attachment theory can contribute to an understanding of problem behaviors in terms of their function, and the mental health professional can educate foster and adoptive parents concerning the "function" of the child's behavioral problems. Sometimes parents need to be taught to look beyond the obvious. If parents do not comprehend why the child acts the way he does, they miss opportunities to develop the most helpful interventions.[4] It is important for parents to learn, for example, why keeping the parents' attention is so crucial to the child and why negative attention may hold more allure than positive attention. Beyond that, mental health professionals can also help parents understand why a child might risk or seek to elicit hazardous parental engagement such as negative attention or even physical abuse (Speltz, 2000).

Parents typically know that certain behaviors from the child are undesirable, inappropriate, dangerous, noncompliant, provocative, and/or strange. Their focus often becomes a single-minded desire to eliminate or expunge the bad behavior. However, for children with serious emotional disturbances, the conduct problems often serve functions, as mentioned in chapter four and summarized here in the Attachment Function Tools, Table 6.2. The obvious behaviors can be deceptive or misleading to parents, distracting them from the deeper issues. Without learning about function—the underlying purpose—parents can take the behavior problems too personally and become less objective in their problem solving. The behaviors continue to escalate or proliferate and the parents try to contain, control, punish, or eliminate these behaviors that refuse to go away. The possible explanation for this is that the function remains strong, the child's view of the world remains the same, and he continues to cling stubbornly to his overlearned strategies.

---

[3] They can be given rudimentary information through informal discussion and/or via online information at www.fosterparentcollege.com, where the course on Reactive Attachment Disorder provides the basics.

[4] Parents are typically advised to curb the natural tendency to quiz the child about why they acted up. Instead parents are encouraged to work toward their own understanding of why.

1. Control of proximity: to control the physical and psychological proximity of caregivers (Speltz, 1990)

2. Reinstatement of contact: to reinstate contact with and interventions from caregiver after interruptions (Speltz, 1990)

3. Reduction of anxiety: to reduce anxiety and insecurity related to unreliability of caregiver's availability (Speltz, 1990)

4. Communication of needs: to communicate care-giving needs (Speltz, 1990)

5. Regulation of caregiver: to regulate the caregiver's behavior to fall in line with the child's goals (Marvin & Stewart, 1990)

6. Provision of self-protection: to provide self with protection normally reserved for caregivers (Lieberman & Pawl, 1988)

7. Reduction of danger: to reduce danger and increase safety (Crittenden & Claussen, 2000)

8. Ventilation of feelings: to vent frustration safely (Crittenden & Claussen, 2000; Speltz, 1990)

9. Improvement of survivability: to survive (Bowlby, 1969)

10. Coercion of interaction: to coerce an affectional bond (Bowlby, 1969)

11. Protection by caregivers: to receive protection from predators (Ainsworth, 1978)

12. Reduction of risk of abuse by the caregiver (Crittenden & Claussen, 2000)

13. Obtainment of parental attention and approval (Crittenden & Claussen, 2000)

TABLE 6.2

Similar to the work of Spetz (1990), "parent sensitivity training" is a necessary part of our parent training and consultation approach. The emphasis is placed on looking past the obvious conduct problems to the underlying purpose or function.[5] It focuses on raising the parent's level of awareness, sensitivity, and responsiveness to the child. Understanding how the child has related to past caregivers can inform us about function or purpose and ongoing strategies.

It's important to reemphasize here that misbehavior and conduct problems, strange as it may seem, can function as attachment behaviors. That is, bad behavior can fit into a strategy to bring the caregiver into proximity and to step up involvement with the child. Current misbehavior can be an adaptation or maladaptation to insensitive or unreliable caregivers in the past.

The purpose of parent sensitivity training is not simply academic. We examine the functions of behavior problems not only to stimulate the parents to think differently, but also to generate ideas for teaching the child to ask for and achieve what he needs. If we know, for example, that the child steals food from the pantry as a result of his neglect and resultant survival behavior (e.g., function #9), then we can offer better ways to reassure the child of availability. Instead of simply focusing upon the bad behavior of stealing, we look to the function, which allows us to provide the child with a backpack full of food, or canned goods under his/her bed, etc.

Parents need to be taught that the obvious behavior problems of a child do not always accurately indicate what the child needs. Dozier's (2000) studies of infants with attachment problems (and prior in utero drug exposure) show they rebuff caregiving; therefore, parents must be exquisitely sensitive to the fact that the infant's behavior sends a confusing signal to them about what s/he really needs. Parents must find ways to meet the child's needs sensitively even in the face of rejection and withdrawal.

---

[5] This approach is similar to functional behavioral analysis (FBA), as seen in school psychology, which examines the purpose a behavior serves for the child (Haynes & O'Brien, 1990) in the home and school environment. One function mode examined by FBA addresses what the child is communicating about a need through his behavior problem (Lazarus, 1989). While behavior or conduct problems are of immediate concern to parents and professionals, what can be more telling and revealing is why the child does what he does. It is important to identify those "controllable environmental events" related to behavior (Gresham, Watson, & Skinner, 2001). Some of these events may either correlate to or even cause the conduct problem. General categories of functions associated with conduct problems include: social attention; access to "tangibles;" escape from "aversive tasks;" avoidance of other people; and internal excitement or stimulation (Carr, 1994). This broader list of functions reminds us that often multiple causes or functions are related to conduct problems. The specific functions of conduct problems from attachment theory, however, most typically center on social attention and avoidance of other people.

Parent sensitivity also fosters the positive tendency of parents to wonder, to analyze, and to get to the bottom of why their children do what they do. Although it may often be fruitless to ask your children why they do what they do, it can be most instructive for parents to be constantly asking themselves why the child acts in certain ways. Thinking in terms of purpose or function can be very illuminating. It also can allow the parents to distance themselves emotionally from the child's problems, not in some cold-hearted fashion, but in a way that allows them to remain more objective and less paralyzed by strong, negative emotional responses.

Let's return to the case of Maggie and examine the 10 behavior problems in terms of their attachment functions (AF). As you can see from Table 6.3, Maggie's behavior problems serve a number of functions.

LYING: In Maggie's case (and with many other maltreated children) lying has served multiple functions. One function that lying may have served is to reduce danger around her caregivers (AF #7). If caregivers do not know the truth, for example, they might not be angry or they might not punish the child. If a child is raised by volatile, punitive, or even dangerous caregivers, he learns to reduce danger by denying or lying about mistakes he has made, rules he has violated, or things he has taken from others. Historically, Maggie may have learned to avoid the wrath of parents by telling lies to get her out of scrapes. Overall, Maggie might continue to reduce parental scrutiny and attention (and punishment) by keeping them in the dark.

Conversely, another function of lying may be to obtain or increase the attention, albeit negative attention, of caregivers. Although this may not be the case with Maggie specifically, many maltreated children become expert at engaging in debates (e.g., question and answer) with caregivers over the truth (e.g., regulation of caregiver). The process of debating secures these children some modicum of attention, albeit negative attention (AF # 5). Foster and adoptive parents can find themselves in the role of Grand Inquisitor, probing for the truth or cross-examining the child endlessly.

STEALING: Maggie may be using stolen items as "transitional objects"—items that make her feel connected to the mother. This may function to reduce anxiety about her mother's availability (AF #3). The stealing may also coerce the mother into the role of

Applying Functions to Understanding Maggie

Behavior Problem	Function(s)
Lying	Reduction of danger (avoidance of punishment)
	Regulation of caregiver (keeping parent engaged in question and answer)
Stealing	Ventilation (dealing with anger by stealing from parent or another)
	Reduction of anxiety (reducing feelings of insecurity)
	Coercion (forcing parental involvement)
Food stealing and hoarding	Survival
Running off on own	Control of proximity (engaging the parent in a game of hide-and-go-seek to keep her close)
	Communication of needs (indirectly expressing need for caregiving)
Aggressive behavior toward younger children	Ventilation (safe displacement onto those lower in hierarchy)
Over-dependency	Reduction of anxiety (regulating closeness by hanging on)
Bedtime problems	Reduction of danger (drawing parent close during times demanding separation and disengagement)
Parentified behavior	Communication of needs (indirectly expressing need for caregiving)
Fake behavior and compulsive agreement	Reduction of danger (using compliance to reduce caregiver-child conflict)
Poor eye contact	Expression of anger toward caregiver without open defiance (discourage caregiving behavior without open protest)

TABLE 6.3

policing the child, thereby keeping her intimately connected to the child (AF #10).

FOOD STEALING AND HOARDING: In many instances, the function of food stealing and hoarding is ultimately survival (AF #9) and self-protection (AF #6). When caregivers historically have not provided food, children in feral fashion provide for themselves.

RUNNING AWAY: The function of running away may be to compel the caregiver to find the child. This may serve to reinstate involvement with the caregiver (AF #2). Oddly, the child runs away to bring the parent close (AF #10). Of course, children run away for a variety of other reasons as well.

AGGRESSIVE BEHAVIOR TOWARD OTHER CHILDREN: One attachment function of aggression might be to ventilate anger toward helpless targets rather than toward caregivers (AF #8). When children have been raised by maltreating parents, they often learn to suppress anger felt toward their caregivers. Felt anger may then be directed or "displaced" onto hierarchically safer targets.

OVER-DEPENDENCY: Shadowing or clinging behavior may insure (coerce) caregiving behavior (AF #10) and proximity of the caregiver (AF #1). This overdependent behavior may also reduce anxiety about separation from the caregiver (AF #3), and it may increase the chances of receiving interaction with the caregiver (AF #2) and insure protection by the caregiver (AF #1).

BEDTIME PROBLEMS: Maggie's problems at bedtime may function to keep her caregivers close (AF #1) at the time when some separation is required. If children have felt most vulnerable at bedtime, coercing parental involvement at bedtime may have served to lower anxiety about lurking dangers (AF #7).

PARENTAL BEHAVIOR: When children like Maggie evidence parental behavior, they often have learned this role around caregivers who were deficient in caregiving.[6] In some ways, parental behavior and caregiving of other children may reduce anxieties about being alone. Additionally, caregiving behavior toward the parent figure provides some way for the child to maintain proximity to the adult (AF #1).

---

[6] Refer to the discussion of the A3 pattern.

FAKE BEHAVIOR AND COMPULSIVE AGREEMENT: Maggie's so-called fake behavior may serve to reduce conflict with the caregiver and thereby reduce interpersonal danger (AF #7).[7]

POOR EYE CONTACT: When children show poor eye contact, this may suggest that they feel unsafe around the caregiver. Poor eye contact may function to reduce danger related to expected conflict (AF #7). If the child, for instance, disagrees with or feels anger at his parent, he might avoid eye contact as a way of sidestepping conflict or revealing his anger.

TEACHING PARENTS ABOUT SOCIAL LEARNING APPROACHES

Foster or adoptive parents arrive for mental health services with concerns about their child's "presenting complaints." These parents also often have expectations about the mental health professional's role:[8] to get rid of or to contain the child's problem behavior.

Social learning approaches used by parents can stabilize children with serious emotional and behavioral problems (Chamberlain & Reid, 1991), even children who have been hospitalized in psychiatric facili-

---

[7] This could be a vestige of the A3 pattern.

[8] Mental health training and consultation begins with gathering background information from the parents and child, including, but not limited to the child's age, grade, prenatal history, developmental history, placement history, trauma history, permanency plan, the family constellation, parent roles, how long the foster or adoptive parents have been resource parents, onset of problems, and antecedents, as well as how various persons in the family view the problems, how they have handled the problems, and what has worked, not worked, and worked temporarily. We also inquire about the nature of relationships in the family, extended family, and the marriage. We ask about the range of problems the child shows and then seek information on strengths. We ask whether the parents feels the placement is in jeopardy, and more importantly about whether there is any imminent danger to or from the child. We routinely ask about medications—psychiatric and other. We try to get a sense of the patterns the child has shown in terms of conduct problems and get a sense of the relationships he has developed within the present and past families. We also seek to uncover how he views himself, parents, and others. We ask about school, friendships, academics, and how the child handles authority at school. We seek information on remaining allegiances to biological family members or other significant individuals. We ask about ongoing contact or visitation and its impact on the child. Importantly, we seek information on the child's attachment relationships, his ability to vocalize feelings, and his capacity to negotiate with adults.

ties. Social learning approaches that are discussed with and taught to foster and adoptive parents include an overall explanation of operant conditioning and its principles of reinforcement, punishment, and extinction. Parents are also, on a case-by-case basis, instructed in social learning approaches,[9] including

- Teaching children to cooperate
- Using behavior tracking
- Emphasizing encouragement
- Setting up behavior contracts
- Limit setting
- Employing time-out

These approaches are explained as ways of providing positive, clear-cut structure for children and offering incentives to help children control acting-out, decrease noncompliant behavior, increase cooperation, and reinforce new, pro-social behaviors. In consultation with foster and adoptive parents, we also address a number of specific issues and caveats, such as

1. Parent training should focus on instructing parents to use "limit setting" to ensure child safety and to employ the minimal amount of coercion for maintaining some "order" in the parent-child relationship. Some parents need to be advised that their expectations for order, compliance, and safety are excessive and can worsen conflict battles.

2. Pinpoint conduct problems that require limit setting. Distinguish between annoying and harmful behaviors and between what must be ignored or dealt with respectively. Interventions by parents tend to weaken if they are overused or blanketly applied to the point that the child becomes "parent deaf."

3. Focus on cooperation from the child rather than strict compliance.

4. Use of the Premack principle: first, do this, then you can have that; or when you've done this, then you can do that.

---

[9] It is beyond the scope of this book to cover social learning approaches in detail. A three-part series on Positive Parenting (www.fosterparentcollege.com) covers the essential social learning approaches we teach to parents. Parents are often directed to this Web site or are given a suggested reading list, including *Off-Road Parenting: Practical Solutions for Difficult Behavior* (Pacifici, Chamberlain, & White, 2002).

It is important to point out here that, when used alone, behavior modification approaches (e.g., time-out procedures) often fail with attachment-disordered children. These approaches are apt to produce superficial changes in "surface behavior," while underlying, negative working models generate new conduct problems. It is only when containment approaches are used jointly with the other treatment components that deeper, lasting changes appear.

Admittedly, some children do not respond to positive reinforcement in the way we would expect; indeed, foster, kinship, and adoptive parents report that with some children positive reinforcement stimulates all manner of negative behaviors and responses. The positives may clash with the child's negative working model and with his low self-esteem (e.g., "I don't deserve praise, and I'll prove it to you.") Or, positives may violate the child's strategy of relating to adults in essentially negative, conflictful, and confusing ways (see disorganized/disoriented attachment pattern in chapter two). In such instances, judicious use of positives may be preferable.

APPLYING SOCIAL LEARNING TOOLS TO MAGGIE

Let's return to the case of Maggie and examine her 10 conduct problems and how we might instruct her foster parents to manage with social learning tools.

LYING: Teach foster parents to ignore the lie and reward the truth when appropriate. Reduce the number of questions parents ask of the child. Cross-examining a child or lecturing the child on lying may provide negative attention, which is sufficient reward to maintain the lying behavior. Encourage and reinforce any honest expression of need, opinion, and goals (see Teaching Negotiation later in this chapter). Lying may relate to Maggie's fake, overly agreeable style (possible A3 strategy) with the parents. Parents may need to be advised that expecting impeccable truth-telling from Maggie may be an overly ambitious wish in the short run.

STEALING: Teach parents to encourage Maggie to ask for things she needs and/or wants. Teach parents to encourage Maggie to earn things by doing chores or extra work. Show Maggie that she can actively attain and obtain her goals. Teach parents to track when stealing occurs. It might be found that Maggie steals prized possessions from the bedroom of her older brother whenever the foster parents spend special one-on-one time with him.

FOOD STEALING AND HOARDING: If a child has come from deprivation and neglect, consider encouragement that reassures her about availability of food. Do not lock food away unless the situation is a safety or health concern. Teach parents to encourage Maggie to ask for food, for seconds, and for specific food items she likes and to reward her for expressing her needs or preferences.

RUNNING AWAY: Instruct parents to monitor Maggie closely (e.g., through behavior tracking and limit setting) and to reward her for either staying close or asking to explore. Teach parents to be more engaging with Maggie when they are around strangers or to be more attentive during the times when she is likely to run off. Parents may need to learn that their undivided, uninterrupted attention is likely the ultimate reward for Maggie.

AGGRESSIVE BEHAVIOR TOWARD OTHER CHILDREN: Look at whether Maggie vocalizes anger (i.e., use behavior tracking to establish when, how, and toward whom she verbalizes anger). Reward Maggie for directly and verbally expressing anger toward adults, especially parent figures. At the same time, teach parents to reward Maggie for cooperating, getting along, and resolving differences with other children.

OVER-DEPENDENCY: Ask parents to reconsider the idea of limiting peer involvement. Keeping Maggie from other children may make problems worse, in that she has no other recourse than to turn to her parent for attention, i.e., negative attention. Unless Maggie is abusing other children, it may be wiser to encourage that social involvement but with close supervision and tandem rewards for appropriate interactions.

BEDTIME PROBLEMS: Provide Maggie with a bedtime routine including one-to-one time. Teach parents to reward her for remaining in bed.

PARENTAL BEHAVIOR: Look for ways to praise Maggie for being an assistant. Punishing Maggie rigidly for caregiving behavior may set up a divide which is unnecessary and unproductive—it may diminish self-esteem and put Maggie in a position of obtaining negative attention.

FAKE BEHAVIOR AND COMPULSIVE AGREEMENT: Stay vigilant for any real, genuine, assertive behavior and reward baby steps.

POOR EYE CONTACT: Rather than forcing Maggie's eye contact, it may be preferable to get her to assertively articulate how she feels toward her parents (e.g., "I don't want you to tell me what to do"). Rewarding her for identifying how she feels and saying it honestly to the adult may result in greater comfort with parents and a resultant increase in eye contact.

TEACHING PARENTS ABOUT THE NEED FOR INCREASED VERBALIZATION AND FOSTERING NEGOTIATION

It is vital for mental health professionals to train foster and adoptive parents about (1) helping their children to increase verbalization about their feelings and needs; and further (2) teaching their children to negotiate with caregivers about their needs. The verbalization of feelings and needs may be a prerequisite to negotiation. Foster and adoptive parents need to understand that the child enters their home with conclusions (and related feelings) about caregivers that affect how they behave. The children's working models are not always conscious or articulated. Training of foster and adoptive parents can focus on how to initiate change by eliciting statements, thoughts, and feelings from the child about himself, his caregivers, and life in general. Parents need to hear that if only the visible behavior or undesirable behavior is eliminated or targeted, little or no impact may follow on the invisible but fathomable, underlying issues which influence the child's behavior toward others (Speltz, 1990). Parents can learn the importance of inviting the child to say how she feels and what she believes.

INCREASING VERBALIZATION OF FEELINGS

In general, maltreated (e.g., abused or neglected) children employ fewer "state words" or vocalize fewer negative feeling words (Crittenden & Claussen, 2000). This poverty of affective words may render them ill-equipped to comprehend what they are going through and to vocalize to others how they feel. Parents are often stymied by the lack of cues or prone to misinterpreting signals from the child. This interferes with the formation of an effective caregiver-child partnership. Affected by a sense (i.e., context) of danger, children may employ one or both of the following two strategies: (1) compulsive-compliance (A4), in which abused children inhibit negative affect and exhibit compliant behavior or (2) compulsive-caregiving (A3), in which the neglected child inhibits negative affect and exhibits "false positive" affect and caregiving to the parent. I recall one foster parent who reported how excited she was when her 11-year-old son kicked a hose caddy and swore at it in frustration, right in front of her! This was something he had never felt comfortable doing in the past. Again, the reason for the foster mother's enthusiasm was that the child, extremely over-compliant and inhibited around adults in the past, finally let loose with some feelings. His history of oppression by and lack of toleration from the caregiver is in sharp contrast to the early home environment of children who have not been intimidated by maltreatment.

It's especially important in parent training and mental health consultation that we focus upon underlying, non-verbalized feelings and the working model. Case in point, a 16-year-old boy who never had a birthday party in the past was placed in a foster home that intended to remedy that unacceptable omission. A large party was planned, but as they day approached the boy began acting out to sabotage the event, i.e., to prevent the celebration on his behalf from occurring. He may have expected inevitable disappointment (e.g., "Good things never happen to me because I don't deserve them.") This probable unverbalized expectation and related cynical feeling had gone unspoken and yet impacted his conduct.

In parent training and mental health consultation, foster and adoptive parents are taught to use a gentle challenge to the child's conclusions by perhaps inviting or urging the child to identify how he is feeling. (This approach can be aided by teaching parents principles of Cognitive Behavior Therapy [CBT].[10]) In one case the child finally stated his personal conclusion: "Mothers ruin your life." He had felt that about his birth mother, who had repeatedly abandoned him, and his conclusions about the foster mother were based upon that earlier feeling. Once that sentiment was elicited, it could be worked with, acknowledged, and gently challenged.

Parent training can focus on how parents can elicit feelings from their children in words. It's essential for parents to help their kids vocalize the underlying negative working model (see Table 6.4 for several conclusions reached by maltreated children). Parents can be provided with a list of conclusions that maltreated foster and adopted children have come to concerning meeting of needs, separation, safety, caregiver availability, attention, self-worth, and expression of feelings, especially anger or other negative emotions.[11]

Foster, kinship, and adoptive parents might benefit from training about whether a child might need to articulate feelings, when those feelings go unverbalized. Training can also focus on ultra-sensitivity

NEGATIVE WORKING MODEL ASSUMPTIONS

- I cannot meet my needs in the context of a parent-child relationship.
- Parents leave you.
- I keep myself safe.
- Big people hurt little people.
- Strangers are more available than family.
- Others get all the attention and I get none.
- I am unlovable and will prove it to you.
- It's best to keep my true feelings and thoughts to myself.
- I don't get mad; I get even.
- I have to force adults (and others) to provide caregiving for me.

TABLE 6.4

[10] Cognitive behavior therapy (CBT) approaches have shown promise in helping patients, adult and child, to identify underlying thoughts and beliefs. These underlying thoughts, beliefs, etc. can be viewed as working model assumptions. While CBT has not been validated specifically with RAD or other attachment disorders, it has been found effective with co-morbid disorders such as ADHD, PTSD, and PDD (Reineke et al. 2003; SAMSA model programs, 2005). CBT addresses risk factors which include impaired interpersonal trust, self-injury, and aggression toward others. It has been designed to treat children from 3 to 18 years of age who have significant emotional and behavioral problems following exposure to trauma, including traumatic loss of loved ones, physical abuse, sexual abuse, domestic violence, and out-of-home placement (foster care, group homes, and residential treatment centers), among other things. It focuses on correcting negative assumptions and on helping the child and caregivers to understand strong emotions and situations that predictably set off a child's emotional outbursts. Of course at the root of CBT is an understanding of feelings and thoughts which are sometimes veiled, self-defeating, irrational, and recalcitrant, i.e., negative working model assumptions. Parents, with the help of the mental health professional, must discover or probe the underlying sentiments and beliefs the child clings to—by what assumptions they operate. Getting a handle on those feelings and getting them out in the light of day is invaluable. Submerged, unvocalized, denied, they hold great power over the child and the relationships around him.

[11] Before focusing on verbalization and teaching foster and adoptive parents to help the child verbalize feelings, it is essential to know how able the child is developmentally to express needs to the caregiver and how capable the caregiver is to respond to the child's expression of needs.

to what the child's words mean and how to translate the meaning of what the child has said and left unsaid (O'Connor & Zeanah, 2003). It is important to teach parents that certain verbalizations of feelings are normal and expectable in children and that their *absence* may be abnormal diagnostic.

Foster parents can be instrumental in helping the child identify and voice previously unspoken feelings in the home. Importantly, they can recognize and focus on situations in the home in which the foster child fails to express normal levels of frustration, anger, jealousy, etc. Identifying what's *not said* by the child is as important, if not more so, than what the child does say. It's essential to see the child's behavior problems and then to identify the corresponding verbalizations that are missing. Here is how we often suggest parents can focus on what is missing: 1) Look for the normal protesting that the child emits daily when she is not intimidated into silence and nominal compliance. 2) List the events that your other, non-frightened children complain, protest, argue, differ, and nag about and see if those moments, segues, and circumstances are handled similarly by your acting-out child. 3) Use scaffolding[12] approach to help the child who either is unwilling or unable to articulate protest. The foster parent, rather than letting the moment pass unnoticed, can gently press the child to make some statements about his negative feelings in those situations. Of course, with the most disturbed, attachment-disordered children, resistance is strong. Acting out may continue unabated, all the while the child vigorously denies feeling any anger whatsoever.

Returning to the case of Maggie, let's examine the behavior or conduct problems in terms of the missing verbalizations and probable underlying (non-verbalized) negative working model. Table 6.5 provides Maggie's 10 usual conduct problems and the suspected, corresponding, non-verbalized feelings. An example of how the mental health professional can confer with foster and adoptive parents would be to discuss with them the probable non-verbalized feelings behind each of the child's conduct problems. As you can see from the table, Maggie has poor eye contact and is not expressing feelings in interactions with parents. Interestingly, when she feels lectured to or corrected or

---

[12] Scaffolding is defined as the support of fledgling attempts at expression of feeling. It involves suggesting ways to express, identifying situations that could benefit from expression of feelings, along with modeling ways of expressing feelings and wants in words. With scaffolding the parent prompts, encourages, and invites expression of feelings.

directed into some activity she doesn't agree with, she averts her gaze from her caregiver. At the same time, Maggie verbalizes no feelings of disagreement, protest, or frustration with the parents' request. Foster parents, in situations like this, need to be taught or advised to use scaffolding at this point, e.g., "I see you looking away. You may not want to listen to me or to what I have asked. Can you tell me that?"

APPLYING NEGATIVE WORKING MODEL ASSUMPTIONS TO MAGGIE	
BEHAVIOR/CONDUCT PROBLEM	NON-VERBALIZED FEELING
Lying	If I tell you the truth, you will hurt me.
Stealing	It does no good to ask for what I want.
Food stealing and hoarding	You don't take care of my basic needs.
Running off on own	I have to force you to pay attention.
Aggressive behavior toward younger children	It's safer to express anger felt with you (parent) toward smaller individuals.
Over-dependency	You will abandon me unless I watch you constantly.
Bedtime problems	You will abandon me unless I watch you constantly.
Parentified behavior	If I take care of your needs, you give me some attention.
Fake behavior and compulsive agreement	If I admit to different goals or unpleasant feelings, you will punish me.
Poor eye contact	It's better not to protest directly.
TABLE 6.5	

FOSTERING NEGOTIATING SKILLS

In addition to learning about how to provide "affective education" (including verbalization of feelings) to their children, foster and adoptive parents need instruction about the importance of negotiation of differences in the partnership with the child. A great deal of attachment research focuses upon the goal-corrected partnership, the fourth stage of attachment formation (see chapter one). The partnership between parent and child is unequal by necessity.[13] Typically, for example, the young child is not allowed to make the household rules, to set bedtime, and generally run the house.

Even with frightening, abusive parents, children can hold a great deal of influence, although often the influence involves subterfuge, e.g., secret and solitary behaviors. These behaviors are antithetical to negotiation and partnership in that they are unilateral and avoidant. The child typically has given up on meeting needs within a recipro-cal parent-child dyad, so she finds alternative, single-handed ways of addressing her needs. In an abusive or neglectful relationship with a caregiver, the child feels totally disempowered. If she has ever tried at all, she negotiated from a position of total weakness. She had limited input. Foster and adoptive parents can benefit from the knowledge that it is often essential to give the child more rather than less con-trol in a variety of situations and to teach them to negotiate (Speltz, 1990). Speltz emphasizes in his "communication skills" training the process of teaching parents to encourage and model for their children how negotiation works. If the child cannot uphold his end of the ne-gotiation, the parent is encouraged to "fill in the blank" until the child learns. Speltz acknowledges that at times parents must make unilat-eral decisions with input from their child. He also clarifies that more important than consensus or agreement between parent and child is the "process of trying to reach agreement" in a way that accentuates the child's sense of input into the parents' decisions. Parents need to be instructed that children who come from maltreatment back-grounds (with attendant attachment issues) have learned little about overt, verbally mediated, mutual, reciprocal co-regulation of a relation-ship. With the A3 and A4 child, for example, he either caregives or complies compulsively in an effort to engage the parent. In so doing, he suppresses any negative affect and in an elliptical fashion achieves a modicum of parent attention and a hint of input into the parents' decisions. The compliance, caregiving, suppression, and ellipse are

---

[13] Goal-corrected partnership, discussed earlier, is the fourth stage in attachment formation and reflects the fact that the child's goals and those of his parent often necessarily differ. The differences can be resolved by negotiation. In essence, negotiation recognizes individuality and automony while retaining or preserving some partnership or unity. The relationship is reciprocal but asymmetrical in that the parent and child influence each other; however, the parent oftentimes could be considered prominent in influence, albeit not in every way or in every instance.

evidence of the lack of a healthy goal-corrected partnership governed by reciprocity and negotiation of discrepant needs.

Much study has examined a central issue of negotiation, the negotiation of comings-and-goings—under what circumstances the caregiver can separate, for how long, etc. However, in our clinical experience partnership implies much more, for example, teaching co-regulation, negotiation, power sharing, and learning to give and take. Some children have learned little about how to regulate their parents' behavior in normal ways. Many foster children from backgrounds of maltreatment have concluded that they have little or no (positive) influence upon their parents. Thus, they often learn to influence their parents in oblique, strange, manipulative ways. Unfortunately, they have not learned to get their needs met positively within the context of the parent-child relationship.

Operant conditioning and social learning approaches often de-emphasize or ignore the importance of negotiations of difference between the parent and child. Indeed, if the child does try to negotiate with the parent, this is seen as negative, unwanted, and as another example of the child's noncompliance. It's seen as a problem rather than an opportunity (Speltz, 1990). With that in mind, parents in many training programs are taught to discount or overlook verbal protests by the child and to employ isolation (time-out) to discourage ongoing protest.[14] The emphasis, pure and simple, is on compliance training to the exclusion of teaching negotiation skills (Speltz). Sadly, the parent and child are not taught to discuss and negotiate issues regarding separation, rules, and differing goals. However, in our approach we address this issue head-on. Some foster and adoptive parents have the expectation that children should obey, conform, and comply without protest and negotiation, which may be regarded as whiney complaining or back talk. Without learning about the importance of partnership and negotiation and with over-reliance on demanding strict compliance, these parents may miss golden opportunities to help the child develop negotiation skills. These parents do not learn about the importance of interpersonal cooperation and the limitations of simple compliance.

When addressing negotiation skills, we teach the parents to gauge how, as half of a dyad with their child, they are capable of reciprocal

---

[14] In our own approach to parent training and mental health consultation social learning is part of an eclectic, synergistic approach.

influence. Does the parent allow the child to exert any control in their relationship (Speltz, 1990)? Also the parent may need to be exquisitely sensitive to when the child is failing to negotiate and press for meeting of needs within a relationship.

The negative working model renders the foster or adopted child skeptical of his ability to negotiate with caregivers for the purpose of meeting his needs or goals. A host of problems ensue when the child feels that parents can or will not help him meet his needs, and when he feels that he is powerless to get them to help him. Table 6.6 is a list of immature/maladaptive behaviors along with corresponding mature/functional behaviors related to either verbalization of feelings or attempts at negotiation or skills in negotiation. Foster and adoptive parents with parent training and mental health consultation are instructed to look for what is missing in the child's repertoire or in their usual interactions, especially with adults.

Foster and adoptive children who lack self-esteem and a sense of efficacy within relationships, who have failed to develop a sense of partnership, and who do not have the skill or willingness to negotiate often resort to the immature/maladaptive behaviors listed in Table 6.6. The mental health professional needs to teach and consult with the foster or adoptive parents to identify which negotiations do *not* occur. The mental health professional can help the parents see that the problematic child often employs strategies which are indirect, while missing the usual opportunities that non-abused children take to influence their parents, to make their needs known, and to gain positive attention from parents. Two productive suggestions for sensitizing parents to a child's lack of negotiation attempts and skills are (1) to ask them to recall other children they've raised who had/have rudimentary negotiation skills and were appropriately assertive; then, to contrast that child against the problematic child and his lack of negotiation; and (2) to point out times and places during the day with their child when the parents' and child's goals typically diverge or clash (e.g., the child is asked to get dressed for school, the child is asked to entertain himself, and the child is asked to wait his turn for parental attention); then to invite the parents to track whether the child says how he feels and negotiates what he wants.

Whenever there are differences in goals, the child should be expected to feel frustrated. It's important for the parents to note if, how, and when the child expresses that frustration. Again, the absence of expressed frustration may not be a good sign. Any child who cannot or

BEHAVIORS RELATED TO NEGOTIATION	
IMMATURE/MALADAPTIVE	MATURE/FUNCTIONAL
Smiling compliance	Child asserts that he doesn't want to.
Failure to complain	Child states that he doesn't like it.
Absence of protest	Child claims that it's unfair.
Lack of verbalization of anger	Child vocalizes that he is angry.
Rote acceptance	Child disagrees with the caregiver.
Lack of affect/ostensible indifference	Child shows spontaneous feeling in response to something he does not want to do.
No begging or questioning	Child asks and persists in asking.
No persuasion	Child tries to convince parent with words.
Missing overt statement of opinion	Child shares thoughts and beliefs with caregiver.
Failure to assertively go for what they want	Child asserts his goal and his plan.
Secret and solitary behaviors	Child is not afraid to be himself.
Temper tantrums	Child verbalizes his anger.
Pouting	Child verbalizes his anger.
Rolling of eyes in disapproval	Child verbalizes his anger.

TABLE 6.6

does not openly assert his need for a parent's undivided and/or uninterrupted attention, for example, may resort to bad behavior to exert control over the parent's time and focus. Also, the child who complies habitually and reflexively in situations where other age-mates would predictably grouse or wheedle may resort to clandestine ways to meet needs. In situations where children lack faith in negotiations with caregivers based upon history, foster and adoptive parents may need training and consultation to permit and encourage a healthy negotiation process with the child.

APPLYING NEGOTIATION TOOLS TO MAGGIE

LYING: While lying should not be condoned and may need to be addressed with contingencies (see Teaching Parents About Approaches to Social Learning earlier in this chapter), parents need to realize that Maggie can be taught to assert honest feelings and thoughts and to negotiate for what she wants. The emphasis should be on inviting, prompting, and rewarding Maggie for pushing for the meeting of her goals. If she passively complies or acquiesces without putting forth what she wants and what her goals are, she is choosing the secret and solitary approach to meeting needs. Essentially she remains self-parenting.

STEALING: Parents need to be instructed about the need for Maggie to ask for (even pester and demand) what she wants from adults. Children from normal backgrounds can badger quite effectively. While caving into whiney children serves little purpose, teaching compulsively compliant children how to bargain, negotiate, and perhaps achieve some of what they want, can be beneficial.

FOOD STEALING AND HOARDING: Parents can be taught about the system of giving Maggie some control over food intake, selection of food items, occasional snacks, etc. She may need to learn to negotiate around food issues by being encouraged to ask for second helpings and to develop a menu of favorite foods.

RUNNING AWAY: If Maggie's running off functions to gain contact with a busy or otherwise involved parent, emphasis should be placed on negotiating for attention. One family gave a child coupons redeemable for attention, which empowered the child to gain attention by presenting the chit to the parent. At that point, if the parent was occupied, the parent at least took some time to make an appointment to connect with the child. This is the essence of a goal-corrected partnership.

AGGRESSIVE BEHAVIOR TOWARD YOUNGER CHILDREN: Given her lack of normal, expectable push-back, assertion, protest, and negotiation (and her ostensible compulsive-compliance), Maggie is bottled up and displaces onto targets from which she fears no retaliation. Again, parents need to see the importance of identifying the negative feelings their child has toward them and then encourage the child to identify those feelings. Together they can work toward negotiating solutions openly and perhaps reduce the source of anger in the process.

OVER-DEPENDENCY: Parents can be instructed that Maggie does not use age-appropriate ways to establish connection and negotiate for more attention, so she must "ask" for it in unrelenting, behavioral fashion (see Running Away above).

BEDTIME PROBLEMS: Maggie could be encouraged to help develop a bedtime routine that would be more reassuring to her. Parents could be instructed to negotiate with Maggie about what could make her feel more comfortable at bedtime. Maggie might need more parent involvement but is unable or unwilling to express it. This need could be negotiated and addressed if it were out in the open.

PARENTAL BEHAVIOR: Foster parents need to be informed that some historic behavior cannot simply be expunged. There may be some harmless ways to retain some parts of the parental role. The parents could negotiate with Maggie, allowing her to provide some non-hurtful caregiving to other children. They could also negotiate a procedure in which Maggie would first consult with the parents before rushing into parental behavior. Parents could negotiate a role with Maggie which engages her as a "deputized assistant" to them.

FAKE BEHAVIOR AND COMPULSIVE AGREEMENT: Foster parents may need to be instructed to see these behaviors as less desirable alternatives to healthy negotiation and assertiveness. When Maggie reflexively agrees, the parent could point it out to her and help Maggie come up with what she wants and give input into the parents' decision.

POOR EYE CONTACT: Foster parents can be taught that when Maggie averts her gaze, she might be failing to vocalize displeasure or disagreement or to provide input to the parent, instead she is passive-aggressively checking out. Foster parents may need to learn how to teach Maggie to vocalize such remarks as "I don't like that" or "I don't want to," honest expressions which can potentially launch the whole negotiation process. Parents could be taught to respond to the honest statement of displeasure with comments such as, "Let's talk about what you don't like," or "What would you rather do?"

PROMOTING POSITIVE ENCOUNTERS

Maltreated foster children often send mixed messages to foster parents about caregiving. Some behaviors discourage parent involvement. That is, they do not permit the parents to have positive encounters with their children. Negative behaviors, i.e., conduct problems, invite increases in parenting, caregiving, negative attention, etc. That is, the parent feels instinctively protective, alarmed, or displeased by the foster child's conduct problems and is drawn toward intervening as caregiver but often negatively or even punitively. For instance, when the child steals, the parent feels compelled to confront, investigate, question the child, seek out the truth, obtain an apology, express his disappointment in the child, and mete out consequences for the misdeed. Thus, the stealing heightens parental involvement, though it may be negative. Indeed, many of the maltreated child's conduct problems seem to coerce (see discussion of C3 child) or insure a certain, perhaps constant, level of negative attention from caregivers. Sometimes parents see this as the child engaging in a "power struggle" with them or in the child being a "control freak." Sadly, the relationship with the child is viewed as a battleground—a struggle over who will be in charge of the child's life. This interpretation of the problem as a "control battle," while not totally inaccurate, may set the stage for the family to preclude the child from having any control or say-so in his world. Some parents report to me that they have been advised by attachment therapists to insist that the child surrender control to them in all matters. Unfortunately, this perpetuates the struggle and defines the nature of the relationship in ways that are very familiar to the child. And for the parents, it defines the child's behavior negatively, rather than as a pathway the child has been on to survive. Essentially, mental health consultation and parent training efforts should be directed at improving a positive "secure base" that the parent offers the child and interesting the child in using that secure base (O'Connor & Zeanah, 2003). Children from maltreatment backgrounds often do not know how to utilize the foster or adoptive parent as a source of security, or they have used conduct problems to achieve some sense of engagement with the parent figure, and correspondingly, some modicum of security. This sets the stage for very few positive encounters. Simply put, it can leave the child mired in the past and can take the fun out of parenting.

With some attachment-disordered children, positives connote something threatening or unfamiliar. Reading the child's behavior sensitively can allow the parent to gauge when the child is open to positives, how much positive interacting the child can accept, what manner of positive interaction the child can tolerate, and how to recognize times and circumstances when the child is relatively open to positive interaction. Ironically, the child may perceive positive, nurturing, harmonious interactions with parent figures as frighteningly alien and unacceptable.

When conflicts permeate almost every aspect of a parent-child relationship, the parent may need to be asked by the mental health professional to step back from the struggle and insert caregiving to the child that involves positive surprises, which can allow for an altering of the child's working model.

APPLYING POSITIVE-ENCOUNTER TOOLS TO MAGGIE

LYING: Instead of asking Maggie about homework, parents might take a holiday from cross-examination and not even mention homework or school. If school problems and homework have become the total focus of family time, parents may need to consider relinquishing school problems to the school. This might permit some positive, relaxing, rewarding exchanges with the child at home.

STEALING: Foster parents can be taught to see Maggie's stealing as potentially a way of staying connected with them while at school. They might then proactively provide Maggie with items to take to school which keep her connected to the home (this might also involve negotiation); she may then feel less like "stealing" these items. Rather than punishing her for taking things, the parent's role can be changed to allow more positive encounters with Maggie, e.g., arranging ways for her to feel less anxious about being separated from them during the school day.

FOOD STEALING AND HOARDING: The foster parents can be coached to provide Maggie with a backpack filled with wholesome food items which she can port wherever she goes to reassure her about availability. By including an inventory in the backpack and regularly checking the contents against the inventory list, the parent is less of a policeman and more a supplier. This rearranges the dynamics from Maggie's being anxiously (i.e., negatively) concerned about food availability to the foster parents' taking on a reassuring, providing (i.e., positive) role.

AGGRESSIVE BEHAVIOR: Teaching the parents that it is desirable and preferable to have Maggie vocalize negative affect toward them may allow the parents to appreciate her fledgling attempts at assertion around them. The parents' allowance of some dialogue and disagreement can reduce Maggie's tendency to displace onto weak targets, such as small children and pets.

OVER-DEPENDENCY: Parents may be taught the possible benefits of providing Maggie with one-on-one time proactively. Parents can supply Maggie with a walkie-talkie with which she can experiment with "distance contact." It can be reassuring to Maggie for the parents to initiate some of the contact.

BEDTIME PROBLEMS: Parents can receive information about separation anxiety and how it can be reduced with rituals, blankies, baby monitors, and sometimes a pet. Maggie's separation anxiety might be reduced with a baby monitor. These parenting tips might allow them to end their day on a positive note.

PARENTAL BEHAVIOR: Instructing parents about allowing or salvaging some part of the parental role can reduce negativity and frustration toward Maggie. Some children, like Maggie, benefit when they are asked to be assistants to the parent. If Maggie insists on remaining the parent, the parents might be coached to pay her for parental behavior she historically would have freely provided. This may externalize the rewards and incidentally point out to Maggie how widespread her parenting is. Parents should also refrain from criticizing Maggie's parenting. After a month, monetary rewards should be terminated. Children, once paid, often do not enjoy unremunerated duties as much.

FAKE BEHAVIOR AND COMPULSIVE AGREEMENT: Parents may benefit from instruction in how fake behavior and compulsive agreement might be unhealthy and that encouragement of genuine expression of emotion may be necessary. Parents, with a slight attitude adjustment, can express pride in Maggie's occasional approximations of real emotion and noncompliance.

POOR EYE CONTACT: Parents may need to learn that eye contact happens more easily with some children when you are laughing with them. Forcing eye contact should be kept to a minimum.

In general, parent training and mental health consultation should focus on reducing the stress of constant conflict with the child. It should emphasize interventions by the parent that keep interactions upbeat and positive wherever possible.

Parent and family impact on the child is preeminent. Essentially, the core of intervention with a formerly maltreated child is the foster, kinship, or adoptive family environment. However, families can get caught up in patterns that simply reinforce and perhaps maintain conduct problems. An example of this is the family whose adopted son, under constant surveillance because of his misbehavior over the past five years, has now developed a pattern which he is as used to is he is ostensibly opposed to. Sadly, the parents and child can become locked into negativity. It's important in our parent training and mental health consultation to stress that discipline must be judicious. Parents need to be advised to stay realistic in their expectations for change in their child and in how much control they attempt to gain over the child. Friedrich (2002) emphasizes with parents the centrality of "sensitivity." The goals are "to enhance the sensitivity of the caregiver, to provide the child with more control rather than less, to reduce caregivers' expectations for rapid change (and encourage acceptance of the child's basic temperament and personality), to unlink contingencies between the child's behavior and his or her perceived permanency within the family, and to emphasize reinforcement and positive exchanges of affection (when the child wants it) rather than punitive consequences that tend to erode the quality of family relationships" (Friedrich).

As discussed in chapter five, foster and adopted children with attachment issues can have measurable, negative impact on parent figures (and on other family members), who often respond in predictable, and perhaps negative, fashion. Yet, when it comes to helping the child, the foster or adoptive parents can be the greatest helpers. In fact, there may be no superior or more radical intervention for such children than living in the non-abusive, nurturing home of the foster or adoptive family (Sroufe et al., 2002).

TEACHING PARENTS ABOUT THEMSELVES

The foster or adoptive parent as a sensitive and reliable caregiver has the potential to reduce the child's insecurities and to influence the child's negative working model (Delaney & Kunstal, 1997). It is important, then, for parent training and mental health consultation to focus on the foster and adoptive parents, their manner of caregiving, and on the issues that impact their caregiving (Speltz, 1990). In our experience it can be helpful to introduce three parent-specific topics into parent training and mental health consultation: 1) the foster or adoptive parents' own attachment issues; 2) the foster or adoptive parents' predominant parenting style; and 3) common foster parent responses, myths, and missteps.

THE FOSTER OR ADOPTIVE PARENTS' OWN ATTACHMENT ISSUES

While studies have demonstrated that the birth parent or original caregivers of children with attachment issues may have their own unresolved attachment-related trauma (Main & Solomon, 1990), little attention has been paid to "issues" of the foster and adoptive parents and how they might relate to parenting (Speltz, 1990).[15]

In talking with parents about their own attachment issues, we typically discuss their relationships to significant individuals in their life, past and present. We often discuss with them the "echoes" from their own past that might be activated by or become embroiled with their child's attachment issues. We also speak candidly, but non-judgmentally, about how their own attachment issues might exacerbate their child's insecurities.

In discussing attachment issues, we typically share with foster and adoptive parents a portion of a chapter entitled "The Cost to Parents and Families" from *Small Feats: The Everyday Heroics of Foster and*

---

[15] Beyond educating the foster and adoptive parents about how their expectations and conclusions about attachment-related issues impact the way they parent their children, it is crucial to instruct parents about family-systems issues which influence their foster or adoptive child or vice versa. Some attachment researchers contend that a complete understanding of attachment must examine attachment in the context of family (Marvin & Stewart, 1990). We will limit our focus here to parents, although it often is essential to work with the entire family system or with individual family members in eductional and therapeutic ways. See *Healing Power of the Family*, Delaney (1997) for how to maximize work with troubled children.

Adoptive Parents (Delaney, 2003). This chapter, among other things, discusses several attachment-related issues that impinge on parenting. These include infertility issues; attachment relationships with their own parents; relationships to their siblings; unresolved developmental issues; significant losses; and exposure to abuse. We also discuss with them the highlights of chapter five's section entitled, "How Foster and Adoptive Parents' Own Attachment Issues Affect Their Response to the Troubled Child" (p. 59).

APPLYING PARENT ISSUES TO MAGGIE

LYING: Maggie's parents may feel that lying undermines the basis of all closeness to the child. It offends their belief that truth and trust are the bedrock of family and other close relationships. This may suggest that the parent needs an overly close relationship which Maggie cannot handle. Her deceit may keep her at a safe distress from her foster parents. While it is important to teach children to tell the truth, feeling demolished by their ongoing lies may indicate a certain naiveté or neediness in the parent.

STEALING: Maggie's parents may feel threatened by her demands on them, and they may discourage her from begging, pleading, and arguing for what she wants. Squelching that tendency across the board can drive Maggie to secret and solitary behaviors, which suggest that she does not believe she can have her way around adults. The parents' expectation about verbal expression of feeling and negotiation are crucial to focus upon. Although it is important not to simply let kids have their way all the time, if they feel it never serves any purpose to express what they want, they will "go underground" to get their needs met.

FOOD STEALING AND HOARDING: Maggie's parents may feel threatened by food stealing because it constitutes an avoidance of themselves as the "source of all nurturing." This can result in the parents' locking food away and perpetuating the child's sense that the insensitive, stingy parents have their own cache of food which is guarded jealously.

AGGRESSIVE BEHAVIOR: If Maggie's adoptive parents abhor conflict and appropriate expression of anger by themselves, by their mate, and by their children, they may unrealistically squelch any verbalized dissent, which can drive Maggie toward more behavioral, aggressive outlets.

OVER-DEPENDENCY: Some foster and adoptive parents, e.g., Maggie's parents, feel that their role is to keep the child moving forward developmentally at all costs. Regression, backsliding, and dependency are discouraged and unappreciated. Parents who disapprove of the child's immaturity and neediness can compound the problem by forging ahead.

BEDTIME PROBLEMS: Maggie's parents may send mixed signals to her at bedtime, and they may suffer from their own separation issues. This can exacerbate normal levels of bedtime problems into full-blown crises.

PARENTAL BEHAVIOR: If Maggie's adoptive mother feels threatened by and competitive toward her, especially when it comes to parenting the other children, she may guard her place as mother in the home at all costs. This puts the mother at odds with Maggie, a child who has an equally strong need to parent.

FAKE BEHAVIOR AND COMPULSIVE AGREEMENT: Maggie's adoptive mother did not dislike the compulsive compliance and agreement, nor did she view that as a problem. (At the same time, she found Maggie's "fakey" behavior distasteful.) If a parent is unaware that compulsive agreement or compliance might not be healthy for a child (and perhaps if they have A3 tendencies themselves), mental health consultation and training may need to address the parent's discomfort with negative affect.

POOR EYE CONTACT: While poor eye contact bothered Maggie's adoptive mother, she did not make the connection between the need for expression of feelings and poor eye contact.

As you can see below, parent issues can collide with issues the child demonstrates. Indeed, in parent training and consultation parents can be instructed about how their own expectations and issues can interact in significant ways with the child's problems.

THE FOSTER OR ADOPTIVE PARENTS' PREDOMINANT PARENTING STYLE

Another approach to parent training and mental health consultation is to discuss with the parents the impact they have on their foster or adopted child related specifically to their parenting style.[16] The task of pinning down their style permits exploring parental attitudes and expectations for themselves and their children. It can further lead to discussion of what parents feel a good parent is. Coincidentally, it may lead to discovery of expectations of what a good child is and what his role is. Essentially, a focus on parenting style helps us to identify the parent's own relevant working models. Very few parents spend time analyzing what kind of parenting style they have, and yet it may be helpful for them to know their predominant style and how it may relate to their children's development (Baumrind, 1995). Here are four styles which we allude to in teaching parents[17]:

1. ENGAGED AND AUTHORITATIVE: The engaged and authoritative parenting style involves parents who are both demanding and yet responsive. We explain that this may be the most effective parenting approach.

2. UNENGAGED, NEGLECTING, AND REJECTING: The unengaged, neglecting, and rejecting parenting style describes parents who are neither demanding nor responsive.

3. RESTRICTIVE AND AUTHORITARIAN: The restrictive and authoritarian parenting style involves parents who are demanding but not responsive.

4. LENIENT AND PERMISSIVE: The lenient and permissive parenting style involves parents who are responsive but not demanding.

Overall, parents are asked to rate which style they most closely ally with or resemble. Some will, understandably, see themselves as a mix. Others will be somewhat lost in trying to self-evaluate. Sometimes it is helpful at this point to discuss two central factors related to the four types of parenting styles: demandingness and responsiveness.

Demandingness in parenting means firm discipline and monitoring of children's behavior. Parents who are demanding directly confront rather than manipulate and thus, they might incur open disagreement. These demanding parents also closely monitor and supervise their children and expect a lot from their children.

---

[16] The purpose of this training is not to sow doubt or to allow parents to wallow in self-recrimination. So many foster and adoptive parents already feel blamed by professionals for causing their child's pre-existing problems.

[17] Since these Baumrind (1995) terms for parenting style are not "user friendly," we often use the following labels in their place: 1) warm and structured, 2) seen but not heard, 3) my way or the highway, and 4) warm but undemanding. We also explain parenting styles in common language the parents can relate to better.

Responsiveness in parents includes affective warmth and empathy, "high-investment parenting of the child and taking into account the wishes and feelings of the child" (Baumrind, 1995).

As might be expected, consulting with and teaching foster and adoptive parents about themselves can, at times, be tricky. The therapist needs to establish rapport with the parents and gauge carefully if, when, and how to introduce the subject of their own issues (as they relate to the child). Sometimes dealing with parenting styles that are observable can be less threatening to the parent than immediate probing of his/her working models and attachment issues.

COMMON FOSTER AND ADOPTIVE PARENT RESPONSES, MYTHS AND MISSTEPS

The third topic for parent training and mental health consultation focuses upon common foster and adoptive parent responses (see chapter five), myths (Delaney, 2000), and missteps. We typically explain the foster or adoptive parent responses by covering several hallmark responses from our work (Delaney, 1997). Parents are also instructed in the myths or misconceptions they might have related to caregiving the foster or adoptive child, especially if they are neophytes. We discuss myths such as "love is enough," i.e., the expectation that all the child needs is a parent's love, and "the past is behind us," i.e., historic issues do not impact the present and future course of the child. We also discuss common missteps made by foster and adoptive parents raising a troubled child. This commonly brings up four subtopics.

1. Foster and adoptive parents need to be instructed that the urge to normalize the child can conflict with how ready the child is to become normal.

2. Setting up unrealistic expectations, such as expecting the child to speak with impeccable truthfulness immediately after placement, can frustrate both child and parent.

3. Some adoptive families are simply too intrusive with newly adopted children. For example, some parents may expect their child to quickly engage in discussions of their emotional and psychological status or to respond favorably to physical affection within weeks or months of adoption. Some experts advise patience and a desensitization approach, in which intimacy on various levels is approached slowly, in a step-wise fashion with the child in control of the pace (Friedrich, 2002).

4. Foster and adoptive parents can take misbehavior too personally. Understanding the child's patterns, developmental path, and strategies (which often served survival needs) can provide parents with a historic perspective that relieves pressure. Additionally, knowledge and inquisitiveness can be an antidote to taking things too personally.

In sum, it's important for parents to receive training on the fact that their response to children's behavior problems may be based upon more than the child's conduct alone (Speltz, 1990). That is, it might relate to their own attachment issues, parenting styles, myths, and missteps.

CONCLUDING REMARKS

Parent training and mental health consultation is predicated on the notion that the foster, kinship, or adoptive family provides the milieu for positive changes in children's lives. Training and consultation need to focus on helping the parents understand and engage the child in the most productive fashion possible by teaching parents how to reinterpret conduct problems; educating parents about social learning approaches; instructing parents to increase the child's verbalization of the underlying negative working model and to allow the child to negotiate differences; advising parents about how to increase positive encounters between themselves and the child; and consulting with the parents about their own issues, parenting styles, and potential missteps.

7 REACTIVE ATTACHMENT DISORDER AND ATTACHMENT THERAPIES

"Complex problems have simple, easy to understand, wrong answers."
—H. L. Menken

If you are a mental health professional or a professional helper of children and families, you undoubtedly have treated children who have been diagnosed with RAD. You yourself may have diagnosed children with that label. Chances are you have been made aware of the growing backlash against the proliferation of the RAD diagnosis and the promulgation of a harsh and potentially dangerous subset of attachment therapies. You may have pondered the vast difference between the official RAD symptoms spelled out in the DSM-IV and the ubiquitous "unofficial" RAD symptoms found on the Internet and in select writings of a subgroup of attachment therapists (see chapter three).

If you are a foster, kinship, or adoptive parent, you have almost certainly heard of the diagnosis of RAD (Reactive Attachment Disorder). You may have a child or children who carry that diagnosis. What you may not be aware of is the raging controversy about the diagnosis. Therapists and parents alike have frequently heard about Reactive Attachment Disorder, but may be uninformed about the swelling controversy about maverick, coercive attachment therapies. A recent task force on the issue lamented, "Although criticism of the controversial attachment therapies has been widespread in mainstream professional and scientific circles, efforts to disseminate these criticisms and concerns to the lay public have been minimal, and most foster or adoptive parents are probably unaware of the risks and poor foundation for some treatment claims" (Chaffin et al., 2006). The experts on attachment theory and the RAD diagnosis are alarmed about the "misuse and overuse" of the diagnosis. What's more, they are opposed in no uncertain terms to the simplistic, potentially dangerous forms of therapy proposed by a subgroup of "attachment therapists" who use coercive approaches[1] (Chaffin et al.; Friedrich, 2002; O'Connor & Zeanah, 2003).

---

[1] Controversies have emerged related to a coterie, circle, or subgroup of attachment therapists who employ a subset of scientifically unproven, possibly hazardous techniques or treatments involving coercion.

Attachment therapy, which is unclearly defined and about which there is no clear agreement as to definition, is an infant field and encompasses a wide variety of approaches. While some of the approaches are controversial, discredited, and even banned in some states, "not all attachment-related interventions are controversial" (Chaffin et al., 2006). These noncontroversial interventions, grounded in traditional, mainstream attachment theory, utilize approaches which are widely approved and focus on improving caregiver sensitivity and responsiveness to the child. They provide safety, stability, predictability, nurturing, and patience. They emphasize improving the caregiver-child relationship and increasing caregiver-child encounters that are central to aiding the attachment process and improving the quality of attachment relationships between the child and caregiver.

This chapter focuses on the following topics:

1. The RAD Controversy

2. The Proliferation of the RAD Diagnosis

3. Pronouncements Against the Use of Holding Therapies

4. A Laundry List of Symptoms from the Unofficial RAD Diagnosis

5. The Lack of Research on RAD and Extreme Coercive Therapies

6. The Disconnect Between a Subgroup of Controversial Attachment Therapists and Attachment Research

7. Promising Treatment Approaches

8. Sympathy for Foster, Kinship, and Adoptive Parents

THE RAD CONTROVERSY

The diagnosis of Reactive Attachment Disorder has stirred up a hor-net's nest in the mental health and social services fields. With the increased use of the RAD label over the past decade, has come a growing controversy and debate over what RAD is, how to treat it (Chaffin et al., 2006; Hanson, 2002), and how to view attachment therapy.[2] The controversy has been heightened, of course, by the deaths to and injury of children treated by a subgroup of controversial attachment therapists. The Houston Chronicle (Sowers, 1997) listed the sensational, tragic cases wherein holding therapy was employed. A Web site targeting attachment therapists essentially as "quacks" lists therapists they believe use "bad science" to justify their dubious, coercive, maverick treatments of children purported to have

RAD. Importantly, thoughtful, respected leaders in the field of attachment study have a growing concern that the RAD label will lead to a "backlash" against the children carrying that label. Indeed, in clinical practice, I have seen grave reluctance by therapists to treat children alleged to have RAD.

To date, there has been little formal, concerted opposition to the subset of radical attachment therapies. Legislation attempting to control the practice has been passed in only one state, Colorado, considered by some to be the epicenter of attachment therapies.

This chapter on the RAD controversy is not intended to undermine the many foster and adoptive parents raising children with serious and severe emotional and behavioral problems. These parents, and the professionals who attempt to help them and the children, contend with the most difficult children in our "system of care" (Friedrich, 2002). As I have pointed out in other publications, society has, in essence, asked foster and adoptive parents to provide a "psychiatric children's hospital without walls," often with little support and guidance. Additionally, the dearth of adoption-competent or foster care-competent mental health services to support the parents in their job of helping and raising their disturbed children is an inexcusable, nationwide problem. This lack of specially trained mental health professionals contributes to the desperation of foster and adoptive parents looking for a solution to the problems of raising disturbed children.

THE PROLIFERATION OF THE RAD DIAGNOSIS

Over the past decade, there has been an upsurge in the use and misuse of the diagnosis of RAD, which has been used to depict a broad range of conduct problems and faulty relationships between children

---

[2] Controversial attachment therapies include any approaches which involve coercive tactics, such as physical and emotional provocation of a child, aversive tickling, extreme isolation of the child, total control of the child's needs by the parent(s), emphasis on the child's complete submission and surrender, holding therapy, and/or rebirthing approaches. These controversial attachment therapies often base their approach upon rage theory, an unsupported theory decidedly unrelated to mainstream attachment theory and research. In this chapter, I refer to these alarming, unrecommended therapies as a "subset" of controversial, maverick, radical, non-scientific, or coercive attachment therapists. These controversial therapies should not be confused with the positive efforts of therapists who base their attachment work on mainstream attachment theory and sound research.

and caregivers (Hanson, 2002). The upsurge or proliferation is very disconcerting, since, for one thing, it is being incorrectly applied to older children, teenagers, and even adults, though RAD is a disorder of infants and young children. Also, the unofficial RAD diagnosis with its laundry list of symptoms has become a huge umbrella covering multiple diagnoses. Zeanah (2002) stated that "the (RAD) diagnosis tends to be made whenever maltreatment is known or suspected in the history of a child referred for psychiatric problems, although this is only one of several criteria required for diagnosis." This knee-jerk diagnosis of a child with RAD is often unhelpful and inaccurate, and it unfairly saddles a child with a label that follows him around—once a RAD child, always a RAD child, is the common misconception. It also frightens families from taking a child into their home, given the fear that this child could become "the next Ted Bundy."

RAD, in its official diagnosis, is "one of the least researched and most poorly understood disorders in the DSM-IV... the incidence rates and course of RAD is not well established" (Chaffin et al., 2006). Overlap with other disorders can lead to diagnostic confusion. There is much overlap with PTSD, conduct disorder, autism, and PDD, as well as some genetic syndromes and odd social habits associated with institutional care. The APSAC task force cautions, "It should not be assumed that RAD underlies all or even most of the behavioral and emotional problems seen in foster children, adoptive children, or children who are maltreated.... Several much more common and demonstrably treatable diagnoses—with substantial research evidence linking them to a history of maltreatment—may better account for many of these difficulties... RAD is presumed to be very uncommon" (Chaffin et al.). Some of the issues which are thought to be attachment issues may arise more from stress, transitory after-effects of abuse, transition among and between placements, and cultural issues.

The APSAC task force warns professionals: "Attachment-related problems may be under-diagnosed, over-diagnosed, or both simultaneously... there are no studies examining diagnostic accuracy among the increasing numbers of children who are maltreated being described by clinicians as having an attachment disorder.... A child described as having RAD may actually fail to meet formal diagnostic criteria for the disorder, and consequently, the label should be viewed cautiously" (Chaffin et al., 2006).

The unofficial RAD diagnosis (described in chapter three) includes characteristics of the child (e.g., antisocial behavior, disordered eating, counterfeit emotions, problems with eye contact, toileting problems, etc.) which stray significantly from the official DSM-IV diagnosis. On the face of it, the unofficial RAD diagnosis has a strong appeal because it "captures" the characteristics widely seen in maltreated children. Friedrich (2002) comments, "This may explain why many adoptive parents are attracted to the promise of intensive attachment therapies; they make the understandable assumption that a therapist who can so accurately describe (diagnose) their child should be able to effectively treat the child as well." Unfortunately, there is not factual basis for this describe-to-treat assumption.

While there is much to be gained by using attachment theory to understand children who come from horrific, traumatic backgrounds, the unfortunate overuse and misuse of the RAD diagnosis undermines the credibility of attachment theory (Sroufe et al., 2002). Additionally, the overuse and misuse of the RAD diagnosis labels children with a condition seen by some as virtually untreatable, incurable, or only treatable by a special cadre (i.e., subgroup) of controversial attachment therapists who employ coercive approaches.[3]

PRONOUNCEMENTS AGAINST THE USE OF HOLDING THERAPIES

Serious researchers and bona fide experts on attachment state that we have a very perplexing and alarming situation occurring with RAD. While they sympathize with foster and adoptive parents who are raising and struggling with seriously troubled children, they witness that these parents are being mislead by the (false) promise of controversial attachment therapists that espouse unsupported rage theories and coercive therapies, including holding therapy.[4] Sroufe et al. (2002), one of the leading attachment researchers, asserts: "I am especially concerned about doing anything with these children that replicates a cycle of violence and control, poking and prodding until the child submits." O'Connor & Zeanah (2003) add: "Clearly, these approaches have no role in the treatment of children and cannot be justified on any basis."

---

[3] "Practitioners working with children who are maltreated must be vigilant to avoid what some have called the 'allure of rare disorders' (Haugaard, 2004a). Mental health and related fields have a long history of diagnostic fads, when rare or esoteric diagnoses become fashionable and spread rapidly through the practice world, support groups, and the popular press.... It is important not to diagnose an uncommon and dramatic disorder when the diagnosis of a common but less exciting disorder is more appropriate" (Chaffin et al., 2006).

Recognized experts in the attachment field assert categorically that holding therapy and its permutations are *not* therapeutic, are punishing and must never be used. They also come out against the "boot camp" parenting approach which enshrines "commanding respect" and unquestioning compliance.[5] Foster, adoptive, and kinship parents should turn a jaundiced eye on those who would exhort them and train them to be "drill sergeant" parents who force compliance through practices like performance of heavy chores, or withholding of food. Our approach as outlined in the previous chapters emphasizes increased sensitivity, understanding of function, the importance of negotiation, and partnership. Partnership is, in our estimation, superior to capitulation or total compliance.

One program, labeled "Basic German Shepherd," suggests a sit down, lie down, roll-over-and-play-dead approach. The name connotes denigration of children from unfortunate backgrounds. Arguably, this type of insensitive parenting replicates the dictatorial backgrounds of abuse from which the children come. While there is great merit for children, disturbed and undisturbed, to have humane, reasonable rules, structure, guidance, and predictability, lock-step compliance training is not advisable. The attitude of "when I say 'jump,' you ask how high on the way up" smacks of Paris Island rather than loving firmness. "Professionals who utilize such approaches are modeling the appropriateness of coercion to often desperate parents using their service. Sadly, the boot camp approach 'licenses' parents to act in kind" (Friedrich, 2002). Foster and adoptive children deserve better from professionals than the

---

[4] Holding therapy includes "coercive, restraining, or aversive procedures such as... aversive tickling... enforced eye contact... requiring children to submit totally to adult control over all their needs... reparenting... or techniques designed to provoke cathartic emotional discharges." Holding therapies and other coercive approaches are not representative of the range of interventions and aproaches used by therapists guided by attachment theory and research. "Attachment therapies that seek to demonstrate dominance and control over the child may duplicate the dynamics of abuse experiences and reinforce rather than ameliorate relationship problems" (Chaffin et al., 2006).

[5] Supporters of rage theory may advise parents to use coercive "attachment parenting," analogous in many ways to coercive therapies, which include isolating the child, restricting social contacts, enforcing hard labor, time-outs where the child must not move, and restricting all food and beverage. In other words, the parent is in total charge. The emphasis is on total, unquestioning compliance with parental directives. "From this perspective, parenting a child with an attachment disorder is a battle, and winning the battle by defeating the child is paramount" (Chaffin et al., 2006).

non-empirical, coercive approaches being touted by some as the treatment of choice for RAD children.

One researcher points out a "strikingly manipulative quality" to the approach of the attachment therapies in terms of psychological interventions that have the potential to reduce the child's already delicate trust in the behavior of adults (Spletz, 2002). Speltz attests that "intensive attachment therapy" (e.g., controversial, coercive) may place the child at a high risk of emotional (or physical) injury and thus requires the highest levels of evidence justifying its use. He concludes that until such time that truly scientific study is done with randomized clinical trials of a well-specified coercive attachment or holding therapy, "it is both unethical and dangerous to involve a child in this form of treatment." The bottom line according to some experts is that controversial attachment therapies should be identified as invalidated treatment as well as potentially dangerous (Mercer, 2002). At this time no empirical evidence supports the assertion that such therapy is more effective, or even as effective, when compared with accepted, evidence-based approaches (Spletz).

A LAUNDRY LIST OF SYMPTOMS FROM THE UNOFFICIAL RAD DIAGNOSIS

Over the past 10 years, RAD has become a catchall, wastebasket diagnosis. If a child has a history of exposure to abuse, neglect, and/or sexual exploitation, and if the child is having serious emotional or behavioral problems, there's a good chance someone has given this child a diagnosis of RAD (Speltz, 2002). Although it is clearly and officially a diagnosis reserved for infants and young children, older children, adolescents, and even adults are labeled with RAD. Children with a host of severe emotional and behavioral challenges which probably are more accurately part of other syndromes are lumped under the RAD diagnosis. The APSAC task force asserts: "These types of lists are so nonspecific that high rates of false-positive diagnoses are virtually certain. Posting these types of lists on Web sites that also serve as marketing tools may lead many parents or others to conclude inaccurately that their children have attachment disorders" (Chaffin et al., 2006).

Previously or simultaneously, these children often have been diagnosed with one or all of a "short list" of psychiatric disorders, usually including RAD, ADHD/ODD, bipolar or mood disorder, PTSD, CD, or Autistic Spectrum Disorder. These diagnoses often more accurately reflect problems of the child and may have empirically based treatment interventions that could be used (Speltz).

THE LACK OF RESEARCH ON RAD AND EXTREME COERCIVE THERAPIES

Despite the widespread use of the diagnosis of RAD and controversial attachment therapies, there are currently no validated, objective measures of RAD, nor are any evidenced based treatments now available (Hanson, 2002; Speltz, 2002). More specifically, there is currently no reliable diagnosis of attachment disorder with proven validity, including the DSM-IV reactive attachment disorder (RAD). Statements that coercive attachment therapy is not only effective, but should be considered "best practice" for RAD are wild, unsupported claims. Overall, no evidence shows that these controversial, radical attachment therapies are more effective or even as effective as mainstream approaches. Speltz criticized three "quasi-experimental" studies of attachment therapy for glaring problems with design of the study and measurement of the symptoms. In one of the three studies, the greatest improvement occurred before therapy began, i.e., spontaneous remission of symptoms.

One of the most notable problems with the measurement of symptoms of RAD is that controversial, non-scientific attachment therapists assert that "the only valid measure of the symptoms of an attachment disorder is the mother's report" (Hanson, 2002). The hallmark sign of RAD is seen then as the child's ability to conceal emotional problems from even the most skilled clinicians, but to "behave with vicious hostility when alone with the mother." Additionally, there is no public confirmation of the mother's report and no assessment of the child's purported attachment problems in a variety of settings and with multiple caregivers (e.g., teachers, therapists, etc.), which is a requirement of the DSM-IV RAD diagnosis (Hanson).

THE DISCONNECT BETWEEN A SUBSET OF CONTROVERSIAL ATTACHMENT THERAPIES AND ATTACHMENT RESEARCH

Despite frequent assertions by maverick attachment therapists and their use of terms referencing attachment, no actual, proven connection exists between coercive attachment therapy and the attachment theory of John Bowlby (1982), the father of attachment theory (Speltz, 2002). Further, researchers have warned that the brand of "attachment therapy" promulgated by certain attachment centers is antithetical to attachment theory and research (Chaffin et al., 2006 ; Friedrich, 2002). Overall, it's not only the use and misuse of the RAD diagnosis, but the underlying "hydraulic theory" or rage theory (which justifies so-called "attachment therapies approach") that alarms researchers; one expert concluded that "the entire underlying rationale for the intervention is faulty" (Hanson, 2002).

There are a number of fundamental problems with the underlying rationale of attachment therapists:

1. Proponents of maverick, coercive "attachment therapy" are out of touch with attachment theory and research when referring to a child as "unattached" (Speltz, 2002). Children develop attachments, though the quality or type of attachment and corresponding strategies may differ. Sroufe et al. (2002), a leading expert on attachment, states about attachment, "It (attachment) is going to happen, although the form it takes may not be optimal to that child.... They're rejecting the caregiver before this individual has a chance to reject them; ultimately it becomes difficult for these children to engage positively with others."

2. A second problem with the underlying rationale is the hydraulic or rage theory approach to the psyche, which claims that a buildup of rage causes symptoms.[6] Consequently—the reasoning goes—therapy must result in a discharge of rage before the child can attach. Beverly James (1994) views coercive therapies advocating the "discharge of emotion" as an enormous obstacle to thinking accurately about therapy. The hydraulic view of the child puts the problems squarely

---

[6] Rage theory asserts that the attachment-disordered child's rage must be purged for the child to attach normally. Children with suppressed rage are seen as controlling, manipulating, dishonest, superficial, self-centered, resisting authority, and engaged in unrelenting power struggles. These children are described by supporters of these non-scientific theories as actively avoiding trusting attachment relationships and at high risk of becoming psychopaths, such as Jeffrey Dahmer. There is no data to support the dire prediction that children with attachment disorders develop into psychopathic personalities. This theory has spawned a variety of therapies with names such as "rage therapy," "rage reduction therapy," and "z therapy." They employ emotional and physical provocation to force the child to vent his/her anger. The emphasis is not placed on the present home or caregiver-child relationship but the view is that there is a "healthy family with a sick child." Emphasis then, is on the child's individual pathology and resistance which must be "broken down." It is important that parents are aware that there is little or no scientific support for rage theory or the concept of suppressed rage, which in short asserts that the child cannot attach to others because of pent-up anger interfering with the attachment process.

inside the child. Attachment experts voice concerns that use of rage therapy, z therapy, rage reduction therapy, and the like "suggest that the problem is inherent in the child, a highly individual notion that is in direct contrast to attachment as a relational process" (Friedrich, 2002).

3. A third problem with the controversial, maverick attachment therapy view is "recapitulation," i.e., the notion that it is possible to rewind or rework developmental sequence by redoing at a later time the stages the child did not complete in his earlier development. The statement that children are "developmentally arrested" or "stuck in the past" has no basis in developmental research. Children, as we pointed out earlier in this book, do not stop developing; rather, development takes different pathways, some of which are quite abnormal.

4. A fourth problem with the approach of maverick attachment therapists centers on the capitulation of the child to the therapist and parents (Speltz, 2002). Coercive approaches smack of "thought reform" and frankly brain washing, which may replicate the child's abusive past and finds no support in attachment theory/research. Speltz adds that the child needs a sense of more control, not giving over all control through surrender. In my own view, it is more important to teach cooperation than compliance.

5. The fifth and most daunting problem with radical attachment therapy is its tragic association with child deaths during therapy. Holding therapies carry with them serious risks of death and injury that are unacceptable given the existence of evidence-based approaches that carry much less risk. Speltz (2002) remarks: "Treatments that involve relatively higher levels of risk... are required to meet higher levels of scientific evidence (because of the probability of 'iatrogenic effect')." No data supports the use of controversial attachment therapy.

Over the past decade, radical attachment therapy has attempted to address some of the concerns, the disconnects between mainstream theory and research, and its radical approach to intervention. In his opinion, Speltz (2002) speculates that these more recent integrations of holding therapies with mainstream scientific work "largely represent a post hoc effort to legitimize highly controversial methods that would otherwise remain on the fringe of mental health treatment" (Speltz). Dozier (2003) also attests that, in the end, neither holding nor any other coercive therapies "emanate in any logical way from attachment theory or from attachment research... and they may subject the child to terrifying or traumatic conditions."

PROMISING TREATMENT APPROACHES

Importantly, treatment for severely disturbed foster and adoptive children should be preceded by a competent, objective, "multiple source" assessment of the child and family (Hanson, 2002). As a precondition of intervention, the child should be living in a safe home and have, within that home environment, consistency, predictability and control. Divesting a child of all sense of control is contrary to sensitive parenting. As seen in chapter six, treatment of children with severe emotional and behavioral problems should provide a combination of mental health consultation to the parents and parent training. Treatment interventions should include the foster or adoptive parents, who provide the most useful information about the child but also serve as the greatest catalyst for positive change—especially when equipped with tools such as contingency management (social learning approaches), an understanding of attachment principles, and negotiation skills. Parent training should focus upon enhancement of parental sensitivity to the child's cues and to the needs the child expresses in behavioral terms. Parent training that focuses on interpreting, (i.e., decoding) the meaning of conduct problems is essential (Speltz, 2002). As pointed out in the previous chapter, parents need to be better informed about how their own expectations and unresolved issues can compound the child's problems. With the number of common but challenging conduct problems often seen in foster and adoptive children (e.g., eating disorders, impulsivity) the mental health professional should draw from Cognitive Behavior Therapy (CBT) and Behavior Therapy (BT), which have shown great promise in helping children (Barkley, 1997; Gore, Vander Wal, & Thelan, 2001).

Of course, treatment should first address any homicidal, suicidal, or other behaviors dangerous to self or others. Treatment should attend to safety plans and reduction and management of any immediate crises that jeopardize placement or individuals (Hanson, 2002).

The mental health consultation and parent training should also focus upon unresolved traumatic events; PTSD is often left untreated (Friedrich, 2002). While assessing for attachment problems in the child is important, attachment theory does not provide all the answers. In my clinical experience, I have found that therapy should not get mired in the past, but should study past trauma and relate it to present functioning within the family.

Even when RAD is the correct, official diagnosis, it often is accompanied by PTSD, ADHD, CD, anxiety disorders, or compulsive disorders. When these disorders coexist with RAD, they may more accurately indicate core problems of the child; and they have evidence-based treatment approaches available for them (Friedrich, 2002). Emerging and promising practices include approaches that address the moderation of aggressive behavior (a huge issue in many foster and adoptive children), which is addressed by Webster-Stratton and Hammon (1997). In addition, approaches are available for issues related to the improvement of caregiver-child relationships (Marvin & Stewart, 1990). It's also crucial to obtain good medical and psychiatric care for children. Many of today's foster and adopted children are benefitting from psychotropic medications.

In general, working with severely troubled foster and adoptive children requires the use of an evidence-based, multi-modal approach, i.e., an eclectic but coordinated set of interventions. When specific approaches are not yet empirically proven, mental health providers should, at a minimum, strive toward the use of approaches which are informed by and compatible with research.

SYMPATHY FOR FOSTER, KINSHIP, AND ADOPTIVE PARENTS

Troubled foster and adopted children can tax even the most experienced parents, caseworkers, therapists, and other helping professionals. For many of the most severe youngsters, we simply do not have easy answers. There is no quick fix—no magic bullet. "To the extent that practitioners and caregivers recognize this fact, they will avoid novel treatments promising a quick cure" (Hanson, 2002). Unfortunately, many caregivers "are desperate for any intervention that promises rapid change (within days instead of months or years)" (Speltz, 2002).

One noted therapist stated, "Professionals who work with maltreated children know how challenging many of these children can be, whether in their birth homes, foster homes, or adoptive placements. I personally have found them among the most difficult children with whom I have ever attempted therapy (Friedrich, 2002)." In my 25 years of work with foster and adoptive parents, I have observed many devoted and skillful parents struggle mightily with their troubled children. They seek answers to the questions raised only by those living with severely disturbed children.

While I do not agree with the controversial, coercive attachment therapist approach to working with children and families, I have met many foster and adoptive parents who have felt very supported by these therapists. The apparent dedication of many of these therapists to the parents and to the child, unfortunately, is not matched by data to support their treatment approach. And yet the myth abounds that radical attachment therapies are the answer, the magic bullet. Parents will "seek out providers with convictions, even when the interventions these providers use pose grave potential risk" because they "feel unsupported within the current mental health system" (Boris, 2003). Admittedly, nondirective, individual therapy with children having severe emotional problems is rarely effective, especially when used as a solitary intervention, according to Speltz (2002).

CONCLUDING REMARKS

The take-away message of this chapter is that Reactive Attachment Disorder is a diagnosis shrouded in much controversy. The *official* RAD diagnosis, which in itself has limitations, bears little resemblance to the so-called "RAD diagnosis" with its laundry list of unofficial symptoms. Of great concern is the overuse and misuse of RAD in the field of foster care and adoption. Of even greater concern is the attempt to justify the use of extreme, punitive, maverick, coercive attachment therapies on the bases of inaccurate theory and weak or absent research. The subset of controversial attachment therapies fall outside of both attachment theory and research, and these approaches have been vilified by many notable attachment researchers. Sadly, many desperate foster and adoptive parents, who struggle with severely disturbed children and youth, are offered coercive attachment therapy as if it were evidence based and the "treatment of choice." Clearly, the use of this unsubstantiated, high-risk approach is not best practice and is not in the best interest of foster and adoptive children. (This appears to be one more example of how foster and adoptive children and their families often receive substandard dental, medical, and mental health services.) The bottom line is that any treatment having the potential to cause injury or trauma to the child should never be utilized.

In closing, I'd like to make some final suggestions for mental health professionals and foster and adoptive parents:[6]

1. Reevaluate children who have been labeled with the RAD diagnosis to see if they have been misdiagnosed and may actually have other, more accurate diagnoses.

2. Do not employ the unofficial RAD diagnosis.

3. Do not use the RAD diagnosis with children in middle childhood and older.

4. Keep in mind that attachment issues are relational issues, not problems exclusively confined to the child.

5. Avoid any treatment approaches which endanger the child, demonize the child, retraumatize the child, or exploit the child's insecurities.

6. Avoid all physically coercive approaches.

7. Avoid using individual therapy approaches which isolate the child from parents and foster a "pseudo" attachment to the therapist.

8. Embed therapy, consultation, or parent training in the larger system attempting to help the family; work with the treatment team, including the caseworker, teacher, physician, etc.

9. Emphasize the value of attachment theory and research in informing your interventions; but remain eclectic and evidence based.

10. Avoid blaming the foster and adoptive parents for the child's ongoing emotional and behavioral problems.

---

[6] The reader is directed to Appendix A of this book for the recommendations from the *Report of the APSAC Task Force on Attachment Therapy, Reactive Attachment Disorder, and Attachment Problems* (Chaffin et al., 2006).

Afterword

The potential of attachment theory and research to improve mental health and other services to foster and adoptive parents and their children remains undiminished despite undeniable controversies. The promise of attachment study lies in the area of increasing the understanding for clinicians and parents of why children do what they do. Uncovering the reasons for a child's ongoing difficulties allows for better understanding. It helps us to appreciate the meaning beneath the obvious behavior problems and to see those problems as clues and signals, rather than as simply something to expunge. In the mental health field, an inordinate emphasis is placed on diagnosis and lists of symptoms. At the same time, too little emphasis is placed on understanding the purpose and function of the symptoms. It's extremely important and helpful to comprehend the message and address the suffering behind the behavior problems. Seeing conduct problems as attachment behaviors is essential in order to do this. When we look at noxious actions as proof of a lack of attachment, we miss the true, underlying meaning of "bad behavior." Problem behaviors are often signs, oddly, of hope. They amount to a desperate child's enigmatic overture, invitation, or coercion of involvement with their parent and others. As long as the child is seeking ways to keep parents involved, albeit negatively, there is still reason for optimism.

If attachment theory provides nothing else, it offers us a colored thread upon which we can tug. We follow that thread and trace its course into the multi-hued garment of the child's past and present life.

Appendix A

The APSAC (American Professional Society on the Abuse of Children) Task Force is a national society focused on the plight and welfare of abused, neglected, and exploited children. It has comprehensively evaluated the controversy surrounding Reactive Attachment Disorder (RAD) and non-scientific attachment therapies and has issued the following recommendations. We list these recommendations in their entirety from the *Report of the APSAC Task Force on Attachment Therapy, Reactive Attachment Disorder, and Attachment Problems* (February, 2006, pp. 86-87) with the permission of Sage Publications.

RECOMMENDATIONS

1. Recommendations regarding diagnosis and assessment of attachment problems.

    a. Attachment problems, including but extending beyond RAD, are a real and appropriate concern for professionals working with children who are maltreated and should be carefully considered when these children are assessed.

    b. Assessment guidelines.

        (1) Assessment should include information about patterns of behavior over time, and assessors should be cognizant that current behaviors may simply reflect adjustment to new or stressful circumstances.

        (2) Cultural issues should always be considered when assessing the adjustment of any child, especially in cross-cultural or international placements or adoptions. Behavior appearing deviant in one cultural setting may be normative for children from different cultural settings, and children placed cross-culturally may experience unique adaptive challenges.

        (3) Assessment should include samples of behavior across situations and contexts. It should not be limited to problems in relationships with parents or primary caretakers and instead should include information regarding the child's interactions with multiple caregivers, such as

teachers, day care providers, and peers. Diagnosis of RAD or other attachment problems should not be made solely based on a power struggle between the parent and child.

(4) Assessment of attachment problems should not rely on overly broad, nonspecific, or unproven checklists. Screening checklists are valuable only if they have acceptable measurement properties when applied to the target populations where they will be used.

(5) Assessment for attachment problems requires considerable diagnostic knowledge and skill, to accurately recognize attachment problems and to rule out competing diagnoses. Consequently, attachment problems should be diagnosed only by a trained, licensed mental health professional with considerable expertise in child development and differential diagnosis.

(6) Assessment should first consider more common disorders, conditions, and explanations for behavior before considering rarer ones. Assessors and caseworkers should be vigilant about the allure of rare disorders in the child maltreatment field and should be alert to the possibility of misdiagnosis.

(7) Assessment should include family and caregiver factors and should not focus solely on the child.

(8) Care should be taken to rule out conditions such as autism spectrum disorders, pervasive developmental disorder, childhood schizophrenia, genetic syndromes, or other conditions before making a diagnosis of attachment disorder. If necessary, specialized assessment by professionals familiar with these disorders or syndromes should be considered.

(9) Diagnosis of attachment disorder should never be made simply based on a child's status as maltreated, as having experienced trauma, as growing up in an institution, as being a foster or adoptive child, or simply because the child has experienced pathogenic care. Assessment should respect the fact that resiliency is common, even in the face of great adversity.

2. Recommendations regarding treatments and interventions.

    a. Treatment techniques or attachment parenting techniques involving physical coercion, psychologically or physically enforced holding, physical restraint, physical domination, provoked catharsis, ventilation of rage, age regression, humiliation, withholding or forcing food or water intake, prolonged social isolation, or assuming exaggerated levels of control and domination over a child are contra-indicated because of risk of harm and absence of proven benefit and should not be used.

        (1) This recommendation should not be interpreted as pertaining to common, widely accepted treatment or behavior management approaches used with reason, such as time-out, reward and punishment contingencies, occasional seclusion or physical restraint as necessary for physical safety, restriction of privileges, "grounding," offering physical comfort to a child, and so on.

    b. Prognostications that certain children are destined to become psychopaths or predators should never be made based on early childhood behavior. These beliefs create an atmosphere conducive to overreaction and harsh or abusive treatment. Professionals should speak out against these and similar unfounded conceptualizations of children who are maltreated.

    c. Intervention models that portray young children in negative ways, including describing certain groups of young children as pervasively manipulative, cunning, or deceitful, are not conducive to good treatment and may promote abusive practices. In general, child maltreatment professionals should be skeptical of treatments that describe children in pejorative terms or that advocate aggressive techniques for breaking down children's defenses.

    d. Children's expressions of distress during therapy always should be taken seriously. Some valid psychological treatments may involve transitory and controlled emotional distress. However, deliberately seeking to provoke intense emotional distress or dismissing children's protests of distress is contra-indicated and should not be done.

    e. State-of-the-art, goal-directed, evidence-based approaches that fit the main presenting problem should be considered when selecting a first-line treatment. Where no evidence-based option exists or where evidence-based treatment op-tions have been exhausted, alternative treatments with sound theory foundations and broad clinical acceptance are appropriate. Before attempting novel or highly unconventional treatments with untested benefits, the potential for psychological or physical harm should be carefully weighed.

f. First-line services for children described as having attachment problems should be founded on the core principles suggested by attachment theory, including caregiver and environmental stability, child safety, patience, sensitivity, consistency, and nurturance. Shorter term, goal-directed, focused, behavioral interventions targeted at increasing parent sensitivity should be considered as a first-line treatment.

g. Treatment should involve parents and caregivers, including biological parents, if reunification is an option. Fathers and mothers should be included if possible. Parents of children described as having attachment problems may benefit from ongoing support and education. Parents should not be instructed to engage in psychologically or physically coercive techniques for therapeutic purposes, including those associated with any of the known child deaths.

3. Recommendations for child welfare.

a. Treatment provided to children in the child welfare and foster care systems should be based on a careful assessment conducted by a qualified mental health professional with expertise in differential diagnosis and child development. Child welfare systems should guard against accepting treatment prescriptions based on word-of-mouth recruitment among foster caregivers or other lay individuals.

b. Child welfare systems should not tolerate any parenting behaviors that normally would be considered emotionally abusive, physically abusive, or neglectful simply because they are, or are alleged to be, part of attachment treatment. For example, withholding food, water, or toilet access as punishment; exerting exaggerated levels of control over a child; restraining children as a treatment; or intentionally provoking out-of-control emotional distress should be evaluated as suspected abuse and handled accordingly.

4. Professionals should embrace high ethical standards concerning advertising treatment services to professional audiences and especially to lay audiences.

a. Claims of exclusive benefit (i.e., that no other treatments will work) should never be made. Claims of relative benefit (e.g., that one treatment works better than others) should only be made if there is adequate controlled trial scientific research to support the claim.

b. Use of patient testimonials in marketing treatment services constitutes a dual relationship. Because of the potential for exploitation, the Task Force believes that patient testimonials should not be used to market treatment services.

c. Unproven checklists or screening tools should not be posted on Web sites or disseminated to lay audiences. Screening checklists known to have adequate measurement properties and presented with qualifications may be appropriate.

d. Information disseminated to the lay public should be carefully qualified. Advertising should not make claims of likely benefits that cannot be supported by scientific evidence and should fully disclose all known or reasonably foreseeable risks.

REFERENCES

AACAP. (2002). *Reactive Attachment Disorder*. Retrieved September 21, 2005, from www.aacap.org/publications/factsfam/85.htm

Adoption and Foster Care Analysis and Reporting System. (2003). AFCARS Report #8: Preliminary estimates published March 2003. Washington, DC: U.S. Department of Health and Human Services, Administration for Children and Families, Administration on Children, Youth and Families, Children's Bureau. Retrieved July 23, 2004, from http://www.acf.hhs.gov/programs/cb/publications/afcars/report8.htm

Ainsworth, M., Blehar, M., Walters, E., & Wall, S. (1978). *Patterns of attachment: A psychological study of the strange situation*. Hillsdale, NJ: Erlbaum.

American Psychiatric Association. (1994). *Diagnostic and statistical manual of mental disorders (4th ed.)*. Washington, DC: Author.

Anastopoulos, A., Smith, J., & Wien, E. (1990). Counseling and training parents. In R. Barkely (Ed.), *Attention-deficit hyperactivity disorder: A handbook for diagnosis and treatment* (pp. 373-393). New York: Guilford Press.

Anthony, J. & Cohler, B. (Eds.). (1987). *The invulnerable child*. New York: Guilford Press.

Bank, L., Patterson, G., & Reid, J. (1987). *Delinquency prevention through training parents in family management*. The Behavior Analyst, 10(1), 75-82.

Barkley, R. (1997). *ADHD and the nature of self-control*. New York: Guilford Press.

Bates, J., & Bayles, K. (1988). Attachment and the development of behavior problems. In J. Belsky and T. Nezworski (Eds.), *Clinical implications of attachment* (pp. 253-294). Hillsdale, NJ: Erlbaum.

Baumrind, D. (1995). *Child maltreatment and optimal caregiving in social contexts*. New York: Garland Press.

Belsky, J., & Nezworski, T. (Eds.). (1998). *Clinical implications of attachment*. Hillsdale, NJ: Erlbaum.

Benson, P., Sharma, A., & Roehlkepartain, E. (1994). *Growing up adopted: A portrait of adolescents and their families*. Minneapolis: Search Institute.

Berliner, L. (2002). *Why caregivers turn to attachment therapy and what we can do that is better*. APSAC Advisor.

Boris, N. (2003). Attachment, aggression and holding: A cautionary tale. *Attachment & Human Development*, 5(3), 245-247.

Bowlby, J. (1969). *Attachment and loss*. (Vols. 1-2). New York: Basic Books.

Bowlby, J. (1973). *Attachment and loss: Vol. 2. Separation: Anxiety and anger*. New York: Basis Books.

Bowlby, J. (1982). *Attachment and loss: Vol. 1. Attachment* (2nd ed.). New York: Basic Books.

Bowlby, R. (2004). *Fifty years of attachment theory*. London: Karnac Pub.

Brazelton, T. & Cramer, B. (1990). *The earliest relationship: Parents, infants, and the drama of early attachment*. Reading, MA: Addison-Wesley.

Bretherton, I., Ridgeway, D., & Cassidy, J. (1990). Assessing internal working models of the attachment relationship: An attachment story completion task for 3-year-olds. In M. Greenberg, D. Cicchetti, & E. Cummings (Eds.), *Attachment in the preschool years: Theory, research, and intervention* (pp. 273-310). Chicago: University of Chicago Press.

Bryson, K., & Casper, L. (1999). Coresident grandparents and grandchildren. *Current Population Reports*. P23, No. 198. Retrieved September 21, 2005, from http://www.census.gov

Buenning, W. (2005). RAD checklist. *Reactive attachment disorder treatment (RAD): Healing with love and limits*. Retrieved from http://www.reactiveattachmentdisordertreatment.com/ssi/checklist.html

Byrne, J. (2003). Referral biases and diagnostic dilemmas. *Attachment & Human Development*, 5(3), 249-252.

Cadoret, R., & Riggins-Casper, K. (2000). Fetal alcohol exposure and adult psychopathology: Evidence from an adoption study. In R. Barth, M. Freundlich, & D. Brodzinsky (Eds.), *Adoption & prenatal alcohol and drug exposure: Research, policy, and practice*. Washington, DC: Child Welfare League of America.

Carlson, E. (1998). A prospective longitudinal study of disorganized/disoriented attachment. *Child Development*, 69(4), 1107-1128.

Carr, E. (1994). Emerging themes in the functional analysis of problem behavior. *Journal of Applied Behavior Analysis*, 27(2), 393-399.

Casey Family Services, The Casey Center for Effective Child Welfare Practice. (2003, October). *Promising practices in adoption-competent mental health services: A white paper*. New Haven, CT: Author.

Chaffin, M., Hanson, R., Saunders, B., Nichols, T., Barnett, D., Zeanah, C., et al. (2006). Report of the APSAC task force on attachment therapy, reactive attachment disorder, and attachment problems. *Child Maltreatment*, 11(1), 76-89.

Chamberlain, P. (2001). What works in treatment foster care. In M. Kluger, G. Alexander, & P. Curtis (Eds.), *What works in child welfare* (pp. 157-162). Washington, DC: CWLA Press.

Chamberlain, P., & Reid, J. (1991). Using a specialized foster care community treatment model for children and adolescents leaving the state mental hospital. *Journal of Community Psychology*, 19(3), 266-276.

Chamberlain, P., & Smith, D. (2003). Antisocial behavior in children and adolescents. In A. Kazdin & R. Weisz (Eds.), *Evidence-based psychotherapies for children and adolescents* (pp. 282-301). NY: Guilford Press.

Chisholm, K. (2000). Attachment in children adopted from Romanian orphanages: Two case studies. In P. Crittenden & A. Claussen (Eds.), *The organization of attachment relationships: Maturation, culture and context* (pp. 171-189). New York: Cambridge.

Cicchetti, D. (2004). An odyssey of discovery: Lessons learned through three decades of research on child maltreatment. *The American Psychologist, 59*(8), 731-741.

Cicchetti, D., Cummings, E., Greenberg, M., & Marvin, R. (1990). An organizational perspective on attachment beyond infancy: Implications for theory, measurement, and research. In M. Greenberg, D. Cicchetti, & E. Cummings (Eds.), *Attachment in the preschool years: Theory, research, and intervention* (pp. 3-50). Chicago: University of Chicago Press.

Crittenden, P. (1988). Relationships at risk. In J. Belsky & T. Nezworski (Eds.), *Clinical implications of attachment* (pp. 136-167). Hillsdale, NJ: Erlbaum.

Crittenden, P., & Claussen, A. (2000). Adaptation to varied environments. In P. Crittenden & A. Claussen (Eds.), *The organization of attachment relationships: Maturation, culture, and context* (pp. 234-250). New York: Cambridge.

Cunningham, E. (1998). A large-group community-based, family systems approach to parent training. In R. Barkley (Ed.), *Attention-deficit hyperactivity disorder* (394-412). New York: Guilford Press.

Dalby, J., Fox, L., & Haslam, R. (1982). Adoption and foster care rates in pediatric disorders. *Journal of Developmental and Behavioral Pediatrics, 3*(2), 61-64.

Delaney, R. (1997). *Healing power of the family: An illustrated overview of life with the disturbed foster and adopted child.* Oklahoma City: Wood 'N' Barnes Pub.

Delaney, R. (1998). *Raising Cain: Caring for troubled youngsters/repairing our troubled system.* Oklahoma City: Wood 'N' Barnes Pub.

Delaney, R. (2000). *Safe passage: A summary of the "parent 2 parent" program.* Oklahoma City: Wood 'N' Barnes Pub.

Delaney, R. (2003). *Small feats: Unsung accomplishments and everyday heroics of foster and adoptive parents.* Oklahoma City: Wood 'N' Barnes Pub.

Delaney, R., & Kunstal, F. (1997). *Troubled transplants: Unconventional strategies for helping disturbed foster and adopted children (2nd ed.).* Oklahoma City: Wood 'N' Barnes Publishing.

Deutsch, M. (1990). Psychological roots of moral exclusion. *Journal of Social Issues, 46*(1), 21-25.

Dollard, J., & Miller, N. (1950). *Personality and psychotherapy: An analysis in terms of learning, thinking, and culture.* New York: McGraw-Hill.

dosReis, S., Zito, J., Safer, D., & Soeken, K. (2001). Mental health services for youths in foster care and supplemental security income disabled youth. *American Journal of Public Health, 91*(7), 1094-1099.

Dozier, M. & Albus, K. (2000). Attachment issues for adopted infants. In R. Barth, M. Freundlich, & D. Brodzinsky (Eds.), *Adoption & prenatal alcohol and drug exposure: Research, policy, and practice* (pp. 171-197). Washington, DC: Child Welfare League of America.

Dozier, M. (2003). Attachment-based treatment for vulnerable children. *Attachment & Human Development*, 5(3), 253-527.

Egeland B., & Stroufe, L. (1981). Attachment and early maltreatment. *Child Development*, 52(1), 44-52.

Ellis, A. (1999). *How to make yourself happy and remarkably less disturbable.* Atascadero, CA: Impact Publication.

Erikson, E. (1968). *Identity: Youth and crisis.* New York: Norton.

Fahlberg, V. (1979). *Attachment and separation.* Lansing: Michigan Dept. of Social Services.

Fahlberg, V. (1991). *The child's journey through placement.* Indianapolis, IN: Perspectives Press.

Fanshel, D. (1977). Status changes of children in foster care. In S. Chess & A. Thomas (Eds.), *Annual progress in child psychiatry and child development.* New York: Brunner/Mazel, Inc.

Fanshel, D., Finch, S., & Grundy, J. (1990). *Foster children in a life course perspective.* New York: Columbia University Press.

Foster Parent College (2006). *Positive parenting.* Eugene, OR: Northwest Media, Inc. Available at www.fosterparentcollege.com

Foster Parent College (2006). *R.A.D.: Reactive attachment disorder.* Eugene, OR: Northwest Media, Inc. Available at www.fosterparentcollege.com

Fox, N., Kimmerly, N., & Schafer, W. (l991). Attachment to mother/attachment to father: a meta-analysis. *Child Development*, 62(1), 210-225.

Fraiberg, S. (1980). *Clinical studies in infant mental health.* New York: Basic Books.

Friedrich, W. (2002). Points of breakdown in the provision of services to severely disturbed foster and adopted children. *APSAC Advisor*, 14(4), 11-13.

George, C., Kaplan, N., & Main, M. (1985). *The attachment interview protocol* (3rd ed.). Unpublished manuscript, University of California at Berkley.

Green, J. (2003). Are attachment disorders best seen as social impairment syndromes? *Attachment & Human Development*, (5)3, 259-264.

Greenberg, M., & Speltz, M. (1988). Attachment and the ontogeny of conduct problems. In J. Belsky & T. Nezworski (Eds.), *Clinical implications of attachment* (pp. 177-208). Hillsdale, NJ: Erlbaum.

Greenberg, M., Cicchetti D., & Cummings, E. (Eds.). (1990). *Attachment in the preschool years: Theory, research, and intervention.* Chicago: University of Chicago Press.

Gresham, F., Watson, T., & Skinner, C. (2001). Functional behavioral assessment: Principles, procedures, and future directions. *The School Psychology Review*, 30 (2), 156-72.

Group for the Advancement of Psychiatry. (1966). *Psychological disorders in childhood*. New York: Author.

Halfon, N., Flint, R., & Inkelas, M. (2002, September). *Child health agency roles in health services for children in foster care*. UCLA Center for Healthier Children, Families and Communities. Health Services for Children in Foster Care. Policy Brief No. 3. Retrieved July 16, 2004, from http://www.healthychild.ucla.edu/Publications/documents/Child%20Health%20Agency%20Roles%20brief%200902.pdf

Hans, S., Bernstein, V., & Sims, B. (2000). Change and continuity in ambivalent attachment relationships from infancy through adolescence. In P. Crittenden & A. Claussen (Eds.), *The organization of attachment relationships: Maturation, culture, and context* (pp. 277-299). New York: Cambridge.

Hanson, R. (2002). Reactive attachment disorder: What do we really know about this diagnosis? *APSAC Advisor, 14*(4), 10-12.

Haynes, S. & O'Brien, W. (1990). Functional analysis in behavior therapy. *Clinical Psychology Review, 10*, 649-668.

Ingersoll, B. (1997). *Daredevils and daydreamers: New perspectives on attention-deficit/hyperactivity disorder*. New York: Doubleday.

James, B. (1994). *Handbook for treatment of attachment-trauma problems in children*. New York: MacMillan.

Johnson-Reid, M., & Barth, R. (2000). From maltreatment report to juvenile incarceration: The role of child welfare. *Child Abuse and Neglect, 24*(4), 505-520.

Jones, K., & Ervin, R. (1999, October). Functional behavioral assessment: Looking beyond feeling good about ourselves. *Communiqué, 28* (2), 23-24.

Kagan, J. (1984). *The nature of the child*. New York: Basic Books.

Kazdin, A., & Weisz, J. (Eds.). (2003). *Evidence-based psychotherapies for children and adolescents*. New York: Guilford Press.

Lazarus, R. (1989). Constructs of the mind in mental health and psychotherapy. In A. Freeman, K. Simon, L. Beutler, & H. Arkowitz (Eds.), *Comprehensive handbook of psychotherapy*. New York: Plenum.

Lieberman, A. (2003). The treatment of attachment disorder in infancy and early childhood: Reflections from clinical intervention with later-adopted foster care children. *Attachment & Human Development, 5*(3), 279-282.

Lieberman, A., & Pawl, J. (1988). Clinical applications of attachment theory. In J. Belsky & T. Nezworski (Eds.), *Clinical implications of attachment* (327-347). Hillsdale, NJ: Erlbaum.

Lieberman, A., & Pawl, J. (1990). Disorders of attachment and secure base behavior in the second year of life: Conceptual issues and clinical intervention. In M. Greenburg, D. Cicchetti, & E. Cummings (Eds.), *Attachment in the preschool years: Theory, research, and interveniton*. Chicago: University of Chicago Press.

Lochman, J., Barry, T., & Pardini, D. (2003). Anger Control Training for Aggressive Youth. In A. Kazdin & J. Weisz (Eds.), *Evidence-based psychotherapies for children and adolescents*. New York: Guilford Press.

Mahler, M., Pine, F., & Bergman, A. (1975). *The Psychological birth of the human infant: Symbiosis and individuation*. New York: Basic Books.

Main, M., & Hesse, E. (1990). Parents' unresolved traumatic experiences are related to infant disorganized attachment status: Is frightened and/or frightening parental behavior the linking mechanism? In M. Greenberg, D. Cicchetti, & E. Cummings (Eds.), *Attachment in the preschool years: Theory, research, and intervention*. (pp. 161-184). Chicago: University of Chicago Press.

Main, M., & Solomon, J. (1990). Procedures for identifying infants as disorganized/disoriented during the Ainsworth Strange Situation. In M. Greenberg, D. Cicchetti, & E. Cummings (Eds.), *Attachment in the preschool years: Theory, research, and intervention*. (pp. 121-160). Chicago: University of Chicago Press.

Marsenich, L. (2002). *Evidence-based practices in mental health services for foster youth*. Sacramento: California Institute for Mental Health.

Martin, H., & Rodeheffer, M. (1980). The psychological impact of abuse on children. In G. Williams & J. Money, *Traumatic abuse and neglect of children at home*. Baltimore: John Hopkins Press.

Marvin, R., & Stewart, R. (1990). A family systems framework for the study of attachment. In M. Greenberg, D. Cicchetti, & E. Cummings (Eds.), *Attachment in the preschool years: Theory, research, and intervention*. (pp. 51-86). Chicago: University of Chicago Press.

Masterson, J. (1972). *Treatment of the borderline adolescent*. New York: Wiley-Interscience.

McDermott, J., Fraiberg, S., & Harrison, S. (1969). Residential treatment of children: The utilization of transference behavior. In S. Chess & A. Thomas (Eds.), *Annual Progress in Child Psychiatry and Child Development*. New York: Brunner/Mazel, 1969.

McNamara, J. (1990). Structuring for safety: Parenting adoptive children who were sexually abused. In J. McNamara & B. McNamara (Eds.), *Adoption and the sexually abused child* (pp. 47-62). Portland, ME: University of Southern Maine.

Mercer, J. (2002, Fall-Winter). Attachment therapy: A treatment without empirical support. *Scientific Review of Mental Health Practice*, 1 (2).

Merriam-Webster Dictionary (11th ed.). (2003). Springfield, MA: Merriam-Webster.

Miller, J., Tansy, M., & Hughes, T. (1998). Functional behavior and effective intervention between problem behavior and effective intervention in schools. *Current Issues in Education*. Retrieved September 21, 2005, from http://cie.ed.asu.edu/volume1/number5

Minuchin, P., Colapinto, J., & Minuchin, S. (1998). *Working with families of the poor*. New York: Guilford Press.

O'Connor, T., & Zeanah, C. (2003). Attachment disorders: Assessment strategies and treatment approaches. *Attachment & Human Development,* 5(3), 223-244.

Pacifici, C., Chamberlain, P., & White, L. (2002). *Off-road parenting: Practical solutions for difficult behavior.* Eugene, OR: Northwest Media, Inc.

Partridge, S., Hornby, H., & McDonald, T. (1986). *Learning from adoption disruption.* Portland: University of Southern Maine.

Pearson, G. (1968). *A handbook of child psychoanalysis.* New York: Basic Books.

Polansky, N., Gaudin, J., Ammons, P., & Davis, K. (1985). The psychological ecology of the neglectful mother. *Child Abuse and Neglect,* 9, 265-275.

Pound, A. (1982). Attachment and maternal depression. In C. Parkes & J. Stebenson-Hinde (Eds.), *Attachment in human behavior.* New York: Basic Books.

Reinecke, M., Dattilio, F., & Freeman, A. (Eds.). (2003). *Cognitive therapy with children and adolescents: A casebook for clinical practice (2nd ed.).* New York: Guilford Press.

SAMHSA, (2005). *Trauma focused cognitive behavior therapy.* Retrieved September 21, 2005, from http://modelprograms.samhsa.gov/pdfs/Details/TFCBT.pdf

Schneider-Rosen, K. (1990). The developmental reorganization of attachment relationships: Guidelines for classification beyond infancy. In M. Greenberg, D. Cicchetti, & E. Cummings (Eds.), *Attachment in the preschool years: Theory, research, and intervention* (pp. 185-220). Chicago: University of Chicago Press.

Soares, I., Fremmer-Bombik, E., Grossmann, K., & Silva, M. (2002). Attachment representation in adolescence and adulthood: Exploring some intergenerational and intercultural issues. In P. Crittenden & A. Claussen (Eds.), *The organization of attachment relationships: Maturation, culture, and context* (pp. 325-342). Cambridge: Cambridge University Press.

Sowers, L. (1997, July 30). *Of human bonding: Attachment disorder is in the news but misunderstood.* Houston, TX: Houston Chronicle.

Speltz, M. (1990). The treatment of preschool conduct problems: An integration of behavioral and attachment concepts. In M. Greenberg, D. Cicchetti, & E. Cummings (Eds.), *Attachment in the preschool years: Theory, research, and intervention* (pp. 399-426). Chicago: University of Chicago Press.

Speltz, M. (2002). Description, history, and critique of corrective attachment therapy. *APSAC Advisor,* 14(4), 4-8.

Spieker, S., & Booth, C. (1988). Maternal antecedents of attachment quality. In J. Belsky and T. Nezworski (Eds.), *Clinical implications of attachment* (95-131). Hillsdale, NJ: Erlbaum.

Steele, H. (2003). Holding therapy is not attachment therapy: Editor's introduction to this invited special issue. *Attachment & Human Development*, 5(3), 219-220.

Steinhauer, P. (2001). *The least detrimental alternative: A systematic guide to case planning and decision making for children in care*. Toronto: University of Toronto Press.

Sroufe, L. (1988). The role of infant-caregiver attachment in development. In J. Belsky & T. Nezworski (Eds.), *Clinical implications of attachment*. Hillsdale, NJ: Erlbaum.

Sroufe, L., Erickson, M., & Friedrich, W. (2002). Attachment theory and attachment therapy. *APSAC Advisor*, 14(4), 4-6.

Task Force on permanency Planning for Foster Children. (1990). *Kinship care: The double-edged dilemma*. Rochester, NY: Author.

Titi, D. (2002). Maternal depression and child—mother attachment in the first three years: A view from the intermountain West. In P. Crittenden & A. Claussen (Eds.), *The organization of attachment relationships: Maturation, culture, and context* (pp. 190-213). Cambridge: Cambridge University Press.

van IJzendoorn, M. (1995). Adult attachment representations, parental responsiveness, and infant attachment: A meta-analysis on the predictive validity of the Adult Attachment Interview. *Psychological Bulletin*, 117(3), 387-403.

Vizziello, G., Ferrero, C., & Musicco, M. (2002). Parent-child synchrony of interaction. In P. Crittenden & A. Claussen (Eds.), *The organization of attachment relationships: Maturation, culture, and context* (pp. 38-60). Cambridge: Cambridge University Press.

von der Lippe, A., & Crittenden, P. (2000). Patterns of attachment in young Egyptian children. In P. Crittenden & A. Claussen (Eds.), *The organization of attachment relationships: Maturation, culture, and context* (pp. 97-114). Cambridge: Cambridge University Press.

Webster-Stratton, C., & Hammon, M. (1997). Treating children with early-onset conduct problems: A comparison of child and parent training interventions. *Consulting & Clinical Psychology*, 65, 93-109.

Wiltse, K. (1985). Foster care: An overview. In J. Laird & A. Hartman (Eds.), *A handbook of child welfare: Context, knowledge, and practice* (pp. 565-584). New York: Free Press.

Zeanah, C. (1996). Beyond insecurity: A reconceptualization of attachment disorders of infancy. *Journal of Consulting & Clinical Psychology*, 64(1), 42-52.

Zeanah, C., Smyke, A., & Dumitrescu, A. (2002). Attachment disturbances in young children. II: Indiscriminate behavior and institutional care. *Journal of the American Academy of Child and Adolescent Psychiatry*, 41(8) 983-989.

Related Publications

Goldstein, J., Freud, A., & Solnit, A. (1973). *Beyond the best interests of the child*. New York: Free Press.

Greenspan, S., & Lieberman, A. (1988). A clinical approach to attachment. In J. Belsky & T. Nezworski (Eds.), *Clinical implications of attachment* (387-414). Hillsdale, NJ: Erlbaum.

Jarratt, C. (1978). *Adopting the older child*. Boston: Harvard Common Press.

Kempe, C., & Halfer, R. (Eds.). (1972). *Helping the battered child and his family*. Philadelphia: Lippincott.

Minuchin, S. (1974). *Families & family therapy*. Cambridge: Harvard University Press.

Parkes, C., & Stevenson-Hinde, J. (Eds.). (1982). *The place of attachment in human behavior*. New York: Basic Books.

Redl, F., & Wineman, D. (1951). *Children who hate: The disorganization and breakdown of behavior controls*. Glencoe, IL: Free Press.

Rose, T., & Rose, D. (1985). Adoption, foster care, and group homes for handicapped children. In J. Laird & A. Hartman (Eds.), *A handbook of child welfare: Context, knowledge, and practice* (pp. 693-705). New York: Free Press.

Sameroff, A., & Emde, R. (1989). *Relationship disturbances in early childhood: A developmental approach*. New York: Basic Books.

Sperling, M. (1974). *The major neuroses and behavior disorders in children*. New York: Aronson.

Spitz, R. (1965). *The first year of life: A psychoanalytic study of normal and deviant development of object relations*. New York: International Universities Press.

Swire, M., & Kavaler, F. (1977). The health status of foster children. *Child Welfare, 56*(10), 635-653.

Whittaker, J. (1985). Group and institutional care: An overview. In J. Laird & A. Hartman (Eds.), *A handbook of child welfare: Context, knowledge, and practice* (pp. 617-637). New York: Free Press.

Williams, G., & Money, J. (Eds.) (1980). *Traumatic abuse and neglect of children at home*. Baltimore: John Hopkins University Press.

Woolf, G. (1990). An outlook for foster care in the United States. *Child Welfare, 69*(1), 75-81.

INDEX

parent training, 66-102, 106, 111-113
partnership, 12-13, 30, 32
permissive parenting, 99
poor eye contact, 34, 69, 75, 77, 81, 85, 92, 95, 98
positive encounters, increasing, 67-69, 81, 92-96, 102
protest, 17-18, 89
protest-despair-detachment sequence, 16-18, 26
proximity, 49
psychopathology, 42-43

Reactive Attachment Disorder (RAD), 2, 22, 26, 33, 35-37, 39, 40, 48, 66,
    71, 83, 102-115
reenactment, 30, 42-52, 59, 61, 63
reinterpretation of conduct problems, 64-66, 68-77, 102
rejecting, parenting style of, 64-65, 99
response, foster and adoptive parent response, 9-10, 44, 47-48, 52-65, 71-
    74, 81-92, 100-101, 107

secure (Type B) attachment, 21
secure base, 9, 15, 93
securely attached children, 9, 14-15, 18, 27-28
selective attachments, 11
separation, 4, 24, 17, 30, 94, 98
social learning, 66-69, 77-81, 87, 102, 112
stealing, 19, 34, 37, 47, 67, 69, 73-75, 79, 85, 90, 92, 93, 97
strategies of attachment, 3, 10, 13, 17, 21-23, 42-43, 56-57, 109
survival, 5-6, 47, 49, 64, 72-73, 76, 101
symptoms of RAD, 36-39, 41, 102-115

temperament, 3, 6, 11
Type A, 21-22, 26, 28, 31, 51, 56, 67, 70, 76-77, 80, 87, 98
Type B, 21
Type C, 21, 23-26, 46, 51, 56, 58-59, 63, 70, 92
Type D, 21, 25-26, 56, 58-59, 70
training parents, 66-102, 107, 111-113
treatment of attachment problems, 102-115

unofficial symptoms of RAD, 33, 37-41, 48, 102-115

verbalization of emotion, 20, 29, 31-32, 62, 66, 68-69, 73, 78, 80-92, 94,
    102

working models, 13-15, 18-19, 27-30, 45, 52-55, 68, 81-83, 93, 99-100

Author Biography

Richard J. Delaney, Ph.D. is an internationally acclaimed clinical psychologist who works closely with foster, kinship, and adoptive parents and with agencies that serve troubled youngsters. He is the author of several books on attachment issues, foster care and adoption, including: *Troubled Transplants* (with Dr. Frank Kunstal), *Raising Cain, The Healing Power of the Family*, and *Small Feats: The Everyday Heroics of Foster and Adoptive Parents*.

Dr. Delaney was one of the central experts in the PATH curriculum developed by Spaulding for Children for pre-service training of foster and kinship parents. He is the principle investigator and codeveloper of Foster Parent College (www.fosterparentcollege.com), an online, in-service training curriculum for foster, kinship and adoptive parents. He is an instructor for the mental health certificate in adoption program at Portland State University (PSU). He is lead faculty of a Casey Family Services-PSU-funded distance education project to train mental health professionals to work with adoptive parents and their children. Dr. Delaney is the principal investigator of a federal grant to train caseworkers on-line about foster care issues. In all of his work, Dr. Delaney's approaches stress the healing power of families and creative and positive strategies to help children.

Dr. Delaney is available for consultation and conference/seminar presentations. Please contact his publisher at: 800-678-0621 or info@woodnbarnes.com.

NOTES

NOTES